"*Tradition, creeds, liturgy, retrieval,* .... seldom used in the Baptist world; at least they are not used in a positive sense! However, the contributors to *Baptists and the Christian Tradition* make a compelling case this should not be the case. This is an excellent work written by some of Baptists' finest thinkers. We have needed a book like this for a long time and now we have it."

—**Daniel L. Akin**, president, Southeastern
Baptist Theological Seminary

"*Baptists and the Christian Tradition* is a tremendous contribution to the very important debate over whether evangelical Baptists must surrender our doctrinal distinctives in order to engage the Great Tradition. The authors respond with a resounding 'no.' Baptists, they argue, can and must position Baptist life within the larger Christian tradition and must do so not only doctrinally but also liturgically. The authors are absolutely right, and this book is a must-read for pastors, professors, and students."

—**Bruce R. Ashford**, provost and dean of faculty,
Southeastern Baptist Theological Seminary

"Baptists have often been accused of being sectarians by other ecclesial traditions. Unfortunately, sometimes we've deserved it! That is why this book is so timely. *Baptists and the Christian Tradition* makes a case for a winsome vision of catholicity that is distinctively Baptist, convictionally evangelical, and warmly ecumenical. The editors have assembled a first-rate group of scholars to address this vision from a variety of complementary perspectives. Baptist pastors, theologians, and other ministry leaders should find much worth reflecting upon as they seek to embody Jesus's prayer that his followers will be one, just as he and the Father are one."

—**Nathan A. Finn**, provost and dean of the university
faculty, North Greenville University

"Many associate the word 'Baptist' with a narrowly sectarian mentality. But as this collection of astute essays demonstrates, the Baptist tradition has, in the main, positioned itself in continuity with the historical and global church. This helpful book will help those who want to affirm Baptist distinctives without slicing themselves off from the broader Christian tradition. It is possible to be a Baptist with catholic sensibilities!"

—**Gavin Ortlund**, senior pastor, First Baptist Church, Ojai, CA

"As an interpreter of Scripture proud to have been nurtured in the Baptist tradition, this volume displays the vast riches of the past as well as providing an orientation toward hope for the future. I am eager to share with my students that which unites Christian denominations as well as the distinctives of this vast and influential body of believers."

—**Amy Peeler**, associate professor of New Testament, Wheaton College

"This book provides must-read contributions on Baptist thought and practice. Each contribution is a worthwhile exercise in historical theology that provides a framework for looking backward and recognizing the classic distinctives and gifts of Baptist theology to the church, often while looking forward and offering proposals for how the Baptists of today can be more ecumenical, humble, and most importantly faithful. This collection represents the best that Baptist theology has to contribute through its focus on Scripture, theology, worship, and mission."

—**Madison N. Pierce**, assistant professor of New Testament, Trinity Evangelical Divinity School

"Evangelical Baptists have as much right to the great tradition of Christian orthodoxy as any other group, and they should act like it by owning up to what this constellation of first-rate scholars calls 'Baptist catholicity.' Embracing the final authority of the Bible for Christian faith, these authors call fellow Baptists to interpret and apply the sacred contents of the Bible in communion with the saints, with guidance from the past. Baptist faith is not a new, uniquely modern form of religion. It is part of what we sometimes call the small-*c* catholic church. And dismissals of the wisdom gained through centuries of orthodox Christian faith and practice are a recipe for heresy and sin. May God bless our Baptist churches with a season of renewal as they appropriate the riches of church history."

—**Douglas A. Sweeney**, dean and professor of divinity, Beeson Divinity School

BAPTISTS

and the

CHRISTIAN TRADITION

BAPTISTS
and the
CHRISTIAN TRADITION

TOWARDS AN EVANGELICAL
BAPTIST CATHOLICITY

edited by

MATTHEW Y. EMERSON
CHRISTOPHER W. MORGAN
R. LUCAS STAMPS

ACADEMIC
NASHVILLE, TENNESSEE

Baptists and the Christian Tradition
Copyright © 2020 by Matthew Y. Emerson, Christopher W. Morgan,
and R. Lucas Stamps

Published by B&H Academic
Nashville, Tennessee

ISBN: 978-1-4336-5061-1

Dewey Decimal Classification: 230.6
Subject Heading: BAPTISTS--DOCTRINES
/ WORSHIP / SACRAMENTS

Cover design by Emily Keafer Lambright.
Photo ® Nuntiya/shutterstock.

Printed in the United States of America

1 2 3 4 5 6 7 8 9 10 VP 25 24 23 22 21 20

To David Dockery and Timothy George,
pioneers of Baptist catholicity and champions
of the faith once delivered to the saints.

CONTENTS

ABBREVIATIONS

B&H   Broadman and Holman
SBC   Southern Baptist Convention
JSNTSS   *Journal for the Study of the New Testament Supplement Series*
SPCK   Society for the Propagation of Christian Knowledge
IVP   InterVarsity Press
NPNF   Nicene and Post-Nicene Fathers
ANF   Ante-Nicene Fathers
AH   *Against Heresies*
JETS   *Journal of the Evangelical Theological Society*
S&T   *Sword and Trowel*
PRSt   Perspectives in Religious Studies
NAC   New American Commentary
SJT   *Scottish Journal of Theology*
ODNB   Oxford Dictionary of National Biography

FOREWORD

Timothy George
Beeson Divinity School

S everal years ago Mark Noll wrote an article titled "So You're a Baptist—
What Might That Mean?" in which he asked: "What is the best way
to take account of the world's self-described Baptists? Do they constitute
a movement with any real cohesion? Or is the term 'Baptist' so flexible
that it designates only a loosely defined collection of heterogeneous frag-
ments clustered haphazardly in one vaguely outlined section of the world
Christian landscape?"[1]

That last question refers to the fact that more Baptists reside in
North America than anywhere else—this despite the fact that Baptists
are a considerable presence in some non-Western regions, such as Nigeria,
Brazil, and Nagaland in India. In his article "The Baptist Exception,"
Philip Jenkins observes that this fact makes Baptists an outlier among
world Christian communions. In most Christian communions, Global
South Christians have strongly outpaced their Northern world counterparts. Jenkins also cautions: "Mere numbers say nothing about the nature
of faith or the quality of practice."[2]

The nature of faith and the quality of practice, among Baptist
Christians especially, are major concerns of the essays in this volume.
Each of the contributors is a convinced Baptist committed to an open
engagement with the Great Tradition of Christian believing and thinking across the centuries. They are advocates of what has been called

---

[1] Mark Noll, "So You're a Baptist—What Might That Mean?" *Books and
Culture* 17, no. 4 (July/August 2011): 92.

[2] Philip Jenkins, "The Baptist Exception," *Christian Century*, May 10, 2017, 61.

"Baptist catholicity." This approach presupposes a critical, but charitable, engagement with the whole church, both past and present, along with the desire to move beyond the false polarities of an Enlightenment-based individualism on the one hand and a pastiche of postmodern relativism on the other.

This project is revisionist only in the sense that it dares to challenge the (fairly) recent telling of the Baptist story primarily in terms of the negatives of dissent and nonconformity. It is possible to so emphasize certain Baptist distinctives, such as believer's baptism, congregational church governance, separation of church and state, and so on, that the weightier matters of Christian faith are neglected—the Bible, the Trinity, salvation by grace alone, and even Jesus's prayer that his disciples would be one, as he and the Father are one (John 17:20–26). Baptists began as a small, persecuted minority in pre-revolutionary England. As ardent advocates of religious freedom, Baptists have always reacted against the imposition of practices and beliefs they deemed unbiblical. This has sometimes led to our magnifying fences while neglecting foundations. Fences have their place in marking out ecclesial identity, but without a solid foundation, the fences will not long endure.

Seen in a broader context, this volume is part of a deeper Protestant impulse to reclaim the foundations of historic Christian orthodoxy—and to do so precisely as confessional, evangelical Baptists. In the nineteenth century, the Oxford movement attempted to do this within the Anglican tradition. The "Catholic Luther" is a theme rehearsed among Augsburg Christians since the Reformation. The work of Nevin and Schaff at Mercersburg is another part of this trajectory. More recently, the late Thomas C. Oden, with his work on patristic exegesis and his call for paleo-orthodoxy, has inspired many in this direction, both within and beyond his own Methodist tradition. Scott Swain and Michael Allen have done something similar for their fellow Presbyterians. Among Baptists, we should note the work of the recently formed Center for Baptist Renewal along with other appeals to Baptist catholicity by Baptist theologians Curtis Freeman, Steve Harmon, and Elizabeth Newman.

Coursing through all these movements, and reflected in the essays in this volume, are three convictions: History counts. Theology matters. Retrieval for the sake of renewal. To take these statements seriously is to recognize the church as a community of memory, a community not only of baptized believers, as Baptists are wont to define the church, but also a community of "remembering believers." Retrieval for the sake of renewal is also an exercise in humility. We must learn to listen before we can speak. Our hearts must become teachable, pliable, docile—from the Latin *docilitas*, the word Calvin used to describe his own conversion—before we are able to offer instruction to others. This means, among other things, that we must overcome the obstacle of inattentiveness and the culture of competition. All of this points to the centrality of Jesus Christ, who is at once the Savior of the world and the Lord of the church.

ACKNOWLEDGMENTS

We thank a number of friends and colleagues, without whom this book would not have been possible. First, we are grateful to Nathan Finn for believing in this book and for his invaluable support and guidance in the early phases of this project's development. Second, we want to thank B&H Academic, and especially Jim Baird, Chris Thompson, Sarah Landers, and Renée Chavez, for their support of this volume and for their warm and wise guidance throughout the whole process. Third, we are grateful to each of the contributors for investing themselves in this project. Fourth, we thank Elliott Pinegar and Maigen Turner for their editorial and administrative assistance. Fifth, we owe an enormous debt of gratitude to our wives, who inspire and support us in countless ways. Finally, we are most deeply grateful to God our Father, who has saved us through our Lord Jesus Christ by his Holy Spirit. We pray that this volume is to the glory of our triune God, in whom the whole church is built up together as one body.

INTRODUCTION

Baptists and the Christian Tradition: What Hath Nicaea to Do with Nashville?

Matthew Y. Emerson,
Christopher W. Morgan,
and R. Lucas Stamps

In recent years, desire appears to have grown among evangelicals, including evangelical Baptists, for a stronger rootedness in the Christian tradition. Evangelical believers (perhaps especially millennials) appear to have a growing hunger for ancient liturgical forms of church worship. Evangelicals across the theological spectrum are asking how and why millennials are drawn to more traditional forms of worship and an interest in early church doctrine and practice.[1] Further, from an academic standpoint, conservative evangelical scholars are likewise seeking a retrieval of patristic doctrinal formulations and precritical interpretive methods. One recent example is Michael Allen and Scott Swain's *Reformed Catholicity*.[2] And from an ecclesial perspective, evangelical churches are longing for a greater sense of transcendence in worship and a more robust and multilayered expression of "the faith that was once for all delivered to the saints" (Jude 3 ESV).

---

[1] See, for example, Gracy Olmstead, "Why Millennials Long for Liturgy: Is the High Church the Christianity of the Future?" *American Conservative*, January 14, 2014, https://www.theamericanconservative.com/articles/why-millennials-long-for-liturgy/.

[2] Michael Allen and Scott R. Swain, *Reformed Catholicity: The Promise of Retrieval for Theology and Biblical Interpretation* (Grand Rapids: Baker Academic, 2015). In their introduction, Allen and Swain highlight a number of recent trends from across the theological landscape toward retrieving the Christian past.

1

Some evangelical churches are experiencing attrition precisely along these lines, as discontented believers flee the sometimes shallow waters of low-church evangelicalism for higher ecclesiastical, liturgical, and sacramental ground. Others, though, such as Sojourn Church in Louisville, Kentucky,[3] Redeemer Fellowship in Chicago, Illinois, and Redeemer Fellowship in Kansas City, Missouri, are seeking to combine conservative evangelical theology with more traditional forms of worship. These churches cooperate with the Southern Baptist Convention—and indeed are among the largest congregations in our denomination. This is not, in other words, an ivory tower discussion but a conversation occurring among Southern Baptists and at growing Southern Baptist churches.

In an academic Baptist context, several prominent Baptists in the United Kingdom[4] as well as a cadre of moderate Baptists in North America[5] have been engaged in ongoing projects to reenvision Baptist identity within the context of the broader Christian tradition. But with some important exceptions, these contemporary movements toward "Baptist catholicity" have been relatively unengaged by conservative Baptists in North America. *Baptists and the Christian Tradition* seeks to

---

[3] Sojourn Church is under the worship direction of Mike Cosper, whose *Rhythms of Grace* seeks to retrieve traditional and ancient worship practices in a contemporary context. See Mike Cosper, *Rhythms of Grace: How the Church's Worship Tells the Story of the Gospel* (Wheaton, IL: Crossway, 2013).

[4] Many of the volumes in Paternoster's Studies in Baptist History and Thought series highlight this interest among British Baptists.

[5] Several moderate Baptist theologians who sometimes identify themselves as "Bapto-Catholics" serve as useful dialogue partners. See the programmatic manifesto "Re-Envisioning Baptist Identity: A Manifesto for Baptist Communities in North America (1997)," authored by Mikael Broadway, Curtis Freeman, Barry Harvey, James Wm. McClendon Jr., Elizabeth Newman, and Philip Thompson, http://www.baptistcenter.net/confessions/Re-envisioning_Baptist_Identity.pdf. See also Steven R. Harmon, *Towards Baptist Catholicity: Essays on Tradition and the Baptist Vision* (Eugene, OR: Wipf & Stock, 2006); Harmon, *Baptist Identity and the Ecumenical Future: Story, Tradition, and the Recovery of Community* (Waco, TX: Baylor University Press, 2016); Barry Harvey, *Can These Bones Live? A Catholic Baptist Engagement with Ecclesiology, Hermeneutics, and Social Theory* (Grand Rapids: Brazos, 2008); and Curtis W. Freeman, *Contesting Catholicity: Theology for Other Baptists* (Waco, TX: Baylor University Press, 2014).

fill this lacuna by exploring some ways conservative evangelical Baptists might better situate Baptist faith and practice within the historic Christian tradition.[6]

Evangelical Baptists need not surrender their doctrinal distinctives to engage this conversation, nor should they seek simply to mimic the beliefs and practices of other traditions. Baptists have much to teach as well as much to learn from the broader body of Christ. Still, Baptist convictions and catholic sensibilities are not mutually exclusive. Indeed, some of the concerns of Baptist catholicity, such as the desire for a more robust sacramentalism, have important precedents in the Baptist tradition itself. Thus this work aims to be both retrospective and prospective—looking back to the best of the Baptist tradition while pointing the way forward for evangelical Baptists in the changing ecclesial and cultural landscape of the twenty-first century.

This volume includes authors from a variety of higher educational institutions, as well as minority authors. We hope that this reflects the catholic spirit the volume intends to champion. The opening essay by Christopher Morgan and Kristen Ferguson sets the stage by examining the important

---

[6] When we use the term "catholic," we do not mean "Roman Catholic." Rather, we are taking up the older meaning of catholic as "universal" or "worldwide" (Greek, *katholikos*: *kata*, "through" + *holos*, "the whole"). In this sense, catholicity is one of the four marks of the church, as confessed in the Nicene Creed: "I believe in one, holy, catholic and apostolic church." While the New Testament most often speaks of the church (*ekklesia*) in local terms, it also makes reference to the church in this collective, universal sense (e.g., Eph 1:22; 3:21; 5:23). To confess the church's catholicity, then, is to embrace its universal scope and its worldwide dimension—the body of Christ that transcends space and time, province and denomination. A uniquely *Baptist* catholicity seeks to situate the Baptist vision within this broader body of Christ. As the Protestant Reformation was a renewal movement within Western Christianity, so also the Baptist vision is a renewal movement within Protestantism—a renewal within a renewal, we might say. So as we call the church to greater faithfulness to Scripture (as we understand it in terms of Baptist distinctives), so also we seek to learn from other traditions as well. We are especially indebted to what many have called the "Great Tradition" of Christian reflection on the gospel and its triune God. Other Baptist groups and theologians have utilized the notion of "Baptist catholicity" or "Bapto-catholicity" (see, for example, the manifesto "Re-Envisioning Baptist Identity"), but we are seeking to stake a claim for a particularly *evangelical* expression of this impulse.

theme of Christian unity in Scripture and how Baptists have received this teaching. The remaining essays explore how Baptists might interface with the Christian tradition and the broader body of Christ on a number of different fronts, including foundational Christian doctrines (such as the Trinity and the incarnation), essential Christian practices (such as worship, baptism, and the Lord's Supper), and pressing contemporary issues (such as interdenominational relations and racial tensions). The appendix is a response to our work written by a moderate Baptist ecumenical theologian, Steven Harmon. As conservative evangelical Baptists, we part ways with Harmon on some important issues. But we consider him a kind of fellow traveler on the road to recovering the Christian past for the sake of contemporary Baptist renewal, and we gladly welcome his perspective from a different sector of the Baptist movement.

1

Baptists, the Unity of the Church, and the Christian Tradition

CHRISTOPHER W. MORGAN
and KRISTEN FERGUSON

Introduction: Unity Matters

As Baptists, we prize the autonomy of the local church and the priesthood of believers; at the same time, we also cooperate in a common mission to plant churches, mobilize missionaries, educate pastors, and provide relief to those in need. We combine our resources to do more together than we would otherwise be able to do on our own. This cooperation has been transformational, accomplishing much for the cause of God's kingdom. But many are concerned that this cooperation is crumbling. The decline of denominationalism, questions concerning institutional effectiveness, financial challenges, generational priorities, diversity of cultural under-standings, conflicts among powerful personalities and agencies, and the manifold array of ministry networks are commonly cited as factors in this perceived weakening.

Another factor is rarely mentioned: our theology of the unity of the church. Without a strong understanding of the theological basis for the unity of the church, practical reasons for unity can eventually shift and fracture. Our historical context will change, generations will cling to dif-ferent priorities, financial strategies will vary, and institutional structures and systems will adapt accordingly. But our cooperation does not have to be like "a rope of sand" but rather can be "cables of steel"[1] if wed together with and sustained by the reality of our union with Christ and each other. Our cooperation can be grounded on the biblical teaching about our unity as his church, living in community, believing his truth, and serving his mission. Our deep-seated conviction concerning the unity of Christ's church can more consistently drive our genuine love for one another, our willingness to listen to each other humbly amid cultural and generational differences, and our commitment to serve alongside each other even when we may differ on matters that are not of the essence of Christianity.

Unity matters—theologically and practically. It can be traced throughout redemptive history, is embedded throughout Christian theology, and has implications for the everyday operations of local church life. Unity is a core doctrine of our faith that should inform our hearts and propel our practice.

This chapter will discuss matters related to what the Bible says about unity, especially the unity of the church. We will first consider the historical narrative of redemption and discover that unity is personal, communal, and cosmic. We will then highlight specific aspects of the nature of unity, namely, that unity is covenantal, transcendent, missional, and inaugurated. We will further explore the highly practical teaching on unity found in the Bible by advocating that unity is indeed possible. Finally, we will end the chapter with a review of Baptist confessions and why unity is, and ought to be, Baptist. Because this topic is so vast and integrated into the rest of theology, we will follow Ephesians as a guide and incorporate John 17 along the way.

---

[1] This language was used by W. A. Criswell in his presidential address at the 1970 SBC annual meeting in Denver, Colorado. See Baptist Press, "Criswell Urges SBC: Hold Fast to Doctrine, Missions,"news release, June 1, 1970, http://media.sbhla.org.s3.amazonaws.com/3003,01-Jun-1970.pdf. See also James L. Sullivan, *Rope of Sand with Strength of Steel* (Nashville: Convention Press, 1974); and Roger S. Oldham's insightful article "Synergy, Cooperation, and Autonomy: The Southern Baptist Experience," *Journal of the Mid-America Baptist Theological Seminary* (2017), https://www.mabts.edu/sites/all/themes/midamerica/uploads/Oldham%20article%20jp%20edit%201%20proof1.pdf.

Unity Is Personal, Communal, and Cosmic

Throughout history, God's plan has been to unite all things in Christ, "things in heaven and things on earth" (Eph 1:10). In the grand narrative of God's Word, we see that God's plan incorporates personal, communal, and cosmic spheres as he unites people to himself, unites people to one another, and even unites the cosmos in Christ.[2]

The Bible begins with God. From all eternity, our triune God exists. The Father, Son, and Spirit are perfectly one and yet exist as distinct persons within that divine unity. The triune God has created everything by his word in a way that pleases him and is good for his creation (Genesis 1–2; John 1). Genesis repeats, "And God saw that it was good," indicating that God has embedded his goodness in his creation (1:4, 10, 12, 18, 21, 25, 31). God's declaration that humanity was created in his own image sets us apart as uniquely able and responsible to show his likeness to the rest of creation (Gen 1:26). Unstained from sin, Adam and Eve each were personally united to God without fear, enjoyed communion with one another without shame, and were together commissioned for dominion over creation without the curse.

Temptation soon confronted Adam and Eve, and, in disobeying God's righteous rule, they severed the unity woven into God's good creation. The rapid and definite fall of Adam and Eve took place as Eve saw, took, ate, and gave to Adam, and he finally ate too. The image bearers of God then realized that they were each personally distanced from God. Knowing they were naked, they were ashamed and hid from him in fear (Gen 3:7–10). Their communion was devoured by sin when they experienced alienation from one another, assigning blame and bearing guilt (vv. 10–13). Evicted from their perfect home, the couple knew their sin had brought strife and relational conflict as they were sent away from God's presence (vv. 15–24). "Through their disobedience, sin entered and disrupted their relationship to God, to each other, and to creation. Adam's

---

[2] This chapter builds on Christopher W. Morgan, "Toward a Theology of the Unity of the Church," in *Why We Belong: Evangelical Unity and Denominational Diversity*, ed. Anthony L. Chute, Christopher W. Morgan, and Robert A. Peterson (Wheaton, IL: Crossway, 2013), 19–36.

sin, while personal and historical, is also communal and cosmic, plunging all humanity into sin (Rom 5:12–21) and resulting in a creation that longs for freedom (8:18–28)."[3]

Thankfully, the biblical story continues to reveal that God himself would bring peace through a mission of reconciliation. God not only brought peace, but his own Son is called "our peace" as he orchestrates personal and communal reconciliation within this cosmic plan of restoration (Eph 2:14). Through his death and resurrection, the Son offers full forgiveness of sin and brings unity in all three spheres. As individuals, we are united to Christ in his death and resurrection, in which we are given every spiritual blessing, including redemption, forgiveness, reconciliation, adoption, and an eternal inheritance (1:3–14; 2:1–10). As the church, we are each united to Christ, who in turn unites us to one another as his people, regardless of our ethnicity or past sin (2:11–22; 3:1–6). Finally, the cosmos is being united by the work of Christ toward complete reconciliation in the new creation (1:9–10; 3:9–11).

In the fullness of time, the work of reconciliation will be complete, and we will see realized the plan of God to unite all things in Christ (1:9–10). Believers will each receive the promised inheritance because of their personal union with Christ (1:11–14). Christ's bride, the corporate people of God (5:22–23; Rev 19:6–9), will be united with Christ at the marriage supper of the Lamb (Rev 19:6–9). As a united people, we will comprise every tribe, tongue, and nation (Rev 5:9), primarily identified no longer by our diversity but by our union with our Savior (Eph 2:14–15). Finally, the entire cosmos will pass away so that the new creation, rightly ordered and subjected to Christ, can take its place. Personally, communally, and cosmically, God's plan of unity will ultimately be fulfilled.

From the foundation of the world until the fullness of time, God's plan is to bring all things into union with Christ. Although humanity was created to experience perfect unity, its fall into sin has severed the unity between God and humanity, between one person and another, and between humanity and creation. Through Christ's saving work, which

---

[3] Morgan, 20.

we receive by faith, we are reconciled to God, to one another, and to creation. We await the consummation of history, at which time our union with Christ, one another, and the new creation will be fully realized. This plan of unity, as Ephesians reiterates, is all for the glory of our Creator, Sustainer, Redeemer, and Savior.

Unity Is Covenantal

Between the cross and new creation, the church testifies to the true reconciliation found only in Christ. As each member of the body is united to Christ, so the body as a whole is united to each of its members. According to Ephesians, to experience and demonstrate this communion among believers, we must not dissolve the theological realities that define biblical unity but instead must uphold them as fundamental prerequisites on which that unity relies.

Ephesians describes entrance into the new covenant church as based not on the law (2:15) but on the death and resurrection of Christ (1:3–14; 2:1–10). The chosen, holy, forgiven, and redeemed children of God (1:3–14) were alienated from God but through the atonement of Christ, have been united to him (2:1–10). Further, having been raised from the dead and seated at God's right hand in the heavenly places, Christ is not only the necessary access point of unity but also now is given as "head over all things to the church, which is his body" (1:20–23 ESV). Foundationally, the church is the new covenant people of God, each member of which is personally reconciled to God.

Paul unveils the mystery of God's plan for corporate unity by describing the inclusion of the Gentiles in the people of God (2:11–12). By nature of their birth, Gentiles were outside of Israel and thus had no hope that the Messiah would benefit them in any way.[4] After reminding them of this hopeless state, Paul reveals that Gentiles are now welcome in the new covenant and "brought near by the blood of Christ" (v. 13).

---

[4] F. F. Bruce, *The Epistle to the Colossians, to Philemon, and to the Ephesians,* New International Commentary on the New Testament, ed. Ned B. Stonehouse, F. F. Bruce, and Gordon D. Fee (Grand Rapids: Eerdmans, 1984), 294.

Those who were once without even the promise of hope can now be full participants in God's plan of reconciliation, regardless of their standing in the old covenant.

Therefore, the church is not only the new-covenant people reconciled to God but is also the new-covenant people reconciled to one another (2:11–22). As one new humanity, the once divided Jew and Gentile are together united in Christ (2:15). Christ is "our peace" and establishes among us a sort of unity that negates the worldly divisions that often define societal norms (2:14). Where there was once a "wall of hostility" (2:14), there is now common access to the Spirit of God and one new building that has Christ as its perfect cornerstone (2:18–21).

Although this new covenant invites both Jew and Gentile, it does not permit entrance apart from Christ. In Ephesians 2, we see Paul exhort those who believe in Christ to be united on the basis of faith in Christ, not right of birth. Conversely, Ephesians 5 prohibits this newly united people from being "partners" with immoral people (5:7). Andrew T. Lincoln describes this forbidden partnership as bearing "the connotation of intimate involvement and participation with the other party."[5] Having become "light" through their union with Christ, Paul's readers are now not to identify themselves with darkness through partnering with unbelievers in sinful acts (2:1–3; 5:8). Therefore, Paul promotes a unity that defies cultural boundaries, but not a unity that denies Christ.

While there certainly are practical reasons to cooperate with those outside the church, the biblical sense of unity relates to church unity. Individuals who had nothing in common now have the most vital thing in common: Christ. The theological realities of our new identity in Christ reorient our social affinities and bring reconciliation where division once persisted.[6] We were separated people, strangers alienated from one another. Now, as one new man (2:15), fellow citizens of a new

---

[5] Andrew T. Lincoln, *Ephesians*, Word Bible Commentary 42, ed. Bruce M. Metzger, David A. Hubbard, and Glenn W. Barker (Grand Rapids: Zondervan, 1990), 326.

[6] See Jarvis Williams and Thomas R. Schreiner, *One New Man: The Cross and Racial Reconciliation in Pauline Theology* (Nashville: B&H, 2010).

kingdom (2:19), and building blocks in the new holy temple (2:21), we are one in Christ.

Ephesians thus stresses that our personal union with Christ through his saving work is necessary for new covenant unity. This theological basis for unity grounds our cooperation for a common cause. It provides ample motive for reordering allegiances that once defined our social interactions because our new identity in Christ determines our closest bonds.

Unity Is Transcendent

The unity of the church not only defines our relationships with other believers; it also pictures God himself. As individuals are united to Christ and those individuals to one another, truth about God is displayed. Throughout Ephesians, Paul demonstrates how God reveals his divine attributes through uniting believers to Christ:

> according to the riches of his grace that he richly poured out on us with all wisdom and understanding. (1:7–8)

> the immeasurable greatness of his power toward us who believe, according to the mighty working of his strength. (1:19)

> so that in the coming ages he might display the immeasurable riches of his grace through his kindness to us in Christ Jesus. (2:7)

> so that God's multi-faceted wisdom may now be made known through the church to the rulers and authorities in the heavens. (3:10)

In the unveiling of his plan for the unity and restoration of the cosmos through Christ, God reveals his grace, wisdom, power, and kindness.

United to Christ and to one another, we partially display God's character in our lives. By walking in good works, we follow after our Father (2:10). Once dead but now alive, we who are united to Christ are new creatures who no longer walk according to the way of the world but walk in good works, making it our aim to imitate the Father as he exposes to light the works once done in darkness (2:1–20; 4:1; 5:11–14).

Individually and collectively, we now exhibit God's character to the world as we "walk in a manner worthy of [our] calling" (4:1 ESV). As the church, we are called to live in unity (4:3, 13), holiness (4:24 ESV), light (5:8), and wisdom (5:15), all of which reflect our God. As we walk accordingly, we bear God's image to the world and glorify him by partially displaying who he is.

Our union with Christ and with one another also points to God's unity. In Eph 4:1–6, Paul writes:

> I, the prisoner in the Lord, urge you to live worthy of the calling you have received, with all humility and gentleness, with patience, bearing with one another in love, making every effort to keep the unity of the Spirit through the bond of peace. There is one body and one Spirit—just as you were called to one hope at your calling—one Lord, one faith, one baptism, one God and Father of all, who is above all and through all and in all.

Paul grounds the reality of the oneness of the church in the oneness of God. The Father, Son, and Spirit are all mentioned in this passage, but the emphasis is on God's unity even amid the uniqueness of each person. In God's eternal plan, he displays his oneness through our unity as his church.

Similarly, in his high priestly prayer Jesus draws a connection between his own unity with the Father and our oneness as his church. The Father reveals himself to his people through Christ. He says he has manifested the Father's name to the people whom the Father has given him, and he has made known to them the Father's words; thus they now believe that the Father sent the Son (John 17:5–8). Jesus then identifies an exchange between the Father and himself: Christ gives back to the Father those people initially given to him by the Father (v. 10). Further, Jesus highlights that the love and glory experienced between the Father and the Son are displayed in his people as they are one (vv. 10, 23).

Jesus also prays that those people who believe that the Father sent the Son would themselves be one. The oneness of God's people is established in the oneness of the Father and the Son. Jesus prays for the unity of his people three times (vv. 11, 21, and 22). The rationale for each request is striking. Their basis is the Father's oneness with the Son: "even as we are one" (v. 11 ESV); "just as you, Father, are in me, and I in you" (v. 21 ESV); and "even as we are one" (v. 22 ESV). Incredibly, oneness with each other in Christ both displays and is rooted in the unity of our triune God.

Unity Is Missional

Our unity with Christ and with each other also testifies to the world that we have been reconciled to God—and that others can be too. Biblical unity reaches inside the church to bind us together in Christ, and it reaches out to all people in hope that they too might be united to Christ and his church. At least two missional obligations spring from our own union with Christ. First, we help others to be reconciled to God through sharing the gospel. Second, we enhance the believability of the gospel by living in unity.

In Ephesians Paul urges Jewish and Gentile believers to be unified as one new humanity (2:13–22). His intent for unity does not end there, however. While Paul sees unity as uniquely experienced by believers, his mission is to bring more people to Christ (3:8–11). Paul models the mission of unity in his call to preach to the Gentiles:

> This grace was given to me—the least of all the saints—to proclaim to the Gentiles the incalculable riches of Christ, and to shed light for all about the administration of the mystery hidden for ages in God who created all things. This is so that God's multi-faceted wisdom may now be made known through the church to the rulers and authorities in the heavens. This is according to his eternal purpose accomplished in Christ Jesus our Lord. (Eph 3:8–11)

Paul is called to proclaim the truth that Gentiles are now included in the promises of God. They too can be united to Christ. The possibility of Gentile union with Christ is so magnificent to Paul that he considers himself unworthy of the calling to proclaim it (v. 8). The glorious weight of his mission is such an honor to him that he is willing to suffer in pursuit of it (vv. 12–13). Therefore, Paul shares the gospel from an appreciation and amazement that God would unite himself to his people through Christ.

United to Christ and to each other, we accentuate our verbal gospel witness with a visible gospel witness. The surprising union of Jewish and Gentile believers has incredible power to persuade the world that God is at work. Ephesians 3:10 indicates that the unity of the church collectively illustrates the wisdom of God. The oneness of Jews and Gentiles in Christ alerts the rulers and authorities in the heavens that God's plan for cosmic unity is moving forward (1:10): "By her very existence as a new humanity, in which the major division of the first-century world has been overcome, the Church reveals God's secret in action and heralds to the hostile heavenly powers the overcoming of cosmic divisions with their defeat."[7] In a fallen world, where disunity pervades, the presence of true unity among believers serves as a window to God's plan for the cosmos and attests to the gospel's power to change lives.

John 17 also highlights God's missional purpose in the unity of believers with God and the unity of believers with one another. Jesus prays that through the word and the unity of believers, the world would believe in him: "I do not ask for these only, but also for those who will believe in me through their word, that they may all be one, just as you, Father, are in me, and I in you, that they also may be in us, so that the world may believe that you have sent me" (vv. 20–21 ESV). The message of the gospel is the means by which the world will believe in Christ (v. 20), and the unity of the believers testifies to the validity of that message (v. 21). The oneness of believers demonstrates the oneness of the Son and Father and the fact that the Father sent the Son. So our unity does not merely affect our own fellowship; it also provides convincing testimony to the world that the gospel is true. As people hear the word and see it enacted in the unity of believers, the gospel message becomes even more compelling.

Both Ephesians and John 17 not only provide theological reflection on biblical unity but also demonstrate its power to further the gospel.

---

[7] Lincoln, *Ephesians*, 187.

The movement of redemptive history presses forward until all things are united in Christ, things in heaven and things on earth. Believers participate in this cosmic movement toward union by sharing the gospel that unites people to Christ and by living in unity with one another.

Unity Is Inaugurated

As we showcase God's eternal purpose of cosmic unity to the world, we demonstrate that the kingdom of God has already broken into history. Although we await its final completion, a foretaste of the kingdom is already present in the church. God is making all things new, and he has begun to do so with the church. As we live out the unity we have in Christ in this inaugurated state, we see that the church is already one but must also pursue unity.

The church is one. The unity of the church is a current reality. Ephesians presents at least three truths that account for the presence of church unity. Paul teaches that the church is already one through his reflection on Christ's headship, his description of the transformation of the Gentiles, and his teaching on the connection between church unity and the oneness of God.

Ephesians 1:22–23 states that Christ has already been made our head and that all things are already under his feet. Our communion as believers is founded upon the reality of Christ's headship over us. With Christ as our head, we are together submitted to his authority over us as we live in this world (compare 5:23). Michael Horton points out, "The church is always on the receiving end in its relationship to Christ; it is never the redeemer, but always the redeemed; never the head, but always the body."[8] Together as a unified body, we require the direction and leadership of our head, Christ (4:15). Just as Christ is already the head of the church, so the church is already one under his headship.

---

[8] Michael S. Horton, *People and Place: A Covenant Ecclesiology* (Louisville: Westminster John Knox, 2008), 31.

We know that the church is already one also because the inclusion of the Gentiles is a present reality. Ephesians 2:11–22 clarifies that Jew and Gentile, once separated by the wall of hostility, are now one new humanity, members of one household, fellow citizens, and parts of the same temple joined together in Christ. Paul's description of this unity rests on a temporal distinction: "remember that at one time" (v. 11) versus "but now" (v. 13). The Gentiles are now one with the Jews because of the work of Christ. They are not waiting for this unity to occur in the future but are encouraged to enjoy it now.

Finally, we see that the current unity of the church is an accurate reflection of the unity of God. In his comments on Eph 4:3–6, John Stott maintains:

> We must assert that there can only be one Christian family, only one Christian faith, hope and baptism, and only one Christian body, because there is only one God, Father, Son, and Holy Spirit. You can no more multiply churches than you can multiply Gods. Is there only one God? Then he has only one church. Is the unity of God inviolable? Then so is the unity of the church.[9]

The church manifests the reality of God's nature, and thus the church is already one because God himself is one.

Note that unity marks the church as a whole, or what is often called the universal church. Unity also marks the local church. As we previously noted, the reconciliation of Jews and Gentiles into one new people is across a vast scale. It is sweeping, salvation-historical, and global, and it requires belief in some sort of universal church. Yet the very fact that the reconciliation of Jews and Gentiles into this one new people serves as a showcase of God's eternal purposes of cosmic unity also requires the church's visibility, and thus the local church.[10]

---

[9] John R. W. Stott, *The Message of Ephesians: God's New Society*, 2nd ed., The Bible Speaks Today (Downers Grove, IL: InterVarsity Press, 1992), 151.

[10] For more on the local and/or universal church, see Morgan, "Theology of the Unity," 19–36. For more on the church in Baptist history, see Anthony L. Chute, Nathan A. Finn, and Michael A. G. Haykin, *The Baptist Story: From*

In sum, Ephesians describes unity as a present characteristic of the church. The church is not anticipating Christ to become its head but submits to his authority now. Gentiles do not await union with Jews but can enjoy full fellowship now. And the oneness of the church will not eventually display the oneness of God but does so now.

The church pursues unity. Although the church's unity is a present reality, Paul teaches that the church must continue to pursue unity as well. Ephesians 4:1–3 exhorts the church to live according to its calling, "making every effort to keep the unity of the Spirit through the bond of peace." The church is not the creator of this unity, but the church is required to strive to guard and promote the unity that has already been established by the Spirit.[11]

The church is already one, but the church is not yet fully one. This already/not yet reality characterizes not only church unity but other attributes of the church as well. Donald Bloesch observes:

> The church is already one, but it must become more visibly one . . .
> in faith and in practice. The church is already holy in its source
> and foundation, but it must strive to produce fruits of holiness in
> its sojourn in the world. . . . The church is already apostolic, but it
> must become more consciously apostolic by allowing the gospel
> to reform and sometimes even overturn its time-honored rites
> and interpretations.[12]

Similarly, Paul presents the paradox of the "already" and the "not yet" throughout Ephesians. He says the church is the fullness of Christ (1:23) but must still be filled (3:19; 4:13). The church is the one new humanity

---

English Sect to Global Movement (Nashville: B&H, 2015). For more on a central figure in such debates, see James A. Patterson, *James Robinson Graves: Staking the Boundaries of Baptist Identity*, Studies in Baptist Life, ed. Michael A. G. Haykin (Nashville: B&H, 2012).

[11] Edmund P. Clowney, *The Church*, Contours of Christian Theology (Downers Grove, IL: InterVarsity Press, 1995), 79.

[12] Donald Bloesch, *The Church: Sacraments, Worship, Ministry, Mission*, Christian Foundations (Downers Grove, IL: InterVarsity Press, 2002), 103.

(2:14–18) but must grow into a mature humanity (4:13) and put on the new humanity (4:20–24). In the same way, as the church, we are already one in Christ, yet we must live out our oneness in humility, gentleness, patience, and love (4:2).

Unity Is Possible

By God's grace, such unity is possible. Paul urges the church to prize unity and calls us to live together in a way that fosters unity and does not undermine it. Ephesians 4:1–6 encourages the church to exhibit the moral qualities necessary for unity; Eph 4:7–16 explains that diverse gifts are supplied to the church to cultivate unity; and Eph 4:17–32 exhorts believers to engage in actions that build unity.

Having discussed the theological realities of unity in Christ in chapters 1–3, in Eph 4:1–3 Paul calls us to promote the practical outworking of this unity through humility, gentleness, patience, bearing with one another in love, and an eagerness to maintain the unity of the Spirit in the bond of peace. Paul understands that unity must begin in the heart as the local church cultivates the sort of care and kindness that is required when living in community with other sinners saved by grace. John Stott states, "Too many start with structures (and structures of some kind are indispensable), but the apostle starts with moral qualities."[13] The unity of the church, grounded in the theological teachings of chapters 1–3, reminds us that our unity is not based on the perfect harmony of like-minded people with common affinities but is rooted firmly in the gospel, which is marked by grace, forgiveness, love, and sacrifice.

After Paul reiterates the oneness of God and the oneness of the church (4:4–6), Eph 4:7 introduces the diversity of gifts given to the unified church: "Now grace was given to each one of us according to the measure of Christ's gift." The variety of gifts granted to the church is meant to build up the body "until we all reach unity in the faith and in

---

[13] Stott, *Message of Ephesians*, 148.

the knowledge of God's Son" (4:13). Paul sees the gifts given by Christ to the church as tools to be utilized to promote unity, especially regarding the faith and the knowledge of Christ (4:13).[14] As every believer engages in ministry through his or her gifts, the church together progresses toward spiritual maturity in Christ.

Moral qualities and gifts in the body both are supplied by God to make unity possible. Ephesians 4:17–32 addresses the actions of believers that directly affect the unity of the local churches. As members of one another, the church is to replace the old self with the new (vv. 20–24) in several ways: by putting away falsehood and speaking the truth (v. 25), resolving anger quickly (v. 26), not stealing but working and giving generously (v. 28), and not speaking corruptly but building each other up (v. 29). More generally, Paul summarizes that the church must not be characterized by bitterness, wrath, anger, clamor, or slander but instead must be kind, tenderhearted, and forgiving of one another (vv. 31–32). He reminds them again that these new habits grow out of an appreciation of the theological reality that "God in Christ forgave you" (v. 32 ESV). Each of these commands has a direct impact on the quality of community life as believers live as one.

Paul's logic in the practical teachings of Ephesians 4 is dependent on chapters 1–3. Just as it is possible for God to make alive those who were once dead (2:1–4), to make citizens those who were once strangers (3:19), or to make a new humanity out of those who were once hostile (3:14–15), so too it is possible for the redeemed to live out their oneness in Christ. The apparent unlikelihood of unity in the church—because of our differences, disagreements, and divisions—makes unity a powerful witness to the world and evidence of our salvation in Christ. The supernatural ability to lay down our own egos, agendas, preferences, and habits for the sake of others continues to demonstrate that God indeed has made us one as he is one.

---

[14] Harold W. Hoehner, *Ephesians: An Exegetical Commentary* (Grand Rapids: Baker Academic, 2002), 553.

Unity Is Baptist?

Unity is clearly biblical and thoroughly Christian. As the Christian tradition and much of this volume underlines, we believe in the church, marked by unity, holiness, truth, and universality.

But is unity Baptist? Some might suggest that Baptist unity is an oxymoron. After all, Baptist churches are notorious for division, and the number of Baptist denominations is hard to track without an advanced degree in statistics. Baptist denominations and institutions have splintered over Calvinism/Arminianism, education, revivals, missions, slavery, the Sabbath, creation/evolution, the inerrancy of the Bible, the role of women, cooperative structures, and more. And Baptist churches have split over much less as well.

From such matters, many might conclude that Baptists have nothing to say about unity. To be sure, more still needs to be said, and a thorough doctrine of the unity of the church for Baptists remains to be developed.[15] But Baptists have addressed the topic of church unity, and in a wide variety

---

[15] See Christopher W. Morgan, "Baptists and the Unity of the Church," *Journal of Baptist Studies* 7 (Feb. 2015): 4–5. "First, note the many-faceted applications and contexts: unity within local church, unity in relationships among believers and families in the local church, unity within denominational agencies, unity within a denomination, unity among segments of denominations (state, associational, organizations), unity in ministry action and vision (Cooperative Program, missions, etc.), unity among different denominations, unity among ethnicities, and social structures, and unity with all believers in all true churches. Second, consider the breadth of sources: Baptist confessions, church covenants, catechisms, institutional documents, theological works, commentaries on key passages, pastoral books, ecclesiologies—let alone a wide selection of sermons by representative Baptists. Third, note the wide variety of types of Baptists and how various stripes would approach a theology of church unity differently. Fourth, consider ever-changing historical contexts and how each distinct context shapes the theology of church unity. Unity when under persecution, unity when successful, unity amidst denominational rivalry, and unity amidst evangelical marginalization all affect how unity is discussed and understood. Plus, unity would need to be evaluated in its absence by examining the all-too-common Baptist splits—in denominations, organizations, and local churches. Praxis (or even the lack thereof) teaches much about theology, especially a theology of church unity."

of ways. Some of the most important of these include Baptist confessions of faith.[16] Examples of references to biblical unity with Christ and with one another found within Baptist confessions include the following:[17]

Thomas Helwys Confession, 1611. The Helwys Confession makes mention of the church as united to one another, the church as one yet many congregations, and the local church as the body of Christ. The confession also teaches that one local church ought not challenge any prerogative of any other, that the Lord's Supper is an illustration of the church's communion with Christ, and that the members of the church ought to love one another.

First London Confession of Faith, 1644. The First London Confession of Faith provides ample description of Baptists' conviction regarding unity. In summary, it explains that the unity of believers is tied to the unity of the Trinity and the union of each believer to Christ. In the local church, believers are to have and value communion with one another as well as to endure the faults and sins of others in patience. Likewise, the local church, though itself a unique body, should also walk together with other local churches, who are fellow members of one body in the common faith under Christ.

Second London Confession, 1689. The Second London Confession also includes an abundance of doctrinal teaching on unity for Baptists. To stress Baptist unity with other Christians and to avoid persecution, the

---

[16] See many Baptist confessions at http://baptiststudiesonline.com/confessions -of-faith/. In personal conversation, Baptist historian Tony Chute observed that the very fact that we have multiple confessions says something in and of itself about Baptists and the unity of the church. Multiple confessions can be good, but their existence does underline our tendency to keep adding distinctions from each other.

[17] For more details on what these confessions teach about church unity, see Morgan, "Baptists and the Unity," 4–23.

confession asserts that it follows the example and even most of the wording of other significant Christian confessions.[18]

The confession teaches that Christ alone is the head of the church,
and church membership is understood as covenantal. The unity of the
church is applied to the one universal church as well as to local churches.
Church members are urged to prize unity by viewing the church as more
significant than their personal offenses with others, praying for the good
and success of all churches, living in community with one another, and
serving one another for the mutual good. Baptism is a sign of our union
with Christ, and the Lord's Supper is a bond and pledge of our union
with Christ and with each other. The confession ends as it begins, stressing the unity of Baptists with other Christians. Baptists share the core of
Christian beliefs in common with other Christians, strive to keep theological disagreements in perspective, and seek to unite and show as much
agreement with other believers as possible. The confession notes that the
unity of the church still exists amid—and is consistent with—the reality
of some disagreements within local churches and denominations. The
unity of the church is also consistent with the recognition of levels of
significance of various doctrines: those of the essence of Christianity and
those of personal conviction or liberty. As a result, the confession urges
those who hold to the doctrines of the essence of Christianity to put

---

[18] For the context of these confessions, see James M. Renihan, "Confessing
the Faith in 1644 and 1689," The Reformed Reader, http://www.reformedreader
.org/ctf.htm: "This Confession, influential as it is, may perhaps best be understood
against its historical and theological backgrounds. It did not appear out of the
blue, the product of a sudden burst of theological insight on the part of an author
or authors, but in the tradition of good Confession making, it is largely dependent
on the statements of earlier Reformed Confessions. A quick glance will demonstrate that it is based, to a large degree, on that most Puritan of documents, the
Westminster Confession of Faith of 1647. A closer inspection will reveal that it is
even more intimately related to the revision of the Westminster Confession made
by John Owen and others in 1658, popularly known as the Savoy Declaration
and Platform of Polity. In almost every case the editors of the Baptist Confession
follow the revisions of the Savoy editors when they differ from the Westminster
document. In addition, the Baptists make occasional use of phraseology from the
First London Confession. When all of this material is accounted for, there is very
little . . . that is new and original to the 1677/89 Confession."

aside smaller differences, embrace each other in love and meekness, and give each other liberty on smaller matters.[19]

Baptist Faith and Message, 1925, 1963, 2000. The three Baptist Faith and Message editions speak very little about the doctrine of the unity of the church. The Scriptures are said to be "the true center of Christian union," but the unity of the church is not mentioned explicitly in the sections on the church, baptism and Lord's Supper, the kingdom, evangelism and missions, or stewardship. The 1963 edition adds (and the 2000 edition retains) material on the universal church but nothing on unity.

Instead, the Baptist Faith and Message speaks of "cooperation." The confession urges individual members of churches and the churches themselves to cooperate with one another for the organization of associations and conventions for kingdom purposes. These organizations should carry no authority over the believers, the churches, or each other; they should remain voluntary and advisory, cooperating for missions, education, and benevolence ministries.

The article on cooperation continues, "Christian unity in the New Testament sense is spiritual harmony and voluntary cooperation for common ends by various groups of Christ's people." There is a reference not to church unity but to "Christian unity," and this unity is not theologically grounded but practically defined. The article adds that cooperation among Christian denominations is "permissible and desirable" (1925 BFM) when the goal is right and when there is "no violation of the conscience or compromise of loyalty to Christ and his Word."[20]

---

[19] The Philadelphia Confession of Faith, 1742, essentially follows the Second London Confession of 1689, so there is no need to rehearse it here. Interestingly and sadly, I could find no direct teaching on the unity of the church in the following important Baptist confessions: the Principles of Faith of the Sandy Creek Association, 1758; the New Hampshire Confession of Faith, 1833; and the Abstract of Principles, 1859. For more, see Morgan, "Baptists and the Unity," 4–23.

[20] "Comparison of 1925, 1963 and 2000 Baptist Faith and Message," Southern Baptist Convention, http://www.sbc.net/bfm2000/bfmcomparison .asp. See under "Cooperation."

The Baptist Faith and Message urges churches to work together, Christians to work together, and denominations to work together. The confession also calls for Christians to work with all people "of good will in any good cause,"[21] acting in love without compromising loyalty to Christ and his truth.

So, is unity Baptist? Yes, but the unity of the church is not as much of a driving force as it was and as it should be. The best of what we do have on the unity of the church in Baptist confessions stems from the earlier Baptists. The Second London Confession stands head and shoulders above the others in terms of coverage and depth on the unity of the church, with the next closest being the First London Confession. Yet much of the best material in Baptist confessions on the unity of the church was stressed out of necessity, to avoid persecution and to avoid being understood as schismatic or heretical. Further, while a good portion of the material on the unity of the church was indeed written by Baptists, quite a bit of the Second London Confession was borrowed—copied verbatim from the Westminster Confession and the Savoy Declaration—and thus originated with Anglicans, Nonconformists, and Puritans. The 1742 Philadelphia Confession of Faith also references church unity, but it was based on the Second London Confession.

The unity of the church apparently has not been framed theologically in Baptist confessions since 1742. This means that a large portion of the best material on church unity in Baptist confessions is more than 300 years old, borrowed from other Christian traditions, and partially occasioned by the need to avoid persecution.

The language of "cooperation" has emerged as the basis for working together. While a fine term in what it stresses (cooperation is indeed good and desirable), it seems to shift the approach from "we work together because we are united together in Christ" to "we cooperate because of shared goals and mission" (which is also good but less permanent and more dependent on extensive relationships). This might inadvertently

---

[21] "Comparison of 1925, 1963 and 2000 Baptist Faith and Message": "The Christian and the Social Order."

ground our unity in practical concerns rather than on a theology of church unity.

It is also important to note that the ways Baptists have understood and articulated the doctrine of the unity of the church have been heavily shaped by the historical context. When Baptists were under persecution by the Church of England, unity was prized and sought after. When Baptists pursued evangelism on the American frontier, unity often took a back seat. When denominational distinctives were highlighted, unity was often neglected. When historic Christian teachings were being redefined by theological liberalism, unity with churches of mainline denominations seemed like disloyalty to Christ and his truth. When denominational agencies and seminaries were led largely by theological moderates and the neoorthodox, unity felt like compromise. And when Christians are increasingly persecuted around the globe and marginalized in this pluralistic age, true church unity again seems vital.

And church unity *is* vital—but not just because of the current context. The unity of the church is a core doctrine of the Christian faith. The unity of the church is an essential spiritual reality for every believer in Christ. The unity of the church is a beautiful goal in God's eternal plan. And the unity of the church is a transformative agent in God's mission. We are united to Christ, indeed to the whole Trinity. In Christ, we are united to each other and are now constituted as the people of God, the church. Our unity as the church grounds our common mission and obliges our cooperation. This cooperation includes churches working together, Christians working together, and, as much as is good and possible, denominations working together for kingdom purposes.

2

Baptists, *Sola Scriptura*, and the Place of the Christian Tradition

RHYNE R. PUTMAN

New Orleans Baptist Theological Seminary

With his 2004 novel *The Mysterious Flame of Queen Loana*, the late Italian novelist and philosopher Umberto Eco explored the relationship between cognition, memory, and literary knowledge. Eco told the story of Yambo, a sixty-something antiquarian book dealer who awoke in a hospital with a peculiar case of amnesia. Though he remembered nothing about his own life or family, he could recall very specific details from every book, article, and poem he had ever read.

Yambo retained what Eco described as his "public memory," but no "episodic memory" remained. With his public memory Yambo remembered the characters, twists, and turns of great works of fiction, but without his episodic memory he had no recollection of the context in which he had read them. Eco defined episodic memory as the memory that "establishes a link between who we are today and who we have been, and without it, when we say *I*, we're referring only to what we're feeling now, not to what we felt before, which gets lost, as you say, in the fog."[1] For the

---

[1] Umberto Eco, *The Mysterious Flame of Queen Loana*, trans. Geoffrey Brock (New York: Harcourt, 2005), 13.

remainder of the novel, Yambo attempts to unravel his life story through the pages of the books and magazines that shaped his early life, hoping to find some semblance of what had been lost.

This postmodern tale of segregated memory serves as a fitting analogy for the relationship between many Baptists and the Christian tradition. Many Baptists have a clear grasp of the public memory of Scripture but have little or no episodic memory of the broader tradition that formed them. They may be orthodox in their theological conclusions and competent as interpreters of Scripture, but they have forgotten or never really understood the role tradition has played in shaping their knowledge. In their historical amnesia, many Baptists have affirmed the substance of the great ecumenical creeds—the doctrines of the Trinity, the true divinity and humanity of Jesus, and so on—but have given little or no formal recognition to the role these creeds play in shaping their interpretation of Scripture and their public worship.

Baptists have often been accused (sometimes justly) of rejecting the authority of tradition as a source for doing theology. Some Baptists have misunderstood the nature of tradition, the classical Protestant conception of *sola Scriptura* ("Scripture alone"), and the historical relationship of Baptists to the tradition of the early church. This chapter will explore how Baptists can maintain their commitment to *sola Scriptura* while also appropriating the Christian tradition in a normative manner.

A Funny Breed without a Creed?

"We have no creed but the Bible!" This oft-repeated slogan sums up what many in Baptist and free church traditions have believed about the Protestant Reformation and *sola Scriptura*. In their version of church history, the Bible came toe-to-toe with church tradition and won. Christians came to their senses and realized they had the Bible and the Holy Spirit and need not waste their time with "vain repetitions" of dusty old creeds. In this view, Bible-believing Christians certainly should not speak of creeds or confessions as having any kind of normative value.

One antitraditional stream in Baptist history, *naïve biblicism*, repudiates any and all creedal or confessional statements not explicitly found in

Scripture.[2] Naïve biblicists insist Scripture must be interpreted in complete isolation from tradition.[3] The most notable representative of this view was the nineteenth-century Irish-American clergyman Alexander Campbell (1788–1866). A Baptist for seventeen years (1813–1830), Campbell went on to lead one of the largest schisms in Baptist history, a movement known by his followers as the Stone-Campbell Restoration Movement. As a self-declared "Reformer," Campbell envisioned a thoroughgoing reconstruction of primitive Christianity devoid of all ecclesial practices not explicitly mentioned in Scripture (e.g., church constitutions, missionary societies, and instrumental worship).[4] Believing that creeds and confessions functionally usurp biblical authority, Campbell and his disciples crusaded against their use in Baptist churches.[5]

Campbell demanded that interpreters of the Bible use the Bible's language when explaining it. Creeds such as the Nicene Creed are exercises in "speculative theology" that only convolute pure biblical truth with "scholastic jargon" better off forgotten than remembered.[6] Campbell ultimately found the creeds pointless: "As far as is known on the earth, there is not in 'the Book of Life of the Lamb slain from the foundation of the world,' the name of any person who was either converted or sanctified to

---

[2] I unashamedly describe myself as a *biblicist* in the sense that I am committed first and foremost to the full authority and complete truthfulness of Scripture, yet, following Kevin Vanhoozer, I distinguish between *naïve biblicism* and *critical biblicism*. See Vanhoozer, "May We Go beyond What Is Written After All? The Pattern of Theological Authority and the Problem of Doctrinal Development," in *The Enduring Authority of the Scriptures*, ed. D. A. Carson (Grand Rapids: Eerdmans, 2016), 790–92.

[3] Timothy George labels this position *nuda scriptura* or *scriptura solitaria*. See George, "An Evangelical Reflection on Scripture and Tradition," *Pro Ecclesia* 9, no. 2 (May 2000): 206.

[4] Alexander Campbell, *The Christian System* (Pittsburg, KY: Forrester & Campbell, 1839), 285. Campbell cites *homoousios* from the Nicene Creed as an example of this unhelpful terminology.

[5] James E. Tull, *Shapers of Baptist Thought* (Valley Forge, PA: Judson, 1972), 106–18; H. Leon McBeth, *The Baptist Heritage: Four Centuries of Baptist Witness* (Nashville: Broadman, 1987), 379–80. Campbell's first target was the Philadelphia Confession of 1742, a statement of faith adopted by the Redstone Baptist Association, of which Campbell's Brush Run church was a part.

[6] Campbell, *Christian System*, 130–31.

God by any of these controversies about human dogmas, nor by any thing learned from the canons or creeds of all the Councils, from that of Nice to the last Methodistic Conference."[7]

Though Campbell's self-identification as a Baptist was short-lived, his influence on American Baptists was pervasive and enduring. By 1830 hundreds of Baptist churches in Kentucky, Tennessee, and Virginia had left their associations to become Church of Christ and Disciples of Christ congregations affiliated with Campbell's "restoration."[8] The Landmark controversy that divided Southern Baptists in the latter half of the nineteenth century developed partly in response to Campbell's own schismatic, antitradition teaching.[9]

Even if Campbell's unique brand of antitraditionalism and ecclesiology had never gained widespread acceptance in Baptist life, another strand of *libertarian anticreedalism* played a considerable role in the late-twentieth-century controversy known as the "Conservative Resurgence" (or, to its detractors, the "Fundamentalist Takeover") of the Southern Baptist Convention.[10] These anticreedal Baptists, once associated with the "moderate" arm of the SBC, opposed any authoritative appeal to historic confessions as binding or central to Christian communion.[11]

---

[7] Campbell, 131.

[8] As many as half of the Baptist churches in Kentucky became "Christian" or "Disciples" congregations during Campbell's lifetime. See J. H. Spencer, *A History of Kentucky Baptists: From 1769 to 1885*, vol. 1, rev. Burrilla B. Spencer (Cincinnati: J. R. Baumes, 1885). Spencer described the rise of "Campbellism" as a "raging epidemic" in Kentucky churches that replaced the spirit of worship with "bitter cavil about creeds, confessions of faith, and church constitutions" (597–98).

[9] See James E. Tull, *A History of Southern Baptist Landmarkism in the Light of Historical Baptist Ecclesiology*, Baptist Tradition Series (New York: Arno, 1980).

[10] For a critical assessment of the relationship between Campbell's anti-traditionalism and later libertarian anticreedalism, see Timothy George, "Southern Baptist Ghosts," *First Things* 93 (May 1999): 18–24.

[11] See R. Albert Mohler Jr., "Southern Baptist Identity: Is There a Future?" in *Southern Baptist Identity: An Evangelical Denomination Faces the Future*, ed. David S. Dockery (Wheaton, IL: Crossway, 2009), 28–29. Mohler makes the helpful distinction between the "truth party" (i.e., the confessionalists) and the "liberty party" (i.e., the moderates) to describe the agendas of the two major parties in the SBC controversy.

They used Campbell's ironic "no creed" credo, but this group's version of anticreedalism, unlike Campbell's, was neither biblicist nor completely against appeals to tradition.[12]

For libertarian Baptists, the slogan "No creed but the Bible!" was a battle cry, the hermeneutical equivalent of "Get off my lawn!" They interpreted *sola Scriptura* as a statement more about interpretive freedom than about biblical authority. Private judgment trumps ecclesial authority in the interpretation of Scripture. In the words of one libertarian Baptist:

> Early Baptists echoed Martin Luther's conviction-filled affirmation of *sola scriptura*, "scripture alone." And they did so because they wanted to be free "from" all other religious authorities. . . .
>
> Over the years some Baptists have almost forgotten it. So it must be said again and it must be said loudly this time: BAPTISTS ARE A NON-CREEDAL PEOPLE! . . . Historically, Baptists have resisted any and all creeds.[13]

The moderates described Baptists as "a funny breed, a churchly crowd without a creed."[14] For them, the moment Baptists articulate expectations of doctrinal orthodoxy for their pastors, missionaries, or seminary professors, they have ceased to be Baptists.[15] After all, Baptists fiercely

---

[12] Campbell's biblicism was evident in his subscription to the dictation theory of inspiration, in which "God spoke to man in his own language . . . as one person converses with another." See Campbell, *Christian System,* 16; cf. Tull, *Shapers of Baptist Thought,* 106–9. The libertarian Baptists had no such emphasis on the doctrine of Scripture. As David Dockery and Timothy George observe, "Sometimes the phrase 'no creed but the Bible' is just a shibboleth for neither creed nor the Bible." David S. Dockery and Timothy George, *The Great Tradition of Christian Thinking: A Student's Guide,* Reclaiming the Christian Intellectual Tradition (Wheaton, IL: Crossway, 2012), 68.

[13] Walter B. Shurden, *The Baptist Identity: Four Fragile Freedoms* (Macon, GA: Smyth & Helwys, 1993), 14.

[14] Grady C. Cothen and James M. Dunn, *Soul Freedom: Baptist Battle Cry* (Macon, GA: Smith & Helwys, 2000), 83.

[15] E. Glenn Hinson, "Baptists and Evangelicals—What Is the Difference?" in *Are Southern Baptists "Evangelicals"?,* ed. James Leo Garrett Jr., E. Glenn Hinson, and James E. Tull (Macon, GA: Mercer University Press, 1983), 173–74.

resist *creedalism*, the "insistence upon formal subscription to a statement of belief, in exactly those words."[16]

Many Baptists in the moderate wing of the SBC had no problem endorsing or even writing confessions of faith, but they typically denied them any significant place in theological formation or denominational governance.[17] This aversion to confessional authority is expressed in the preamble to the 1963 Baptist Faith and Message: "Throughout their history Baptist bodies, both large and small, have issued statements of faith which comprise a consensus of their beliefs. Such statements have never been regarded as complete, infallible statements of faith, nor as official creeds carrying mandatory authority."[18]

Libertarian Baptists have reluctantly accepted some forms of tradition but are skeptical about its having any normative influence over the interpretation of Scripture or the rule of the local church. They understand *creeds* and *confessions* to be very different kinds of statements of faith. According to their definition, creeds *prescribe* what Christians should believe, while confessions merely *describe* what Christians already believe.[19] Libertarian Baptists are convinced that creeds are a threat to religious liberty, personal autonomy, academic freedom, and the autonomy of

---

[16] Millard J. Erickson, *The Concise Dictionary of Christian Theology*, rev. ed. (Wheaton, IL: Crossway, 2001), s.v. "creedalism."

[17] See Cecil E. Sherman, "Freedom of the Individual to Interpret the Bible," in *Being Baptist Means Freedom*, ed. Alan Neely (Charlotte: Southern Baptist Alliance, 1988), 11. Freeman admits, "Our churches have ignored them for the most part. We have had a loose theology. Experience has been the rite of entrance to our churches."

[18] Preamble, "Comparison of 1925, 1963 and 2000 Baptist Faith and Message," sbc.net/bfm2000/bfmcomparison.asp. The 2000 Baptist Faith and Message takes a more confessional tone: "Baptist churches, associations, and general bodies have adopted confessions of faith as a witness to the world, and as *instruments of doctrinal accountability*. We are not embarrassed to state before the world that these are doctrines we hold precious and as *essential to the Baptist tradition of faith and practice*" (italics mine).

[19] Fisher Humphreys, *The Way We Were: How Southern Baptist Theology Has Changed and What It Means to Us All* (New York: McCracken, 1994), 52; Cothen and Dunn, *Soul Freedom*, 83–84.

the local church.[20] However, both naïve biblicists and libertarian Baptists often misunderstand the nature of tradition, the Protestant relationship to it, and its formative role in early Baptist thought.

The Nature of Tradition

In the broadest, nontheological sense of the word, *tradition* (from the Latin verb *tradere*) describes any information, belief, or custom passed along from one individual or group to another.[21] It is the corporate memory of any community, whether that community be familial, religious, vocational, or academic.[22] Tradition transmits culturally significant beliefs and customs such as worldviews or religious rituals, as well as more picayune things such as family recipes or athletic superstitions. Even common sense and human language are parts of a larger tradition people acquire from living in community with others.[23] Tradition is everywhere, and it shapes how everyone thinks about the world.[24]

Despite this ubiquity of tradition, many in the history of Western philosophy going back to Plato have questioned its usefulness in attaining knowledge. For a rationalist like Descartes, a person becomes a critical thinker when he doubts everything learned from tradition and begins

---

[20] See Walter B. Shurden, "Freedom for Theological Education," in *Being Baptist Means Freedom*, 57–68.

[21] The Latin terms *traditio* and *tradere*, as well as the Greek terms *paradosis* and *paradidomi*, can be used to describe a transfer of physical property, or they can be used metaphorically to describe something "handed down" from one generation to the next. See Yves Congar, *The Meaning of Tradition*, trans. A. N. Woodrow (San Francisco: Ignatius, 2004), 9–10. New Testament authors also use forms of *paradidomi* to describe something or someone physically handed over, as is the case in the arrest of Jesus (Matt 27:18, 26; Mark 15:10, 15; John 19:16; Rom 4:25).

[22] See Anthony C. Thiselton, "Knowledge, Myth, and Corporate Memory," in *Believing in the Church: The Corporate Nature of Faith*, compiled by the Doctrine Commission of the Church of England (Wilton, CT: Morehouse-Barlow, 1981), 45–78.

[23] Thiselton, 50–51.

[24] Alister E. McGrath, *The Genesis of Doctrine: A Study in the Foundation of Doctrinal Criticism* (Oxford, UK: B. Blackwell, 1990), 177.

to reason for himself.[25] Empiricists like Hume dismiss tradition because they believe firsthand experience and evidence are the only means to attaining knowledge. Many Christian theologians influenced by these Enlightenment-era epistemologies also shunned the broader tradition in favor of individualistic religion that gave epistemic primacy to the individual interpreter and private religious experience.[26]

Tradition may be fallible, but complete skepticism toward all forms of tradition is, epistemically speaking, an untenable position. All people begin their search for knowledge within a framework of tradition or inherited knowledge, not in a vacuum. Beliefs form within traditions, and all major beliefs—whether religious, scientific, or historical—comprise individual and corporate elements.[27] So, what role does tradition play in Christian theology? The answer must be nuanced carefully, because the term *tradition* has many meanings in the New Testament, church history, philosophy, and theology.

First, the Christian faith itself is a tradition in the broadest sense. Like Judaism before it, the Christian "faith that was delivered to the saints once for all" (Jude 3) is a tradition that includes a common metanarrative as well as a distinctive set of worldview-shaping beliefs, practices, and values. Every element of Christian corporate memory was built on what came before. The traditions of the Old Testament shaped Jesus and his teaching. His life and teaching gave rise to the apostolic faith ultimately preserved in Scripture. Creeds developed over time as a means of explaining Scripture and defending Christian truth to particular contexts. Today the faith is transmitted through the preaching and disciple-making ministries of local churches. All people who confess Christ as Lord join in

---

[25] See René Descartes, *Meditations on First Philosophy*, AT VII 17–23.

[26] Friedrich Schleiermacher (1768–1834), known as the father of modern theology, was one of the most important advocates of this experiential model of theology. Perhaps the most significant Baptist voice in this vein was Walter Rauschenbusch (1861–1918), who rejected the substance of the ecumenical creeds as something alien to the teaching of Jesus and the New Testament. See Walter Rauschenbusch, *A Theology for the Social Gospel* (New York: Macmillan, 1917), 24–26.

[27] Kevin J. Vanhoozer, *The Drama of Doctrine: A Canonical Linguistic Approach to Christian Doctrine* (Louisville: Westminster John Knox, 2005), 157.

the tradition and are charged with passing the tradition along through evangelism and discipleship.[28]

This tradition also entails numerous "smaller-T" traditions, ranging from sweeping categories like *Protestant* and *Orthodox* to more specific denominational groupings such as Lutheranism or Methodism. Tertiary differences between members of traditions such as these create even smaller subsets, such as Reformed Baptists and Arminian Baptists. Groups who have rejected the consensus of the broader Christian tradition in favor of theological or ethical innovation are deemed heretical or unorthodox. They have created new traditions outside this grand Christian tradition.

Second, Scripture itself is part of the larger Christian tradition. It may seem odd or even unsettling to call Scripture "tradition," especially when Christians so often juxtapose Scripture and tradition as contradictory sources of religious knowledge. Though Scripture is the only God-breathed, inerrant source of written revelation, it is, strictly speaking, a form of written tradition that preserves the corporate memory of Israel and the early church. Furthermore, the formation of the canon—that is, the process by which the church, under the leadership of the Holy Spirit, recognized the sixty-six books of the Bible as Scripture—was itself a post-biblical development of that tradition.[29]

Third, Scripture contains and transmits tradition. Some might object that biblical writers themselves oppose tradition.[30] After all, Jesus speaks critically of the "tradition of the elders" advocated by the Pharisees and the scribes (Matt 15:1–9; Mark 7:1–13). He accuses them of exchanging the explicit command of God for "human tradition" (Mark 7:8). Jesus does not mince words on the matter: "You nullify the word of God by *your tradition* that you have handed down" (Mark 7:13; italics added). In his letters, Paul acknowledges his former zeal for Jewish tradition but

---

[28] For a helpful overview of this process, see Michael F. Bird, *What Christians Ought to Believe: An Introduction to Christian Doctrine through the Apostles' Creed* (Grand Rapids: Zondervan, 2016), 29–42.

[29] Harmon, *Towards Baptist Catholicity*, 43–44.

[30] Wendell Holmes Rone, *The Baptist Faith and Roman Catholicism* (Kingsport, TN: Kingsport Press, 1952), 20.

asserts that the gospel has usurped its place in his life (Gal 1:11–16). He likewise warns Colossian Christians against heresy rooted in "human tradition" (Col 2:8).

Yet biblical writers also use the language of tradition to describe the reception and transmission of their own teaching. Paul commands Timothy to "hold on to the pattern of sound teaching" he has received from him and to "guard the good deposit through the Holy Spirit who lives in us" (2 Tim 1:13–14). Paul likewise tells the Thessalonian Christians to "stand firm and hold to the traditions you were taught, whether by what we said or what we wrote" (2 Thess 2:15). He praises the Corinthian church because they "hold fast to the traditions" he "delivered [*paredōka*]" to them (1 Cor 11:2). The practice of the Lord's Supper is in this category (1 Cor. 11:23). Even the gospel message itself is a tradition Paul receives and passes along: "I passed on [*paredōka*] to you as most important what I also received [*parelabon*]: that Christ died for our sins according to the Scriptures, that he was buried, that he was raised on the third day accord- ing to the Scriptures" (1 Cor 15:3–4). Peter condemns false prophets who ignore the tradition "delivered [*paradotheisēs*] to them" (2 Pet 2:21).

Before the New Testament was formed, there was an unwritten oral tradition concerning the life, death, burial, and resurrection of Jesus—the *kerygma*. The early church had creeds and hymns that predated the New Testament Epistles (cf. 1 Tim 3:16; Phil 2:5–11).[31] Through the means of divinely inspired authors who transmitted this tradition, Scripture has perfectly preserved God's revelation in history for his people. Without these traditions written down in Scripture, there would be no way of knowing about Israel, Jesus, or the early church, for tradition provides humans' only access to the past.

Finally, the greater Christian tradition entails the ongoing interpre- tation and application of Scripture in the life of God's people across time and place. The Christian tradition is the historical, corporate response of the people of God to the Word of God as they are led by the Spirit

---

[31] Bird, *What Christians Believe*, 19–21; cf. Steven E. Fowl, *The Story of Christ in the Ethics of Paul: An Analysis of the Function of the Hymnic Material in the Pauline Corpus* (Sheffield, UK: Sheffield Academic Press, 1990).

of God in all truth. Faithful Christians have never sought to add or take away from "that faith which has been believed everywhere, always, and by all people,"[32] but they have always sought to understand Scripture and apply it to their own context. From the very beginning, Christian theologians understood their primary task to be the careful preservation and transmission of the biblical message. In the words of Irenaeus, "For the faith being ever one and the same, neither does one who is able to discourse at great length regarding it, make any addition to it, nor does one, who can say little, diminish it."[33]

Interpretations of Scripture have been passed along in numerous ways, including through the unwritten "rule of faith" (*regula fidei*) that guided biblical interpretation in the early church, the creeds formulated in response to various heretical sects, and commentaries. The ancient creeds (from the Latin *credo*, meaning "I believe") were summary statements of belief that served to define orthodoxy for the broader Christian communion. The creeds also aided a valuable pedagogical goal in the ancient world, preparing new converts for baptism and ensuring they were committing their lives to the right gospel.[34]

The creeds most recognized throughout the Christian world are known as the *ecumenical creeds*. The term *ecumenical* comes from a Greek word meaning the "inhabited world" (*oikoumenē*). Ecumenical creeds express beliefs universally recognized among Christian churches. Three creeds are recognized as ecumenical by Western Christians: the Apostles' Creed (ca. AD 200), the Nicene Creed (325/381), and the Athanasian Creed (sixth century).[35] In addition to these, the Definition

---

[32] Vincent of Lérins, *The Commonitory* §2.3.

[33] Irenaeus I.3, quoted in J. Stevenson, ed., *A New Eusebius: Documents Illustrating the History of the Church to AD 337*, rev. W. H. C. Frend (Grand Rapids: Baker, 2013), 125.

[34] Thomas C. Oden, "The Faith Once Delivered: Nicea and Evangelical Confession," in *Evangelicals and Nicene Faith: Reclaiming the Apostolic Witness*, ed. Timothy George (Grand Rapids: Baker, 2011), 5.

[35] Though the Orthodox Church only officially accepts the Nicene Creed, the Apostles' and Athanasian Creeds nevertheless express the common faith of the patristic era.

of the Council of Chalcedon (451) is also received as authoritative in both Eastern and Western Christianity. The discussion that follows will focus on the Apostles' and Nicene Creeds and the Chalcedonian Definition.

The late-second-century Apostles' Creed (*Symbolum Apostolicum*), once widely believed to have been written by the twelve apostles, reads like a view of the Bible from thirty thousand feet. The creed summarizes the gospel story with little theological specificity. It contains a triune formula but makes no effort to explain the relations within the Godhead (what theologians call the "immanent Trinity"). Rather, its focus is on the activities and roles of the distinct persons of the Trinity (i.e., the "economic Trinity").

Over time, it became clear that the church needed more precision in its creedal language. Emperor Constantine called the Council of Nicaea, the first ecumenical council, in AD 325 to deal with the growing controversy over Arianism. Arius was a fourth-century Alexandrian presbyter who insisted Jesus was a Godlike being but denied he was eternally God in the same way the Father was. The Nicene Council rejected this position and described Jesus as "very God of very God" and as "being of one substance with the Father."[36] Responding to several christological and pneumatological heresies that emerged throughout the fourth century, the Council of Constantinople (381) had to revisit the Nicene Creed. This revised creed (sometimes known as the "Niceno-Constantinopolitan Creed") includes more details about the incarnation of Christ and a more robust statement on the Holy Spirit.

Prompted by early fifth-century heresies that divided Christ's person (Nestorianism) and confused Christ's two natures (Eutychianism), the Council of Chalcedon put forward the Chalcedonian Definition in 451. This definition incorporates the insights of the previous councils and sums up what "the prophets have taught concerning Him,"[37] what Jesus

---

[36] "Nicene Creed," Christian Classics Ethereal Library, https://www.ccel.org /creeds/nicene.creed.html.

[37] "The Chalcedonian Definition of the Faith," in T. Herbert Bindley, *The Oecumenical Documents of the Faith* (London, 1899), 297.

himself taught, and what has been handed over by the creeds. The definition states plainly that Jesus is truly God and truly human, one person in two distinct natures, "without confusion, without change, without division, without separation."[38]

The church fathers and councils occasionally employed new concepts and terms to explain the meaning of biblical texts (e.g., *Trinity*, *homoousios*), but they did not see such development as a mutation of the faith received—they were simply making explicit what was implicit in biblical teaching. They sought to offer biblically shaped answers to the new challenges posed to them. As Richard Hanson argued, these developments were necessary because "theologians of the Christian Church were slowly driven to a realization that the deepest questions which face Christianity cannot be answered in purely biblical language, because *the questions are about the meaning of biblical language itself.*"[39] The early church never saw these developments as violations of biblical authority. The church was convinced that it was merely the steward of the unchanging faith preserved in Scripture.

The Reformers, *Sola Scriptura*, and Christian Tradition

One common misconception about the Protestant Reformation is that the Reformers rejected tradition altogether in favor of "Scripture alone."[40] While it is true that some Reformers had a negative outlook on tradition, particularly some of our Anabaptist cousins, this was

---

[38] "Definition of the Union of the Divine and Human Natures in the Person of Christ: Council of Chalcedon, 451 A.D., Act V," Historical Documents of the Church, *The (Online) Book of Common Prayer*, https://www.bcponline.org.

[39] R. P. C. Hanson, *The Search for the Christian Doctrine of God: The Arian Controversy, 318–381* (London/New York: T&T Clark, 1988), xxi, emphasis added.

[40] For a critical evaluation of this misconception, see Anthony N. S. Lane, "*Sola Scriptura?* Making Sense of a Post-Reformation Slogan," in *A Pathway into the Holy Scripture*, ed. Philip E. Satterthwaite and David F. Wright (Grand Rapids: Eerdmans, 1994), 297–327.

not the general sentiment of the Reformation.[41] Magisterial Reformers such as Luther and Calvin found much to appreciate in the church fathers and creeds, even if they were frequently critical of them. The Reformers did not discard tradition altogether but rather rejected a particular view of tradition that placed it on the same level as Scripture. The vast majority of patristic and medieval theologians understood the relationship between Scripture and tradition much the same way the Reformers understood it.

By the time of the Reformation, two broad theories of tradition had developed, views the Dutch historian Heiko Oberman later labeled "Tradition I" and "Tradition II."[42] Tradition I is a one-source theory of revelation that treats Scripture as the only source of divine revelation. On this view, postbiblical tradition is merely the church's Holy Spirit–guided interpretation of the divine revelation found in Scripture. Most patristic and early-medieval theologians tacitly held a one-source theory of revelation.[43]

Tradition II, by contrast, is a two-source theory of revelation that posits the tradition of the church as another source of revelation equal to Scripture in its authority. The earliest known proponent of Tradition II, Basil of Caesarea (ca. 330–379), defended nonscriptural liturgies and practices as secret, unwritten traditions passed down from the apostles:

> Of the dogmas and proclamations that are guarded in the Church, we hold some from the teaching of the Scriptures, and

---

[41] See Alister E. McGrath, *Reformation Thought*, 3rd ed. (Malden, MA: Blackwell, 1999), 154–56. Thomas Müntzer (1489–1525) and Caspar Schwenckfeld (ca. 1489–1561) elevated the private interpretation of Scripture over and against creeds and confessions. Other Anabaptists, however, employed the creeds in their teaching and preaching. Balthasar Hubmaier (1480–1528) used the Apostles' Creed as a guide for Christian prayer. See his "Twelve Articles in Prayer Form," in *Balthasar Hubmaier: Theologian of Anabaptism*, trans. and ed. H. Wayne Pipkin and John H. Yoder (Scottdale, PA: Herald, 1989), 234–40.

[42] See Heiko A. Oberman, *Forerunners of the Reformation: The Shape of Late Medieval Thought*, trans. Paul L. Nyhus (New York: Holt, Rinehart and Winston, 1966), 51–120.

[43] For an overview of relevant sources, see Keith A. Mathison, *The Shape of Sola Scriptura* (Moscow, ID: Canon, 2001), 19–48.

others we have received in mystery as the teachings of the tradition of the apostles. Both hold the same power with respect to true religion. . . . For if we attempt to reject non-scriptural customs as insignificant, we would, unaware, lose the very vital parts of the Gospel, and even more, we would establish the proclamation merely in name.[44]

Debates over papal authority and canon law in late-medieval thought served as catalysts for the development of a more explicit two-source theory of revelation.[45] Two-source theorists view Scripture as an insufficient source of revelation that must be supplemented by tradition. For example, Johannes Brevicoxa listed four sources of revelation in addition to Scripture: (1) oral or written apostolic traditions not found in Scripture or deducible from it; (2) histories written by the faithful; (3) truths deduced from those other categories; and (4) truths more recently revealed by God to the Catholic Church.[46]

Since the Council of Trent (1545–1563), many Roman Catholic theologians have used a two-source theory to justify several of their distinctive dogmas, including the immaculate conception of Mary and papal infallibility. The most recent version of the *Catechism of the Catholic Church* seems to affirm a two-source theory: "Sacred Tradition and Sacred Scripture . . . flowing out from the same divine well-spring, come together in some fashion to form one thing and move towards the same goal. . . . *Both Scripture and Tradition must be accepted and honored with equal sentiments of devotion and reverence.*"[47]

---

[44] Basil the Great, *On the Holy Spirit* 27.66, trans. Stephen Hildebrand (Yonkers, NY: St. Vladmir's Seminary Press, 2011). This view developed into a position that the church has always used secret rites (*disciplina arcani*) passed along by the apostles but not included in Scripture. See Philip Schaff, *History of the Christian Church* (New York: Charles Scribner's Sons, 1910), 2:232–35.

[45] Alister E. McGrath, *The Intellectual Origins of the European Reformation*, 2nd ed. (Malden, MA: Blackwell, 2004), 137–44.

[46] John Brevicoxa, "A Treatise on Faith, the Church, the Roman Pontiff, and the General Council," in Oberman, *Forerunners of the Reformation*, 72–73.

[47] See *Catechism of the Catholic Church*, 2nd ed. (New York: Doubleday, 2012), 31, italics mine.

The Reformation doctrine of *sola Scriptura* was a scathing criticism of Tradition II. Like many who came before them, the Reformers believed Scripture to be the only necessary source of divine revelation. This aspect of Scripture is its *material sufficiency*. To call Scripture materially sufficient does not imply that it provides exhaustive knowledge of God, his will, or his world. Rather, it means that Scripture provides us with all the content necessary for salvation, faith, and ongoing obedience in the Christian life.[48] Other sources, such as tradition, reason, culture, or experience, may be helpful tools in theology but pale in comparison to the infallible authority of Scripture. The Bible is the supreme source and only norming norm of Christian theology.[49]

Some medieval theologians considered Scripture materially sufficient but insisted that an infallible ecclesial interpretation was necessary for understanding its contents.[50] The Reformers had witnessed theological abuses among the church's doctrinal teachers and denied them this kind of authority.[51] They believed Scripture illumined by the Holy Spirit was clear enough to be understood without a magisterium dictating its meaning for interpreters. This quality of Scripture is its *formal sufficiency*. With its formal sufficiency, Scripture helps us interpret Scripture, and it contains within itself all "the means by which the Lord can lead us into greater covenant faithfulness."[52]

While the Reformers did not reject tradition, neither did they uncritically embrace it. As Jaroslav Pelikan has convincingly argued, the Reformers lived within the tension of "Catholic substance" and the

---

[48] The Westminster Confession of Faith 1.1, ligonier.org/learn/articles/westminster-confession-faith/.

[49] Baptist theologian Matthew Barrett provides an excellent overview of this doctrine in his *God's Word Alone: The Authority of Scripture* (Grand Rapids: Zondervan, 2016), 332–71.

[50] Vincent of Lérins (d. 445) touted this opinion in his *Commonitorium*.

[51] A. N. S. Lane, "Scripture, Tradition, and Church: An Historical Survey," *Vox Evangelica* 9 (1975): 39–40, 42–45; cf. Calvin, *Institutes*, 4.8.10–12.

[52] Timothy Ward, *Words of Life: Scripture as the Living and Active Word of God* (Downers Grove, IL: InterVarsity Press, 2009), 115.

"Protestant principle."[53] Like all catholic Christians, Luther and Calvin professed the theological consensus of the first five centuries (*consensus quinquesecularis*), so well expressed in the ecumenical creeds. But their *sola Scriptura* commitment kept them from granting those councils primary authority. They had sharp words for conciliarists and papists who suggested ecumenical councils had authority to establish new doctrine.

In his 1539 work *On the Councils and Churches*, Luther defined a true council as one that "should confess and defend the ancient faith, and not institute new articles of faith against the ancient faith."[54] Luther expressed gratitude to the Council of Nicaea for defending biblical truth against Arianism but found many of its other conclusions to be inconsequential and irrelevant to the ongoing Christian life.[55] Luther remarked that the Council of Ephesus "only defended the old faith against the new notion of Nestorius" and that no one can "take any examples from it" that "give the councils authority to establish new or different articles of faith."[56] Though he accepted the Chalcedonian Creed as a faithful restatement of biblical teaching, he still asserted that "Scripture is far more reliable than all councils."[57]

Calvin put tradition, including the creeds, in a category of "external means or aids by which God invites us into the society of Christ and holds us therein."[58] His assessment of the councils and their creeds was similar to Luther's: "We willingly embrace and reverence as holy the early councils, such as those of Nicaea, Constantinople, Ephesus I, Chalcedon and the like, which were concerned with refuting errors—*in so far as they relate to the teachings of the faith*. For they contain *nothing but the pure and genuine exposition of Scripture*, which the holy fathers applied

---

[53] Jaroslav Pelikan, *Obedient Rebels: Catholic Substance and Protestant Principle in Luther's Reformation* (New York: Harper & Row, 1964), 11–14, 60–63.

[54] Martin Luther, "On the Councils and the Church," trans. Charles M. Jacobs and Eric W. Gritsch, in *Luther's Works*, vol. 41, ed. Jaroslav Pelikan (Philadelphia: Fortress, 1966), 135–36.

[55] Luther, 68.

[56] Luther, 105.

[57] Luther, 119.

[58] Calvin used this phrase as the title of book 4 of the *Institutes*.

with spiritual prudence to crush the enemies of religion who had then arisen."[59] For Calvin, the creeds and traditions of the ecumenical councils are of value as long as they represent faithfully the greater, more primary authority of inspired Scripture.[60]

The Earliest Baptists and the Creeds

Few Baptists have formally acknowledged the ecumenical creeds, but it has been clear from the beginning that they have been indebted to the creeds. With the Protestant Reformers, the earliest Baptists uniformly affirmed the supreme authority of the Bible, but they did not refrain from engaging with the broader Christian tradition or even using the ecumenical creeds as instruments of theological accountability.[61]

"Things Necessary for a Christian Man to Believe"

The Particular Baptist confessions clearly reflect the language of the ecumenical creeds, but Particular Baptist theologians rarely addressed the creeds directly.[62] One noteworthy exception was the pastor Hercules Collins (d. 1702), who adapted the Heidelberg Catechism (1563) for an audience of English separatists. In addition to an extended critique of infant baptism, one of the most notable alterations Collins made to Heidelberg was including the full texts of the Nicene, Athanasian, and Apostles' Creeds, which he claimed "ought thoroughly to be believed and

---

[59] Calvin, *Institutes*, 4.9.8, italics mine.

[60] Calvin, 4.9.1–11.

[61] For a comprehensive overview of early Baptist beliefs about biblical authority, inspiration, and inerrancy, see L. Russ Bush and Tom J. Nettles, *Baptists and the Bible*, rev. ed. (Nashville: B&H Academic, 1999).

[62] For example, the Second London Confession (1677/1689), following the Westminster Confession (1646) and the Nicene Creed, describes the Trinity as "three subsistences . . . of one substance," the Son as "eternally begotten of the Father," and the Holy Spirit as "proceeding from the Father and the Son" (2.3). The wording of 8.2 mirrors Chalcedon.

embraced by all those that would be accounted Christians."[63] In answer to the question "What are those things which are necessary for a Christian man to believe?" Collins quoted the Apostles' Creed, which he believed contained the "sum of the Gospel."[64]

Collins defended his use of the creed against critics who would question its validity because of its human composition: "I beseech you do not slight it because of its form, nor antiquity, nor because supposed to be composed by men; neither because some that hold it maintain some errors, or whose conversation may not be correspondent to such fundamental principles of salvation." Collins then added another principle that extends to all Christian tradition: "That whatever is good in any, owned by any, whatever error or vice it may be mixed withal, the good must not be rejected for the error or vice sake, but owned, commended, and accepted."[65] For Collins, the acknowledgment of error in tradition need not entail the dismissal of all tradition. The creedal baby must not be discarded with its ecclesial bathwater.

"No Devisers or Favourers of Novelties"

While the Particular Baptists were usually mum on the ecumenical creeds, many of the early General Baptists gave considerable attention to them. Sometimes this was simply by appropriating language of the creeds in their confessions, as in the *Short Confession of Faith* by John Smyth (1570–1612), the first General Baptist. Smyth's statement on the incarnation closely resembles the wording of Chalcedon: "Jesus Christ is true God and true man . . . the Son of God taking to himself, in addition,

---

[63] Hercules Collins, *An Orthodox Catechism: Being the Sum of Christian Religion Contained in the Law and Gospel* (London, 1680; Knightstown, IN: Reformed Baptist Faith & Family Ministry, 2014), 5, https://www.thecalvinist.net/etc/1680%20Orthodox%20Catechism%20(Hercules%20Collins).pdf. The language here reflects art. VIII of the Thirty-Nine Articles of Religion (1563).

[64] Collins, 5.

[65] Collins, 5.

the true and pure nature of a man, out of a true rational soul, and existing in a true human body."[66]

Other seventeenth-century General Baptists invoked the creeds to defend the *consensus quinquesecularis* from those within their ranks who had succumbed to heterodoxy. Free Will Baptist scholar Matthew Pinson has shown early General Baptists to be thoroughly entrenched in the Nicene and Reformed traditions, knowing nothing of the radical individualism later associated with Baptist life.[67] When engaged in dialogue with their Anglican counterparts, they used tradition as an apologetic for the antiquity and orthodoxy of their faith.[68]

Thomas Grantham (1634–1692) authored *Christianismus Primitivus* (1678), the first systematic theology in the Baptist tradition. Grantham was a most competent biblical exegete and apologist. Like Calvin, Grantham was fluent in the resources of tradition, interacting with figures such as Ambrose, Augustine, Chrysostom, Jerome, and Tertullian.[69] Grantham effectively used ancient creeds to establish a common ground with Anglicans and other Protestant dissenters. Placing a composite of the Nicene and Apostles' Creeds alongside the *Standard Confession* (1660) of General Baptists, he sought to establish their continuity. Of these creeds Grantham wrote:

> Since there hath been several Confessions of Faith published, among which that called the *Apostles Creed*, and the *Nicene* do

---

[66] John Smyth, *Short Confession of Faith in XX Articles*, 6; quoted in William L. Lumpkin, *Baptist Confessions of Faith* (Valley Forge, PA: Judson, 1959), 100.

[67] See J. Matthew Pinson, *Arminian and Baptist: Explorations in a Theological Tradition* (Nashville: Randall, 2015), 153–82.

[68] Explicit references to the creeds in English Baptist writing became more infrequent after the Toleration Act of 1689 gave likeminded Protestant dissenters the freedom of worship. See Michael Smith, "The Early English Baptists and the Church Fathers" (PhD diss., Southern Baptist Theological Seminary, 1982), 145–46. Steve Harmon adds that the Enlightenment and the rise of radical individualism in Baptist life were also contributing factors to this diminished interaction with creeds. See Steven R. Harmon, "Baptist Confessions of Faith and the Patristic Tradition," in *Perspectives in Religious Studies* 29, no. 4 (2002): 349–58.

[69] Pinson, *Arminian and Baptist*, 165.

seem to be of most venerable estimation, both for Antiquity, and the solidity of the matter, and for their excellent brevity, we do hereby declare to the world that we assent to the Contents thereof, as we find them both digested and comprehended in these ensuing Articles, that all men may know that we are no devisers or favourers of Novelties or new Doctrines.[70]

By using the creed in this way, Grantham demonstrated there was no disagreement between Baptists and the Church of England in the essentials of the faith. As an early proponent of Baptist catholicity, he hoped the use of these ancient creeds "might be a good means to bring to a greater degree of unity . . . many of the divided parties professing Christianity."[71] Even though Anglicans and Baptists differed in practices, especially regarding baptism, both traditions eschewed heresies and new doctrines contrary to the creeds.

"A Means to Prevent Heresy in Doctrine"

In 1678, General Baptists from the Midlands composed the Orthodox Creed, the only Baptist confession to include the full texts of ancient creeds. This document, most likely crafted by Thomas Monck, served two major purposes. First, it sought to unite English Protestants around points of doctrinal agreement. Second, it sought to counter heretical teachings surfacing in the General Baptist camp. General Baptist pastor Matthew Caffyn (1628–1714) had been preaching a Hoffmanite Christology that denied Jesus a true human nature.[72] Caffyn, driven largely by a naïve biblicist methodology, eventually denied the doctrines

---

[70] Thomas Grantham, *Christianismus Primitivus* (London: Francis Smith, 1678), 2.59–60.

[71] Grantham, 61.

[72] Lumpkin, *Baptist Confessions of Faith*, 295–96. Five years before writing the Orthodox Creed, Thomas Monck published *A Cure for the Cankering Error of the New Eutychians* (London, 1673) as a response to this teaching.

of the Trinity and the deity of Jesus. Many General Baptists in his circle of influence became Socinian or Unitarian.[73]

With the Orthodox Creed, the General Baptists again used ancient creeds to exhibit their orthodoxy and continuity with the early church. Article 38, "Of Three Creeds," is a reworking of article 8 of the Thirty-Nine Articles of the Church of England (1571). With the Thirty-Nine Articles, the General Baptists contended that the Nicene, Athanasian, and Apostles' Creeds "ought thoroughly to be received and believed":[74]

> For we believe, they may be proved, by the most undoubted authority of holy Scripture, and are necessary to be understood by all Christians; and to be instructed in knowledge of them, by the ministers of Christ, according to the analogy of faith, recorded in the sacred scriptures, upon which these creeds are grounded, and catechistically opened, and expounded in all Christian families, for the edification of young and old, which might be a means to prevent heresy in doctrine, and practice, these creeds containing all things in a brief manner, that are necessary to be known, fundamentally in order for our salvation; to which end they may be considered, and better understood of all men.[75]

General Baptists saw no inconsistency in affirming the Bible's unique authority and also the use of creeds. They asserted, "No decrees of popes, or councils, or writings of any person whatsoever, are of equal authority with the sacred scriptures,"[76] but maintained that the substance of the creeds is thoroughly biblical and derived from the Bible's authority. They also encouraged the use of these creeds in disciple-making because

---

[73] Pinson, *Arminian and Baptist*, 166–69; cf. A. C. Underwood, *A History of the English Baptists* (London: Carey Kingsgate, 1947), 127.

[74] The Thirty-Nine Articles statement is itself a revision of art. 7, "The three Credes," in Forty-Two Articles by Thomas Cranmer (1553). The acceptance of these three creeds was commonplace in the Reformation. See Gerald R. Bray, "Whoever Will Be Saved: The Athanasian Creed and the Modern Church," in George, *Evangelicals and Nicene Faith*, 45–46.

[75] Orthodox Creed (1678), art. 38.

[76] Orthodox Creed (1678), art. 37.

they contain summary statements of all biblical teaching "necessary to be known . . . [for] our salvation." The modern myth that Baptists have never used creeds or confessions to provide doctrinal accountability is undermined by General Baptists' explicit statement that the creeds provide "a means to prevent heresy in doctrine."[77] Furthermore, the historical example of Caffyn should also give readers pause about neglecting the ancient creeds.[78]

"Neither Creed-Makers nor Creed-Imposers"

Another key piece of evidence against the anticreedal claim that Baptists have never used creeds for theological accountability comes from the pen of General Baptist Joseph Hooke, whose *Creed-Making and Creed-Imposing Considered* (1729) affirmed both religious liberty and the need for pastors and teachers to maintain fidelity to the theological substance of creeds and confessions.[79] Hooke stated plainly that Baptists are "neither . . . *Creed-Makers* nor *Creed-Imposers*," but he did not use this phrase to mean there is no place for human creedal formulations or no function for creeds in church discipline.[80]

Against naïve biblicists who contested the use of extrabiblical language, Hooke defended the production and use of creeds and confessions:

> If Men would bind us, *in expressing our Faith*, to use no Word but what is found in Number of Syllables in Holy Scripture, *they would bind us to a hard Law . . . whereby is condemned all Exposition that is not pieced together with bare laying together of Texts of Scripture.* And they would certainly bind themselves to a hard Law too, which would *tie* them from *Preaching*, and *Discoursing*, and *Writing* of any *Point of Faith.* They might indeed

---

[77] Orthodox Creed (1678), art. 38.

[78] Pinson, *Arminian and Baptist*, 166–69.

[79] Pinson, 162–63.

[80] Joseph Hooke, *Creed-Making and Creed-Imposing Considered, and the Divinity of Christ and the Doctrine of the Trinity Defended* (London: J. Darby and T. Browne, 1729), 9, italics in the original.

read the Holy Scriptures, but by no means *expound*, *comment*, or *paraphrase* upon them; for that would be to mix some Words of Men with the Word of God, *professing* and *declaring* them to be *true*, and therefore to be *believed* which is the *very thing* they scruple and seem to start at.[81]

Hooke argued that without the ability to express briefly the content of Scripture or give it explanation, preaching and teaching are futile. Though Hooke defended the development of creedal formulations, he denied any human authority the right to "make creeds" or invent or establish doctrine independently of Scripture. God alone makes the creed, or the "thing or Proposition to be believed."[82]

Hooke specified an appropriate use of creeds and confessions in church discipline consistent with religious liberty. Creeds must never be imposed on nonbelievers. Though Christians should seek to convert non-Christians from other religious traditions, they should never punish them for disbelieving the creeds. Hooke believed Christians should seek gently to restore apostates who have denied the faith in times of persecution, but never by violence or oppression. Many of these apostates were never true converts in the first place. Hooke likewise renounced imposing creeds on "weak believers" who do not yet understand their contents, noting a clear difference between the "professed Ignorance" of new believers and the "willful Opposition" of apostates and heretics.[83]

With these caveats aside, Hooke was convinced of the propriety of using creeds and confessions for doctrinal accountability.[84] False authorities teach contrary to the creeds using doctrine "dishonourable to God and dangerous to the Souls of Men." Such teaching "must not be tolerated." The "*true Articles of Faith ought not be opposed*, any more than we ought to *impose* that upon weak People which they are not able

---

[81] Hooke, 4–5.
[82] Hooke, 3.
[83] Hooke, 6–7.
[84] Pinson, *Arminian and Baptist*, 163.

to understand."[85] Heretics must not be allowed to abide in the church, but this exercise of church discipline does not entail civil punishment. Threatening them with violent inquisitions was the practice of popes, not the true churches of Christ. These early Baptists saw no contradiction in affirming both biblical authority and creeds, nor did they understand the use of creeds as instruments of theological accountability to be in conflict with their strong convictions about religious liberty.

The Ongoing Role of Tradition in Baptist Life

Amnesia of and suspicion toward tradition have been recurring problems in Baptist life, but tradition is an essential element of our discipleship and theological heritage. Every reader of the Bible reads it through the lens of tradition, whether that tradition comes from a creed, a confession, a pastor, a favorite Sunday school teacher, or a parent. Every disciple belongs to the greater Christian tradition that has been unfolding since the first century. This tradition will continue to develop until the Lord returns, because there will always be a need for faithful followers of Jesus under the leadership of the Spirit who are committed to expressing the authority of Scripture in their churches, communities, and world.

As Baptists, we belong to a distinctive theological tradition. We make a strong commitment to the supreme authority of the Bible in what we believe and practice. Our distinctive church practices, such as regenerate church membership and insistence on believer's baptism, are extensions of this belief. Like the church fathers and the Reformers before us, we hold Scripture alone to be the inspired, infallible, and inerrant Word of God. It is the only source of revelation we need. But our commitment to *sola Scriptura* does not mean we read the Bible by ourselves or have nothing to learn from Christians who came before us.

The distinction some anticreedal Baptists make between creeds as normative standards of faith and confessions as voluntary, purely descriptive statements of faith is an arbitrary distinction often shaped by an

---

[85] Hooke, *Creed-Making and Creed-Imposing*, 8.

ill-informed historiography of the ancient church, the Reformation, and early Baptist life. A creed, like a confession of faith, is a verbal expression of belief. A confession of faith, like a creed, draws certain parameters around what a group believes. Both serve as statements of definition and membership affiliation. The ancient creeds of the Christian church speak broadly about what all Christians believe—the essentials of the faith. They provide a common ground for catholicity—our fellowship with Christians of other (small-*t*) traditions. The later confessions give more clarity and definition to what small-*t* traditions believe and practice in their ecclesial contexts.

Baptists throughout history have affirmed both *sola Scriptura* and the ecumenical creeds of antiquity. Early Baptists would have seen the choice proffered by some between inquisitional creedalism and an "anything goes" approach to biblical interpretation as a dangerous false dichotomy. Yes, creeds and confessions can provide a means for sound instruction and accountability to biblical teaching. But Baptists of every stripe have recognized that creeds should never be imposed on people in such a way that they violate conscience or religious liberty.

Our choice to covenant together under creeds and confessions, as well as to use them as instruments of doctrinal accountability in our local churches and denominational entities, in no way contradicts our affirmations of religious liberty and freedom of conscience. Even E. Y. Mullins (1860–1928), the great advocate for "soul competency," insisted creeds and confessions were necessary for the survival of denominations and faith traditions: "A denomination controlled by a group who have no declared platform is heading for the rocks." Yet the call to mutual theological accountability is not tantamount to inquisitional creedalism. As Mullins explained:

> The Baptist denomination has never allowed creeds to be imposed upon it by others. But Baptists have always insisted upon their own right to declare their beliefs in a definite, formal way, and to protect themselves by refusing to support men in important places as teachers and preachers who do not agree with them. . . . If a group of men known as Baptists consider

themselves trustees of certain great truths, they have an inalienable right to conserve and propagate those truths unmolested by others inside the denomination who oppose such truths. The latter have an equal right to unite with another group agreeing with them.[86]

The summaries of New Testament truth found in creeds and confessions help safeguard communities of faith from theological error, but we subscribe to them voluntarily. Recovery of the ancient creeds can provide Baptists with a robust confessional understanding of their theological heritage and a clearer understanding of the God revealed in the Bible.

All the resources of tradition, whether creedal, confessional, ecclesial, or pastoral, have a type of authority. Throughout history, God has called individuals and corporate bodies to proclaim (not invent) his Word. Pastors are called to preach, and teachers are called to teach. If local churches and their teachers cannot speak authoritatively on behalf of the Word of God, then it is best for them to read the Bible publicly and sit down without a sermon or explanation of the text.

But the Bible itself is a witness to its need for interpretation and explanation. In the book of Nehemiah, we learn that the Levites expounded the Law for the people, "*making it clear* and *giving the meaning* so that *the people understood* what was being read*" (8:8, NIV; emphasis added). The Ethiopian eunuch needed Philip to explain the meaning of Isaiah 53 (Acts 8:30–35). Peter acknowledged the challenge of understanding Paul's letters and warned against their distortion by false teachers (2 Pet 3:15–16).

As long as the Lord tarries, there will always be a need for the people of God to interpret the Word of God, and there will always be a need for concise ways to talk about its contents. Creeds and confessions are an important part of that interpretive tradition. Those who transmit the tradition are authorized, or deputized, to relay the Word of God. Yes, the

---

[86] E. Y. Mullins, "Baptists and Creeds," in E. Y. Mullins, *The Axioms of Religion,* comp. R. Albert Mohler Jr., ed. Timothy George and Denise George (Nashville: B&H, 1997), 189–90.

derivative authority of traditions, creeds, and confessions is fallible and is in no way a rival to the Word of God. Even so, we need not neglect or ignore this tradition. This derivative authority is like the light of the sun reflected off the moon. Moonlight, though only a pale reflection, is often needed in the darkness of night. In the same way, the creeds and confessions of tradition can be helpful sources of luminescence as we wander through this dark world, even if they are not themselves the source of light.

3

Baptists, Classic Trinitarianism, and the Christian Tradition

MALCOLM YARNELL

Southwestern Baptist Theological Seminary

One of the earliest attempts to portray Baptist theology was written by Daniel Featley, a Calvinist Episcopalian.[1] This self-satisfied polemicist took a decisive stand against the English Baptists in his report of a debate between him and a group of Baptists, held in Southwark on October 17, 1642. In his 1645 preface documenting that earlier event, Featley argued from guilt by association that the "Catalogues of Heretiques" demonstrated nearly all theological errors derived from this bizarre religious school he called "the Anabaptists." Featley likewise accused Baptists of sourcing heresy through erasing the clergy-laity distinction, elevating women immorally by baptizing them alongside men, and endangering England's entire social structure with their advocacy of religious liberty.[2]

---

[1] Bill J. Leonard, "Sex, Class, and Religious Freedom: Daniel Featley vs. the Early Baptists," *Baptist History & Heritage* 53, no. 1 (2018): 26–42.

[2] Daniel Featley, *The Dippers Dipt. Or the Anabaptists Duck'd and Plung'd Over Head and Eares in a Disputation at Southwark* (London: Nicholas Bourne, 1645), "The Preface to the Reader," C2ᵛ-C3ᵛ.

It was the seminal doctrines of the authority of Scripture and of God as Trinity that Featley chose to emphasize first during the debate in Southwark, ignoring his interlocutor's efforts to begin with baptism. He led off with the Trinity and the Bible, because he wanted to demonstrate the Baptists were unfit to teach, being "so imperfect in the fundamentall poynts of Catechisme."[3] He pressed the Baptists in particular over the eternal generation of the Son and the double procession of the Holy Spirit, trying to bait his interlocutors into denying the deity of two of the three divine persons with a proposed misinterpretation of John 17:3.[4] The Baptists, led by a pastor named Cufin (a Welsh form of the sur-name Kiffin, also spelled Kiffen), deflected Featley's sophisticated feint and quickly returned the conversation to ecclesiology. William Kiffen's views here are important, because he was instrumental in the growth and preservation of the Particular Baptist movement and was a leading signa-tory for both the First and the Second London Confessions of Faith, the most important Particular Baptist confessions.[5]

Featley's scurrilous report is theologically interesting because it dem-onstrates that Baptists have, from their earliest years, been required to define doctrinal matters they assumed were held in common with other Christians.[6] From its perspective, the Baptist movement did not begin its journey with an effort to redefine the classical doctrines of the Christian faith, but with an effort to ensure the Christian faith was genuinely experienced in conversion and properly expressed in church and soci-ety. While an Anglican like Featley felt it important to begin with the trinitarian nature of Christian baptism, the Baptists were concerned to identify the correct recipient of Christian baptism.

---

[3] Featley, 4.

[4] Too clever by far; even the officiating gentry were confused by what Featley was trying to assert. Featley, 2–3.

[5] The critical material on this leading Baptist patriarch is being gathered by Larry J. Kreitzer in multiple volumes, beginning with *William Kiffen and His World (Part 1)*, Re-Sourcing Baptist History: Seventeenth Century Series (Oxford: Centre for Baptist History and Heritage, 2010; corrected ed., 2018).

[6] Featley's book is also interesting from the perspectives of history, literature, and art, as a perusal of its illustrative and argumentative material evince.

In spite of their general presuppositions regarding classical Trinitarianism, this fundamental doctrine of the faith has nonetheless periodically proven a point of contention among the Baptists. In this essay, we wish to demonstrate that classical Trinitarianism has been the default position of the overwhelming majority of Baptists, even as they also sought to remain biblical in their language and to show deference for personal freedom. To establish this point, we shall begin with a survey of representative Baptist confessions, catechisms, and covenants, before proceeding to a summary review of representative systematic theologians. We conclude with an answer to the question of whether classical Trinitarianism must be embraced by Baptists.

First, however, a preliminary taxonomy is required. The classical Christian understanding that God is eternally three yet one has typically utilized the language of "substance" or "essence" as well as "persons" and "Trinity." For instance, *The Oxford Dictionary of the Christian Church* defines the doctrine of the Trinity as "the central dogma of Christian theology, viz. that the One God exists in Three Persons and One Substance. This doctrine is held to be a mystery in the strict sense, in that it can neither be known by unaided human reason apart from revelation, nor cogently demonstrated by reason after it has been revealed."[7] Similarly, Gregg Allison, an evangelical historical theologian, states, "The church has historically believed that 'God eternally exists as three persons, Father, Son, and Holy Spirit, and each person is fully God, and there is one God.'"[8] The Doctrinal Basis of the Evangelical Theological Society agrees, "God is a Trinity, Father, Son, and Holy Spirit, each an uncreated person, one in essence, equal in power and glory."[9] These statements

---

[7] *The Oxford Dictionary of the Christian Church*, 2nd ed., ed. F. L. Cross and E. A. Livingstone (Oxford: Oxford University Press, 1983), s.v. "Trinity, Doctrine of the."

[8] Note that Allison does not use the language of "essence" in this preliminary definition, although he does use it later in his chapter. Gregg R. Allison, *Historical Theology: An Introduction to Christian Doctrine* (Grand Rapids: Zondervan, 2011), 231.

[9] "Doctrinal Basis," Evangelical Theological Society, accessed June 19, 2019, https://www.etsjets.org/about.

indicate the classical doctrine of the Trinity employs the language of ontology, the language of relationality or personhood, and the numeric language of three with one.

Baptist Confessions

An analysis of the language used in twelve major Baptist confessions deriving from the seventeenth century and continuing into the twenty-first century indicates that the language of ontology, relationality, and/or Trinity is not entirely universal (see Table 1). Of these twelve confessions, two chose not to use the classical language of ontology, including either "substance," "essence," "nature," or "Godhead" in their definitions. Five chose not to use the classical language of relationality, such as "person" or "subsistence," nor of "generation" or "begotten" with regard to the Son, nor of "procession" with regard to the Holy Spirit. In addition, three of the twelve chose not to use the classical language of "Trinity" or "triune," nor of "Three" with "One" when speaking of God. Finally, only half of the twelve official confessions chose to use all three types of classical terminology to indicate the full definition of a unitary ontology, a multiple relationality, and a numeric Trinity.

John Smyth, the first pastor of an English Baptist church, wrote two documents carrying the title of Short Confession. The first, written in 1609, only cursorily mentions the doctrine of God and has none of the classical language, although it is recognizably Trinitarian in its claim for God being "one" and also "Father, Son, and Holy Spirit."[10] The second, written in 1610, was signed by Smyth and forty-two other English Baptists in that first congregation. It uses all three forms of the classical language, including ontology, relationality, and threeness with oneness: First, God, "being three" is "nevertheless one." Second, the Son is "begotten," while the Spirit is "proceeding from the Father and the Son." Third,

---

[10] William L. Lumpkin, *Baptist Confessions of Faith*, 2nd rev. ed., ed. Bill J. Leonard (Valley Forge, PA: Judson Press, 2011), 93.

there is no division or separation in "essence, nature, property, eternity, power, glory, or excellency" between the three persons.[11]

Reflecting the ambivalence toward classical language in this first set of confessions, the General Baptists demonstrated a penchant for striving to use biblical language but without entirely letting go of classical language. For instance, the General Baptist Faith and Practice of Thirty Congregations of 1650 traces a biblical basis for claiming there is a unity between the Son and the Father, and also the Holy Spirit. However, in spite of perhaps implying both ontological and economic threeness with oneness, there is no explicit use of the classical terminology.[12] The Standard Confession of 1660, approved at a national level by the General Baptists, is similarly reticent to use the classical language of ontology and relationality, preferring instead to privilege biblical language. This confession follows the Apostles' Creed in positing faith in "one" who is Father and Son and Holy Spirit, but goes beyond that ancient creed by stating, "these three are one."[13]

With the Orthodox Creed of 1678, the General Baptists finally confessed a robust classical doctrine of God. Article III states, "In this divine, and infinite being, or Unity of the Godhead, there are three Persons or Subsistences, the Father, the Word, or Son, and the Holy Spirit, of one Substance, Power, Eternity, and Will, each having the whole Divine Essence, yet the Essence undivided. The Father is of none, neither Begotten nor Proceeding; the Son is Eternally Begotten of the Father; the Holy Ghost is of the Father, and the Son, proceeding." The confession then said the whole Trinity should be worshiped as God: "We worship and adore a *Trinity* in Unity, and a *Unity* in Trinity, three Persons, and but *one God*." This doctrine of the Trinity is "the foundation of all our Communion with God." In the next article, the deity of the Son is

---

[11] In a unique turn of phrase regarding generation, Smyth's second confession states the Father "hath begotten his Son from everlasting Word of the Father, and his wisdom." A Short Confession, art. 3, in Lumpkin, 96.

[12] The Faith and Practice of Thirty Congregations, art. 20, in Lumpkin, 165.

[13] Standard Confession, arts. I, III, and VII, in Lumpkin, 207–9; see also http://www.baptistcenter.net/confessions/Standard_Confession_1660.pdf.

affirmed in such a way that neither Arianism nor Socinianism could possibly be held: Christ is wholly "Begotten of the Father" and is "not a *God by Office*, but a God by Nature, *Coequal*, *Coessential*, and *Coeternal*, with the Father and the Holy Ghost."[14]

The language here intentionally reflects the three classical creeds held in common with Roman Catholics as well as the Church of England, the Presbyterians, and the Congregationalists. Indeed, the Orthodox Creed includes all three ancient creeds—the Apostles' Creed, the Nicene Creed, and the Athanasian Creed. These three formulae "ought thoroughly to be received, and believed. For we believe they may be proved by most undoubted Authority of holy Scripture, and are necessary to be understood of all Christians; and to be instructed in the knowledge of them, by the Ministers of Christ." If the people are catechized in these Trinitarian creeds, they "might be a means to prevent Heresy in Doctrine, and Practice, these Creeds containing all things in a brief manner, that are necessary to be known, fundamentally, in order to our salvation."[15] There is little doubt the General Baptist churches, when led by such orthodox stalwarts as Thomas Monck and Thomas Grantham, were classical in their Trinitarianism. However, it must be remembered the reason they felt compelled to adopt such a strong statement was due to the heretical Christology of Matthew Caffyn, a long-lived and influential General Baptist Messenger active in Kent and Sussex.[16]

The Particular Baptists, on the other hand, employed classical language in both of their major confessions. The London Confession of 1644, originally known as "The Confession of Faith, Of Those Churches which are commonly (though falsly) called Anabaptists," developed from a number of previous sources, largely within the English Separatist

---

[14] Orthodox Creed, arts. III and IV, in Lumpkin, 301–3; see also http://baptist studiesonline.com/wp-content/uploads/2007/02/orthodox-creed.pdf.

[15] Orthodox Creed, art. XXXVIII, in Lumpkin, 317–18.

[16] See the editor's preface to *An Orthodox Creed*, ed. Madison Grace (Fort Worth: Center for Theological Research, 2006), i-iii. Clint Bass, in a forthcoming book on "The Caffynite Controversy," traces the development of both Caffyn's heretical Christology and the back-and-forth nature of the General Baptist Assembly's responses into the eighteenth century.

tradition.[17] This is important, for the Separatists and their Baptist descendants primarily argued against their Anglican and Puritan fore-fathers regarding ecclesiology rather than theology. The first Particular Baptists confessed together, "In this God-head, there is the Father, the Sonne, and the Spirit; being every one of them one and the same God; and therefore not divided, but distinguished one from another by their severall properties; the Father being from himselfe, the Sonne of the Father from everlasting, the Holy Spirit proceeding from the Father and the Sonne."[18] The language of "properties" reflects classical person-alism, while "God-head" indicates a classical ontology, and the use of "one and same" alongside "every" and "another," with the Father, the Son, and the Holy Spirit coming under consideration, indicates a classical numerical affirmation.

The Second London Confession, published by the Particular Baptists in 1677, and reissued in 1688, attempted to maintain continu-ity both with the 1644 Baptist confession and with the Presbyterian Westminster Confession, as far as was possible. This is why the Second London Confession has so many structural similarities with that of the Westminster Assembly of thirty years earlier. However, a compar-ison of chapter 2, section III of both documents reveals differences. For instance, the Baptist version is twice the length of its Presbyterian exemplar, prefers to speak of "subsistences" rather than "persons," and speaks of "relative properties" and "personal relations."[19] There is no significant change in doctrine in spite of the different terms, as they were treated synonymously by John Calvin.[20] The Particular Baptists were not slavish in their borrowing but creatively adapted the earlier statement.

---

[17] Jay Collier, "The Sources behind the First London Confession," *American Baptist Quarterly* 21 (2002): 197–214.

[18] London Confession, art. II, in Lumpkin, *Baptist Confessions of Faith*, 144.

[19] The Second London Confession, in Lumpkin, 237.

[20] John Calvin, *Institutes of the Christian Religion*, ed. John T. McNeill, trans. Ford Lewis Battles, Library of Christian Classics (Philadelphia: Westminster John Knox, 1960), 1.13.5.

At the turn of the eighteenth century, the General Baptists continued to struggle with Caffynite Christology. The General Baptist confessions of 1703 and 1705 resorted to the full panoply of classical language in order to affirm orthodox Trinitarianism.[21] For their part, the Trinity did not excite much interest among the Particular Baptists until the Salters' Hall controversy erupted in the summer of 1719. As I discuss elsewhere, the three dissenting denominations in London, which counted Particular Baptists and General Baptists as one denomination for the sake of ecumenical action, divided over the propriety of requiring subscription to a confession affirming the Trinity. The division, however, should not be seen as an up-or-down vote for or against the classical Trinity. Rather, the desire to maintain freedom of conscience against an intolerant state, which recently required subscription to classical language, coupled with the desire to maintain the sufficiency of Scripture against extrabiblical tradition, set orthodox proponents against one other. Major evangelical figures, including Isaac Watts and Edmund Calamy, characterized the division as entirely unnecessary and refused to participate in it. One unexpected and important result from my rehearsal of the primary evidence from the Salters' Hall Controversy was the discovery that all sides agreed the diminishing of the Son's authority vis-à-vis the Father should be deemed nothing less than Arianism.[22]

After Salters' Hall, the Baptist denominations in England and America largely consolidated around simple confessional statements using classical language with haphazard freedom. The most prominent early American confession, the Philadelphia Confession, printed by Benjamin Franklin in 1743, took up the Trinitarian statements of the

---

[21] For the texts of these General Baptist confessions, the Brief Confession (1703) and the Unity of the Churches (1705), see appendices D and E in Clint Bass, *The Caffynite Controversy* (Oxford, UK: Centre for Baptist History and Heritage, Regent's Park College, Oxford University, forthcoming, 2020), used with permission).

[22] Yarnell, "'The Point in Question' at Salters' Hall: Baptists Contending for Trinity, Scripture, and Freedom," in *Trinity, Creed, and Confusion: The Salters' Hall Debates of 1719*, ed. Stephen Copson (Oxford, UK: Centre for Baptist History and Heritage, forthcoming).

Second London Confession verbatim.[23] Perhaps because of its Calvinism, the Philadelphia Confession was "not always received with enthusiasm" on the American frontier.[24] The first article in the confession of the prominent Sandy Creek Association, which exercised profound influence upon revivalist Baptists in the South, explicitly employed ontological and numerical terms but merely implied Trinitarian relationality.[25] The New Hampshire Confession, crafted as a moderating statement for Calvinists and Arminians in 1833, achieved widespread use among American Baptists after its inclusion in J. Newton Brown's *The Baptist Church Manual* in 1853 and J. M. Pendleton's *Baptist Church Manual* in 1867. It used summary ontological, relational, and numerical terms in its second article, "On the True God." After affirming divine unity and some divine attributes, the New Hampshire Confession says this one true God is "revealed under the personal and relative distinctions of the Father, the Son, and the Holy Spirit." Perhaps to ward against a Modalistic construal of that statement, the document said the three are "equal in every divine perfection."[26]

When the Southern Baptist Convention drafted The Baptist Faith and Message in 1925, a confession that exercised great influence upon Baptists worldwide due to the large Southern Baptist missionary presence, they relied heavily upon the structure and terminology of the New Hampshire Confession. They recast the Trinitarian sentence of the second article about the one God to read, "He is revealed to us as Father, Son, and Holy Spirit, each with distinct personal attributes, but without division of nature, essence, or being."[27] This sentence unfortunately may be read in a Modalist fashion, since divine ontology is subsumed within the divine economy of revelation. The 1963 revision did little to improve

---

[23] Lumpkin, *Baptist Confessions of Faith*, 363–64.

[24] Lumpkin, 368.

[25] Lumpkin, 374.

[26] The New Hampshire Confession, art. ii, in Lumpkin, 379; see also "New Hampshire Confession," Historic Baptist Documents, http://baptistdocuments.tripod.com/nhampshire.htm.

[27] "Comparison of 1925, 1963 and 2000 Baptist Faith and Message," art. II, "God," accessed June 20, 2019, http://www.sbc.net/bfm2000/bfmcomparison.asp.

the situation with, "The eternal God reveals Himself to us as Father, Son, and Holy Spirit, with distinct personal attributes, but without division of nature, essence, or being." However, the 2000 revision added the word "triune" after "eternal," thus precluding a Modalist interpretation by locating Trinitarian ontology before the Trinitarian economy of revelation: "The eternal triune God reveals Himself to us as Father, Son, and Holy Spirit, with distinct personal attributes, but without division of nature, essence, or being."[28] While the doctrine of the Trinity did not evince itself much in the twentieth century in Southern Baptist pulpits, the few references to it sometimes tended toward Modalism.[29]

Baptist Covenants

There are three major communal documents produced by Baptist churches for theological purposes—confessions, covenants, and catechisms. Confessions, typically adopted by more than one church, have an official doctrinal character. Covenants, although they might be similar among various churches, originate within one church during its formative phase. Catechisms are drawn up by pastors for use in introducing younger people to the faith. We now turn our attention from evaluating presentations of God as Trinity in confessions to consider the Trinitarian claims of representative covenants.

Charles W. Deweese states, "A church covenant is a series of written pledges based on the Bible which church members voluntarily make to God and to one another regarding their basic moral and spiritual commitments and the practice of their faith. A covenant deals mainly with conduct (although it contains some doctrinal elements), while a

---

[28] Cf. Benjamin S. Cole, "Significance of 1 Word Noted in SBC's Updated Statement of Beliefs," Baptist Press, November 4, 2003, http://www.bpnews.net /16997/significance-of-1-word-noted-in-sbcs-updated-statement-of-beliefs.

[29] Herschel H. Hobbs, "God the Father," chap. 1 in *What Baptists Believe* (Nashville: Broadman Press, 1964). Hobbs stated, "God is one Person (Deut. 6:4) who reveals himself in three manifestations as Father, Son, and Holy Spirit." A few pages later, he clarified, "All three Persons are present at all times, with each being the more prominent revelation at given stages of history."

confession of faith centers more heavily on beliefs. The basic meaning of a covenant resides in divine/human relationships in the context of church membership."[30] Covenants are helpful for discerning Baptist beliefs about classical Trinitarianism due to their divine orientation. So, who is the God with whom Baptists make a local church covenant? The doctrine of the Trinity, along with the doctrines of Christ and gospel and authority, appear often in church covenants, being considered important, even causative. However, these doctrines are not detailed.

While leading the first Baptist church in Amsterdam in 1609, John Smyth pictured the church covenant as communal participation in the economic Trinity. "[T]he covenant is this: I wilbe their Father . . . and we shalbe his sonnes calling him Father by the Spirit, whereby we are sealed."[31] "The oldest surviving covenant" from among the Particular Baptist churches mentions "the Lord" thrice but does not define God in Trinitarian terms.[32] The popular covenant of Benjamin and Elias Keach, printed in 1697, likewise treated the covenant in loosely economic Trinitarian terms.[33] The Sandy Creek tradition may have offered the first covenantal commitment with definite if rudimentary classical Trinitarian language: "We take the only living and true God to be our God, one God in three persons, Father, Son, and Holy Spirit."[34] Brown's manual offered a very popular covenant that begins with a paragraph describing both personal salvation and confessional baptism in unmistakably Trinitarian terms.[35]

---

[30] Charles W. Deweese, *Baptist Church Covenants* (Nashville: Broadman Press, 1990), viii.

[31] Deweese, 25.

[32] Deweese, 29. "Covenant of Broadmead Baptist Church" (1640), in *Baptist Confessions, Covenants, and Catechisms*, ed. Timothy George and Denise George, Baptist Classics (Nashville: Broadman & Holman, 1996), 173.

[33] "Covenant of Benjamin and Elias Keach," in Deweese, 177–79.

[34] "Covenant of Grassy Creek Baptist Church" (1757), in Deweese, 202. I pastored a church that was a direct descendant of this tradition in North Carolina; see "Covenant of Cherokee Creek Baptist Church" (1783), in Deweese, 214.

[35] "Covenant of J. Newton Brown's *The Baptist Church Manual*" (1853), in Deweese, 223. "Doubtless, the church covenant printed in J. Newton Brown's

Deweese surmises that British Baptist churches began to shy away from the use of covenants in the nineteenth and twentieth centuries due to rigid application of church discipline and formulaic habits for many in adopting covenants.[36] Behavioral expectations were stressed among Baptist churches on the American frontier, so ethics increasingly side-lined doctrines.[37] While efforts have been made to spark a renewal of interest in church covenants, Deweese notes seven reasons why covenants underwent decline in America, including formalism, legalism, and an overriding emphasis on church growth.[38] Whatever the reasons for their decreasing use, aside from implicit allusions to the economic Trinity, it is rare to find much more than a cursory mention of "the sacred three," "the holy Trinity," or "the triune name" in a typical church covenant.[39] It is primarily in the southern United States, in both the Sandy Creek tradition and the Charleston tradition, that one finds classical Trinitarian statements in the covenant (although examples also exist in Canada and China).[40] But even the fullest definition only summarily confesses, "That we will take the one living and true God, one God in three persons, Father, Son, and Holy Spirit, to be our God."[41]

Baptist Catechisms

The catechisms produced and used by Baptists were intended to educate young people in the basics of the Christian faith. They are more detailed in their treatment of the doctrine of God as Trinity than the more common

---

Baptist *Church Manual* in 1853 has had a more lasting influence on Southern Baptist churches than any other similar document." Deweese, 15.

[36] Deweese, 36.

[37] Deweese, 56, 59.

[38] Deweese, 88–90.

[39] "Covenant of New Road Baptist Church, Oxford" (1780), "Covenant of Kehukee Baptist Association" (1803), and "Covenant of Baptist Union of Victoria" (1948), in Deweese, 126, 153, 194.

[40] Deweese, 182, 193.

[41] "Covenant of Citadel Square Baptist Church, Charleston" (1868), in Deweese, 165.

covenants. However, they are typically less detailed in their treatment of the Trinity than a full-orbed confession and carry minimal communal authority. This is not to dismiss the influence of catechisms but to note their subsidiary place in official Baptist theology. Indeed, one contemporary proponent of catechisms notes with sadness that many Baptists today see "Baptist" and "catechism" as "mutually exclusive."[42] This was not always the case.

Henry Jessey, the pastor of the church from which the Particular Baptist movement arose, published *A Catechism for Babes, or Little Ones* in 1652. It teaches according to an economic hermeneutic, "There is but one Jehovah, one God the Father, of whom are all things, and one Lord and Saviour Jesus Christ, by whom are all things, and there is one Comforter, which is the Holy Spirit; and these are one."[43] The Trinity is also affirmed according to the economy of salvation.[44] Thomas Grantham, the first Baptist theologian to write a systematic theology, also wrote a catechism for General Baptist use. In the introduction to his 1687 *St. Paul's Catechism*, Grantham affirms in the first article, "that God is One, . . . Who hath revealed himself in the Gospel by the Name of the Father, Son, and Holy Ghost. And these three are one."[45] Developing his catechism according to the six principles in Heb 6:1–2, Grantham includes the Nicene Creed under the second principle, "Of Faith towards God." While he affirmed the eternal generation of the Son and denied the creation of the Son, Grantham did not remark upon the creed's claim that the Son is "of one substance with the Father."[46] He also wrote "that the holy Spirit is God," the "eternal" One.[47]

---

[42] Tom J. Nettles, *Teaching Truth, Training Hearts: The Study of Catechisms in Baptist Life* (Amityville, NY: Calvary Press, 1998), 14–15.

[43] Henry Jessey, "A Catechism for Babes, or Little Ones (1652)," in *Baptist Confessions, Covenants, and Catechisms*, 230. For a delineation of such terms as "ontological" and "economic," when applied to Trinitarianism, see Malcolm B. Yarnell III, *God the Trinity: Biblical Portraits* (Nashville: B&H Academic, 2017).

[44] Jessey, "Catechism for Babes," 237.

[45] Thomas Grantham, *St. Paul's Catechism, or, A Brief and Plain Explication of the Six Principles of the Christian Religion* (London, 1687), 5.

[46] Grantham, 25–26.

[47] Grantham, 30.

Benjamin Keach, in his popular catechism of 1693, treated the Trinity first in the economies of revelation and salvation, but soon after also affirmed classical Trinitarian ontology and relationality. Keach required students to affirm the equality in power and glory of the three—there is no hint whatsoever of eternal submission.[48] Trinitarianism is reinforced again according to the economies of revelation and salvation, but then also according to the baptismal formula of Matthew 28 and the economy of prayer.[49] Nettles notes that Keach's Baptist Catechism was developed from the Westminster Catechism and was subsequently advocated for use among Philadelphia Baptists, Charleston Baptists, and later by Charles Haddon Spurgeon.[50] John Sutcliff, who helped foster the modern missions movement alongside William Carey and Andrew Fuller, also published a catechism in 1783. Sutcliff's eleventh answer required the student to affirm, "The one living and true God does subsist in three distinct persons, bearing the names of Father, Son, and Holy Spirit." However, this question and answer was placed in small print, indicating it was intended only for more advanced students.[51]

James Petigru Boyce, the first president of The Southern Baptist Theological Seminary, published a catechism in 1864, with revisions in the following decade. Boyce treated the Trinity in summary according to the distinction between the persons yet of one "nature," which nature remains beyond human knowledge.[52] John A. Broadus, one of the founding faculty of Southern Seminary, provided a fuller treatment of the Trinity in his catechism of 1892. His sixth lesson, "The Holy Spirit and the Trinity," affirmed the deity of all three persons, denied tritheism, admitted the doctrine's mysterious nature, and noted the baptismal formula

---

[48] Benjamin Keach, "The Baptist Catechism (1693)," in *Confessions, Covenants, and Catechisms*, 241–42.

[49] Keach, 253–54.

[50] Nettles, *Teaching Truth, Training Hearts*, 47–58.

[51] John Sutcliff, "The First Principles of the Oracles of God (1783)," in Nettles, 110, 256.

[52] James P. Boyce, "A Brief Catechism of Bible Doctrine," in Nettles, 170–71.

and the Corinthian benediction as sources for the doctrine.[53] However, it is E. T. Winkler, pastor of the First Baptist Church of Charleston, who gave the fullest treatment of the Trinity in 1857. Beginning with the Great Commission, Winkler not only affirmed the terminology of "Trinity," but also the unity of the Godhead, the distinctions between the persons, the equality of the three in "power and glory," salvation by the Trinity, and the need to worship all three as one. Moreover, Winkler provided an affective hymn, "Praise to the Trinity," to assist in worship.[54] Sadly, the publication and use of catechisms fell out of vogue after the turn of the twentieth century. However, systematic theologians have continued teaching about the Trinity from the seventeenth well into the twenty-first century.

Baptist Systematic Theologians

As with our analysis of the confessions, covenants, and catechisms created by Baptists, we shall herein treat a representative sample of Baptist writing theologians in order to evaluate their positions vis-à-vis classical Trinitarianism. First, it should be noted that the major systematic theologians writing within the Baptist tradition during its first two centuries affirmed the full language and meaning of classical Trinitarianism, often at length. In the next two centuries, systematic challenges undermined the Baptist tradition.

Grantham agreed that while the term *Trinity* is not found in Scripture, it "hath very near affinity with the Language of the Holy Ghost."[55] Moreover, the Son and the Holy Spirit possess "the same Nature or Essence" as the Father, for each one is "Eternal." They may

---

[53] John A. Broadus, "A Catechism of Bible Teaching (1892)," in *Confessions, Covenants, and Catechisms*, 267–68. Broadus later states, "The word 'Trinity' or 'Triunity' means that God is in one sense three and in another sense one."

[54] E. T. Winkler, "Notes and Questions for the Oral Instruction of Colored People (1857)," in Nettles, *Teaching Truth, Training Hearts*, 137–39.

[55] Thomas Grantham, *Christianismus Primitivus, or, the Ancient Christian Religion, in Its Nature, Certainty, Excellency, and Beauty* (London: Francis Smith, 1678), 2.2.3, 40. He depends upon the Johannine Comma to support this claim.

"fitly be called three Persons" due to the application of hypostasis to the Father in Hebrews 1.[56] Grantham took the Apostles' Creed and the Nicene Creed and "digested and comprehended" them to confess the Son is "begotten of the Father" and "of one substance with the Father," while the Spirit "proceeds from the Father and the Son."[57] He also reprinted and commented upon the 1660 Standard Confession of the General Baptists, which he understood to teach "this Trinity is one God" although it lacked classical language.[58]

John Gill, the leading Particular Baptist systematic theologian of the eighteenth century, defended the doctrine of the Trinity in the early years after Salters' Hall. This young pastor showed from Scripture "that there is a Trinity of persons in the Godhead." He first proved divine unity, then divine plurality, specifically threeness, and concluded with the distinct personality of each divine person.[59] He admitted terms like "Trinity, Unity, Essence, and persons" are not found in Scripture, but "we have the things themselves signified by them."[60] Gill's early monograph concluded the three persons "are the same in substance, equal in power and glory."[61] Four decades later, the mature Gill addressed the Trinity again in his systematic theology, stating he could alter nothing he had written before.

Six hefty chapters are devoted to the Trinity in *A Body of Doctrinal Divinity*. Gill begins by establishing divine unity as a "first principle" and refuting the Arian, Sabellian, and Tritheist heresies. Trinitarians assert "there is but one divine essence, undivided, and common to Father, Son, and Spirit, and in this sense but one God; since there is but one essence, though there are different modes of subsisting in it which are called persons; and these possess the whole essence undivided."[62] After surveying

---

[56] Grantham, 2.2.4, 43.

[57] Grantham, 2/2.5.3, 60–61.

[58] Grantham, 2/2.5.3, 65.

[59] John Gill, *The Doctrine of the Trinity, Stated and Vindicated* (London: Aaron Ward, 1731), 2, 4–5.

[60] Gill, 53–54.

[61] Gill, 204.

[62] John Gill, *A Body of Doctrinal Divinity*, New Edition (London, 1839), 125–28.

divine plurality in the Old Testament, Gill discusses the New Testament threeness of God.[63] He then unfolds the revelation of God as triune through the major divine works of creation, providence, and the covenant of grace. Gill laments those who consider the Trinity to be a speculative doctrine, for "it enters into the whole of our salvation, and all parts of it; . . . there is no doing without it."[64]

Gill argues the relations between the persons did not come about as an act of divine will but arise from the divine nature, for the Trinity's nature "exists necessarily." Divine creation is an act of divine willing, but divine existence derives from divine being.[65] The "modes of subsisting" of the Father, Son, and Spirit are "begetting," "begotten," and "breathed," respectively.[66] Eternal generation of the Son is necessary to uphold the Trinity.[67] Gill also clarifies that there may be a subordination in the office of Christ as human, "but not as he is the Son of God." While sonship may imply inferiority among men, it carries no such meaning in the Godhead. Because the Son has the same nature, he is equal in authority and is due the same homage as the Father. Gill firmly rebukes those who "pervert" 1 Cor 15:24, 28 to mean "the sense of subordination and subjection of the Son of God to the Father."[68] Gill's entire theology of the Trinity remains the most mature presentation available among classical Baptist theologians, even after 250 years.

Alas, Baptist Trinitarianism went downhill after Gill. The next most important and popular Baptist systematician was Augustus Hopkins Strong. Rehearsing much the same biblical territory as Gill, Strong nonetheless tested the bounds of classical orthodoxy. Positively, with regard to the "ordering of the Trinity," Strong allows passages describing Christ's inferiority to be ascribed to his humanity. Moreover, a difference in office need not compromise "essential oneness and equality."

---

[63] Gill is careful not to depend entirely upon the disputed Johannine Comma. Gill, 130–36.

[64] Gill, 137–38.

[65] Gill, 141.

[66] Gill, 142.

[67] Gill, 144.

[68] Gill, 148.

Negatively, he concludes, "the divine nature was in some way limited and humbled."[69] Again, on the one hand, Strong holds the line on the oneness of the divine being, the threeness of the divine persons, and contradicts both Arianism and Modalism with the Athanasian creed.[70] On the other hand, he repeats the moderately liberal theologian Isaak August Dorner's doctrine of "one divine personality" alongside the three "modes of subsistence."[71] Happily, Strong agreed with Gill that the processions of the Son and the Spirit are not an act of the divine will, nor do they compromise the equality of the three.[72] Foreshadowing later developments, Strong correlated the Trinity with other doctrines, including not only previously emphasized areas such as revelation and redemption, but also as a "model for human life" in our "social nature."[73]

Among Southern Baptists, John Dagg provided an unattributed precis of Gill's classical arguments from Scripture. He also warned against pressing creaturely analogies: "All such illustrations darken counsel with words without knowledge. What shall we liken to the Lord?"[74] Dagg also offered a compelling description of Trinitarian movement in the covenant of grace.[75] While Dagg largely followed Gill, some other Southern Baptist theologians developed new approaches, while staying, like Dagg, within classical bounds. For instance, Edgar Young Mullins appreciated the contributions of the liberal theologian F. D. E. Schleiermacher regarding method, but he typically adopted conservative conclusions. Thus, while Schleiermacher addressed the Trinity in a postscript, Mullins disagreed[76] and treated the Trinity with the person of the Spirit. Before addressing the Trinity proper, Mullins concluded

---

[69] Augustus Hopkins Strong, *Systematic Theology: A Compendium and Commonplace Book*, vol. 1 (Old Tappan, NJ: Revell, 1907), 314.

[70] Strong, 327–30.

[71] Strong, 331.

[72] Strong, 341–42.

[73] Strong, 351.

[74] John L. Dagg, *A Manual of Theology* (repr., Harrisonburg, VA: Gano Books, 1982; first published 1857), 249.

[75] Dagg, 253–57.

[76] Edgar Young Mullins, *The Christian Religion in Its Doctrinal Expression* (Philadelphia: Judson Press, 1917), 29–30.

"the deity of Christ is a necessary article of faith," argued for Christ's preexistence, and allowed for divine limitation in Christ's incarnation if only as "a mark of the infinite perfection of God." [77] Mullins affirmed the terms "Trinity" and "persons," but said human language must be understood analogously when applied to God.[78] He recognized the difference between the economic and immanent Trinity but correlated the two closely.[79] Like some medieval theologians, Mullins stated that the priority of divine love entails the existence of eternal persons.[80] After rejecting the Unitarian, Modalist, and Tritheist interpretations, Walter Thomas Conner, a student of Mullins, reaffirmed the classical Trinity along with the indivisible working of the three, the "properly qualified" use of "persons," and a realist correlation of the economic Trinity with the "Being" of the immanent Trinity.[81]

Taking a different tack, Mullins's predecessor at Southern Seminary, James Petigru Boyce, followed his Princeton professor, Charles Hodge, in kicking against the goads of classical Trinitarianism. Boyce contradicted Gill's grounding of the personal relations in God's nature: "It is by the will of the Father that he begets the Son, and by the will of the Father and the Son that the Spirit proceeds. The action of the will here is causal, although these relations are eternal and are characteristic of the Godhead. They are the results of the divine activity."[82] Boyce shows no awareness that divine simplicity may be compromised through positing temporal potentialities within the divine being. Boyce providentially recapitulated the ontological unity, personal relationality, and numeric Trinity of classical Trinitarianism. Later, Boyce repeated his grounding of divine ontology in the divine will and affirmed the eternal generation of the Son.

---

[77] Mullins, 167, 180–83.

[78] Mullins, 205–6. Mullins also says, "God is a person," but seems to mean, "God is personal." Mullins, 210.

[79] Mullins, 207–8.

[80] Mullins, 208–9.

[81] Walter Thomas Conner, *Christian Doctrine* (Nashville, TN: Broadman Press, 1937), 120–27.

[82] James Petigru Boyce, *Abstract of Systematic Theology* (repr., Hanford, CA: Den Dulk Christian Foundation, [n.d.]; first published 1887), 107.

However, Boyce also posited an "inequality" among the three "relative to each other as persons."[83] Driven by a desire to prioritize an authoritarian analogy of fatherhood and sonship, Boyce said the Son's inequality is not in nature, but in "official rank and personal relation."[84] After affirming the double procession of the Holy Spirit, Boyce addressed an entire section to "Subordination between the Persons." While maintaining "absolute equality" in nature, he believed 1 Cor 15:24, 28 teaches "inferiority" in office. Moreover, Boyce grounded the relations in the Father's will, who alone is not willed as a person.[85] On the one hand, Boyce properly condemned Arianism. But, on the other hand, he advocated a novel divine ontology.

Teachings similar to those of Boyce have been advanced recently by Bruce A. Ware of Southern Seminary and Wayne Grudem of Phoenix Seminary, who teach there is "eternal functional subordination" (EFS) or "eternal relations of authority and submission" (ERAS) between the Son and the Father.[86] Other Baptist theologians, including the present author and two of the editors of this volume (Emerson and Stamps), have responded with reaffirmations of the Baptist tradition of classical Trinitarianism, considering any eternal subordination too problematic to countenance.[87] Yet other Baptist theologians have, unlike Grudem

---

[83] Boyce, 139.

[84] Boyce, 143.

[85] Boyce, 152–55. James M. Pendleton also posits an inferiority in office alongside an equality in essence between the persons, but without Boyce's ruminations on the willing of the relations. James M. Pendleton, *Christian Doctrines: A Compendium of Theology* (Valley Forge, PA: Judson Press, 1906), 69–71.

[86] Bruce A. Ware, "Response to Malcolm B. Yarnell III, Matthew Y. Emerson, and Luke Stamps," in *Trinitarian Theology: Theological Models and Doctrinal Application*, ed. Keith S. Whitfield (Nashville, TN: B&H Academic, 2019), 132–33. Grudem denies eternal subordination in "being," but affirms eternal subordination in "role or function." He does not indicate how he is able to divide the ontological from the functional, contrary to the tradition exemplified in Grantham. Wayne Grudem, *Bible Doctrine: Essential Teachings of the Christian Faith*, ed. Jeff Purswell (Grand Rapids: Zondervan, 1999), 114n4.

[87] Chris Morgan, the third editor of this volume, also affirms classical Christian theism and classical Trinitarianism in his forthcoming systematic theology, although he does not do so in conversation or debate with Ware and

and Ware, borrowed from the social trinitarian movement, yet without diminishing the authority of the Son and the Holy Spirit. For instance, Paul S. Fiddes developed a pastoral doctrine of the Trinity by drawing upon the mutual relationality of the three.[88] The classical Baptist tradition's emphasis on the equality in power and glory of the divine persons contradicts the proponents of EFS and ERAS.

On the more liberal side of the Baptist ledger, some theologians have experimented with new language, while a few have vacated Christian orthodoxy. William Newton Clarke tried to improve the classical language.[89] He called the economic Trinity, which he believed was revealed, "The Divine Trinity," and the immanent Trinity, which he considered speculative, "The Divine Triunity."[90] Clarke was also troubled by the change in meaning over the centuries in the word, "person." He thus opted to speak of God as "one Person" in the modern sense but "three persons" in the classical sense."[91] In spite of such creative terminology, Newton concluded the doctrine was both "vital" and the "very substance of Christianity," and makes God "richer" to our minds.[92] Harold W. Tribble of Southern Seminary summarized Clarke's innovative language

---

Grudem. See Christopher W. Morgan, *Christian Theology: The Biblical Story and Our Faith* (Nashville: B&H Academic, 2020). On a separate note but related to the above point about Grudem and Ware, egalitarian theologians were the first to criticize Ware and Grudem. Cf. Millard J. Erickson, *Who's Tampering with the Trinity? An Assessment of the Subordination Debate* (Grand Rapids: Kregel, 2009). Complementarian critics have more recently entered the field. See the two essays each of Emerson and Stamps, and of Yarnell in *Trinitarian Theology*, ed. Whitfield. See also the essays of Tyler R. Wittman and Stephen R. Holmes in *Trinity without Hierarchy: Reclaiming Nicene Orthodoxy in Evangelical Theology*, ed. Michael F. Bird and Scott Harrower (Grand Rapids: Kregel, 2019), 141–64, 259–73.

[88] Paul S. Fiddes, *Participating in God: A Pastoral Doctrine of the Trinity* (Louisville, KY: Westminster John Knox, 2000).

[89] James Garrett classifies Clarke first among the "Northern Baptist Liberal Theologians." James Leo Garrett Jr., *Baptist Theology: A Four-Century Study* (Macon, GA: Mercer University Press, 2009), 304–10.

[90] William Newton Clarke, *An Outline of Christian Theology*, 6th ed. (New York: Scribner, 1899), 161.

[91] Clarke, 170–71.

[92] Clarke, 179–81.

of "Triunity" for the laity,[93] while Gary L. Parker similarly pictured God as "one person" with three "personal images."[94] However, R. Kirby Godsey went much further and undermined more than the terminology of the classical Trinity. By denying the priority of biblical revelation, denigrating creeds, and arguing for a nonpropositional reading of Scripture, Godsey denied Christians should worship Jesus; rather, Jesus is to be followed.[95] Christians may confess Jesus as Lord, but this means Jesus is merely "God's light" and not "God's only word."[96] God is not a "person," but "the heart and soul of our being persons."[97] Alongside these innovations, Godsey denied that God is "Father" and universalized the Spirit,[98] effectively removing the Trinity from consideration. While some conservative Baptists have altered classical Trinitarianism, some liberal Baptists have not only altered it but contradicted it.

Must Baptists Embrace Classical Trinitarianism?

Baptists emphasize both the sufficiency of Scripture for doctrinal formation and the freedom for creativity in response to the leading of the Spirit, yet most have also concluded these commitments require, not the surrender, but the utilization of some Trinitarian language from the classical tradition. Four witnesses to this conclusion include two American Baptists and two British Baptists, transcending the divides between left and right, radical and traditional.

---

[93] Harold W. Tribble, *Our Doctrines* (Nashville: Sunday School Board, 1936), 24–26.

[94] Gary L. Parker, "God," in *A Baptist's Theology*, ed. R. Wayne Stacy (Macon, GA: Smyth & Helwys, 1999), 28–29.

[95] R. Kirby Godsey, *When We Talk about God . . . Let's Be Honest* (Macon, GA: Smyth & Helwys, 1996), ix, 120. "There are no right theologies." Godsey, 16. "Doctrinal soundness is arrogant theological nonsense." Godsey, 17.

[96] Godsey, 52, 119, 125.

[97] Godsey, 71–72.

[98] Godsey, 64, 70.

First, while prioritizing *suprema Scriptura*, James Leo Garrett Jr., a cautious Southern Baptist theologian, states, "Creeds, confessions of faith, and decisions of councils and of church leaders are seen as establishing the norms or the conclusions of systematic theology."[99] Second, arguing for a generous and liberal theology, Curtis W. Freeman advocates that Baptists embrace classical Christianity, because "ironically, no group in the wider Christian communion is in greater need of confessing the one faith as delineated in the ancient ecumenical creeds of the church." Freeman resolves Baptist theology must thus be centered on "the revelation of the Triune God in Jesus Christ."[100]

Third, Stephen R. Holmes, a British Baptist proponent of classical Trinitarianism, argues there should be no distinctive Baptist theology of the Trinity. Holmes finds, in an ecumenical mode, "Baptists generally assumed the traditional doctrine of God when it was generally assumed."[101] Finally, Nigel Wright, a radical evangelical formerly of Spurgeon's College in London, believes Trinitarianism remains "the fundamental, defining paradigm by which we interpret Christianity." Rejecting various contemporary challenges to the classical doctrine, Wright reasons that radicals must never surrender the orthodox doctrine of the Trinity.[102] I agree with these four representative contemporary Baptist scholars. To put it more strongly, allowing for some freedom in language due to our respect for biblical precedence and creative liberty, Baptists who outright reject the classical Trinitarian tradition ought to be counted neither Baptist nor Christian.

---

[99] James Leo Garrett Jr., *Systematic Theology: Biblical, Historical, and Evangelical*, vol. 1, 2nd ed. (North Richland Hills, TX: BIBAL, 2000), 26, 206–8.

[100] Curtis W. Freeman, "Toward a Generous Orthodoxy," in *Evangelicals and Nicene Faith: Reclaiming the Apostolic Witness*, ed. Timothy George (Grand Rapids: Baker, 2011), 116–17.

[101] Stephen R. Holmes, *Baptist Theology* (New York: T&T Clark, 2012), 7–8, 72.

[102] Nigel G. Wright, *The Radical Evangelical: Seeking a Place to Stand* (London: SPCK, 1996), 13–27.

Table 1

The Use of Classical Trinitarian Language in Twelve Baptist Confessions

Baptist Confession, Article(s)	Year Adopted	Uses Ontological Language of "Substance," "Essence," "Nature," or "Godhead"	Uses Relational Language of "Person," "Subsistence," or "Generation" ("Begotten") with "Procession"	Uses Numerical Language of "Trinity," "Triune," or "Three" with "One"
A Short Confession of Faith, 2–3	1610	Yes	Yes	Yes
The London Confession, II	1644	Yes	Yes	No
The Faith and Practice of Thirty Congregations, 20	1651	No	No	No
The Standard Confession, VII	1660	No	No	Yes
Second London Confession, 2	1677	Yes	Yes	Yes
The Orthodox Creed, III and XXXVIII	1678	Yes	Yes	Yes
The Brief Confession, I	1703	Yes	Yes	Yes
The Unity of the Churches	1705	Yes	Yes	Yes
Principles of Faith of the Sandy Creek Association, I	1816	Yes	No	Yes

The New Hampshire Confession, 2	1833	Yes	Yes	Yes
The Baptist Faith and Message, II	1925	Yes	No	No
The Baptist Faith and Message, II	2000	Yes	No	Yes

Sources: William L. Lumpkin, *Baptist Confessions of Faith*, 2nd rev. ed., ed. Bill J. Leonard (Valley Forge, PA: Judson Press, 2011); Clint Bass, *The Caffynite Controversy* (Forthcoming), appendixes D and E; The Baptist Faith and Message (Nashville: Southern Baptist Convention, 2000)

4

Baptists, Classic Christology, and the Christian Tradition

R. Lucas Stamps
Anderson University

Introduction

There is a sense in which the Baptist vision is reducible to the personal and ecclesial experience of the forgiving and transforming presence of the crucified and risen Christ. All of the Baptist distinctives are grounded in and flow from this fundamental experience.[1] Baptists reserve church membership and its initiating rite, baptism, only for those who can give credible attestation to a believing encounter with the only Son of God, the Word made flesh, Jesus Christ. Our polity assumes this saving experience among all the people of God, and our social and political posture is predicated upon its possibility for all and only those who freely accept the Savior's promises and demands. Since faith in Jesus Christ is prerequisite to membership in the new covenant, no attempts at premature confirmation or state-sanctioned coercion are permissible. Even as explicit affirmations of creedal language concerning the person of Christ have waxed and waned in the Baptist movement, this fundamental Christocentric orientation has never flagged among biblically faithful

---

[1] For an exposition of Baptist distinctives see R. Stanton Norman, *The Baptist Way: Distinctives of a Baptist Church* (Nashville: B&H, 2005).

Baptists. Nevertheless, this chapter will argue that the earliest Baptists were indeed explicitly indebted to the language and concepts of Nicene and Chalcedonian orthodoxy, that the eclipse of these categories often signaled a regression in the Baptist vision, and that a recovery of these creedal affirmations in our own day is a key to Baptist theological renewal and missiological reinvigoration.

The chapter will proceed in three steps. The first section will briefly survey the development of classical Christological orthodoxy in the early centuries of the church, especially in terms of the seven ecumenical councils and the various heresies they addressed. The second section will examine key defenders of classical Christology in the Baptist tradition. The concluding section will explore how a recovery of this Christological heritage may serve to renew contemporary Baptist faith and practice.

Classic Christology: A Very Brief Overview

As scholars of the New Testament and early Christianity have increasingly argued in recent years, the exalted status of Jesus of Nazareth in Christian faith and devotion goes all the way back to the earliest strata of Christianity's development.[2] Without in any way attenuating their commitment to Jewish monotheism, the earliest Christians came to believe Jesus is to be identified[3] with God himself, possessing the attributes and prerogatives of, and even receiving the worship owed to, Israel's God. Texts from the Old Testament were interpreted in a way that allowed for personal distinctions within the one God of Israel and particularly

---

[2] See, for example, Richard Bauckham, *Jesus and the God of Israel: God Crucified and Other Studies on the New Testament's Christology of Divine Identity* (Grand Rapids: Eerdmans, 2008); Larry W. Hurtado, *Lord Jesus Christ: Devotion to Jesus in Earliest Christianity* (Grand Rapids: Eerdmans, 2003); Simon J. Gathercole, *The Pre-Existent Son: Recovering the Christologies of Matthew, Mark, and Luke* (Grand Rapids: Eerdmans, 2006); and Matthew W. Bates, *The Birth of the Trinity: Jesus, God, and Spirit in New Testament and Early Christian Interpretations of the Old Testament* (Oxford, UK: Oxford University Press, 2015).

[3] The language of "divine identity" comes from Bauckham's impressive studies of New Testament Christology. See Bauckham, *Jesus and the God of Israel*.

for the preexistence of Christ in the divine life. This "prosopological" reading strategy appears to go back to Jesus himself, who interpreted Psalm 110 as an address of Yahweh to himself.[4] New Testament teaching on the identity and mission of Jesus placed a kind of "exegetical pressure" on the church to account for both the unity of and the distinction between the three persons identified with the one true God: Father, Son, and Holy Spirit.[5]

The early centuries of the church witnessed several attempts to account for how Jesus Christ could be both God and man. The Logos Christology of Justin Martyr sought to demonstrate how Jesus is the Word or Reason permeating all created reality. In a dialogue with his Jewish interlocutor, Trypho, Justin interpreted the Old Testament story as a witness to the preexistent Logos.[6] Irenaeus viewed the biblical narrative as a divine economy (God's unfolding redemptive plan) that has as its hypothesis (its basic gist or master plan) the recapitulation of all things in the Word made flesh.[7] Tertullian gave the church the basic grammar that would come to be accepted as the orthodox doctrine of the triune God, the *Trinitas*: one nature in three persons.[8] Origen developed the notion that the Son is inseparable from the Father and is distinguished from the Father in terms of his eternal generation: the Father never exists "even for

---

[4] See the discussion of prosopological exegesis in Bates, *Birth of the Trinity*.

[5] Stephen R. Holmes, *The Quest for the Trinity: The Doctrine of God in Scripture, History and Modernity* (Downers Grove, IL: InterVarsity Press Academic, 2012), 54.

[6] Justin Martyr, *Dialogue with Trypho*, trans. Thomas B. Falls, ed. Michael Slusser and Thomas P. Halton (Washington, DC: Catholic University of America Press, 2003).

[7] See Irenaeus of Lyons, *Against the Heresies*, trans. Dominic J. Unger (New York: Paulist, 1992); Irenaeus, *On the Apostolic Preaching*, trans. John Behr (Crestwood, NY: St. Vladimir's Seminary Press, 1997). For a treatment of these themes in Irenaeus, see John J. O'Keefe and R. R. Reno, *Sanctified Vision: An Introduction to Early Christian Interpretation of the Bible* (Baltimore: John Hopkins University Press, 2005), 33–44.

[8] Tertullian, *Against Praxeas*, trans. Ernest Evans (London: SPCK, 1948). See also Timothy David Barnes, *Tertullian: A Historical and Literary Study* (Oxford, UK: Oxford University Press, 1985).

a single moment, without begetting [his] wisdom."[9] These second- and third-century attempts to explain the deity of Christ sometimes suffered from hints of subordinationism, at times viewing the Son of God as a kind of middle category between the Father and the created world, but they remained important steps in the development of the doctrines of the Trinity and of the incarnation of the Second Person for the redemption of the world.

The controversies of the fourth century forced the church to seek greater clarity on the equality of the divine persons.[10] The debate was sparked by the Egyptian priest Arius, who argued that the Son was indeed preexistent to his incarnation but was the first and greatest of the Father's created beings. "There was once when he was not" was Arius's summary statement. This controversy precipitated the convening of the Council of Nicaea in 325, which came to be considered the first of the ecumenical (that is, worldwide) councils.[11] The council fathers decisively rejected the Arian heresy and affirmed that the Son of God is consubstantial, of the same substance (Greek, *homoousios*) with, the Father. The creed that emerged from the council declared that Christ is the only Son of God, who became incarnate, suffered, died, rose from the dead, ascended to the Father, and will one day return to judge the living and the dead. In the decades that followed, many in the imperial and ecclesiastical establishment reverted to a kind of semi-Arian position, but courageous leaders such as Athanasius of Alexandria defended the Nicene settlement. In a crucially important work, *On the Incarnation*, Athanasius argued that

---

[9] Origen, *On First Principles*, trans. John Behr, 2 vols. (Oxford: Oxford University Press, 2018), 1.2.2.

[10] For the historical and theological background to the fourth-century controversies, see Khaled Anatolios, *Retrieving Nicaea: The Development and Meaning of Trinitarian Doctrine* (Grand Rapids: Baker Academic, 2011); and Lewis Ayres, *Nicaea and Its Legacy: An Approach to Fourth-Century Trinitarian Theology* (Oxford, UK: Oxford University Press), 2004.

[11] On the seven ecumenical councils, see Leo Donald Davis, *The First Seven Ecumenical Councils (325–787): Their History and Theology* (Collegeville, MN: Liturgical Press, 1983).

humanity's Savior must be both God and man, a truth evidenced in Christian confession and worship.[12]

As the fourth century wore on, it became apparent that a second council was needed to clarify the church's position on the identity of the Son (as well as to fill out its statement of belief in the Holy Spirit, whose divinity had been challenged by a group known as the *Pneumatomachi*, or the Macedonians). In the lead-up to the council, three theologians ministering in the region of Cappadocia were especially influential. The brothers Basil of Caesarea and Gregory of Nyssa, along with their good friend Gregory of Nazianzus, were instrumental in defending and explicating the Nicene doctrine. Particularly important was the terminological clarification the Cappadocian Fathers made regarding the three persons of the Trinity.[13] At Nicaea, the Greek terms *ousia* and *hypostasis* were seen as roughly synonymous ways of naming the divine essence shared by the three persons, so much so that the council expressly forbade anyone from speaking of three *hypostases* in the Trinity. But what term should be used to speak of the three?

The Greek *prosopon* was a serviceable term, mirroring the Latin use of *persona* that developed in the West from the writings of Tertullian, but it was easily misinterpreted in modalistic ways—as if the persons were simply distinct modes of revelation of a unipersonal God. The Cappadocian Fathers chose instead to co-opt, as it were, the term *hypostasis* and utilize it as a way of distinguishing the three.[14] Its close relation to *ousia* left intact the emphasis on divine unity—there are not three gods—but gave the church a way of distinguishing three real relations of origin within the divine life: the unbegotten Father, the eternally begotten Son, and the eternally proceeding Holy Spirit. The second ecumenical council that

---

[12] Athanasius, *On the Incarnation*, trans. John Behr (Yonkers, NY: St. Vladimir's Seminary Press, 2011).

[13] On the Cappadocians' role in these terminological clarifications see Anatolios, *Retrieving Nicaea*, 23–24.

[14] There were precedents for using *hypostasis* to name the three, going back to Origen. See the discussion in Gilles Emery, *The Trinity: An Introduction to the Catholic Doctrine of the Triune God*, trans. Matthew Levering (Washington, DC: Catholic University of America Press, 2011), 61.

met at Constantinople in 381 reaffirmed the Nicene doctrine of the Son's consubstantiality with the Father and provided a fuller statement on the Holy Spirit, who proceeds from the Father[15] and is coequal and coeternal with the Father and the Son.

The resulting creed, commonly referred to as the Nicene Creed but more accurately titled the Niceno-Constantinopolitan Creed, summarizes the church's teaching as follows:

> I believe in one God, the Father Almighty, Maker of heaven and earth, and of all things visible and invisible.
>
> And in one Lord Jesus Christ, the only-begotten Son of God, begotten of the Father before all worlds; God of God, Light of Light, very God of very God; begotten, not made, being of one substance with the Father, by whom all things were made.
>
> Who, for us men for our salvation, came down from heaven, and was incarnate by the Holy Spirit of the virgin Mary, and was made man; and was crucified also for us under Pontius Pilate; He suffered and was buried; and the third day He rose again, according to the Scriptures; and ascended into heaven, and sits on the right hand of the Father; and He shall come again, with glory, to judge the quick and the dead; whose kingdom shall have no end.
>
> And I believe in the Holy Ghost, the Lord and Giver of Life; who proceeds from the Father [and the Son]; who with the Father and the Son together is worshipped and glorified; who spoke by the prophets.
>
> And I believe one holy catholic and apostolic Church. I acknowledge one baptism for the remission of sins; and I look for the resurrection of the dead, and the life of the world to come. Amen.[16]

---

[15] Of course, relatively early on, Western Christians began to add "and the Son" (*filioque*) to the Creed's statement on the Spirit's procession. On the *filioque* controversy see Holmes, *Quest for the Trinity*, 147–64.

[16] The Nicene Creed, accessed March 14, 2018, https://www.ccel.org/creeds /nicene.creed.html.

The first two ecumenical councils made clear the true deity of the Son and his incarnation and redeeming work for the salvation of the world, but the centuries that followed witnessed several rigorous debates about how divinity and humanity are related in the person of the Son. The canons of the Council of Constantinople had already addressed one pernicious heresy about the incarnation, namely, the teaching of Apollinaris. According to the Apollinarians, the Son of God assumed only a human body in his incarnation, with the person of Son essentially functioning in place of the human soul. Gregory of Nazianzus's argument against the Apollinarians proved decisive: the unassumed is unhealed.[17] In other words, if there is any part of humanity that the Son did not assume—that is, take to himself in personal union—then that part of human nature remains untouched by his redeeming work. The incarnation was comprehensive; the Son assumed all that it means to be human, sin excepted, in order to save humanity to the uttermost.

In the fifth century, another heresy arose that warranted a response from the orthodox. The patriarch of Constantinople, Nestorius, had shown reticence about speaking of Mary as the *theotokos*, the God-bearer, because he feared it would communicate the notion that Mary somehow gave birth to Christ's divinity. Perhaps instead *christotokos*, the Christ-bearer, would better communicate the sense that Christ partook of Mary's humanity. But Cyril of Alexandria discerned the potential threat that Nestorius's position posed to the unity of Christ's person.[18] Who is the one born of Mary? Is it not the only Son of God made man? There is no person there, so to speak, other than the person of the eternal Son. The Nestorian position seemed to divide Christ into two sons, two persons. This position implies there was some already-existing human person who was simply adopted into a unique relationship with the person

---

[17] See Gregory of Nazianzus, "To Cledonius Against Apollinaris (Epistle 101)," in *Christology of the Later Fathers*, ed. Edward R. Hardy (Louisville, KY: Westminster John Knox, 1954), 218–19.

[18] See Cyril of Alexandria, *On the Unity of Christ*, trans. John Anthony McGuckin (Crestwood, NY: St. Vladimir's Seminary Press, 1995). For an impressive and detailed treatment of Cyril's Christology, see Henry van Loon, *The Dyophysite Christology of Cyril of Alexandria* (Leiden: Brill, 2009).

of the Son. If Apollinarianism had sacrificed the distinction of the two natures of Christ to preserve the unity, Nestorianism preserved the distinction at the cost of the unity. The third ecumenical council, meeting at Ephesus in 431, affirmed Cyril's position on the unity of the Son and condemned the Nestorian heresy.

The high-water mark for early Christological orthodoxy came in 451 at the fourth ecumenical council, the Council of Chalcedon, which addressed the precise nature of the incarnation in a more comprehensive way. The statement the council fathers produced defined the person of Christ in terms of two natures, the nature of God and the nature of man, in the one person, or *hypostasis*:

> Following the holy fathers, we all with one accord teach men to acknowledge one and the same Son, our Lord Jesus Christ, at once complete in Godhead and complete in manhood, truly God and truly man, consisting also of a reasonable soul and body; of one substance with the Father as regards his Godhead, and at the same time of one substance with us as regards his manhood; like us in all respects, apart from sin; as regards his Godhead, begotten of the Father before the ages, but yet as regards his manhood begotten, for us men and for our salvation, of Mary the Virgin, the God-bearer; one and the same Christ, Son, Lord, Only-begotten, recognized in two natures, without confusion, without change, without division, without separation; the distinction of natures being in no way annulled by the union, but rather the characteristics of each nature being preserved and coming together to form one person and subsistence, not as parted or separated into two persons, but one and the same Son and Only-begotten God the Word, Lord Jesus Christ; even as the prophets from earliest times spoke of him, and our Lord Jesus Christ himself taught us, and the creed of the fathers has handed down to us.[19]

---

[19] The Definition of the Council of Chalcedon, accessed March 14, 2018, https://reformed.org/documents/chalcedon.html.

This hypostatic union of two natures in one person warded off the full range of Christological heresies that had arisen in the early centuries.[20] Against Arianism, the Definition of Chalcedon maintained that the Son is consubstantial with the Father as his eternally begotten Son. Against Apollinarianism, it argued for the Son's assumption of both a body and a rational soul. Against Nestorianism, it affirmed that the one born by Mary, the *theotokos*, is "one and the same Son, and only begotten, God the Word, the Lord Jesus Christ," whose two natures are united without division or separation. Against another heresy, Eutychianism—which had maintained that the Son's two natures had merged into a kind of third, combined nature—the Definition affirmed that the two natures retain their distinctive properties without confusion or change. So, in sum, Chalcedon laid down the coordinates for the orthodox doctrine of the incarnation: true God (against the created Son of the Arians), true man (against the partial incarnation of the Apollinarians), two distinct natures (against the merged nature of the Eutychians), and one united person (against the divided persons of the Nestorians). These parameters did not so much *explain* the mystery of the incarnation as *preserve* the mystery against false teachings threatening to surrender one or more aspects of the biblical revelation of the person of Christ.

The last three ecumenical councils are sometimes neglected or subordinated to a lesser status when compared to the first four, but they represent important clarifications regarding the implications of Chalcedonian Christology. The fifth ecumenical council, the Second Council of Constantinople, convened in 553 to condemn some of the remaining Nestorian books not anathematized at Ephesus. In condemning the so-called Three Chapters of Nestorian writings, the council fathers once again affirmed the unity of the person of Christ against attempts to divide him into two sons.

---

[20] Heresy has often aided the church in clarifying its doctrinal positions, especially as they are expressed in the creeds. As Emery, *The Trinity*, 59, writes, "In their teaching function, the creeds pay special attention to the true expression of the faith by avoiding the errors that disfigure it. . . . Consideration of an error enables one to discover the depth of the truth, and a more profound knowledge of the truth helps one to discern the root of the error that opposes it."

The sixth ecumenical council, the Third Council of Constantinople (680–81), clarified Chalcedon's two-nature Christology by rejecting monothelitism, the belief that there is in the person of Christ only one will. The key opponent of this heresy in the lead-up to the council, Maximus the Confessor, applied Gregory's maxim "the unassumed is unhealed" to this new challenge to Christ's two natures.[21] If Christ did not assume a human will, the very locus through which sin entered the human race, then how can fallen human wills be redeemed and restored? The council's Dyothelite position affirmed that Christ has two wills: the will of God, which he shares eternally with the Father and Spirit, and the will of man, which was perfectly conformed to the divine will, as the Gethsemane narrative teaches.

The final ecumenical council, the Second Council of Nicaea (787), took up the challenge of the Iconoclasts, who argued that images of Christ and saints used in Christian worship represented a violation of the second commandment against graven images. The principle defender of the use of icons in the years before the council was John of Damascus.[22] John maintained that attempts to portray the divine essence or actual worshiping of icons would indeed be idolatrous, but, because God the Son took on true humanity, representations of Christ (and the saints in union with Christ) are not idolatrous. To reject their use would amount to a rejection of the Son's true incarnation.[23]

Much more could be said about the classical Christology that developed in the patristic era. Other important themes include the *communicatio*

---

[21] For an introduction to Maximus, including the texts of some of his more important works, see Andrew Louth, *Maximus the Confessor*, The Early Church Fathers (London: Routledge, 1996).

[22] See John of Damascus, *Three Treatises on the Divine Images*, trans. Andrew Louth (Crestwood, NY: St. Vladimir's Seminary Press, 2003).

[23] The Protestant Reformation witnessed its own iconoclastic controversy, with many Reformation groups coming to reject the use of icons as idolatrous. For a compendium of documents on these controversies, especially as they played out in England, see David J. Davis, ed., *From Icons to Idols: Documents on the Image Debate in Reformation England* (Cambridge, UK: James Clarke, 2015).

idiomatum, or communication of attributes[24] (which maintains that the attributes of both natures are communicated to the person of Christ); the tensions between the Alexandrian Logos-flesh Christologies and the Antiochene Logos-man Christologies[25] (resolved in the church's decisive rejection of both Apollinarianism and Nestorianism); the practice of partitive exegesis[26] (which sought to discern whether a given passage is speaking about the Son of God as such or about the Son of God in terms of his incarnational mission); and the so-called *extra Calvinisticum*, to use an admittedly anachronistic term[27] (the belief that the Son of God is not limited to or circumscribed by his human nature). But this brief summary of the classical view of Christ, developed in the seven ecumenical councils, will serve as the necessary background for the following exploration of how the earliest Baptists took up these important patristic themes.

Classic Christology in Early Baptist Thought

The story of the earliest Baptists, who emerged from seventeenth-century English separatism, actually comprises two stories: the General Baptists, who trace their beginnings to the 1600s and 1610s through the work of John Smyth and Thomas Helwys, and the Particular Baptists, whose beginnings lie in the 1630s.[28] Despite their disagreements over the Calvinistic doctrines of grace—with the General Baptists opting

---

[24] See the discussion in Aloys Grillmeier, *Christ in Christian Tradition*, vol. 1, *From the Apostolic Age to Chalcedon (451)*, rev. ed., trans. John Bowden (Atlanta: John Knox, 1975), 436–37.

[25] Grillmeier frames his treatment of early Christology in terms of these two schools of thought.

[26] On the practice of partitive exegesis, especially as employed by Cyril of Alexandria, see Matthew R. Crawford, *Cyril of Alexandria's Trinitarian Theology of Scripture* (Oxford, UK: Oxford University Press, 2014).

[27] Because the so-called *extra Calvinisticum* was widely held long before Calvin, David Willis has suggested that it might be better termed the *extra catholicum* or *extra patristicum*; see E. David Willis, *Calvin's Catholic Christology The Function of the So-called Extra Calvinisticum in Calvin's Theology* (Leiden: Brill, 1966).

[28] On Baptist origins see Chute, Finn, and Haykin, *Baptist Story*, 11–38.

for a more Arminian soteriology and the Particular Baptists espousing a more Calvinistic one—both groups were united in their commitment to a believers' church and the ecclesiological implications that flow from it. Only those who make credible professions of faith in Christ should be members of a local church and thus receive its initiating sign and seal of baptism. But throughout most of the seventeenth century, the two groups were also largely united on the classical doctrine of God, the classical doctrine of the Trinity, and, especially important for our present purposes, the classical doctrine of the incarnation. This section will explore one key theologian and one key confession of faith in each of the two Baptist movements: Thomas Monck and the General Baptists' Orthodox Creed; and Hercules Collins (who published a Baptist version of the Heidelberg Catechism) and the Particular Baptists' Second London Confession of Faith.[29]

General Baptist Christology

Thomas Monck was a farmer and General Baptist pastor from the Midlands of England. He stands as one of the most significant General Baptist theologians of the latter half of the seventeenth century. Monck made important theological contributions to the Baptist movement through his own teaching and writing, but he is also noteworthy as the principal author of the influential Orthodox Creed, which demonstrated the General Baptists' substantial theological agreement with their evangelical peers in England.

Monck's most important individual work is *A Cure for the Cankering Error of the Modern Eutychians*. The impetus behind this book was the controversial teaching of a General Baptist pastor, Matthew Caffyn,

---

[29] Choosing to highlight these figures from the 1670s and 1680s unfortunately elides important works and confessional symbols from earlier in the century. It also omits mention of creedal Baptists in later centuries, such as John Gill in the eighteenth century or James Petigru Boyce in the nineteenth. But it should serve as a kind of sampling of the ways in which Baptists sought solidarity with other Christian traditions on the foundational doctrines of the faith.

who had denied that Christ took his human nature from Mary.[30] Caffyn maintained that the Son of God had brought his human flesh from heaven and simply passed "through the Virgin's womb as Water through a Conduit."[31] Monck discerns in this denial of Christ's sharing in Mary's humanity a reversion to the old Eutychian error, which had diminished the true humanity of Christ and its distinction from the divine nature. Monck's book thus has four principal aims: to explicate the classical understanding of the divine essence (as simple, immutable, impassible, and so on), to defend the classical understanding of the Trinity (as one undivided essence, with the persons distinguished only by their eternal relations), to affirm the unity of the person of Christ, and to maintain both the union and the distinction of the two natures in Christ. Monck's mode of argumentation is primarily biblical, with copious scriptural citations throughout, but he is also conversant with the church fathers (including Hilary of Poitiers, Gregory of Nazianzus, and Augustine), the arguments of medieval scholastics, and the formulations of the Reformers and their heirs. He also explicitly cites and echoes the language of the ecumenical creeds, especially the Athanasian Creed, as well as the Chalcedonian Definition.

On the person of Christ, Monck maintains, "We must note how Christ took Man's Nature upon him. Not by turning his Godhead into his Manhood, but by assuming of his Manhood into his Godhead; not by confusion or mixture of substance, but by unity of Person."[32] Here Monck is clearly dependent on the language of Chalcedon and its rejection of the Eutychian notion that the two natures are mixed together, as it were. The natures are related by a union in the person, not by a confusion of essences. Monck goes on to describe the Son's assumption of a complete human

---

[30] For the history of the Caffyn-Monck debate, set within the broader context of Trinitarian reception among seventeenth-century Baptists, see Freeman, *Contesting Catholicity*, 144–59. See also G. Stephen Weaver Jr., *Orthodox, Puritan, Baptist: Hercules Collins (1647–1702) and Particular Baptist Identity in Early Modern England* (Göttingen, Germany: Vandenhoeck & Ruprecht, 2015), 72–74.

[31] Matthew Caffyn, "A Brief Declaration of Faith," in Lumpkin, *Baptist Confessions of Faith*, 225.

[32] Monck, *Cure for the Cankering Error*, 49.

nature: "When, I say, Christ took our Nature upon him, I mean not that he took our flesh only, (as some Hereticks have thought) but the Soul of man also. Forasmuch as he is no half-Savior, but a Redeemer both of Body and Soul."[33] Monck seems to be echoing the argument of Gregory of Nazianzus against the Apollinarians: Christ must assume a body and a soul in order to heal both body and soul. Monck also directly takes on Caffyn's erroneous notion of Christ's celestial flesh: "Even so it is written, Christ was made of a Woman, Gal. 4:4., for he did not pass through her as Water through a Pipe, but took part of her substance."[34] Christ "took the flesh of the Virgin Mary" and is thus "flesh of our flesh."[35]

Monck affirms the Son's consubstantiality with the Father and eternal generation from the substance of the Father. He affirms the Son's true humanity, evinced by many scriptural proofs, and the unity of his person. He maintains the distinction of the two natures—the one immutable, impassible, and simple and the other genuinely human and capable of suffering and dying for the redemption of the world. As mentioned earlier, Monck liberally cites patristic sources, including the language of Nicaea, Constantinople, and Chalcedon. He explicitly takes on the various heresies "contrary to this Doctrine," including Sabellianism, Arianism, Apollinarianism, Eutychianism, and Nestorianism. The work includes not only lengthy expositions of Scripture and traditional formulations but also several catechetical sections. In sum, we might say that Monck's *Cure* is an exemplary model of Baptist catholicity, written by a Baptist pastor-theologian conversant not only in the sacred Scriptures but also in their doctrinal reception in the patristic, medieval, and Reformation eras.[36]

---

[33] Monck, 49.

[34] Monck, 50.

[35] Monck, 51.

[36] In recent years some Baptists have sought to reverse the individualizing trend in Baptist theology and reposition the Baptist vision as a "catholic" renewal movement. See especially Harmon, *Towards Baptist Catholicity*; and Freeman, *Contesting Catholicity*. While Harmon and Freeman approach these issues from a more "moderate" or "post-liberal" orientation, the Center for Baptist Renewal

Monck is also recognized as the principal author of the Orthodox Creed, a confession drawn up in 1678 and adopted by the Midlands General Baptists in 1679.[37] Like the Congregationalists' Savoy Declaration and the Particular Baptists' Second London Confession, the Orthodox Creed follows much of the order and language of the influential Westminster Confession of Faith, demonstrating the General Baptists' desire for a kind of Protestant catholicity with their fellow nonconformists. The creed's statement on the hypostatic union is worth quoting at length:

> We believe the Person of the Son of God, being a Person from all *Eternity existing*, did assume the most pure Nature of Man, (wanting all Personal Existing of its own) into the Unity of his Person, or Godhead, and made it his own; the properties of each Nature being preserved, and this *Inseparable* and *Indissolvable* union of both Natures, and was made by the Holy Ghost, *Sanctifying* our Nature in the Virgins Womb, without change of either Nature, or *mixture of both*; and of two Natures is one Christ, *God–Man*, or *Immanuel*, God with us. Which Mystery exceeds the Conception of Men, and is the wonder of Angels, one only Mediator, Jesus Christ, the Son of God.[38]

Here we see many of the elements of conciliar Christology: the Son's eternal personhood, denial of a distinct human person in the incarnation (against the Nestorian heresy), the distinct and unmixed properties of the two natures (against Eutychianism), and the union of the two natures in

---

has brought together a group of more conservative Baptist pastors and scholars to accomplish a similar end but based on somewhat different premises.

[37] Weaver, *Orthodox, Puritan, Baptist*, 73. As Freeman, *Contesting Catholicity*, 159, 158, notes, the Orthodox Creed "never gained widespread acceptance among General Baptists nor proved to be a basis for unity in the General Assembly." Some General Baptists were reticent to use creedal language, preferring "a simple account of the Godhead." Others were persuaded by Caffyn's views, laying the groundwork for the General Baptists' slide into heterodoxy and eventual decline.

[38] Orthodox Creed, art. 6, accessed March 19, 2019, http://baptiststudieson line.com/wp-content/uploads/2007/02/orthodox-creed.pdf.

the one person of the Son (once again, against Nestorianism). The creed also takes on Caffyn's error by affirming the Son's assumption and sanctification of "our Nature in the Virgins Womb."

Unique among all the major confessions of faith in Baptist history, the Orthodox Creed also includes the full text of the three ecumenical creeds. The creed's introduction to these ancient symbols is taken almost verbatim from the Church of England's Articles of Religion, once again underscoring the Baptists' desire to express the catholic faith in its essential elements:

> The Three Creeds, (*viz.*) *Nicene* Creed, *Athanasius* his Creed, and the Apostles Creed, (as they are commonly called) ought throughly to be received, and believed. For we believe they may be proved by most undoubted Authority of holy Scripture, and are necessary to be understood of all Christians; and to be instructed in the knowledge of them, by the Ministers of Christ, according to the Analogie of Faith, recorded in sacred Scriptures (upon which these Creeds are grounded), and Catechistically opened, and expounded in all Christian Families, for the edification of Young and Old; which might be a means to prevent Heresie in Doctrine, and Practice, these Creeds containing all things in a brief manner, that are necessary to be known, fundamentally, in order to our Salvation; to which end they may be considered, and better understood of all Men, we have here Printed them under their several Titles as followeth.[39]

The full texts of the creeds follow this introduction. So we see both in Monck's personal work and in the statement of faith he drafted an explicit indebtedness to the language and concepts of creedal and conciliar Christology. As we turn to the Particular Baptist tradition, we see the same tendencies in one of its key exemplars, Hercules Collins.

---

[39] Orthodox Creed, art. 38.

Particular Baptist Christology

Hercules Collins was pastor of the Particular Baptist Church in Wapping, London, a position he assumed in 1677.[40] During a time of persecution against nonconformists, Collins was imprisoned in 1683 for violating the requirements of the 1665 Five Mile Act. After his release in 1687, Collins resumed his ministry and moved his congregation to a new location in Stepney. The church continued to flourish, especially after the 1689 Toleration Act under William and Mary. Collins was one of the signatories of the important Second London Confession of Faith, adopted by the Particular Baptists' 1689 general assembly. By the time of his death in 1702, Collins was "regularly preaching to an audience of roughly 700 people, which would have made his congregation one of the largest Calvinistic Baptist works in the city."[41]

In the midst of his courageous preaching and pastoral ministry, Collins was also busy producing a number of theological and polemical treatises. Perhaps the most significant of these was his very first publication, in 1680: a Baptist version of the influential Heidelberg Catechism. While Collins's version of this important Reformed symbol included some revisions to make it more pedagogically clear and more amenable to Baptist ecclesiology, he left most of the catechism largely intact, including those questions and answers concerning the doctrines of the Trinity and the incarnation. For example, consider question 15: "What manner of mediator and deliverer, then, must we seek for? A. Such a one as is very man and perfectly just, and yet in power above all creatures, that is, one who also is very God."[42] The Son's assumption of humanity must entail

---

[40] For more on the life, ministry, and theology of Collins see the introduction by Michael Haykin and Stephen Weaver in their recent reprinting of Collins's Orthodox Catechism: Hercules Collins, *An Orthodox Catechism: Being the Sum of the Christian Religion, Contained in the Law and Gospel*, ed. Michael A. G. Haykin and G. Stephen Weaver Jr. (Palmdale, CA: Reformed Baptist Academic, 2014). For a fuller treatment of Collins's life and theology see Weaver, *Orthodox, Puritan, Baptist*.

[41] Haykin and Weaver, "Introduction," in Collins, *Orthodox Catechism*, 18–19.

[42] Collins, 48.

his utter sinlessness and righteousness. Answer 16: "Because the justice of God requires that the same human nature which has sinned do itself likewise make recompense for sin; but he that is himself a sinner, cannot make recompense for others."[43] And why must the Mediator be truly God? Answer 17: "That He might by the power of His Godhead sustain in His flesh the burden of God's wrath and might recover and restore to us that righteousness and life which we lost."[44]

In the exposition of the second article of the Apostles' Creed, Collins's catechism echoes the patristic principle that Christ is the Son of God by nature (that is, by his eternal generation), while redeemed humans become sons of God by adoption: "Q. 32. For what cause is Christ called the only begotten Son of God, when we also are the sons of God? A. Because Christ alone is the eternal and natural Son of the eternal Father, and we are but sons adopted of the Father by grace for His sake."[45] But the Son's true humanity was necessary for the salvation of the world. He partook of Mary's humanity in order to serve as Mediator:

> Q. 34. What do you believe when you say He was conceived by the Holy Spirit, and born of the virgin Mary? A. That the Son of God, who is and continues true and everlasting God, took the very nature of man, of the flesh and blood of the virgin Mary, through the working of the Holy Spirit, that He might be the true Seed of David, like unto His brethren in all things, sin excepted.[46]

Here we see the broad outlines of the classic doctrine of the incarnation. As the common patristic formula puts it, without ceasing to be what he was (true God), Christ became what he was not (true man).

In an interesting addition to the Heidelberg Catechism, Collins added a final chapter that included the full text of the Nicene and Athanasian Creeds. We have already discussed the important concepts of

---

[43] Collins, 48.
[44] Collins, 49.
[45] Collins, 59.
[46] Collins, 60.

the Nicene Creed, but the Athanasian Creed represents an expansion of the important Nicene doctrines. Touching the person of Christ, the creed affirms that the Son is "of the Father alone, not made, nor created, but begotten."[47] The creed also includes an extensive article on the incarnation of the Son:

> The right faith is, that we believe and confess, that our Lord Jesus Christ, the Son of God, is God and man, God of the substance of the Father, begotten before the world, and man of the substance of His mother born in the world; perfect God, perfect man, of a reasonable soul and human flesh subsisting; equal to the Father as touching His Godhead, inferior to the Father as touching His manhood; who although He be God and man, yet is not two, but one Christ; one, not by conversion of the Godhead into flesh, but by taking of the manhood into God; one altogether not by confusion of substance, but by unity of Person. For as the reasonable soul and flesh is one man, so God and man is one Christ, who suffered for our salvation, descended into hell, rose again the third day from the dead, He ascended into heaven, sits on the right hand of God the Father almighty, from where He shall come to judge the living and the dead. At whose coming all men shall rise again with their bodies, and give an account for their own works: and them that have done good, shall go into life everlasting; and them that have done evil, into everlasting fire.[48]

Here we see the same Christological judgments rendered by the Chalcedonian Definition: the consubstantiality of the Son with the Father, the consubstantiality of the incarnate Son with humanity, the unity of the person of Christ, the distinctive and unchanged properties of his two natures, the Son's assumption of a body and soul, and the major events of the gospel. Given the anti-creedal expressions of certain sectors of contemporary Baptist life, it is truly remarkable that this important seventeenth-century Baptist

---

[47] Collins, 119.
[48] Collins, 120.

theologian had no reservations affirming the three ecumenical creeds and their Christological particulars.[49]

Collins was one of the signatories to the important Second London Confession of Faith, written in 1677 and affirmed by the Particular Baptist general assembly in 1689, after the Toleration Act. This confessional symbol influenced several subsequent Baptist confessions, including its later American counterpart, the Philadelphia Confession of Faith, as well as the Abstract of Principles, the New Hampshire Confession of Faith, and the Baptist Faith and Message. The 1689 confession, a Baptist revision of the Westminster Confession of Faith, represents another important piece of evidence that the earliest Baptists were indeed indebted to the classic Christology they inherited from the Reformers and the medieval and patristic theologians before them. Part of the impetus behind writing the confession was the aberrant teaching of Particular Baptist pastor Thomas Collier, who initially embraced more orthodox opinions but later came to reject certain key tenets of Reformed orthodoxy, including the doctrine of original sin, particular redemption, the Trinity, and the incarnation.[50] Collier rejected the traditional doctrine of the Trinity as amounting to tritheism, believing the Son's human nature to be eternal. Particular Baptist leaders Nehemiah Coxe and William Collins were largely responsible for penning the 1689 confession as a response to this controversy. And again, Hercules Collins added his imprimatur to this key confessional symbol.

On the Trinity, the 1689 confession restates Westminster's orthodox doctrine:

> In this divine and infinite Being there are three subsistences, the Father, the Word or Son, and Holy Spirit, of one substance, power, and eternity, each having the whole divine essence, yet the

---

[49] Weaver, *Orthodox, Puritan, Baptist*, 89–91, also notes places in Collins's individual writings where he affirms the classic doctrine of the incarnation.

[50] For a discussion of the Collier controversy, see Weaver, *Orthodox, Puritan, Baptist*, 74–76. My retelling here is dependent on Weaver's explanation and analysis.

essence undivided: the Father is of none, neither begotten nor proceeding; the Son is eternally begotten of the Father; the Holy Spirit proceeding from the Father and the Son; all infinite, without beginning, therefore but one God, who is not to be divided in nature and being, but distinguished by several peculiar relative properties and personal relations; which doctrine of the Trinity is the foundation of all our communion with God, and comfortable dependence on him.[51]

Thus the 1689 confession uses explicitly creedal language and concepts. God is one in substance or essence and three in subsistences or persons. The persons each have "the whole divine essence" and are distinguished only by their personal properties, the eternal relations of origin.

Similarly, on the doctrine of the incarnation, the confession uses concepts explicitly indebted to the Chalcedonian Definition:

The Son of God, the second person in the Holy Trinity, being very and eternal God, the brightness of the Father's glory, of one substance and equal with him who made the world, who upholdeth and governeth all things he hath made, did, when the fullness of time was come, take upon him man's nature, with all the essential properties and common infirmities thereof, yet without sin; being conceived by the Holy Spirit in the womb of the Virgin Mary, the Holy Spirit coming down upon her: and the power of the Most High overshadowing her; and so was made of a woman of the tribe of Judah, of the seed of Abraham and David according to the Scriptures; so that two whole, perfect, and distinct natures were inseparably joined together in one person, without conversion, composition, or confusion; which person is very God and very man, yet one Christ, the only mediator between God and man.[52]

---

[51] Second London Confession of Faith, in Lumpkin, *Baptist Confessions of Faith*, 253.

[52] Second London Confession, 260–61.

The Son is consubstantial with the Father in his divinity, and in the fullness of time he became true man, partaking in Mary's humanity. The two natures in Christ retain their distinctive properties but are united in an indissoluble union in the person of the Son. The confession reiterates Chalcedon's "alpha privatives" to describe this union: the hypostatic union is without separation, conversion, composition, or confusion. The person of Christ is thus "very God and very man, yet one Christ"—the very language of Chalcedon.[53]

An explicit or implicit dependence upon conciliar language and concepts persisted among certain strands of the Baptist movement over the following centuries. For example, London pastor John Gill, perhaps the greatest Particular Baptist theologian of the eighteenth century, affirmed the use of the creed in his theological method and explained the doctrine of the incarnation in noticeably Chalcedonian ways.[54] Nineteenth-century Southern Baptist theologian James Petigru Boyce also held dear conciliar doctrines such as the eternal generation of the Son.[55]

But some sectors of the Baptist movement witnessed digressions from classic Christology. Already in the seventeenth century, both streams of the Baptist movement had to battle heterodox views of the incarnation, with Collier among the Particular Baptists and Caffyn among the General Baptists as key exemplars of this trend. Among the General Baptists, the regression to heretical opinions was starker, as many came to embrace a version of Unitarianism.[56] Even among more conservative expressions of the Baptist movement, the language of conciliar orthodoxy tended to

---

[53] Thomas Nettles, *The Baptists: Key People Involved in Forming a Baptist Identity*, vol. 1, *Beginnings in Britain* (Fearn, Scotland: Christian Focus, 2005), 37, summarizes well the conciliar nature of the 1689 confession: its "language derives from the vocabulary and concepts of the early church councils and reflects the decisions expressed in the creeds of Nicaea, Constantinople, and Chalcedon."

[54] John Gill, *Complete Body of Doctrinal and Practical Divinity*, 2 vols. (repr., Grand Rapids: Baker, 1978; first published 1839), 1:x–xii; 537–54.

[55] James P. Boyce, *Abstract of Systematic Theology* (Philadelphia: American Baptist Publication Society, 1887). See also Thomas J. Nettles, *James Petigru Boyce: A Southern Baptist Statesman* (Phillipsburg, NJ: P&R, 2009).

[56] On the doctrinal decline among the General Baptists see Freeman, *Contesting Catholicity*, 158–59.

fall out in nineteenth- and twentieth-century Baptist confessions, with more biblicist formulations preferred. The reasons for this shift are varied and not immediately apparent, but without the conceptual apparatus of Nicene and Chalcedonian orthodoxy, Baptist confessions became more ambiguous and open to heterodox interpretations.[57] As we will see in the next section, some Baptists even came to reject creeds and confessions entirely, but this creedless expression of the Baptist faith was not the original posture of the earliest Baptists, as this section has demonstrated.

Classic Christology for Contemporary Baptist Theology and Mission

Over the last couple of centuries, Baptists have sometimes been drawn to the notion of a creedless Christianity: "No creed but the Bible" or "No creed but Christ."[58] But, as we have seen, from the beginning it was not so. The earliest Baptists were as committed as any other Protestant denomination to the Reformation principle of *sola Scriptura*: the Bible alone is the supreme and final court of appeals for all matters of faith and practice. Councils, theologians, and church leaders can err in their theological judgments, but the Bible and the Bible alone is the only inerrant and infallible written revelation from God. But this commitment to *sola Scriptura* did not mean for the Reformers nor for the earliest Baptists that traditional interpretations of Scripture should be jettisoned. The consensus of historic Christian interpretation concerning the cardinal

---

[57] See the discussion in Harmon, *Towards Baptist Catholicity*, 80–81.

[58] Consider, for example, the opinion of W. B. Johnson, the first president of the Southern Baptist Convention: "The value of the Christocratic form of government consists in this, that each acting in reference to Christ alone, all will be conformed to Christ, and thus conformed to each other. And this is the manner by which uniformity is to be secured and preserved, and not by confederations of churches, confessions of faith, or written codes of formularies framed by man, as bonds of union for the churches of Christ." William B. Johnson, *The Gospel Developed through the Government and Order of the Churches of Christ* (Richmond, VA: H. K. Ellyson, 1846), reprinted in *Polity: Biblical Arguments on How to Conduct Church Life*, ed. Mark Dever (Washington, DC: Nine Marks Ministries, 2001), 234.

doctrines of the faith—the Trinity and the incarnation—possesses a kind of derivative authority, under the authority of the Scriptures to the degree it conforms to them.[59] So, the earliest Baptists, while seeking a more thorough reformation concerning the doctrine of the church, were not seeking an overthrow of the church's creedal foundations. When an unhealthy version of biblicism—an "allergy" to postbiblical doctrinal defenses of what the Scriptures teach—crept into the Baptist movement, the churches were left open to heterodoxy, as the rise of Unitarianism among the General Baptists attests.

Theologians and church leaders from a variety of ecclesiastical traditions have begun to rediscover the important role that the church's traditional doctrines can play in renewing the faith for the twenty-first century.[60] This emphasis on "retrieval for the sake of renewal" signals an important development in the contemporary church—a development that, if we may be so bold, might represent a new work of the Spirit of God among the people of God.[61] Despite their perceived or real legacy of creedless Christianity, some Baptists have been full participants in this renewal, and we can pray that many more would join its ranks. In this concluding section, I wish to suggest a few ways in which a rediscovery of the classical understanding of Christ can help to renew the faith and practice of contemporary Baptist churches.

First, in terms of *Baptist theology*, the contemporary articulation of the whole fabric of Christian belief would be strengthened by a thorough engagement with the church's reflection on the mystery at the heart of the faith: the incarnation of the Son of God for the salvation of the world.

---

[59] Reformation historian Heiko Oberman draws a distinction between what he calls "Tradition I" and "Tradition II." According to the former, tradition is seen as an authoritative exegetical guide to Scripture. According to the latter, tradition is seen as a second source of revelation alongside Scripture. The Reformers, and many of the earliest Baptists, would have happily accepted Tradition I while rejecting decisively Tradition II. See Oberman, *Forerunners of the Reformation*, 51–65.

[60] Allen and Swain, *Reformed Catholicity*, 1–15.

[61] Among Baptists, no contemporary writer has been more adamant in emphasizing this theme than Timothy George. See, for example, his introduction in George, *Evangelicals and Nicene Faith*.

For too long, Baptist theology has had an impoverished understanding of and engagement with the Christian tradition. Our engagement with the language, literature, and history of the biblical text has been second to none in evangelicalism. But without the categories provided by the history of interpretation and the history of doctrine, we have sometimes left ourselves open to idiosyncratic ways of synthesizing the biblical teaching.[62] Baptist churches should catechize their members in the basic tenets of the orthodox faith, perhaps through sermon series, baptismal preparation, Sunday School classes, and small group Bible studies.

Baptist colleges and seminaries would do well to expose their students not only to the Reformers and our Baptist forebears but also to the patristic and medieval divines who articulated the foundational truths of God's triune being and the incarnation of the Son of God. Furthermore, renewed attention to the classical doctrine of the incarnation will cast light on the entire range of theological loci: theology proper, humanity and sin, atonement and salvation, church and last things. The whole of human history—indeed, the whole of created reality—finds it scope and key in the mystery of the Word made flesh. The doctrine of salvation is especially implicated in a proper understanding of classic Christology. Salvation belongs to the Lord; so, only God can save. But only one who is truly man—one who has assumed all that it means to be human, body and soul, mind and will—can repair the breach caused by human rebellion. A diminished God or divided Christ would be of no use for this task; only one who is true God and true man, without confusion or division, can be the Savior of the world.

Second, *Baptist worship* would be enriched by a renewal of classic Christology. The traditional patterns and elements of historic Christian worship are designed explicitly to tell the story of the gospel, centered on the person and work of Jesus Christ. Baptist worship has been heavily influenced by what historians of Christian worship have called "frontier liturgy," the worship structure that emerged from nineteenth-century revivalism: a service of songs, followed by an evangelistic sermon and

---

[62] The problems associated with Trinitarian subordinationism and kenotic Christology immediately come to mind.

invitation.[63] There is much to appreciate in this frontier liturgy, chiefly its focus on proclaiming the gospel and calling for a response to its saving promises.

But this structure would be strengthened and deepened by incorporating within it the historic patterns of Christian liturgy: a call to worship from God's Word, private and corporate confessions of sin, an assurance of pardon grounded in Christ's person and work, sermons that weave together more canonical patterns of scriptural interpretation, weekly observance of the Lord's Supper, public confession of the faith once delivered to the saints, benedictions pronounced over God's people, and the commissioning of the church to go out into the world as salt and light. Especially fruitful would be public confession of the faith in the form of ecumenical creeds, which dramatically retell the story of the gospel—the incarnation, life, death, resurrection, ascension, and return of Christ—and the triune God who enacts it.[64]

Finally, *Baptist mission* would be strengthened by a renewed attention to the doctrines of classical Christology. While missionary zeal is not exclusive to Baptists, it has been a distinctive emphasis throughout most of our four-hundred-year history. The modern missions movement was sparked by a Particular Baptist association in eighteenth-century London, with William Carey its principle champion and first missionary.[65] The first American missionary during the modern missions movement, Adoniram Judson, was persuaded of Baptist ecclesiology on his voyage to Burma and remained a powerful advocate for missions among Baptists until his death.[66] Even today, missions and evangelism remain the lifeblood of Baptist spirituality, with Southern Baptists boasting one

---

[63] James F. White, *A Brief History of Christian Worship* (Nashville: Abingdon, 1993), 159–61.

[64] For an attempt to integrate historic patterns of worship into the frontier liturgy, see R. Lucas Stamps and Matthew Y. Emerson, "Liturgy for Low-Church Baptists," *Criswell Theological Review* 14, no. 2 (Spring 2017): 71–88.

[65] Timothy George, *Faithful Witness: The Life and Mission of William Carey* (Birmingham, AL: New Hope, 1991).

[66] Jason G. Duesing, ed., *Adoniram Judson: A Bicentennial Appreciation of the Pioneer American Missionary* (Nashville: B&H, 2012).

of the largest missionary forces in the world through their International Mission Board.

But as Baptists interface with the religions and philosophies of both the Western world and the majority world, what is the content of the gospel message we proclaim? Certainly that Jesus died and rose again for the salvation of the world. But who is this Jesus we proclaim? Once again, a mere man could not save. One who is merely God could not suffer and die. It is precisely the two-nature doctrine of Chalcedon that distinguishes the Christian message from its rivals, even those who espouse some form of monotheism (like contemporary Judaism and Islam) or those who espouse a false version of the gospel events (like Jehovah's Witnesses and Mormons).

So, to the degree that Baptists care about the renewal of our theology, worship, and mission, we should care about the doctrinal truths codified in the classical understanding of the person of Christ. As the fathers of the church demonstrated and the earliest Baptists affirmed, these truths are not some alien imposition on the biblical text; instead, they are better understood as Spirit-illumined truths that enable the church to account for all the Scriptures say about the person of Christ and to defend this teaching against heresy. These doctrines are not theological trivia nor the exclusive preserve of church historians. Rather, they are the heritage and stewardship of all the people of God, including the people called Baptists.

5

Baptists, Classic Ecclesiology, and the Christian Tradition

W. Madison Grace II
Southwestern Baptist Theological Seminary

Introduction

"I believe in the holy catholic church." This affirmation is the basic ecclesial statement of the ancient confessions.[1] It is thus an important expression of belief passed down to us today. Although this affirmation does not elaborate on the doctrine of the church, its inclusion in the early creedal formulas marks it as a central belief of Christianity.

That there has been and should be an ecclesiology is rarely debated. The focus of robust discussion throughout the history of Christianity has been on *what* such an ecclesiology should be. Although a variety of Christian traditions find unity around doctrines relating to such topics as the Trinity and Christology, the doctrine of the church is often a point of disunity. In fact, some have argued the ecumenical movement's stagnation is due to the reluctance of any particular tradition to compromise its ecclesiology.[2] Baptists are no strangers to this. The doctrine of

---

[1] The Apostle's Creed, in Philip Schaff, *The Creeds of Christendom, with a History and Critical Notes: The History of Creeds*, 3 vols. (New York: Harper & Brothers, 1878), 1.22.

[2] For a discussion on what has been called an "ecumenical winter" see the essays in Francesca Aran Murphy and Christopher Aspery, eds., *Ecumenism Today: The Universal Church in the 21st Century* (Burlington, VT: Ashgate, 2008).

the church is among the distinguishing doctrines of any tradition. What constitutes a church member? How and when should one be baptized? What is the nature and practice of the Eucharist? Who has authority, and how should a church be governed? These questions are all important but are answered slightly differently in each tradition.

So, if ecclesiological concerns create and sustain disunity, can there be such a thing as "classic ecclesiology"? The answer is yes—and Baptists have embraced this classic ecclesiology historically. It is the purpose of this chapter, first, to explore what this classic ecclesiology is and, second, to determine how Baptists have articulated a version of that ecclesiology.

Ecclesiology in Broader Tradition

In his High Priestly Prayer, recorded in John 17, Jesus has a great deal to say about the future of those who follow him. "May they all be one, as you, Father, are in me and I am in you. May they also be in us, so that the world may believe you sent me. I have given them the glory you have given me, so that they may be one as we are one" (John 17:21–22). In this prayer it is clear that Jesus is outlining his desire for the unity of those who would believe. It stands to reason that this prayer is offered because of potential threats to that unity in the future. Indeed, soon after the church was formed at Pentecost, factions and divisions arose in various places. In particular we find Paul engaging the question of the church's unity. For instance, he condemns the Corinthians for the divisive groups in their church (1 Cor 1:10–17); in more than one of his letters he calls out the circumcision party for its divisiveness (e.g., Galatians 2); and in his letter to the Ephesians he calls for the unity of the church in this way: "There is one body and one Spirit—just as you were called to one hope at your calling—one Lord, one faith, one baptism, one God and Father of all, who is above all and through all and in all" (Eph 4:4–6). The Jerusalem Council in Acts 15 is an example of multiple communities working together to decide on accepted practices for their own particular churches. Thus, we see that within a few decades of the church's inception, there arose threats of division, and those threats gave rise to discussion of the church's nature.

From the second century onward, discussion of the nature of the church continued. Concern for ecclesiology has been more acute at particular points in the history of Christianity than at others, but it always has been a matter of concern. So, how has orthodox Christianity understood itself in terms of the church? That the term for church (ἐκκλησία) meant "gathering" has not gone unnoticed, but the concept holds a meaning beyond merely a group of people amassed. Churches are not merely "persons gathered in one place"; they have purpose, ritual, belief, and creed. An early example of this richer understanding of "church" can be found in Irenaeus and his confession of faith, which addresses "the Church . . . scattered through the whole world to the ends of the earth."[3] The specific, and important, doctrinal affirmations—purpose, ritual, belief, and creed—in this more expansive definition are intended to represent the tradition and belief of the entire church. According to the logic of early Christians, to deny this understanding calls into question one's standing to be a member of the church. As in Acts 15, here we see a continuing tradition of limiting the constituency of a church to the beliefs, or creed, a particular community may hold.

As time progressed, a variety of beliefs intruded upon the church. Development occurred in how Christianity determined a belief to be true. Bishops aligned with other bishops concerning what had been handed down to them, and a variety of confessions were written expressing beliefs in important doctrines such as the Trinity, Christ, and the Holy Spirit. What is interesting for our purposes is that in early confessions of faith, the church was confessed, but that confession was limited. Over time, confession of the church's nature grew from an acknowledgment of its existence as the locus of the redeemed to include a more robust set of defining characteristics: holiness, catholicity, unity, and apostolicity. These four constitute the marks of the church found in the Nicene Creed: "one, holy, catholic, and apostolic church."[4]

Before discussing these specific marks in detail, it is important to note that classic ecclesiology affirmed both the universal and the local

---

[3] Irenaeus, "Against Heresies," 1.10.1, in Schaff, *Creeds of Christendom*, 2.13.
[4] The Nicene Creed, in Schaff, *Creeds of Christendom*, 1.28.

church. Churches can be conceived of locally, as in house churches or regional churches, and universally, as the one body of Jesus Christ. This is why schism was dangerous in the minds of the church fathers. As the company of the redeemed, believers within the universal church experience a connection with all redeemed communities across the globe. Both the visible and the invisible nature of the church were affirmed by the end of the early church era, though such affirmations were not uniform in expression and would see further development later on. Still, for the early church, the nature of the company of the redeemed needed to be expressed broadly as a church that was one, holy, catholic, and apostolic.

Unity

The confession that the church is one comes from the biblical statements of Jesus and Paul mentioned above. It highlights the commonality among individuals and individual communities, or churches, as there is a commonality through the Spirit among all those in Christ (cf. Eph 4:4). This unity is spiritual in nature, though there is a confessional unity as well. That the church is one is an expression that it is one body, with its head being Jesus Christ (Col 1:18), united through one baptism. Given such a unity, any divisive person would be seen as a false teacher. To be separated from the body is to separate oneself from Christ.

Many schisms in church history were condemned because of their divisive nature (especially the Great Schism and the Reformation), but the conflict between the Novatians and Cyprian led to early church teaching on unity. That conflict revolved around what to do with confessing Christians who had lapsed in their faith (i.e., denied Christ publicly). Ultimately, a group called the Novatians decided to split and exist alongside the church in Carthage. A controversy ensued over the nature of schism and unity in the church, which led Cyprian to write *The Unity of the Catholic Church*. This work, along with Cyprian's letters, codified for many years Christian teaching on the unity of the church and on how to consider those outside the church's union. Cyprian stated:

Whoever dissociates himself from the Church is joined to a counterfeit paramour, he is cut off from the promises of Christ, and neither will he who abandons Christ's church attain Christ's rewards. He is a foreigner, he is deconsecrated, and he is an enemy. He cannot have God as his Father who does not have the Church as his Mother.[5]

In one of his epistles Cyprian also wrote of this controversy and made the famous claim that there is "no salvation outside the church."[6] The unity of the church must be maintained, because the church is the place of Christ and as such is the place of salvation. Separation from the church is a separation from its benefits—chiefly, salvation.

Holiness

The second mark of the church is holiness. Theologically, the church should be considered holy because of the relation she has to the holiness of God—as God is holy, so too is the church made holy. This is seen especially in the picture of the church as the bride of Christ. Ephesians 5:26–27 addresses this relation, as Christ's goal is "to make [the church] holy, . . . to present the church to himself in splendor, without spot or wrinkle or anything like that, but holy and blameless." This holiness is seen also through the Holy Spirit's being given to the church at its inception (Acts 2). The presence of the Spirit makes the church holy. The Spirit not only descended on the disciples at Pentecost but continually comes to new believers (cf. Acts 2:38; 8:14–17; 19:1–5).

Holiness is understood as an essential element of the church, but it also depicts the activity of the people of God. This affirmation was not always specific in church history, however, as John Hammett reminds us: "There was not agreement on *how* holiness was to be related to the

---

[5] Cyprian, *The Unity of the Catholic Church*, 6.1, in *On the Church: Select Treatises*, trans. Allen Brent, Popular Patristics Series 32 (Crestwood, NY: St. Vladimir's Seminary Press, 2006), 157.

[6] Cyprian, *Epistles*, LXXII.21; ANF, 384.

nature of the church."[7] For example, some have detected laxity concerning holiness within the church. The Novatians, mentioned above, were of this mind, as was another schismatic group of the fourth century, the Donatists, who formed a rival church in Carthage and throughout North Africa. Following the Diocletian persecution, the Donatists claimed that those who had broken faith with the church should not be restored and that their administration of the sacraments was invalid. This claim was rejected by their opponents, including Augustine of Hippo. The controversy led to the development of two affirmations. First, that the sacraments are attached to the church and effectual in and of themselves—their holy character remaining intact regardless of who administers them. Second, that the church is both visible and invisible—the church itself is holy but will inevitably have a mixed visible community.

Catholic

The third mark of the church is catholicity. This means that the church is worldwide, or universal. This did not mean merely that the church was geographically diverse—it also included a doctrinal component, at least originally. Writing in the fourth century, Cyril of Jerusalem provided a thorough statement on the catholicity of the church:

> It is called Catholic then because it extends over all the world, from one end of the earth to the other; and because it teaches universally and completely one and all the doctrines which ought to come to men's knowledge, concerning things both visible and invisible, heavenly and earthly.[8]

The concept of catholicity is attached to the universal nature of the church in the common teachings she holds. In one sense, this is simply orthodoxy. A similar understanding of the catholicity of the church is

---

[7] John Hammett, *Biblical Foundations for Baptist Churches: A Contemporary Ecclesiology* (Nashville: B&H Academic, 2005), 55 (italics mine).

[8] Cyril of Jerusalem, *Catechetical Lectures*, 18.23; NPNF2, 7.139–40.

found in Vincent of Lerins, who avers that it entails "that faith which has been believed everywhere, always, by all."[9]

The need to include catholicity as a mark of the church is apparent when one considers the various false teachings condemned as heresies in the early church. For example, in the fourth century Arius of Alexandria taught that Jesus Christ was not eternal—"there was a time when Christ was not." This teaching caused great turmoil in the church and the empire to such a degree that Constantine called for a special council to adjudicate the issue. This was the first ecumenical council, meeting at Nicaea in 325.

Arius was defeated as orthodoxy affirmed the full divinity of Jesus Christ, but we should note the means by which the decision was made. Though the council itself was representative only of those who attended it, its constituency hailed from a variety of places throughout the empire and was able to conclude that a teaching such as Arianism was not in accord with the traditions handed down in their various locations.

Catholicity was intended to assert the commonality, especially doctrinally, that churches share with one another. This belief was a matter of orthodoxy, but the way in which it was understood developed in the following centuries.

Apostolic

The last mark of the church is apostolicity—the church is connected, in some way, to the apostles. For many in the early church, the authority of their teaching was traced through a succession of leaders attached to an apostle. If a church held a belief that was not in accord with apostolic teaching, it was suspect. Tertullian highlighted the necessity of this mark of the church, as the apostles held a derived authority from God, and the "churches [are] from the apostles, the apostles from Christ, Christ from God."[10]

At the heart of this mark is the concept of authority. What makes a church authoritative? Apostolicity helps in answering this question,

---

[9] Vincent of Lerins, *Commonitorum*, 2.6.
[10] Tertullian, *Prescription against Heretics*, 21; ANF 3.252.

primarily through the tradition of authoritative teaching passed down through a local church. A doctrine was true and could be authoritative because it was traced back to an apostle. However, as time marched forward, this authority developed and was ceded to bishops. Additionally, not only was there a succession of teaching passed down that was traced to the apostles; there was a ministry passed down as well. Arguments against a true church's apostolicity would reveal that those making such arguments were beyond the confines of orthodoxy and orthopraxy and, as such, outside the church.

The Early Church

The preceding four marks of the church are helpful in defining the nature of the church to establish a "classic ecclesiology," though they do not address all developments in early Christianity concerning the nature of the church. Those who constitute the church are to have one mind about what they believe. This relates particularly to the nature of salvation, so that those in the church are those who have confessed saving faith in Jesus Christ, which entails a particular understanding of him. The early confessions were intended to clarify for the church the correct way to think about God, the Trinity, and Christ. Early confessions of the church were not intended to define intricately the nature of its community. That community was a place for the people of God and, as such, needed a correct understanding of doctrine so it could truly be the people of God. This is why the church was likened to the robe of Christ, an ark, or a mother in the early church: such conceptions pointed to the nature of the community in its unified relation to God. So, again, for the early church, ecclesiology was summed as "one, holy, catholic, and apostolic church."

Later Ecclesial Developments

As Christianity became more accepted politically and culturally, it also became more intertwined with the state. In the fourth century, much changed for Christianity. It shifted from being a persecuted religion to becoming the established religion of the empire. In the Middle Ages, the concept of the church did not greatly change other than by becoming associated more deeply with the state. The role of the bishop had expanded greatly by this time, and bishops in Rome and elsewhere wielded governmental as well as ecclesiastical power. The church became a powerful force in the government, though not always in the favor of orthodox Christianity.

In 1215 Innocent III called a general council known as the Fourth Lateran Council. Here multiple hallmarks of medieval theology were defined, such as transubstantiation. In the first canon of the council, we can see the council's understanding of the church:

> There is one universal church of believers outside which there is no salvation at all for any. In this church the priest and sacrifice is the same Jesus Christ Himself, whose body and blood are truly contained in the sacrament of the altar under the figures of bread and wine, the bread having been transubstantiated into His body and the wine into His blood by divine power, so that, to accomplish the mystery of our union, we may receive of Him what He has received of us.[11]

The church continued to be viewed as the locus of the redeemed. It was still universal in scope and comprised all true believers. We also see here a development in the church's understanding of its relationship to the redeemed. The broad confessions of the early church did not mention the church as the specific means through which one became redeemed, yet here that theology developed into a confessional reality.

The Reformation is often said to have begun at Wittenberg in 1517, when Luther published his Ninety-Five Theses. Though Luther's reform was focused on the nature of salvation by faith alone, it held ecclesial overtones that would affect the nature of the church. In general, the Reformers redefined the church as the place where the Word is rightly

---

[11] Canon I, Fourth Lateran Council, quoted in *Creeds of the Churches*, ed. John H. Leith, 3rd ed. (Louisville, KY: Westminster John Knox, 1982), 58.

proclaimed and the sacraments are rightly administered, although the Reformers themselves did not always agree on what that entailed. Luther and Zwingli, for example, could not come to agreement on the Lord's Supper and thus could not unite.

As the Reformation on the continent began to settle, confessional ideas concerning the nature of the church emerged. The Augsburg Confession stated, for instance: "It is also taught among us that one holy Christian church will be and remain forever. This is the assembly of all believers among whom the Gospel is preached in its purity and the holy sacraments are administered according to the Gospel."[12] This article confesses the universal nature of the church and expresses the unity found in a church centered on the gospel.

Calvin and other Reformed divines developed their own concepts of the nature of the church, including the twin nature of the church: visible and invisible. Calvin wrote that the foundation of the church was God's "secret election."[13] The church is invisible, related to the mystical union between all believers, and thus known only to God. However, there is also a visible church. "Wherever we see the Word of God purely preached and heard, and the sacraments administered according to Christ's institution, there, it is not to be doubted, a church of God exists."[14]

Lastly, since Baptists find their origins in seventeenth-century England, let us look to the influential 1646 Westminster Confession of Faith, which became the basis for the Baptists' own Second London Confession of Faith. This confession was written as a statement of belief of the Presbyterian elements among the Dissenters of seventeenth-century England. Chapter 25 expresses the nature of the church:

> I. The catholic or universal Church, which is invisible, consists of the whole number of the elect, that have been, are, or shall be gathered into one, under Christ the head therefor; and is the spouse, the body, and the fulness of him that filleth all in all.

---

[12] Art. VII Augsburg Confession, in Leith, 70.

[13] John Calvin, *Institutes of the Christian Religion*, ed. John T. McNeill, trans. Ford Lewis Battles, 2 vols. (Philadelphia: Westminster, 1960), 4.1.2.

[14] Calvin, *Institutes*, 4.1.9.

II. The visible Church, which is also catholic or universal under the gospel (not confined to one nation as before under the law) consists of all those, throughout the world, that profess the true religion, and of their children; and is the kingdom of the Lord Jesus Christ, the house and family of God, out of which there is no ordinary possibility of salvation.

Summary

We have examined the major marks of the church from early Christianity until the seventeenth century. After the patristic era, the effort to continue to speak of the church as unified, holy, catholic, and apostolic continued. As greater divisions occurred within the church, these concepts were not jettisoned. Rather, they were retained with great care and developed with more clarity. Sometimes the marks were defined differently among various traditions, but the four classic marks of the church remained a hallmark of traditional ecclesiology. Thus we can say these marks are constitutive of classic ecclesiology.

Ecclesiology in the Baptist Tradition

Having established classic ecclesiology, we now turn to the question of if and how Baptists are part of this tradition. We will do so by examining various confessions of faith within the Baptist tradition. These corporate confessions represent the broader views of Baptists and thus are more indicative of Baptist ecclesiology than any one theologian or movement.

Precursors

The last two hundred years have seen a variety of opinions concerning the origin of Baptists. Some have claimed Baptists have always existed; others argue they originated with the Anabaptists; but most see them originating historically with the English Separatists. While there is no clear historical link between Baptists and continental Anabaptists, on the nature of the church there is similarity. For instance, in speaking of church discipline, the Schleitheim Confession stated,

> Whoever has not been called by one God to one faith, to one baptism, to one Spirit, to one body, with all the children of God's church, cannot be made [into] one bread with them, as indeed must be done if one is truly to break bread according to the command of Christ.[15]

The Mennonites had a similar view of the church. They understood the church as both visible and invisible:

> Such believing and regenerated men, dispersed throughout the whole earth, are the true people of God or Church of Jesus Christ in the earth, which he loved and for which he gave himself up that he might sanctify it, which indeed he did sanctify through the laver, in the word of life. Of this church Jesus Christ is the Foundation, Head, Shepherd, Leader, Lord, King, and Master. This alone is his adored spouse, holy body, flock, and people and through regeneration his flesh and bones. But even though a huge multitude of deceivers and hypocrites are hidden and live among this church, yet those alone who in Christ are regenerated and sanctified are true members of Christ's body.[16]

These Anabaptist confessions understand the true church as comprising true believers. Whether they take a hard stance on the visible church or allow for an invisible/visible scheme, they understand that membership is limited to the redeemed and reject a mixed community of believers and unbelievers.

There is a clear link between British Baptists and the Separatists in England in the late sixteenth and early seventeenth centuries. In 1596 a group of Separatists wrote A True Confession, later utilized by Particular

---

[15] "The Schleitheim Confession," in Lumpkin, *Baptist Confessions of Faith*, 2nd rev. ed., 26.

[16] "The Waterland Confession," in Lumpkin, 55.

Baptists in composing their own confession. On the nature of the church, A True Confession states:

> Christ hath here in earth a spirituall Kingdome and canonicall regiment in his Church ouer his servants, which Church hee hath purchased and redeemed to himself, as a peculiar inheritance . . . making them a royall Priesthood, an holy Nation, a people set at libertie to shew foorth the virtues of him that hath called them out of darknes into his meruelous light, gathering and vniting them together as members of one body in his faith, loue and holy order.[17]

This confession shows the Separatists understood the church as a kingdom of Christ made up of the redeemed and united into one body.

Early Baptists

What did the first actual Baptists say about the church? A variety of confessions of faith from both John Smyth and Thomas Helwys evince their understanding. For instance, in 1610 Smyth wrote that the church is "a company of the faithful; baptized after confession of sin and of faith, endowed with the power of Christ."[18] This simple confession defines the nature of the church and then points to its authority. At its root is the concept of the church as the company of the faithful. Of course Baptists will argue with others about who those faithful are and who has been constituted the true church through right baptism, but none contest that the church is the locus of the redeemed.

Thomas Helwys expressed a similar understanding of the church in A Declaration of Faith of English People Remaining at Amsterdam in Holland:

> 10. That the church of CHRIST is a company of faithful people (1 Cor 1:2. Eph 1:1) separated frō the world by the word & Spirit

---

[17] "A True Confession," in Lumpkin, 82.
[18] John Smyth, "A Short Confession," in Lumpkin, 95.

of GOD (2 Cor 6:17) being knit vnto the LORD, & one vnto another, by Baptisme. (1 Cor 12:13). Vpon their own confessiō of the faith (Acts 8:37) and sinnes. (Matt 3:6)

11. That though in respect off CHRIST, the Church bee one (Eph 4:4) yet it consisteth of divers particuler congregacions, even so manie as there shallbee in the World, every off which congregacion, though they be but two or three, have CHRIST given them, with all the meanes off their salvacion. (Matt 18:20; Rom 8:32; 1 Cor 3:22). Are the Body of CHRIST (1 Cor 12:27) and a whole Church. (1 Cor 14:23). . . .

12. That as one congregation hath CHRIST, so hath all, (2 Cor 10:7). And that the Word off GOD cometh not out from anie one, neither to anie one congregacion in particuler. (1 Cor 14:36). But vnto everie particuler Church, as it doth vnto al the world. (Col 1:5, 6). And therefore no church ought to challeng anie prerogative over anie other.

13. That everie Church is to receive in all their members by Baptisme vpon the Confession off their faith and sinnes wrought by the preaching off the Gospel, according to the primitive Institucion, Matt 28:19) and practice, (Acts 2:41). And therefore Churches constituted after anie other manner, or off any other persons are not according to CHRISTS Testament.[19]

Note first that Helwys continues with the concept that the church is the company of the redeemed, or "faithful people." This community is related to the Son and the Spirit and shall be one yet diverse. Here he is making room for the difference between a particular congregation and the universal church. Through these statements we can see how the classic marks of the church are present in his thought. Yet he is clear that the church itself is constituted in particular by means of a particular baptism.

---

[19] Thomas Helwys, "A Declaration of Faith of English People Remaining at Amsterdam in Holland," in Lumpkin, 111.

In other words, his ecclesiology is in agreement with classic ecclesiology, but at the same time he critiques other churches who are not constituted by means of believer's baptism.

General Baptists

Throughout the seventeenth century, Baptists wrote numerous confessions of faith. Two major groups of Baptists emerged during this time—General and Particular Baptists. For the General Baptists (those who held to a general atonement) two confessions stand out: The Standard Confession and An Orthodox Creed.

In 1660 the general assembly of General Baptists gathered to write a confession for the whole of the General Baptists in England: A Brief Confession or Declaration of Faith (commonly called The Standard Confession). On the church, it states:

> XI. That the right and only way of gathering Churches, (according to Christs appointment, Matt 28:19, 20) is first to teach, or preach the Gospel, (Mark 16:16) to the Sons and Daughters of men; and then to *Baptise* (that is in English to *Dip*) in the name of the Father, Son, and holy Spirit, or in the name of the Lord Jesus Christ; such only of them, as profess *repentance towards God, and faith towards our Lord Jesus Christ,* (Acts 2:38; Acts 8:12; Acts 18:8). . . .

> XII. That it is the duty of all such who are believers *Baptized,* to draw nigh unto God in submission to that principle of Christs Doctrine, to wit, Prayer and Laying on of Hands, that they may receive the promise of the holy Spirit, (Heb 6:1, 2; Acts 8:12, 15, 17; 19:6; 2 Tim 1:6) whereby they may *mortifie the deeds of the body,* (Rom 8:13) and live in all things answerable to their professed intentions, and desires, even to the honour of him, *who hath called them out of darkness into his marvellous light.*

> XIII. That it is the duty of such who are constituted as aforesaid, *to continue stedfastly in Christs and the Apostles Doctrine, and*

assembling together, in fellowship, in breaking of Bread, and Prayers (Acts 2:42).

XIV. That although we thus declare the primitive way, and order of constituting Churches, yet we verily believe, and also declare, that unless men so professing, and practising the forme and order of Christs Doctrine, shall also beautifie the same with a holy and wise conversation, in all godliness and honesty; the profession of the visible form will be rendered to them of no effect; *for without holiness no man shall see the Lord* (Heb 12:14; Isa 1:11, 12, 15, 16).[20]

Of note in this confession are the particular ways in which the classic marks of the church are formalized. There is no explicit reference to the universality of the church, but the constitutive nature of the church by means of proclamation and baptism places this into the broader teaching of the Reformation's twofold marks of the church: right preaching and right sacraments (to which right discipline was often added).

In addition, and of greater importance, are the concerns for holiness and apostolicity. In articles 12 and 14, holiness is especially highlighted. We see this first in the ways in which members are to come into the church. These Baptists confessed a practice of laying on hands in accord with the teaching of six-principle Baptists. They practiced laying on hands after baptism for the reception of the Holy Spirit in an attempt to ensure each member was indeed indwelt and thus being sanctified in holiness by the Spirit. Second, they called church members to live holy lives. Finally, in article 13 is an argument for a particular form of apostolicity. These General Baptists appealed not to a succession of leadership back to the apostles but to the teaching of the apostles. This form of apostolicity is in agreement with the broader Reformation understanding.

Another General Baptist confession, An Orthodox Creed, was idiosyncratic in Baptist life, for it affirmed and reproduced the three ancient creeds (Apostles', Nicene, and Athanasian). It also followed the form

---

[20] A Brief Declaration or Confession of Faith (London, 1660).

of the Westminster Confession, as did other dissenting confessions. In short, the confession addressed heresies within and was intended to express to those without that Baptists were in accordance with broader orthodoxy and were not to be considered outside the greater tradition. On the nature of the church it states:

> There is one holy Catholick Church, consisting of, or made up of the whole number of the Elect; that have been, are, or shall be gathered, in one Body under Christ, the only Head thereof: Which Church is gathered by Special Grace, and the Powerful and Internal Work of the Spirit; and are effectually united unto Christ their Head, and can never fall away.
>
> Nevertheless, we believe the Visible Church of Christ on Earth, is made up of several distinct Congregations, which make up that one Catholick church, or Mystical Body of Christ. And the Marks by which She is known to be the true Spouse of Christ, are these, *viz.* Where the Word of God is rightly Preached, and the Sacraments truly Administred, according to Christ's Institution, and the Practice of the Primitive Church; . . . And although there may be many Errors in such a Visible Church, or Congregations, they being not Infallible, yet those Errors being not Fundamental, and the Church in the *major*, or Governing part, being not Guilty, she is not thereby unchurched; nevertheless She ought to detect those Errors, and to Reform, according to God's holy Word, and from such Visible Church, or Congregations, no Man ought by any pretence whatever, schismatically to separate.[21]

The church confessed is both universal and local, or invisible and visible. In affirming the universal church, this confession understands it to fulfill the marks of catholicity and unity. Further, the confession affirms the universal church as comprising the elect, known only to God and

---

[21] Thomas Monck et al., "An Orthodox Creed," *Southwestern Journal of Theology* 48, no. 2 (Spring 2006): 163.

who as such will persevere. However, it also confesses that the church is not merely universal—it is the visible churches that constitute the universal. Here the Reformation marks of the church are affirmed, including church discipline. To follow these marks constitutes a church as true. The confession also adds two interesting notes. First, it states that the visible church is not infallible but should always seek to correct its own errors. Second, it affirms that one should not be schismatic. This is an interesting point for a Dissenter or Baptist to make, but it nevertheless affirms the classic desire for unity of the body of Christ.

Particular Baptists

The other major group of Baptists in the seventeenth century was the Particular Baptists. Their most important confessions are the First (1644; pub. 1646) and Second (1677; pub. 1689) London Confessions.

The First London Confession, or A Confession of Faith of Seven Congregations or Churches of Christ in London, was written at the beginning of Particular Baptist life. These churches arose from a fellowship of Separatist Churches in England, and together they wrote the First London Confession, using the Separatist A True Confession as their basis. Concerning the church this confession states:

> Jesus Christ hath here on earth a spiritual kingdom, which is the Church, whom he hath purchased and redeemed to himselfe as a peculiar inheritance; which Church is a company of visible Saints, called and separated from the world by the Word and Spirit of God, to the visible profession of the faith of the Gospel, being baptized into the faith, and joyned to the Lord, and each other, by mutuall agreement, in the practical enjoyment of the Ordinances, commanded by Christ their Head and King.[22]

---

[22] A Confession of Faith of Seven Congregations or Churches of Christ in London (London, 1646), art. XXXIII.

This statement on the church addresses the visible nature of the church and its connection to Christ as a company of saints. Herein one can find overtones of unity, holiness, and apostolicity.

In 1677 the Particular Baptists revised and expanded their confession, modeling it after the Savoy Declaration and the Westminster Confession.

CHAP. XXVI. Of the Church.

1. The Catholick or universal Church, which (with respect to the internal work of the Spirit, and truth of grace) may be called invisible, consists of the whole number of the Elect, that have been, are, or shall be gathered into one, under Christ the head thereof; and is the spouse, the body, the fulness of him that filleth all in all.

2. All persons throughout the world, professing the faith of the Gospel, and obedience unto God by Christ, according unto it; not destroying their own profession by any Errors everting the foundation, or unholyness of conversation, are and may be called visible Saints; and of such ought all particular Congregations to be constituted.

3. The purest Churches under heaven are subject to mixture, and error; and som have so degenerated as to become no Churches of Christ, but Synagogues of Satan; nevertheless Christ always hath had, and ever shall have a Kingdome in this world, to the end thereof, of such as believe in him, and make profession of his Name. . . .

6. The Members of these Churches are Saints by calling, visibly manifesting and evidencing (in and by their profession and walking) their obedience unto that call of Christ; and do willingly consent to walk together according to the appointment of Christ, giving up themselves, to the Lord & one to another by the will of God, in professed subjection to the Ordinances of the Gospel.

7. To each of these Churches thus gathered, according to his mind, declared in his word, he hath given all that power and authority, which is any way needfull, for their carrying on that order in worship, and discipline, which he hath instituted for them to observe; with commands, and rules, for the due and right exerting, and executing of that power. . . .

CHAP. XXVII. Of the Communion of Saints.

1. All *Saints* that are united to Jesus Christ their *Head*, by his Spirit, and Faith; although they are not made thereby one person with him, have fellowship in his Graces, sufferings, death, resurrection, and glory; and being united to one another in love, they have communion in each others gifts, and graces; and are obliged to the performance of such duties, publick and private, in an orderly way, as do conduce to their mutual good, both in the inward and outward man.[23]

The confession has a great deal more to say about the structure and function of the churches, yet these articles point to themes we find in classic ecclesiology. At the beginning of the confession, discussion of the invisible church affirmed catholicity. A close connection to this understanding is seen in the following chapter, "Of the Communion of Saints," which expressed that individual saints constitute and participate in the universal body of Christ. Additionally, both of these affirmations implied the unity of the church based in Christ. Second, the church is understood to have a visible nature in this world, which leads to the affirmation that these visible churches, though they should be pure, might not be so. They are mixed, and some might not be churches at all, an affirmation harkening to ancient schismatic controversies. Third, there is a consistent call for holiness in these articles. This is expressed both individually and corporately, as there is a charge to "walk together" and to "giv[e] up

---

[23] A Confession of Faith Put Forth by the Elders and Brethren of Many Congregations of Christians (Baptized upon Profession of Faith) in London and the Country (London, 1677), arts. XXVI, XXVII.

themselves to . . . one another." Finally, there is a confession of the ordering of the church around Christ, who grants his authority through the Word. This implicitly references apostolicity, since the teachings of the apostles are continued through the teaching of the Word.

Later Baptist Confessions

The seventeenth century proved to be a time of many historic Baptist confessions of faith; as we have demonstrated, these Baptists adhered to the tenets of classic ecclesiology. I will present in brief only two more confessions to show how these principles have continued in Baptist life, especially in the United States. The first is a confession of faith written in the nineteenth century and broadly utilized by many Baptists: The New Hampshire Confession of Faith. The second is the current confession of the Southern Baptist Convention, the largest Baptist body in the world today.

In 1833 a succinct Baptist confession was written from New Hampshire. In the article "Of a Gospel Church," the New Hampshire Confession states:

> A visible Church of Christ is a congregation of baptized believers, associated by covenant in the faith and fellowship of the Gospel; observing the ordinances of Christ; governed by his laws; and exercising the gifts, rights, and privileges invested in them by his word; that its only proper officers are Bishops or Pastors, and Deacons, whose qualifications, claims, and duties are defined in the Epistles to Timothy and Titus.[24]

This confession points to the visible nature of the church and shows its Baptist origin by limiting membership to the visible congregation of "baptized believers." What it does not state are universal aspects of the church, but this should not necessarily be construed as a rejection

---

[24] "New Hampshire Confession of Faith," in Lumpkin, *Baptist Confessions of Faith*, 382.

of that classic mark of the church. The confession was written during a period of Baptist history in which greater emphasis was placed on the local church. Many proponents of Landmarkism would find this confession helpful.

As Southern Baptists found a need to compose a confession of faith in the early twentieth century, the New Hampshire Confession formed the basis for the Baptist Faith and Message. This latter document provided the broad and simple basis for the variety of churches cooperating in the SBC. The orginal 1925 Baptist Faith and Message made explicit reference only to local churches, following the language of the New Hampshire Confession by and large. The Baptist Faith and Message underwent revisions in 1963 and 2000, with a reference to the universal church added in 1963 and retained in 2000. In article VI of the 2000 edition, we find the confession on the church:

> A New Testament church of the Lord Jesus Christ is an autonomous local congregation of baptized believers, associated by covenant in the faith and fellowship of the gospel; observing the two ordinances of Christ, governed by His laws, exercising the gifts, rights, and privileges invested in them by His Word, and seeking to extend the gospel to the ends of the earth. Each congregation operates under the Lordship of Christ through democratic processes. In such a congregation each member is responsible and accountable to Christ as Lord. . . .
>
> The New Testament speaks also of the church as the Body of Christ which includes all of the redeemed of all the ages, believers from every tribe, and tongue, and people, and nation.[25]

Though almost twice as long as the New Hampshire Confession's article on the church, this statement is still quite simple. However, it does provide insight into the classic ecclesiology of Baptists. We find unity in the appeal to being part of the greater body of Christ as well as in the repeated admission of being under Christ's authority. Catholicity can be seen in the inclusion of all "redeemed of all the ages." Apostolicity can

---

[25] "Baptist Faith and Message 2000," in Lumpkin, 515–16.

be seen in the submission to the Word. The holiness of the church is not as explicitly stated as in previous confessions, but in aligning the church with Jesus Christ the confession affirms it implicitly.

How Baptists Are in Agreement with the Broader Tradition

We have defined classic ecclesiology as that which affirms the four marks of the church: unity, holiness, catholicity, and apostolicity. We determined this definition by looking at early church confessions to see what they confessed about the nature of the church. We then briefly examined other major traditions prior to the Baptist movement to demonstrate that this classic ecclesiology remained. Then we studied the tradition of Baptist confessions, especially in the seventeenth century, to see if they confessed a similar ecclesiology—and in general they indeed confessed these classic marks of the church.

Many other Baptist confessions of faith from around the world could have been utilized in this study. Moreover, many other articles in these confessions could be presented to provide a broader view of Baptist ecclesiology. These other confessions either agreed with the examples provided or highlighted the differences Baptists have with other traditions (especially in forms of the sacraments and polity).

Baptists have consistently confessed the classic ecclesiology of Christianity known through the four marks. One cannot deny their desire for unity simply because they separated from other Christians. Their understanding of unity is bound up with their understanding of apostolicity, which they found in the words of the Bible. Other than in a few instances in Baptist history (e.g., Landmarkism), Baptists have also affirmed a connection to a universal church, which we have seen confessed as the invisible church. This also confirms their understanding of unity and catholicity. Finally, though imperfect in practice, Baptists have consistently addressed a need for individuals and churches to walk in holiness, for the bride of Christ is related to her bridegroom, Jesus. These general, or classic, understandings of the church found in the greater tradition are part of the Baptist tradition as well.

6

Baptists, Classic Interpretation, and the Christian Tradition

Patrick Schreiner
Western Seminary

Introduction

Thomas Oden once said, "The history of classic Christianity is primarily a history of exegesis."[1] This is true not only for Christianity in a broad sense but also for the particular Protestant form of Christianity known as Baptist. Denominations arise out of good intentions: careful exegesis and traditions yield results, and Christians differ on these results. Baptists are no different in this sense, and they too have come to certain convictions based on their exegetical processes.

Many, when they think of Baptist interpretation, might assume the distinguishing Baptist distinctive to be liberty of conscience.[2] The 1689 Second London Baptist Confession of Faith states, "God alone is Lord of the conscience, and he has left it free from human doctrines and

---

[1] Thomas C. Oden, *Classic Christianity: A Systematic Theology* (New York: Harper Collins, 2009), xxv.

[2] It was W. B. Johnson who said "no creed but the Bible" at the 1845 Southern Baptist convention, and since then many North American Baptists have been nervous about confessions. Yet Johnson's views on this issue were probably closer to the frontier Restorationists than to early Baptists.

commandments that are any way contrary to his word or not contained in it."[3] While it is thus true that liberty of conscience is one Baptist characteristic, I will contend that it is not the *sine qua non* of Baptist interpretation.[4]

What defined, undergirded, and gave the basis for liberty of conscience was an understanding of the authority of Scripture birthed in the Christian tradition more broadly. In sum, Baptists historically have considered themselves not so much pioneers in interpretation as continuing in the great tradition of the church.[5]

Although early Baptists did not view the creeds and councils as their final authority, they did rely heavily on them for their doctrinal guardrails and evoked the church fathers in their exegesis. Baptists have been explicitly orthodox in their stated continuity with the Trinitarian and Christological consensus of the early church.

While we have much to learn from the history of Baptist interpretation, some developments are not as heartening. Baptist identity is marked by both fluidity and constancy. As I survey Baptist interpretation, I will point out both strengths and weaknesses, pondering how our current moment could progress by resuscitating historic Baptist thought.

---

[3] This same sentence occurs in the 2000 Baptist Faith and Message under art. XVII: Religious Liberty. Most of the paragraph is dedicated to the separation of church and state. Under art. XIV (Cooperation) it states cooperation is desirable only if it involves no violation of conscience.

[4] As will be argued in the latter half of the essay, E. Y. Mullins can be viewed as an example of this view. Additionally, in their survey of Baptist interpretation of Acts, the editors of *Four Centuries of Biblical Interpretation* conclude with the following identifying marks of Baptist interpretation. First, Baptists are clearly biblicists. Second, Baptists are polemicists, responding to other groups or individuals with whom they disagree. Third, Baptist identity is diverse. See Beth Allison Barr et al., eds., *The Acts of the Apostles: Four Centuries of Baptist Interpretation* (Waco, TX: Baylor University Press, 2009), 15.

[5] Harmon, *Towards Baptist Catholicity*, 3, argues, "Baptist confessions issued during the seventeenth century are surprisingly rich with echoes of the patristic doctrinal tradition." Timothy George, introduction to *Baptist Confessions, Covenants, and Catechisms*, 3, asserts, "The idea that voluntary, conscientious adherence to an explicit doctrinal standard is somehow foreign to the Baptist tradition is a peculiar notion not borne out by careful examination of our own heritage."

I will attempt to accomplish the above not in a comprehensive fashion but by focusing on three matters. First, I will look at the Baptist view of Scripture. Every method of interpretation is grounded in a certain conviction about the ontology of Scripture. Second, I will survey three Baptist figures and their exegetical practices. Finally, I will conclude by addressing what it means to retrieve the Baptist tradition, listing strengths and weaknesses of Baptist interpretation.

Historic Doctrine of Scripture

Concealed beneath every exegetical practice is a doctrine of Scripture. Because the Baptist view grew out of the Protestant and Puritan traditions, it historically held to *sola Scriptura*: the Bible is the *ultimate* written authority for Christian faith and practice, because it has a divine nature and origin. The New Hampshire Confession of 1833, in a statement repeated in the Baptist Faith and Message, declares:

> We believe that the Holy Bible was written by men divinely inspired and is a perfect treasure of heavenly instruction; that it has God for its author, salvation for its end, and truth, without any mixture of error, for its matter . . . and [is] the supreme standard by which all human conduct, creeds, and religious opinions should be tried.[6]

E. Y. Mullins, a late-nineteenth- and early-twentieth-century Baptist seminary president, wrote, "For Baptists there is one authoritative source of religious truth and knowledge. To that source they look in all matters

---

[6] One could also look to Thomas Helwys's confession (1611), the Standard Confession (1660–63), the First London Confession (1644), the Second London Confession (1677/89), the Philadelphia Confession (1742), and the Orthodox Creed (1678). See David S. Dockery, "A People of the Book and the Crisis of Biblical Authority," in *Beyond the Impasse? Scripture, Interpretation, and Theology in Baptist Life*, ed. Robinson B. James and David S. Dockery (Nashville: Broadman, 1992), 17–39.

relating to doctrine, polity, the ordinances, worship, and Christian living. That source is the Bible."[7]

In the most important way, this is no different from other Protestant traditions or the historic Christian view. Although the church fathers were not battling along the same fronts, there is evidence their view of the Holy Word aligned with the Protestant recovery. Augustine wrote to Jerome that he learned to "honour those Scriptural books only which are now canonical, that I believe most firmly that no one of those authors has erred in any respect in writing."[8] Irenaeus calls Scripture the "divine Scriptures" and the Bible the "ground and pillar of our faith."[9] He writes, "All Scripture, which has been given to us by God, shall be found by us perfectly consistent."[10] Elsewhere he avers, "The Scriptures are indeed perfect, since they were spoken by the Word of God and His Spirit."[11] Gregory of Nyssa encourages, "Let the inspired Scripture, then, be our umpire, and the vote of truth will surely be given to those whose dogmas are found to agree with the Divine words."[12]

When the Protestant Reformers addressed the doctrine of Scripture, they spoke along similar lines. In a sermon on John 3:16–21, Martin Luther stated of the Bible, "Sooner would the heavens and earth perish than the smallest letter or tittle of his Word would fail."[13] John Calvin commented on 2 Tim 3:16, "We owe to Scripture the same reverence which we owe to God; because it has proceeded from him alone, and has

---

[7] E. Y. Mullins, "Baptists and the Bible," in *Encyclopedia of Southern Baptists*, vol. 1, ed. Davis C. Wooley (Nashville: Broadman, 1958), 141–43.

[8] Augustine, *Epistolae*, 82.i.3.

[9] Irenaeus, AH 2.35.4; 3.9.2; 3.1.1.

[10] Irenaeus, 2.28.3.

[11] Irenaeus, 2.28.2.

[12] Gregory of Nyssa, "On the Holy Trinity, and of the Godhead of the Holy Spirit: To Eustathius," Orthodox Church Fathers, accessed January 1, 2020, https://orthodoxchurchfathers.com/fathers/npnf205/npnf2026.htm#P2526_1733404.

[13] Martin Luther, "A Sermon, in which Christ Presents Himself as Mediator and Saviour, and Passes Judgment on the World and Believers," in *Complete Sermons of Martin Luther*, vol. 2, ed. John Nicholas Lenker, trans. John Nicholas Lenker and others (Grand Rapids: Baker, 2000), 341.

nothing belonging to man mixed with it."[14] English Puritans took up the themes of their Reformation forebears in the Westminster Confession of Faith, stating the Bible "is to be received because it is the Word of God."[15]

Baptist identity is therefore first, foremost, and fundamentally historic, Christian, and Protestant. The liberty of conscience distinctive must be married to the historic tradition from which the Baptist soil was watered.

Although this is the historic Baptist conviction, the line of the Baptist view of Scripture is not straight. Under the influence of biblical criticism, the earlier conviction began to erode, and Baptist scholars began to voice their rejection of it. In the 1860s, Thomas Curtiss, who taught theology at a Baptist college, jettisoned his belief in the infallibility of the Bible because of documentary theories. Ezekiel Robinson, president of Rochester Seminary in the 1870s, and William Newton Clark both concluded that the inerrancy of Scripture was untenable. Crawford Toy, professor of Old Testament at Southern Baptist Theological Seminary, was forced to resign because of his unorthodox views of Scripture.[16]

Beginning in 1960, events occurred that led to the eventual "conservative resurgence," in which the Southern Baptist Convention reoriented itself toward an unambiguous affirmation of biblical inerrancy in the late twentieth century.[17] Other Baptist streams experienced similar pains. The Conservative Baptists broke away from the Northern Baptists

---

[14] John Calvin, "Commentaries on the Epistles to Timothy, Titus, and Philemon," trans. William Pringle, in *Calvin's Commentaries*, 500th anniversary edition, vol. 21 (Grand Rapids: Baker, 2009), 219.

[15] Westminster Confession of Faith 1.4.

[16] I am largely dependent on Pinnock for this overview. See Clark H. Pinnock, "Baptists and Biblical Authority," *JETS* 17, no. 4 (1974). For an overview of Southern Baptists see Slayden A. Yarbrough, "Biblical Authority in Southern Baptist History, 1845–1945," *Baptist History and Heritage* 27, no. 1 (1992): 4–12. See also John E. Steely, "Biblical Authority and Baptists in Historical Perspective," *Baptist History and Heritage* 19, no. 3 (1984): 7–15.

[17] Its detractors called it a "fundamentalist takeover." Rob James and Gary Leazer, *The Fundamentalist Takeover in the Southern Baptist Convention: A Brief History* (Timisoara, Romania: Impact, 1999).

in the 1940s because the Northern Baptists would not accept traditional doctrinal standards.

Although the line of the doctrine of Scripture in Baptist circles veers in a variety of directions, L. Russ Bush and Tom Nettles have convincingly argued that Baptists have a rich heritage of being "people of the book."[18] They demonstrate that the earliest Baptists, John Smyth and Thomas Helwys, affirmed the inerrancy of Scripture as a foundational doctrine. This framework pervaded their confessions and launched the modern missionary movement.

Therefore, the historic Baptist tradition held to the authority of the Scriptures both because it grew out of the Christian, Protestant, and Puritan tradition and because the Scriptures themselves witness to their own authority. Liberty of conscience as a mark of Baptists grew out of this tradition, not in opposition to it. To have the resources to criticize a tradition, one must first sit in that tradition.

Three Soundings

The scope of this chapter allows for only a few soundings from Baptist interpretation. I have chosen three individuals, spread through the centuries. Each person will be examined with an eye to his interpretative practices. Although they are unique in their own rights, these figures are also representative of the Baptist tradition. Benjamin Keach was the most prolific Baptist writer of the seventeenth century; Charles Spurgeon was a famous Baptist preacher of the nineteenth century; and Bernard Ramm wrote a key textbook on hermeneutics in the twentieth century that went through multiple editions. Because of their prominence, these figures helped to form and shape Baptist interpretation for future generations.

---

[18] L. Russ Bush and Tom Nettles, *Baptists and the Bible*, rev. and exp. ed. (Nashville: B&H Academic, 1999).

Benjamin Keach (1640–1704)

Benjamin Keach's writings were not defined by liberty of conscience. He was, according to David Riker, a "catholic reformed theologian."[19] Although Keach denied any supremely authoritative role of tradition, he did not embrace *solo Scriptura*—the view that creeds, councils, and traditions must play no role in guiding scriptural interpretation. He affirmed Scripture not as the *only* authority but as the *supreme* authority.[20] Keach employed conciliar parlance to confirm what a Christian ought to believe.[21] In his preface and introduction to *Preaching from the Types and Metaphors of the Bible*, Keach cites Gregory of Nazianzus, Justin Martyr, Cyprian, and Tertullian and then moves into a discussion of the divine authority of the Bible.[22] He bases his view of the Bible's authority first on Scripture itself but then turns to the testimony of the church: "And as for the Christian Church, it hath with great consistency, and sweet consent, received and acknowledged the books of the Old Testament and New Testament . . . to be divine."[23]

---

[19] David B. Riker, *A Catholic Reformed Theologian: Federalism and Baptism in the Thought of Benjamin Keach 1640–1704* (Milton Keynes, UK: Paternoster, 2008). Arnold protests, arguing he should be labeled a "Reformed Orthodox theologian." Jonathan Arnold, "The Reformed Theology of Benjamin Keach (1640–1704)" (PhD diss., University of Oxford, 2009).

[20] Benjamin Keach, *Light Broke Forth in Wales . . .* (London: William Marshall, 1696), 226, reassured, "Know, noble *Britains*, that we build not our Faith . . . upon the Practice and Custom of Men, Fathers, General Councils, Protestant Reformers or Churches; but upon the Word of God." See Riker, *Catholic Reformed Theologian*, 62.

[21] Benjamin Keach, *A Golden Mine Opened, or, the Glory of God's Rich Grace Displayed . . .* (London: Benjamin Keach and William Marshall, 1694), 85; see Riker, *Catholic Reformed Theologian*, 68.

[22] Benjamin Keach, *Preaching from the Types and Metaphors of the Bible*, 12th ed. (repr.,Grand Rapids: Kregel Academic & Professional, 1972), ix–xiii; first published under the title *Tropologia: A Key to Open Scripture Metaphors* (London: City Press, 1856). In his discussion of types Keach also cites numerous church fathers (225–27).

[23] Keach, xxii.

So, while Keach rejected the ultimate authority of the councils, he interpreted the Bible in conformity with them. His seemingly harsh statements toward councils should be tempered in light of his context. His practice of exegesis was in accord with the councils.

Keach also stood within a major tradition of Reformed theology: federalism. His covenantal scheme shows abundant parallels with other mainstream Reformed thinkers.[24] Keach's interpretation was founded not on charting new paths but on adhering to well-trod ones.

Keach, in continuity with the early Christian tradition, was also quite positive and descriptive concerning allegories. He defined allegory etymologically, as saying one thing in order to understand another, and described analogy as a continuation of a trope, especially of a metaphor. Keach wrote, "The first promise of the Gospel and the whole mystery of redemption to come, is proposed by God himself in this allegory: 'And I will put enmity between thee and the woman and between thy seed, and her seed; it shall bruise thy head, and thou shalt bruise his heel.'"[25] Keach did not seem to have a negative word to say about allegory.

Although Keach followed the tradition of the church, like the other Baptists of his day, he was also a proponent of hermeneutical liberty of conscience. He advocated for credo-baptism, and when he was sentenced to fifteen days in jail for printing material contrary to the Church of England, he was ordered to renounce his heresy. Keach responded, "I hope I shall never renounce those truths."[26] Therefore, it was not that Keach eschewed liberty of conscience in hermeneutics; it was merely grounded in a doctrine of Scripture birthed from the early church.

---

[24] Benjamin Keach, *Display of Glorious Grace: or, The Covenant of Peace Opened* (London: printed by S. Bridge, 1698), iv–v; see Riker, *Catholic Reformed Theologian*, 94. Jonathan W. Arnold, "The Reformed Theology of Benjamin Keach (1640–1704)" (DPhil thesis, Oxford University, 2010). In Arnold's dissertation on Keach he asserts, "As for the overarching doctrine of covenant theology, Keach did not see himself as being an innovator at all. Rather he actually claimed to be a defender of the Reformed tradition, constantly relying on Reformed divines as support for his arguments" (169–70).

[25] Keach, *Types and Metaphors*, 192.

[26] Thomas Crosby, *The History of the English Baptists*, vol. 2 (London, 1738; repr., Lafayette, TN: Church History Research and Archives, 1978), 203.

To summarize, Keach cannot be described solely as having a hermeneutic of liberty of conscience, though this played a part. He was a covenant theologian in continuity with his theological forefathers; he based his view of baptism on an attempt to reform the church, not divide it; he employed the church fathers; and he was a proponent of a form of allegory. All this was based on a historic view of Scripture.

Charles Spurgeon (1834–1892)

Charles Spurgeon was an English Particular Baptist preacher who, before his death in 1892, published a staggering eighteen million words and preached up to thirteen times a week. His sermons were translated into multiple languages and therefore had a wide influence across the world. Much could be said about Spurgeon's hermeneutic, but I will mention only three aspects of his interpretive method.

First, consistent with his Protestant heritage, Spurgeon believed in the inspired and infallible Word of God: Scripture "is the writing of the living God. . . . Each sentence was dictated by the Holy Spirit. . . . This is the book untainted by any error."[27] Spurgeon saw the Scriptures as the supreme authority: "Fathers, schoolmen, reformers, Puritans, bishops, and even ecclesiastical courts are nothing in comparison with this oracle of God."[28] Yet, though Spurgeon saw the Bible as his primary authority, he also "loved the historic confessions and the pious and helpful writings

---

[27] Charles H. Spurgeon, *The New Park Street Pulpit*, vol. 1 (London: Passmore and Alabaster, 1855), 237, 241.

[28] Charles H. Spurgeon, "Essence of a Bible Society Speech," *Sword & Trowel* 18 (April 1882): 163, repr. in Charles H. Spurgeon, *The Complete Works of C. H. Spurgeon*, vol. 85 (Fort Collins, CO: Delmarva, 2015). Spurgeon, quoting Robert William Dale, also said, "A man may believe in the Nicene Creed, and in the Creed attributed to Athanasius, or in the confession of Augsburg, or the confession of the Westminster divines; but if he does not believe in the Sermon on the Mount . . . he has denied the faith, and is in revolt against Christ." *S&T* 21, no. 245 (May 1885): 238; Robert Dale, "The Moral Precepts of Christ" (1884), in *The Congregationalist*, vol. 13, ed. Robert William Dale and James Guiness Rogers (London: Hodder and Stoughton, 1884), 193–94.

of the Reformers and Puritans as well as selected numbers from the early fathers and even some medieval writers."[29]

Duncan Ferguson writes concerning Spurgeon:

> He seldom questioned the categories in the post-Calvinistic theology of seventeenth-century Protestant scholasticism. The Bible was inspired and authoritative. God was sovereign in creation, providence and redemption. Christ the Son of God was sinful mankind's substitute in his atoning sacrifice at Calvary, and human beings are justified by faith in this deed. . . . These mutually dependent Puritan assumptions that Spurgeon adopted constitute the major influence on his interpretation of Scripture.[30]

The point is that Spurgeon's hermeneutic was birthed from his Protestant heritage.

These assumptions lead to the second point. Spurgeon's preaching and interpretation were Spirit-directed and governed by the analogy of faith—the principle that any scriptural text should be interpreted in light of other scriptural texts and in light of the Scripture's major themes. Spurgeon constantly emphasized that interpreters need the Spirit's illuminating power: "The Holy Spirit often sets the Word on a blaze while they are studying it."[31] It is the Spirit of God who "delights to open up the Word to those who seek his instruction."[32] Scripture must also be interpreted in terms of its central message. "No one text is to be exalted above the plain analogy of faith."[33] This allowed Spurgeon to regularly preach on a very short text and veer into similar "spiritual" matters without confining himself to the immediate context of that verse.

---

[29] Tom J. Nettles, *Living by Revealed Truth: The Life and Pastoral Theology of Charles Haddon Spurgeon* (Fearn, UK: Mentor, 2013), 181.

[30] Duncan S. Ferguson, "The Bible and Protestant Orthodoxy: The Hermeneutics of Charles Spurgeon" *JETS* 25, no. 4 (December 1982): 459.

[31] C. H. Spurgeon, "The Talking Book" (sermon), The Spurgeon Archive, accessed November 15, 2019, http://archive.spurgeon.org/sermons/1017.php,

[32] Charles H. Spurgeon, "Lecture 2, On Commenting," The Spurgeon Archive, accessed November 15, 2019, http://archive.spurgeon.org/misc/c&cl2.php.

[33] Spurgeon.

Third, Spurgeon argued we must first understand the Scripture in its literal sense, but this does not disallow "spiritualizing": "The first sense of the passage must never be drowned in the outflow of your imagination."[34] Yet Spurgeon told young preachers they should not be afraid to spiritualize and draw out meanings that may not lie on the surface.[35] Still, he almost always did this in a Christ-centered way.[36] He maintained that Christ was to be the center of every message.

Although Spurgeon regarded the Bible as the supreme authority, he still relied on the Christian tradition to help interpret Scripture. He also followed that tradition's hermeneutical method, which relied first on the literal sense but then proceeded to the spiritual sense. The spiritual sense was controlled by Christocentricity, the analogy of faith, and a Spirit-directed hermeneutic. Like Keach, Spurgeon's hermeneutic cannot be defined solely by appealing to liberty of conscience.

Bernard Ramm (1916–1992)

Bernard Ramm was a Baptist theologian whose academic career began when he joined the faculty at the Bible Institute of Los Angeles (now Biola University). He became a professor of philosophy at Bethel College and Seminary and then professor of religion at Baylor University. One of his most well-known books is *Protestant Biblical Interpretation*, which has

---

[34] Charles Spurgeon, "On Spiritualizing," lecture 7 in *Lectures to My Students*, vol. 1 (London: Passmore and Alabaster, 1881), 108.

[35] Spurgeon, 103. Christian George writes, "Spurgeon's Alexandrian hermeneutic fueled an interpretation of Scripture that perceived the entirety of the canon through the lens of themes, allegories, and illustrations. . . . Though certainly upholding the literal sense of Scripture, Spurgeon's continuation of a tradition that appreciated deeper meanings in the text spurred him to locate underlying patterns throughout Scripture." Christian George, "Jesus Christ, The 'Prince of Pilgrims': A Critical Analysis of the Ontological, Functional, and Exegetical Christologies in the Sermons, Writings, and Lectures of Charles Haddon Spurgeon (1834–1892)" (PhD diss., University of St. Andrews, 2012), 267.

[36] John David Talbert, "Charles Haddon Spurgeon's Christological Homiletics: A Critical Evaluation of Selected Sermons from Old Testament Texts" (PhD diss., Southwestern Baptist Theological Seminary, 1989).

gone through three editions (1950–1980). It served as a hermeneutics textbook for many years and therefore has helped shape and define modern Baptist hermeneutics. I will highlight a few distinctives.

First, Ramm begins the book by saying the science of hermeneutics is needed for two reasons: (1) that we may know what God said, and (2) that we may span the linguistic, cultural, geographical, and historical gaps separating our minds from those of the biblical writers.[37] The emphasis on "what God said" is based, for Ramm, on believing in divine inspiration, and he grounds this in the historic Protestant view. Throughout the book Ramm bases his exegetical method on the divine inspiration of Scripture, and although he claims creeds are not binding, he does employ the creeds: "Judged by their official creeds and confessions, all the major churches of Christendom have accepted the divine inspiration . . . *infallibility* . . . [and] *inerrancy* of the Bible."[38]

Second, Ramm distinguishes historical schools of thought in interpretation, dividing them along the lines of allegorical, literal, devotional, liberal, and neoorthodox.[39] In place of these, Ramm argues for the Protestant system of hermeneutics, which shares much in common with the classicists' system.[40] The assumptions concerning Scripture for Ramm are: (1) the clarity of Scripture, (2) revelation as accommodated, (3) revelation as progressive, (4) Scripture as interpreting Scripture, (5) the analogy of faith, (6) the unity of Scripture, and (7) the distinction between interpretation and application.

On this last point, Ramm advocates for one meaning with multiple applications: "This means that there is only one meaning to a passage of Scripture which is determined by careful study."[41] Ramm also promotes what he calls the "philological principle," or grammatical-historical interpretation. In this method he focuses on the literal over the allegorical,

---

[37] Bernard Ramm, *Protestant Biblical Interpretation: A Textbook of Hermeneutics*, 3rd ed. (Grand Rapids: Baker, 1970), 7.

[38] Ramm, 201.

[39] Ramm, chap. 2.

[40] Ramm, chap. 3.

[41] Ramm, 113.

arguing that all secondary meanings must be based on the literal, which controls the abuse of Scripture:

> The Church Fathers used an uncontrolled allegorical method to find Christian theology in the Old Testament. How do we resolve the competition among the various allegorical schools of interpretation? There is really only one way: grant the prior right to literal interpretation of Scripture and the right of literal interpretation to act as judge and umpire of any proposed allegorical and mystical interpretation of Scripture.[42]

Ramm's work has stood the test of time—going through three editions. Like Keach and Spurgeon, Ramm begins with a historic view of Scripture. He then proceeds to describe the different schools of interpretation, advocating for a "Protestant" view of biblical interpretation. For Ramm this is defined by a spiritual, philological, and doctrinal reading. Yet, compared to Keach and Spurgeon, Ramm also demonstrates some development. He is more negative concerning spiritualization of the text and seems to be tied more strictly to the literal and historical senses.

Retrieving Baptist Interpretation

Although the three soundings lack comprehensiveness, and each figure is unique in his own right, commonalities arise from their interpretive approaches. Differences also map onto their historical placement. Baptist theologians and pastors are molded and shaped by their environment. In this section I will detail some of the key components of Baptist interpretation and point to what we can retrieve while also noting some areas of growth.

---

[42] Ramm, 125. Ramm does qualify what literal interpretation is: "It does not overlook the figures of speech, the symbols, the types, the allegories that as a matter of fact are to be found in Holy Scripture" (126).

Overview

First, all of these figures based their interpretation of Scripture on the *authority of the Scriptures, yet within the bounds of confessionalism*.[43] They believed only the Bible to be inerrant and infallible, but even this belief was grounded in the tradition of the church.[44] While they affirmed *sola Scriptura*, none of them advocated *solo Scriptura*. The Baptist commitment to religious liberty was not historically a pretext for the trampling of tradition.

The interpreters also based their views largely on the church fathers or their Protestant forebears (though Ramm was more critical). Although they emphasized liberty and independence from the creeds as a final authority, they still valued and worked within the creeds' doctrinal lines. Even if not explicit, all three interpreters operated out of the rule of faith.

This is not true of all Baptists. Some have advocated for Biblicism or Landmarkism, sipping from the Enlightenment pool of antagonism to tradition, represented by the slogan "no creed but the Bible."[45] Yet the

---

[43] Harmon, *Towards Baptist Catholicity*, 32, argues that Baptists in North America tended toward *sola Scriptura* but did not explicitly identify other subordinate sources of authority. However, though they may have not explicitly identified them, they did so implicitly.

[44] Harmon, 72, 80, states, "A chronological reading of major confessions of faith issued by Baptist individuals, congregations, associations, and denominational bodies with an eye open for theological language and concepts that cannot be explained by a pure a-traditional radical biblicism, but instead evidence the mediation of language and concepts that are traceable to post-New Testament patristic Christianity, suggests . . . continuities [with] the patristic tradition." Harmon goes on, "These continuities were not necessarily attributable to a conscious engagement with the patristic tradition as a source of religious authority; rather, these continuities were trained from the ecclesiastical bodies out of which the confessing Baptist communities came" (77). Harmon also claims these continuities are most evident in the first century of Baptist existence (80).

[45] Mark Medley surveys the place of tradition as a theological category in ten major Baptist systematic theologies from John L. Dagg (1857) to Stanly Grenz (1994), finding that only a few of them have entered into extensive and constructive consideration of tradition. Millard Erickson's widely used systematic theology gives minimal attention to tradition. Mark Medley, "Catholics, Baptists, and the Normativity of Tradition," *PRSt* 28, no. 2 (Summer 2001):119–30. I found this reference in Harmon, *Towards Baptist Catholicity*, 5.

three key figures we have surveyed held a balanced view of the authority of the Scriptures and the value of tradition.

Second, all three interpreters were *textual, but in different ways*. Each believed that God communicated his message philologically and that the literal sense of the text was the starting point for interpretation. This was birthed in their reliance on Reformational hermeneutics but went back to the church fathers. Yet differences from Reformation interpretation also appeared in these men's work.

Development between Keach and Ramm most likely reflects a historical shift. Writing amid challenges to the authority of the Scriptures, Ramm was harder on allegorizing and spiritual interpretation of the text than was Spurgeon or Keach. Ramm was careful not to have a wooden definition of "literal interpretation," but he was quite pejorative concerning some forms of allegory. Spurgeon and Keach were more open to the spiritual sense, but they still clearly affirmed the authority of the Bible.

Third, all three interpreters were *Christological, but some more than others*. Ian Birch argues the principles that have shaped Baptist reading of Scripture are to regard Christ as the hermeneutical key to Scripture and to read the Bible with a view toward living imaginatively in its story.[46] This is exemplified best by Spurgeon. Ramm had some comments along these lines, but for a hermeneutics book the size of his, it is surprising how little it speaks of Christ, probably reflecting the questions of his day and his hesitancy to spiritualize.[47]

Fourth, all three interpreters had *devotional, homiletical, and spiritual aims*. Exegesis for them was a spiritual task. They spoke of truth as spiritually discerned and noted one cannot be a good interpreter without the working of the Spirit. Therefore, rules and methods can bring a person only so far. God must illumine his Word, and this is a supernatural event.

---

[46] Ian Birch, "Baptists and Biblical Interpretation: Reading the Bible with Christ," in *The "Plainly Revealed" Word of God? Baptist Hermeneutics in Theory and Practice*, ed. Helen Dare and Simon Woodman (Macon, GA: Mercer University Press, 2011), 157.

[47] In the typology section, Ramm had a few lines about Luke 24 and John 5, but his proposal as a whole did not revolve around this idea. But if this is how Jesus taught his disciples to interpret their Bible, then it is a significant oversight.

Fifth, all three did emphasize *the liberty of conscience and/or priesthood of believers, but as a secondary aspect of their positions.* Each Baptist interpreter affirmed the importance of the creeds, spoke of the final authority of Scripture, *and* implied he had liberty to interpret Scripture outside the bounds of historical modes of interpretation when necessary. These three realities were held in balance without cancelling each other out.

Strengths

The common perception of Baptist interpretation is misplaced. It was not all about liberty of conscience; Baptist interpreters were historical in their exegetical processes, pastoral, Christ-centered, and often covenantal in their theological system. Many of their strengths are included in the overview above, but more can be highlighted in summative fashion.

First, *all three figures grounded interpretation in their understanding of the nature of Scripture.* Baptists have historically believed one cannot understand what to do with Scripture until one understands what Scripture is. Ontology determines methodology and therefore precedes praxis. Books on interpretation typically begin with a discussion of the nature of the Bible. A recovery of classic interpretation must begin with an understanding of what Scripture is. Without this preliminary work, the blind are leading the blind.

Second, each interpreter was *consciously historical.* They saw Scripture as the norming norm but demonstrated that they aligned with the Christian tradition.[48] Baptists were not primarily breakaways; they were linked and locked into the catholic *ecclesia.*

Third, they were *interpreters for the larger body of Christ.* The task for them was not purely a scholarly endeavor; they seemed to view themselves as serving the church in their formulation of principles. They spoke not

---

[48] Herschel Hobbs puts it too strongly when he says, "Baptists are not a creedal people. Yet through the centuries they have felt it useful to adopt various confessions of faith." In Herschel H. Hobbs, "Southern Baptists and Confessionalism: A Comparison of the Origins and Contents of the 1925 and 1963," *Review & Expositor* 76, no.1 (1979): 55–68.

only to Baptist circles but to a broader tradition. Ramm's book does not have the label "Baptist" in the title; rather, it is called *Protestant Biblical Interpretation*. He sought to serve a larger tradition than the Baptist one from which he hailed; Spurgeon's sermons and talks were translated into many languages and passed on to believers of many traditions; and Keach was conversant with the larger Protestant covenantal discussion.

Weaknesses

Although Baptist interpreters have many strengths, there are also a few cautionary notes Baptists can draw from a historical overview of their interpretive tradition.

First, *published Baptist treatments of biblical interpretation do not exhibit diversity among their authors*. Of the interpreters I was able to survey, very few (if any) were ethnic minorities or women. This is no doubt linked to historical, cultural, and theological underpinnings. Yet if Baptists believe in the priesthood of all believers, then this must be remedied. The Scripture is a deep well, and a variety of perspectives can unearth more fully its treasure. Baptists have hamstrung their own interpretation by closing off lines to those who could reveal new treasures in the text.

Second, *Baptists should not overemphasize unity around a single interpretive method when the history of Baptist interpretation is so diverse*. Keach had no problem with allegory, and Spurgeon offered positive remarks about the spiritual sense (if grounded in the literal sense), while Ramm had his doubts about allegory. Each of these interpreters followed the signs of his time. While it is true that many spiritual-sense interpretations throughout history have been misguided, it would be equally misguided to reject that type of interpretation as a whole. To equate a high view of Scripture with modern hermeneutics is historically myopic.[49] We

---

[49] Harrelson argues, "Historical criticism of the Bible helps the Christian community and its individual believers to pass on the faith intact." In a positive sense, this could simply mean that history is important to the Christian faith. Amen! But Harrelson means more than this and is pointing to a certain method. Later Harrelson says, "Historical criticism is our *best instrument* in the faithful

must distinguish between hermeneutical positions and the authority of the Scripture. Some hermeneutical positions collide with the truthfulness of Scripture, but many do not, and some labeled "progressive" are actually historic.

Globalism and attacks on the authority of the Scriptures produced uncertainty. To garner some certainty, some in the modern era adopted the historical-critical method to produce singular and definitive answers about "what the Scriptures mean."[50] The only acceptable presupposition in exegesis at times seems to be the historical-critical method.[51] But as we have seen, early Baptists based their views on the early church, and the early church adopted a somewhat different hermeneutic. Yet both affirmed the truthfulness of Scripture.

Modern Baptists need therefore to remember that Christianity transcends modern and postmodern philosophies. We need to hold in balance certainty about the nature of Scripture and charity toward those who appropriate the authoritative Scripture in different ways. This could be called convictional cooperation. Even within the Baptist world, there have been a variety of approaches to the Scripture.

It is vital to sound an alarm when individuals start to deny the Bible's truthfulness. Yet it also is important to note that an interpretation which seems objectionable might not deny the trustworthiness of the Bible but instead might deny an interpretive method to which one has become wed. More gears should exist on our hermeneutical bike than "extremely important" and "not important at all." Baptists are certainly people of

---

passing along of the central core of the biblical heritage." Yet Paige Patterson challenges Harrelson on this point later in the book. See Walter Harrelson, "Passing on the Biblical Tradition Intact: The Role of Historical Criticism," in *Beyond the Impasse?*, 41, 53.

[50] As Harmon, *Towards Baptist Catholicity*, 40–41, notes, champions of radically individualistic interpretations would be shocked to discover how similar their hermeneutic is to radically secular expressions of postmodernism and deconstructionism.

[51] John Newport argues that Baptists must start with the reconstruction and representation of the author's intention, which is the goal of interpretation. He goes onto critique a variety of other approaches. See John P. Newport, "The Challenge of Recent Literary Approaches to the Bible," in *Beyond the Impasse?*, 64–90.

the book. Yet we must also remember that not every disagreement calls for war. If every aberration looks like an enemy, we end up ostracizing friends, who then become opponents.

Third, *Baptists need to continue allowing their contextual lens to widen, resisting atomistic interpretation.*[52] Baptists do not need to play by the rules of the secular or religious academies. They need to read the Bible like Jesus, his disciples, and even the early church. This means following not only modern advances but also ancient practices. Baptists, especially those of an exegetical ilk, should not be afraid to let theological categories intrude on the text. There is no such thing as a pure exegetical process, and there are many more questions to be answered than the two poles of "what it meant" and "what it means." Systematic theology asks questions about what the whole Bible teaches on certain topics, while biblical theology looks at the Scriptures progressively and works inductively from the text—from individual books and from themes that run through the Bible as a whole. However, the two are not like two fighting brothers that need to be reconciled. Rather, they are like the hands and feet of the same person.

Fourth, *Baptists need to place liberty of conscience under the banner of the confessional Christian tradition.* I have argued that liberty of conscience is not the *sine qua non* of Baptist interpretation. Yet E. Y. Mullins in his *The Axioms of Religion* asks what is the distinguishing Baptist principle and states the opposite of what I have argued.

> Is it separation of the Church and State? Or is it the doctrine of soul freedom, the right of private judgment in religious matters and in the interpretation of the Scriptures? Assuredly, these are distinctive Baptist principles. . . . And yet they are scarcely an adequate statement by themselves. . . .
>
> The sufficient statement of the historical significance of Baptists is this: The competency of the soul in religion. . . .

---

[52] For example, Harrelson, "Passing on the Biblical Tradition Intact," 43, advocates for a historical criticism that "does not work on the text of the Bible as a whole but on its particular parts."

Observe then that the idea of the competency of the soul in religion excludes at once all human interference, such as episcopacy and infant baptism, and every form of religion by proxy. Religion is a personal matter between the soul and God.[53]

While "soul competency" for Mullins did not mean something akin to complete freedom in interpretation with respect to affirming or denying core tenets of the faith or traditional interpretive conclusions, and while we should be careful to distinguish between the terms "soul competency," "the priesthood of all believers," and "liberty of conscience," there is here a distinctively modern individualist note to Mullins's description of Baptist distinctives, And although some may identify "Baptist" with Mullins's concept of " soul competency," it is not clear that Mullins understood correctly the implications of justification by faith and the priesthood of all believers in relation to his articulation of the doctrine.[54] Mullins himself admitted that the axiom of soul competency arose from Renaissance humanism, Anglo-Saxon individualism, and the Reformation principle of justification by faith.[55]

Therefore, while liberty of conscience (and the related concepts of soul competency and priesthood of believers) long has been part of Baptist interpretation, it has been conceived of in both respectable and

---

[53] Edgar Young Mullins, *The Axioms of Religion: A New Interpretation of the Baptist Faith* (Philadelphia: Griffith & Rowland, 1908), 50, 53–54.

[54] As Curtis Freeman argued, "although the phrase 'soul competency' as an anthropological concept does not appear in theological discourse before Mullins, it became for many the canonical reading of Baptist heritage: the rock on which all else stood." See Curtis W. Freeman, "E. Y. Mullins and the Siren Songs of Modernity," *Review & Expositor* 96, no. 1 (1999): 35. Two things should be noted about this quote. First, the phrase did not occur before Mullins, and, second, it became the rock on which Baptists stood. This second point might seem to run against the argument of this entire chapter, but the point of this chapter is to show that historically Baptists have not stood solely on this conception. The Baptist past shows that their history is more diverse and probably more historic in their views. Tracing Mullins's "soul competency" back to Roger Williams's "soul liberty" has been shown to be faulty history—see LeRoy Moore, "Roger Williams and the Historians," *Church History* 32 (1963): 441–43.

[55] Mullins, *Axioms of Religion*, 57.

unfortunate ways.[56] It was Luther—the architect of justification by faith alone—who advocated the priesthood of believers as an alternative to Roman Catholicism. As Vanhoozer points out, "Luther never spoke of the priesthood of the believer, in the singular, and neither does the New Testament. The Reformers emphasized the priesthood of all believers not as *isolated* but as *gathered* individuals. . . . The phrase is not a charter for rank individualism."[57] A proper understanding of these concepts coheres with a strong view of personal faith, the local church, and historic Christian tradition, while also denying rank individualism and negative portrayals of tradition. As Timothy George states, no Baptist denies the priesthood of all believers; what is at stake is how this principle is to be understood.[58] Baptists can affirm liberty of conscience while understanding it in light of and under the banner of the confessional Christian tradition.

Conclusion

Baptist interpretation cannot be wholly defined by liberty of conscience. Baptists have intentionally put themselves in the historic, Christian, Protestant stream.[59] They have wrestled with texts in the shadow of the early church and sought to be faithful with what has been given to

---

[56] Timothy George, "The Priesthood of All Believers and the Quest for Theological Integrity," *Criswell Theological Review* 3 (1989): 284, argues we need to distinguish soul competency, religious liberty, and the priesthood of all believers.

[57] Kevin J. Vanhoozer, *Biblical Authority* after *Babel: Retrieving the Solas in the Spirit of Mere Protestant Christianity* (Grand Rapids: Brazos, 2016), 158.

[58] George, "Priesthood of All Believers," 283.

[59] Garrett, *Baptist Theology*, 22, argues, "Baptists have adhered to the Trinitarian and Christological doctrines formulated by the first four ecumenical councils and expressed in the earliest Christian creeds. . . .They seem to have been indebted to various magisterial Reformers: Luther for the supremacy of the Scriptures over tradition, for justification by grace through faith, and the priesthood of all Christians; Zwingli for a memorialist understanding of the Lord's Supper; Bucer for church disciple as essential to the true church, and Calvin for predestination as a major doctrine."

them. They are not just academicians but are spiritually and ecclesiologically minded.

Many Baptist interpreters did not think of themselves as trailblazers; they thought of themselves as walking worn paths, even if those paths had been abandoned in their lifetime. Their aim was not to divide the church but to bring greater clarity and certainty to the faith once for all delivered to the saints.[60]

Yet it is also true that the Baptist river does not run straight. There are still areas in which Baptists can grow. This includes reenvisioning the place of tradition in Baptist interpretation. It would do all of us well to revisit past writings and learn that Baptist interpretation has been grounded on one truth: the reliability of the Scriptures. God has spoken to us through his Word, and with the psalmist we look to that Word and say, "With my whole heart I seek you; let me not wander from your commandments! I have stored up your word in my heart, that I might not sin against you" (Ps 119:10–11 ESV).

---

[60] My thesis is well summarized by Garrett in his opening paragraph to *Baptist Theology*, 1: "The people called Baptists have often identified their churches as 'New Testament churches' and have frequently insisted that they are not creedal people. Some Baptists have 'leapfrogged' over the Christian centuries, while others have posited a 'trail of blood' church succession. Consequently, one may be prone to assume that they owe nothing to the creeds, the church councils, or the theologians of the sixteen centuries prior to the advent of the Baptist movement. But that assumption needs to be challenged and tested."

7

Baptists, Corporate Worship, and the Christian Tradition

TAYLOR WORLEY

Trinity International University

Introduction

Of all the questions we might ask regarding Baptist worship, among the most significant is: What would representatives of the early church make of Baptist worship today? For instance, if first-century Bereans wandered into the Sunday morning service of the local First Baptist Church, what would they notice? What would they recognize? Aside from the differences in language, dress, and other customs, it is worth asking whether our forebears in the early church would find the worship of Baptists today recognizable. Would any of the elements in the service seem familiar?

Admittedly, many innovations in Christian worship have appeared since those earliest days. For their part, Baptists have contributed a few of their own. First, it seems that the endorsement of free or unscripted prayers in worship by early Baptists such as John Smyth and later John Bunyan has been adopted quite broadly.[1] Second, the encouragement of Benjamin Keach, a leader of early Particular Baptists, to embrace the congregational singing of hymns alongside the Psalms has remained and

---

[1] McBeth, *Baptist Heritage*, 91–95.

even flourished.[2] Of course, even these major contributions within the Baptist tradition could be seen as attempts to restore contemporary worship to the simplicity and spontaneity of New Testament forms.[3] Thus, the question remains: What continuity does Baptist worship today have with the historic church? More importantly, however, we must ask: Does such continuity serve an aesthetic function or a missional one? In what follows, I argue for a recovery of historic Christian worship practices for Baptists today. Baptists need not fear or forsake the great liturgical resources of the Christian tradition and should instead harness these tools to celebrate more fully the rich and specific calling that is ours in God's kingdom. Reform, renewal, and fidelity to God's Word will guide us, and we will avoid the influence of conformity or nostalgia.

This case will be primarily theological and biblical rather than historical, for what is most needed in Baptist life today is not more affirmation of historical precedent but instead a deeper reflection on the theological

---

[2] Note that it took Keach twenty years to implement his program of regular Sunday hymn singing during a time of much resistance; see Christopher Ellis, "Baptists in Britain," in *The Oxford History of Christian Worship*, ed. Geoffrey Wainwright and Karen B. Westerfield Tucker (Oxford, UK/New York: Oxford University Press, 2006), 571. We can track the development of this innovation in Garrett's discussion of the evolution of congregational singing within early General and Particular Baptists in England; see Garrett, *Baptist Theology*. Ellis, "Baptists in Britain, 560: "From the beginning Baptists have valued spontaneity in prayer, instruction and challenge in preaching, and a devotional commitment on the part of the congregation that eventually led to the development of congregational hymn singing."

[3] In addition to the polemical writings distancing themselves from Catholics and Anglicans, Baptists embraced a biblical simplicity when it came to their values in worship. For instance, the Second London Confession (1677) describes public worship in chapter 22, "Of Religious Worship, and the Sabbath Days," in this way: "The reading of the Scriptures, Preaching and hearing the word of God, teaching and admonishing one another in Psalms, Hymns, and Spiritual songs, singing with grace in our Hearts to the Lord; as also the Administration of Baptism and the Lord's Supper are all parts of Religious worship of God, to be performed in obedience to him, with understanding, faith, reverence, and godly fear; moreover solemn humiliation, with fastings; and thanksgiving upon special occasions, ought to be used in an holy and religious manner." In Lumpkin, *Baptist Confessions of Faith*, 281.

commitments embodied within our worship. This proposal, then, will proceed in three parts: first, a historical reorientation for understanding the origins of Baptist worship; second, a biblical theology of worship with respect to tradition and liturgy; and third, a set of proposals aimed at protecting the simplicity and spontaneity of Baptist worship in line with the liturgical resources of the great Christian tradition.[4]

Baptist Worship as *Replacement Cultus*

Alongside other strands of the Reformation, the Baptist movement prioritizes worship sourced from the New Testament.[5] Baptist reflection on worship is, in large measure, a sustained consideration of how best to embody the teachings of the New Testament. Of course, Baptists were not the first to consider the New Testament a primary text for worship, and they surely will not be the last. This approach has featured prominently in a broad spectrum of Baptist projects, from the ideologically overzealous (i.e., the Landmark movement) to the more self-critical and intellectually humble, but no matter the sector of Baptist life considered, one will consistently find a majority of churches that endeavor to organize their worship in line with the "New Testament church." Setting aside the historiographical challenges that beset this common Protestant aim, the enduring value of replicating the "New Testament church"

---

[4] The phrase "simplicity and spontaneity" was used by William Brackney to describe the pattern of worship laid down by John Smyth and is retained here as a description of worship in the greater Baptist movement to this day. See William H. Brackney, ed., *Baptist Life and Thought, 1600–1980: A Source Book* (Valley Forge, PA: Judson, 1983), 51; cf. Robert A. Reid, "Music in the Spiritual Life of Baptists," in *Ties That Bind: Life Together in the Baptist Vision*, ed. Gary Furr and Curtis W. Freeman (Macon, GA: Smith & Helwys, 1994), 152–70.

[5] Perhaps, the classic (and most novel) expression of this sentiment can be found in the writings of the early General Baptist leader and forerunner John Smyth (ca. 1570–1612), especially his 1608 *The Differences of the Churches of the Seperation* [sic], which called for a departure from church tradition and a return to what he called "spiritual worship." Cf. C. Douglas Weaver, *In Search of the New Testament Church: The Baptist Story* (Macon, GA: Mercer University Press, 2008).

among Baptists should prove quite illuminating for our purposes.[6] We must inquire into why this attachment remains. In hopes of explaining this phenomenon, we will turn to some of the best studies on early Christian worship.

For the last few decades, Larry Hurtado has argued quite persuasively for a high Christology (i.e., belief that Jesus Christ is God) in the first generations of Christianity, and he has done so through sustained consideration of early Christian worship.[7] To make his case, Hurtado has explored the thoroughly religious landscape into which Christianity was birthed. Despite the ways in which modernity has remembered Roman antiquity for its great thinkers, leaders, and systems of government but quite apart from any meaningful connection to its religion, Hurtado reminds students of early Christianity that the Roman world was, in fact, thoroughly and pointedly religious in many ways. Along with characterizations such as "evil" and "hideous and shameful," the Roman state historian Tacitus disdained Christianity as a "most mischievous superstition."[8] Christians in antiquity were haphazardly labeled "atheists." These disastrous, and often fatal, characterizations of our ancient brethren were not the result of an uncritical estimate of the theological merit of Christianity's profound teachings, but rather represent reactionary animosity generated

---

[6] Cf. Theodore Dwight Bozeman, *To Live Ancient Lives: The Primitivist Dimension in Puritanism* (Chapel Hill, NC: University of North Carolina Press, 1988); Matthew Ward, *Pure Worship: The Early English Baptist Distinctive* (Eugene, OR: Pickwick, 2014).

[7] Larry W. Hurtado, *One God, One Lord: Early Christian Devotion and Ancient Jewish Monotheism* (Philadelphia: Fortress, 1988); Hurtado, *Lord Jesus Christ: Devotion to Jesus in Earliest Christianity* (Grand Rapids: Eerdmans, 2003); Hurtado, *How on Earth Did Jesus Become a God? Historical Questions about Earliest Devotion to Jesus* (Grand Rapids: Eerdmans, 2005); Hurtado, *Why on Earth Did Anyone Become a Christian in the First Three Centuries?* (Milwaukee: Marquette University Press, 2016); Hurtado, *Destroyer of the Gods: Early Christian Distinctiveness in the Roman World* (Waco, TX: Baylor University Press, 2016); Hurtado, *Ancient Jewish Monotheism and Early Christian Jesus-Devotion: The Context and Character of Christological Faith* (Waco, TX: Baylor University Press, 2017).

[8] Jona Lendering, "Tacitus on the Christians," *Livius: Articles on Ancient History*, accessed April 4, 2018, http://www.livius.org/sources/content/tacitus/tacitus-on-the-christians.

by the mere presence of Christians and the threat their simple worship presented to the religious status quo. Roman religion supplied a stable foundation for the entire empire, and the joyous, corporate confession that "Jesus Christ is Lord" in the prayers, praises, and preaching of early Christianity threatened to undo that order.

In describing "how varied, prominent, pervasive and popular the practice of religion was," Hurtado outlines several features of Roman religion that presented particular challenges for Christian worship.[9] First, Roman religion was ubiquitous: "It is in fact difficult to point to any aspect of life in that period that was not explicitly connected with religion. Birth, death, marriage, the domestic sphere, civil and wider political life, work, the military, socialising, entertainment, arts, music—all were imbued with religious significance and associations."[10] Second, not only was religion present everywhere in Roman society, but it was visible and practically unavoidable at every turn: "In the Roman era religion was not only a private affair but was also seen as very much a public aspect of life. Religious ceremony was deliberately intended to be noticed and to engage the entire village or city."[11]

Additionally, Roman religion accounted for a great diversity of gods, religious forms, and practices. With the exception of devout Jews and Christians, the religious practices of all peoples could be successfully assimilated into Roman religion. This was the religious genius that united a world empire, made up as it was of diverse peoples and cultures, with their own sacred mysteries and religious idiosyncrasies. As long as loyalty was paid to Rome itself, the empire seemed to have a syncretistic posture of the more the merrier.[12] Thus it is clear that Roman religion either

---

[9] Larry W. Hurtado, *At the Origins of Christian Worship: The Context and Character of Earliest Christian Devotion* (Grand Rapids: Eerdmans, 2000), 4.

[10] Hurtado, 8–9.

[11] Hurtado, 12.

[12] Along with these broad features, Roman religion made great use of sacred places (e.g., the numerous temples and shrines for various gods found in most Roman cities), images (e.g., cultic representations of gods and divinized emperors), rituals (e.g., from everyday sacrifices in gratitude to the gods to the secretive and elaborate initiation rites of the mystery cults), and meals (e.g., numerous feasts

existed within or made possible much of the social space of that society. Life in ancient Rome was, from top to bottom, thoroughly religious.

Early Christianity could not seek to compete with the sheer scope of Roman religious life. Whereas Roman religion was all-encompassing and ubiquitous—and therefore somewhat generic in appeal and homogenizing in effect—Christianity was intensely personal and immediate. In this vein, Hurtado highlights five overriding features of early Christian worship: intimacy, participation, fervor, significance, and potency.[13] In these ways the worship of early Christians demonstrated a marked departure from the generic and depersonalizing aspects of Roman religion. Christians worshiped with a simplicity of form and spontaneity of spirit.[14]

Hurtado's insights concerning early Christian worship add much to our understanding of the pastoral priorities that surface throughout

---

taking place on temple grounds or in private homes with the remaining meat from animal sacrifices to the gods) to further solidify itself in the lives of its participants. For example, N. T. Wright claims in his recent biography of Paul that the main concern raised by the apostle's sermon on Mars Hill was whether he was calling for the erecting of a new temple or shrine for his god(s). See N. T. Wright, "Athens," chap. 8 in *Paul: A Biography* (New York: HarperOne, 2018).

[13] The intimate fellowship of the earliest Christians took place exclusively within house-church settings, where "brothers and sisters" greeted each other with a "holy kiss" (1 Cor 16:20), partook of a common table (1 Cor 10:17), and enjoyed a thick network of relations. In such settings, all those present—despite the gender-based, socioeconomic, and cultural divisions that defined their lives in Roman society (Gal 3:28)—were called upon to participate fully in the Christian *leiturgia* (literally, "work of the people"). These ritual occasions were marked not only by a common meal but by a host of fervent spiritual exercises (1 Cor 14:26; 12:4–11) and infused with ecstatic joy (Heb 6:4–5). The significance of such "work"—which the apostles related with strategic use of the term *ekklēsia*, as opposed to the more popular term *synagogē* among contemporaneous Jews—was nothing short of fulfilling the ancient expectations of God's covenant with Israel (1 Pet 2:4–12). Moreover the "work" of this new people was uniquely enabled by the power of the Holy Spirit and the gifts he provides (1 Corinthians 12–14).

[14] We should see the apostolic warnings of the New Testament about protecting the fragile fellowship of these worshiping communities (e.g. 1 Corinthians 11; Heb 10:23–25; Jas 2:1–13, 1 John 1) as further confirmation that early Christian worship represented something truly remarkable in its day and age.

the New Testament. Beyond filling out the picture of that foundational period, however, such contextual reading can aid us in understanding something of the enduring nature of Christian worship. While we may have assumed early Christian worship (e.g., that described in the *Didache*) was principally a novel creation of a new religious movement, the actual history will not suffer such shallow understandings. We must embrace a more complex picture of our origins: in some ways consistent with diasporic Jewish religion, Christian worship developed as a simultaneous renunciation of Roman civic religion and a profoundly new iteration of Jewish synagogue practice. For his part, Hurtado describes early Christian worship with the term *replacement cultus*:

> For early Gentile Christians to disdain and renounce the religious practices of their pre-conversion lives meant to turn away from colourful and engaging cultic customs that offered a great deal to devotees. It also meant abandoning a central feature of common life in Roman cities and a major component in the things that united families and peoples. We cannot appreciate early Christian worship unless we keep before our eyes the fact that for Gentile Christians it represented a *replacement cultus*. It was at one and the same time both a religious commitment and a renunciation, a stark and demanding devotional stance with profound repercussions.[15]

Early Christians were identified as much by what religious activities they avoided as by the new forms of worship that embodied their faith. So, any appreciation for "New Testament worship" must not assume a novel originality or primitive austerity but rather must acknowledge the contextual conditions that meant each worship gesture was an act simultaneously of obedience to Christ *and* of disobedience to one's own state, society, and culture. This poignant dynamic is important to note for reasons beyond merely honoring the heroic faithfulness of our ancient sisters and brothers. As we align our worship with what Scripture describes

---

[15] Hurtado, *Origins of Christian Worship*, 4.

from the early church, successive generations of Christians may be organizing their services as a *replacement cultus* without knowing exactly how
or why they are doing so.

While I believe this historical insight could be fruitfully applied
to many Christian denominations and traditions, I wish to pursue it
primarily within the free church tradition and specifically the Baptist
movement. The origins of Baptist worship center on another clear repu-
diation of Roman religion, but in this instance it was the late-medieval
Roman Catholic religion targeted by the Reformers. We can apply the
same notion of *replacement cultus* to the breadth of the Reformation,
because in each strand of the movement, reform involved revising worship practices to one degree or another. In many cases, these revisions
embodied renunciation of Catholic modes of worship. Such changes,
however, were measured, and a great emphasis was also placed on dismantling the divisions between sacred and secular so characteristic of
late-medieval spirituality. As Timothy George concludes, "life itself was
liturgical" for each of the Reformers, and their renewed spirituality made
possible by a recovery of the biblical gospel was meant to permeate every
sphere of the believer's life.[16]

While the Baptists surely appreciated these developments and
embraced the Reformation's concern for a holistic faith that informs life
in the church as well as the world, more reform was needed. Thus Baptist
worship appears more and more to operate as a *replacement cultus* when its
evolution is traced through the influence of the Reformation, Puritanism,
and eventually Separatism. Early Baptists successively abandoned worship
practices deemed idolatrous (i.e., too Catholic). The representative list of
forsaken practices included use of the Prayer Book, feast days and saints'
days, written pulpit homilies, the sign of the cross, bowing and kneeling
in worship, a sacramental understanding of the Lord's Supper, and, principally, infant baptism. "The list shows," David Bebbington reflects, "how

---

[16] Timothy George, *Theology of the Reformers*, 25th anniversary ed. (Nashville:
B&H Academic, 2013), 390; George's reflections on the restoration of the balance
between Word and sacrament in Christian worship are particularly illuminating
with respect to the question of tradition in relation to worship today (390–91).

the earliest Baptists were preoccupied with ensuring that they should flee from all residual traces of Catholic influence, including those recently reintroduced by Archbishop Laud into the Church of England. Worship was their central concern. To purify their services of all hints of idolatry was their overriding aim."[17] From its genesis, then, Baptist worship has been defined principally by that from which it abstains.

Thus many Baptist churches, since the movement's beginning and up to today, operate within a *replacement cultus* framework. Whether or not those churches consciously embrace this historical model, it affects drastically the degree to which Baptist worship today has the capacity to celebrate traditions of worship that predate or issue from outside their movement. The *replacement cultus* model has a built-in appeal in that the strengths of the new form of worship—however meager or great—at least represent an alternative to the false forms of worship dominating the surrounding culture. It is argued (or assumed) that the reforming community should willingly embrace forms of worship that are new, different, or dramatically altered, and any residual sense of loss or regret would likely dissipate over a generation or two.

This phenomenon can perhaps explain why the charge of idolatry and the label "Catholic" were almost synonymous in the early days of the Baptist movement. For at least these reasons, we can now see how it came to pass that tradition as it relates to worship came to be seen with such suspicion. Tradition is the opponent in a *replacement cultus* framework. Continuity should be broken, not restored or affirmed. But let us be clear: there was a difference between the *replacement cultus* of the Reformation and that of the early church. Whereas the early Christians protested false worship in Roman religion, the Reformation—and by extension the Baptist movement—was resisting the false *practice* of true religion. There is, in fact, a world of difference, even if Baptists' self-understanding and historiography does not account for it well.

---

[17] David Bebbington, *Baptists through the Centuries: A History of a Global People* (Waco, TX: Baylor University Press, 2010), 23. The significance of worship for early Baptists is reinforced well by Chute, Finn, and Haykin in their opening chapter "Baptist Beginnings," in Chute, Finn, and Haykin, *Baptist Story*, 11–38.

We come now to the contemporary dilemma of tradition for Baptist worship. Put simply, is there any place for tradition in Baptist worship today? Does the Baptist project, as one form of the ancient *replacement cultus*, preclude any sustained appreciation for connection with the past? Tradition should not be so quickly characterized as *the* enemy. The reality is much more complex than that.[18] Though the *replacement cultus* model has forced the hand of many Baptist churches when it comes to worship, it remains to be seen whether the Baptist movement should continue in this mode. While many Baptists would celebrate Bebbington's conclusion, "Baptists were the people who took Reformation principles to their ultimate conclusion,"[19] we must ask ourselves today whether we have gone too far, or not far enough! In other words, have Baptists stopped short of reforming fully by not reappropriating the best of the great tradition of Christian worship? It is worth reconsidering this historical stance. Just as the early Christians reformed the practices of the Jewish synagogue to maintain fidelity with biblical worship in light of the apostolic witness, so we must follow through with our reforms as we seek to embody the most faithful attempt at biblical worship today. Let us explore Scripture afresh, to this end.

Biblical Theology of Worship: Tradition and Liturgy

A biblical theology of worship is best addressed as a separate work or set of volumes, and indeed we possess several seminal resources by leading scholars.[20] Our question, thus, should be more narrowly focused, and

---

[18] Philip Thompson explores this theme well and reflects: "It is an understatement to say that Baptists in America are of two minds concerning tradition: though only one is a conscious mind." Philip E. Thompson, "'As It Was in the Beginning'(?): The Myth of Changelessness in Baptist Life and Belief," in Philip E. Thompson and Anthony R Cross, *Recycling the Past or Researching History? Studies in Baptist Historiography and Myths* (Milton Keynes, UK: Paternoster, 2005), 185.

[19] Bebbington, *Baptists through the Centuries*, 24.

[20] Daniel I. Block, *For the Glory of God: Recovering a Biblical Theology of Worship*, (Grand Rapids: Baker Academic, 2014); Harold M. Best, *Unceasing Worship: Biblical Perspectives on Worship and the Arts* (Downers Grove, IL: InterVarsity Press,

hence we seek to inquire into what the Bible teaches regarding the place of tradition in expressions of Christian worship. We turn with the biblical scholar N. T. Wright to the liturgical texts within the Bible itself. In *The Case for the Psalms*, Wright invites today's church to return to what he calls her "original hymnbook." He explores these biblical hymns and poems as the transformative texts they were in fact compiled to be. Along with much reflection on how Christians have used the Psalms, Wright unearths at least three layers within the subtle liturgical dynamics of how the Psalms function and what they convey about biblical worship. He examines, in turn, the transformation of time, place, and experience.

First, Wright understands the Psalms as portals to the threshold of eternity, for "the Psalms invite us, first, to stand at the intersection of the different layers of time."[21] He takes Psalm 90 as the preeminent example of this intersection of divine and human time. The psalm opens by confessing God's eternal reign: "Lord, you have been our refuge in every generation. Before the mountains were born, before you gave birth to the earth and the world, from eternity to eternity, you are God" (Ps 90:1–2). While humanity's experience of time is transitory and unpredictable— shaky at best—God's position beyond time is fixed and perfectly stable. The juxtaposition is unrelenting, if not harsh, and the psalm amplifies this divide in verse 9: "For all our days ebb away under your wrath; we end our years like a sigh." The fragility of human life is much more than a foil for divine perfection; our days not only disappear but slip away in pain, anger, and frustration.

Psalm 90 relays more, however, than the plight of our brokenness. It signals a hope for the redemption of human time. When the psalmist recognizes both the fixity of God's reign over time and our living at the mercy of time, worship opens up and into a new form of time—the time of prayer. Prayer invites a moment for divine and earthly time to converge

---

2003); David Peterson, *Engaging with God: A Biblical Theology of Worship* (Downers Grove, IL: InterVarsity Press, 2002); David S. Dockery, James Earl Massey, and Robert Smith, eds., *Worship, Tradition, and Engagement: Essays in Honor of Timothy George* (Eugene, OR: Pickwick, 2018), 48–78.

[21] N. T. Wright, *The Case for the Psalms: Why They Are Essential* (New York: HarperOne, 2013), 37.

in what we might call "liturgical time." Human time cannot bind itself to eternity, but rather God condescends to earthly experience. He hears the prayers of his people. To that end, the psalmist prays: "Teach us to number our days carefully so that we may develop wisdom in our hearts" (Ps 90:12).[22] Again, Wright explains, "To recognize that the Psalms call us to pray and sing at the intersection of the times—of our time and God's time, of the *then* and the *now* and the *not yet*—is to understand how those [seemingly contradictory] emotions [of brokenness and hope] are to be held within the rhythm of a life lived in God's presence."[23] Thus, in the emotional turbulence of Psalms such as 91, 102, 103, and 104, we find joyful adoration alongside mourning and sorrow, but in the midst of such turmoil the Psalms also remind us that God's people are supported solely by the gracious fact that the Lord remembers them.

Second, Wright sees the Psalms as envisioning the transformation of place. The Old Testament sustains Genesis's primary concern with land, and that abiding concern is elevated to the level of spiritual crisis in psalmic worship. More pointedly, the dilemma manifests itself with a personalizing tone: How do we find our way home? The covenant blessing of "promised land" means that the expectation for a placed and flourishing community never departs from the hopeful imagination of our biblical songs. These hymns are predicated on the unabashed belief that geography can be transformed through presence; that places can be engaged by relationship and redeemed into a site of divine homemaking. The imagery of divine homemaking in the Psalms is rich and varied. According to Wright, there is no escaping its dominance as a poetic and theological thread: "Again and again the Psalms celebrate, in almost embarrassingly vivid language, the belief that the creator of the universe has, for reasons best known to him, decided to take up residence on a small hill in the Judean uplands. The living God, the Psalms declare,

---

[22] Paraphrasing v. 12, Wright (*Case for the Psalms*, 38) pleads, "Make us, in other words, to be people who know how to stand at the threshold of human time and God's time, and there to learn both humility and hope."

[23] Wright, 44.

has decided to make his own special home at the point where the fertile western escarpment meets the eastern wilderness."[24]

The Psalms, as Wright emphasizes, are not fixated on some other-worldly or purely abstract notion of place. They are bound, rather, to a specific geographical location: Jerusalem, the city of King David and the site of Christ's death, burial, and resurrection. While the uninitiated reader might assume this preference for Jerusalem to be an arbitrary detail of history, closer inspection reveals it to be anything but. Wright describes Jerusalem as "poised between garden and desert—almost as though God couldn't quite make up his mind whether to settle firmly in a New Eden or to remain camped with his people in their wilderness wanderings."[25] Thus, long before the events of the New Testament, the physical character of Jerusalem bore out the significance of distinctive moments in salvation history and stood as a reminder of the deep covenantal tension between the promises already unfolding and the fulfillment yet to come.

The Psalms name this tension by their contrasting labels for the city. "Zion" houses the throne of God's king and pictures the fulfillment of every blessing entailed by God's promises. Its glory surfaces throughout the book, such as in the rich imagery of Psalms 46 and 133 but with particular emphasis in such Psalms as 2, 9, and 48: "The LORD is great and highly praised in the city of our God. His holy mountain, rising splendidly, is the joy of the whole earth. Mount Zion—the summit of Zaphon—is the city of the great King" (Ps 48:1–2). In other words, "Zion" is the image of what "Jerusalem" could be—the aim of God's covenant and intended destination of his promise. But the city of David is not yet what it could be, and the Psalms account for this reality too. In the same breath, the psalmist can celebrate the anticipated glory of Zion alongside an honest awareness of the city's present struggles: "Pray for the well-being of Jerusalem: 'May those who love you be secure; may there be peace within your walls, security within your fortresses'" (Ps 122:6–7).

In awaiting their future reconciliation, the Psalms focus this specific hope on the status of the temple. As the meeting place for God and

---

[24] Wright, 77–78.
[25] Wright, 78.

God's people, the temple marks the convergence of present and future as well as of sacred and common space.[26] God's people cannot guarantee the security of their meeting place, according to the Psalms, but instead must learn to trust in the generosity and grace of God to make it secure. Psalms beautifully recall the protection motif of Exod 33:22: "The one who lives under the protection of the Most High dwells in the shadow of the Almighty. I will say concerning the LORD, who is my refuge and my fortress, my God in whom I trust" (Ps 91:1–2). Psalm 91—like Psalms 2, 11, 33, and 46—indicates the key to resolving the tension between present and future, sacred and common space: the Lord himself is a sanctuary for his people.[27] Ultimately, then, what we learn through the Psalms' poetry of place is that worship means being present and belonging somewhere, and such belonging is a divine gift that can transform any place into an outpost of God's kingdom (Matt 18:20).

Last, and perhaps most important, Wright traces how the Psalms describe a transformation of the heart. While time- and place-experience are renewed through worship, the human experience itself undergoes profound change and transformation as well. More often than not, such restorative movements in the Psalms begin with honest and heartfelt lament. In the midst of alienation, pain, and distress, Psalm 13 cries out: "How long, LORD? Will you forget me forever? How long will you hide your face from me?" (v. 1). Implied within this hymn of lament is the simple faith that one's cry does not ascend in vain. While Psalm 13 asks "Who sees my suffering?" or "Who knows my pain?" these questions receive their response elsewhere. Psalm 34: "The eyes of the LORD are on the righteous, and his ears are open to their cry for help" (34:15). The

---

[26] The pilgrim psalms, or Songs of Ascents, such as Psalm 122, demonstrate well this concern for the temple of God in the city of God. They reflect both a deep sense of delight for the ministry of the temple and a simultaneous sense of duty to protect and prolong that ministry until the promises are complete.

[27] God's own presence makes a just and good place of this earth. While the Psalms signal a time in which this hope will be fulfilled, the ministry of Jesus in time and space secures the restoration of forsaken places by making his people into a new temple.

Psalms announce that when no one else is within reach, the Lord himself hears and sees.

Such confidence then makes possible a somewhat unexpected turn. Psalm 34's confidence generates an empathetic openness, a reversal of the purely internal focus of lament to an emotional focus on others. Such a turn then issues the call to corporate confidence in the Lord. Psalm 130 begins much like Psalm 13 but concludes with an exhortation to all: "I wait for the LORD; I wait and put my hope in his word. . . . Israel, put your hope in the LORD" (130:5, 7). In just a few brief movements, Psalm 130 reveals the transition from inwardness and potential despair to courageous empathy and mutual concern. "Woe is me!" transforms into "Let us cry out and seek the Lord together." Such dramatic shifts are characteristic of the rich poetic landscapes of the Psalms and the transformative power of biblical worship.

Of course, such transformative moments are offered in and through the Psalms for us, but only because Jesus Christ prays the Psalms and prays them for us.[28] They were his prayers before they became the prayers of the church. That in itself may be enough to draw all Christians back to using the Psalms extensively and creatively in worship. But we must not do so with a sense of servile obligation. Jesus instructs us to worship "in Spirit and in truth" (John 4:23). In light of these rich layers in the Psalms, then, we should feel free to go deeper. Wright reflects: "The Psalms are not only poetry in themselves; they are to be the cause of poetry in those who sing them, together and individually. They are God's gifts to us so that we can be shaped as his gift to the world."[29]

---

[28] Dietrich Bonhoeffer penned a work on the Psalms that for years has been published alongside *Life Together*. In *Prayerbook of the Bible*, Bonhoeffer makes his case for a recovery of the Psalms as the church's prayerbook, and he does so on the basis that Christ himself prayed the Psalter in his own life. Now, by virtue of Christ's representative action on behalf of the church, we can pray these psalms with him and through him. The mediatorial nature of Christ's ministry, in Bonhoeffer's account, is not only richly theological but also fully wedded to the Bible as well. See Dietrich Bonhoeffer, *Life Together and Prayerbook of the Bible*, Dietrich Bonhoeffer Works, vol. 5 (Minneapolis: Fortress, 2005).

[29] Wright, *Case for the Psalms*, 36.

The invitation of the Psalms is to experience the marriage of time with memory, place with presence, and authenticity with others. The liturgical dynamics of the Psalms show us that biblical worship sees the disparate times, places, and experiences of our lives pulled together into the moment, site, and community of God's salvific work. The Psalms can be our model both in maintaining these deep connections in our worship and in beginning to shift from mere anticipation to a more robust participation: "Given the new reality ushered in by Christ's work on the cross and his ongoing high priestly role, the act of Christian worship takes on a new significance—not as an *anticipation* of a future fulfillment, but as a *participation* in a heavenly reality."[30] "Then" becomes "now," "there" enters "here," and "they" merges into "we."

Historic Baptist Worship Today

While we might consider only some churches and some traditions within Christianity as "liturgical," it should be clear that all churches have liturgy. All churches worship with their own sense of order, structure, and routine. The question is not whether a church will be liturgical but to what degree a church will reflect on and take into consideration the deep foundations, rhythms, and structures that undergird its worship habits. For some very important historical reasons, Baptists are among the churches most resistant to valuing liturgy per se. Indeed, Baptist worship from its earliest generations sought freedom from the liturgical impositions of Catholicism and Anglicanism.[31] At this point in the movement's life, however, Baptists must look forward rather than backward and take

---

[30] Cameron Jorgenson, "The Missional Shape of Liturgy," in Derek C. Hatch and Rodney Wallace Kennedy, *Gathering Together: Baptists at Work in Worship* (Eugene, OR: Pickwick, 2013), 139.

[31] It should be noted, however, that early Baptists valued communal worship greatly and esteemed it to be the primary means of spiritual formation in the life of the believer. Cf. Philip E. Thompson, "Practicing the Freedom of God: Formation in Early Baptist Life," in David M. Hammond, ed., *Theology and Lived Christianity*, Annual Publication of the College Theology Society, vol. 45 (Mystic, CT: Twenty-Third Publications/Bayard, 2000), 119–38.

responsibility for the challenges of their own day. Baptists can no longer consider themselves a marginalized movement or persecuted religious minority. The question of free worship has a whole new orientation. We must ask ourselves to what end or for what good should our freedom aim. In other words, whereas Baptist worship was once defined as freedom *from*, it should now be marked by freedom *for*. In what follows, I will make a case regarding the aim of free worship in Baptist life. I believe the guiding values of Baptist life and the best of the Baptist movement can be enhanced and furthered by a more reflective, theological, and missional engagement with the latent liturgical character of our worship.

Before making my constructive proposal, I need to offer one important clarification. There are a number of thoughtful and winsome advocates in Baptist life that argue eloquently for a reengagement among Baptists with the liturgical treasures of the broader Christian tradition.[32] These voices have reinvigorated a helpful conversation about the long-term health and fidelity of Baptist worship, and we are in their debt. I do not presume to understand fully the intentions of their work, but in my estimation most of these efforts focus on bringing Baptist expressions of worship into closer alignment with the more established traditions of Catholicism, Orthodoxy, and Anglicanism. They see something significant missing from Baptist worship and advocate greater conformity with the historic and universal church.

My proposal, on the other hand, does not envisage conformity as the primary goal of worship renewal. Consistency, rather than conformity, should be our aim.[33] I reject conformity as a model on at least two

---

[32] Steven R. Harmon, *Baptist Identity and the Ecumenical Future: Story, Tradition, and the Recovery of Community* (Waco, TX: Baylor University Press, 2016); Anthony R. Cross and Philip E. Thompson, *Baptist Sacramentalism* (Carlisle, UK/Waynesboro, GA: Paternoster, 2003); Stanley Keith Fowler, *More Than a Symbol: The British Baptist Recovery of Baptismal Sacramentalism* (Carlisle, UK: Paternoster, 2002); Paul S. Fiddes, *Tracks and Traces: Baptist Identity in Church and Theology* (Carlisle, UK: Paternoster, 2003); Harvey, *Can These Bones Live?*

[33] With appreciation for Curtis Freeman's efforts toward articulating a "contesting catholicity" for Baptists, this essay offers a more qualified picture of continuity with the past. Here the aim is honest and earnest efforts toward consistency with the best of the Christian tradition. In other words, we want more

grounds. First, one tradition cannot conform to another, because both are in fact evolving in time and along separate trajectories. The image of *the* Catholic or historic church is something of a fabrication in its own right. There are many different expressions of Catholicism, for instance, that vary from place to place and over time. The plurality of such expressions makes conformity a particularly difficult and moving target. Second, conformity is antithetical to the spirit of Baptist life and worship. Making conformity our aim opens us to theological or historical idolatry. Conformity is not the Baptist way and puts inappropriate limits on our goal of a more faithful expression of what God's Word teaches. Also, conformity would never make sense in a Baptist (i.e., historically nonconformist) model. Seeking consistency or a measured continuity, however, allows for free worship to flourish. While conformity places an undue, perhaps impossible, burden on us to re-create or emulate worship expressions incongruous with Baptist life, we should increasingly look for, highlight, and enhance those ways in which Baptist worship already or minimally participates in aspects of historic and universal Christian worship.[34] Conformity would be a fool's errand, but consistency is a responsibility we might be able to fulfill, for the continued health and flourishing of the Baptist movement.

In what follows I offer four brief proposals that seek to make use of the liturgical resources of the Christian tradition for the renewal of Baptist worship today. They are not to be seen as direct implications of

---

continuity than divergence, more commonality than novelty, and more coherence than innovation. Baptist worship should seek to be, in the main, recognizable to all Christians on the essentials of Christian worship and fidelity to Word and sacrament, which is admittedly a tall order for many Baptist churches today. See Freeman, *Contesting Catholicity*, x–xi, 18–20. Freeman is, however, not the primary voice against which this chapter seeks to distinguish itself. For a more straightforward call to retrieval in the tradition see Harmon, *Towards Baptist Catholicity*, 151–77.

[34] For another proposal regarding a *via media* between replicating the past and renouncing it altogether, consider Bruce Ellis Benson's thoughtful deployment of "improvisation" as a category for understanding the give-and-take with tradition in contemporary worship. See Bruce Ellis Benson, *Liturgy as a Way of Life: Embodying the Arts in Christian Worship* (Grand Rapids: Baker Academic, 2013).

what Scripture teaches about worship. Yet, in light of our reconsideration of the Psalms, these proposals need not be seen as departures from or impositions on the character of biblical worship. They issue from ministry experience, and in that way are the product of pastoral improvisation and all-too-human efforts at reinvigorating Baptist churches of which I have been a part.

In each instance, my proposals seek to contextualize the liturgical resources of Christianity to meet the needs of real Baptist congregations today. Such efforts have been undertaken for the sake of greater consistency with signature Baptist principles such as congregational vitality, biblical authority, and gospel centrality.[35] These principles identify the markers of healthy worship in the Baptist tradition.[36] We should not draw upon historical or cross-cultural resources merely for the sake of nostalgia or novelty, but rather to advance strategic evangelistic and pastoral aims. If such renewal efforts do not help us be more faithful to the gospel and the Word of God, they are ultimately of no use to us. Therefore, these proposals should be accepted only if they extend the renewal called for by the Reformation and help Baptists pursue greater fidelity to the whole biblical gospel in our worship.

Whole-Gospel Witness

As much as Baptists consider themselves to be people of the Book, the paucity of Scripture found in many Baptist services today is almost

---

[35] As he envisions the future of Baptist worship, Ellis, "Baptists in Britain," 572, aims in a similar direction: "Yet an awareness of Baptist spirituality, with its concern for devotional warmth, relevant preaching, and freedom in community, will need to offer a critique of future developments as Baptists continue to prize relevance in worship as a priority for missionary congregations."

[36] These proposals are meant to align closely with all that is affirmed in the document "Evangelical Baptist Catholicity: A Manifesto," especially arts. 2, 3, 7, 8, and 10. See R. Lucas Stamps and Matthew Y. Emerson, "Evangelical Baptist Catholicity: A Manifesto," The Center for Baptist Renewal, accessed June 1, 2018, http://www.centerforbaptistrenewal.com/evangelical-baptist-catholicity-a -manifesto.

scandalous. While Scripture certainly supports nearly everything that happens in such services, it is rare to find significant portions of Scripture being read aloud in worship. Baptists would do well to restore such readings to their services in ways that parallel the practices of other traditions. In other more liturgically rich services we find readings of extended passages from the Old Testament and the New Testament in addition to the reading of the sermon text. While many informal prayers and liturgical cues involve direct reference to or even quotations of Scripture, nothing substitutes for a clear and confident reading of an extended passage of God's Word. We cannot consider ourselves those who truly celebrate the revelation of God in the holy Scripture if we fail to put that Word on public display in our services with regularity and consistency.

It should be noted that, alongside the sermon(s) in the secret worship meetings of the early General Baptists, the reading of Scripture was the most prominent feature of the liturgy. Of course, some will consider this portion of the service to be less than ideal for encouraging congregational participation, but that would be shortsighted. Once the regular reading of Scripture, especially longer portions of it, becomes a part of Baptist worship services, congregations will embrace the opportunity to hear from God's Word each week and also have opportunity to meditate upon and more fully grasp it. Of all the practices of other traditions, it seems Baptists are most suited to embrace the call and response that follows Scripture reading in other denominations:

Leader: "This is the Word of the Lord."
Congregation: "Thanks be to God."

By this simple congregational affirmation, all those gathered in the public service can affirm to themselves and to one another in the presence of Almighty God that they indeed receive and embrace his Word afresh. Of course, the specific text of such an affirmation matters less than the clear, concerted effort of the gesture. This rhythm of acknowledging, approving, and affirming the veracity and strength of God's Word can be a source of spiritual renewal for God's people. Though relatively small in terms of adjusting contemporary services, the initiative to restore public readings of Scripture to Baptist worship represents a major step toward healthier worship.

Whole-Gospel Structure

Every service has a liturgy, and every liturgy tells a story.[37] Each liturgy is arranged and sequenced by a set of assumptions about what constitutes proper and orderly worship for God's people. Even the most seemingly arbitrary arrangement of worship elements in the free church tradition demonstrates a set of theological assumptions about how worship should unfold and proceed. In this way, every liturgy relates a narrative of God's meeting with his people.[38] Inevitably there is a beginning, a middle with some sense of climax, and an ending. If a narrative approach seems contrived, it may be that our worship has become so routine that we have lost sight of the underlying order and rationale that determines what is included.[39] Whether or not we recognize it, the sequence is significant. The ordering of our services implies a strong sense of priority within the relationship of each element to the others.

At the risk of sounding simplistic about a complex history, many Baptist services follow a revivalist narrative that highlights the altar call

---

[37] Here I am indebted to Bryan Chapell's *Christ-Centered Worship* and his careful work of establishing liturgy as essentially narratival. See Bryan Chapell, *Christ-Centered Worship: Letting the Gospel Shape Our Practice* (Grand Rapids: Baker Academic, 2009), 15–25; cf. Cosper, *Rhythms of Grace*, 117–50.

[38] Gerrit Immink explains this dynamic in terms of worship's "agenda and script." See F. Gerrit Immink, *The Touch of the Sacred: The Practice, Theology, and Tradition of Christian Worship* (Grand Rapids: Eerdmans, 2014), 10–22.

[39] On the relationship of theology and worship, consider the account given in Reinhard Hütter, "Hospitality and Truth: The Disclosure of Practices in Worship and Doctrine," in Miroslav Volf and Dorothy C. Bass, eds., *Practicing Theology: Beliefs and Practices in Christian Life* (Grand Rapids: Eerdmans, 2002). A similar perspective informs Van Dyk's project of inviting theologians to reflect liturgically in Leanne Van Dyk, ed., *A More Profound Alleluia: Theology and Worship in Harmony*, Calvin Institute of Christian Worship Liturgical Studies (Grand Rapids: Eerdmans, 2005).

as the climax of worship. There are, however, other stories to tell. Without dismissing the immensely significant legacy of revivalism within Baptist life, it is worth pondering whether this model should be the exclusive one. Even a quick historical survey will indicate that Baptist worship differed from this model before and after the Second Great Awakening. It seems somewhat counterproductive to structure the entire service of worship around the hoped-for response of a few. We should at least consider a story that speaks to the majority of the congregation more fully.[40]

Naturally, the story that best serves the gathered believers and the lost in their midst is the gospel itself, for we all benefit from revisiting the gospel together. So, we should aim for a liturgical structure that includes as much of the following as possible: acknowledging the holiness of the God who made us, recognizing our own sin in light of his transcendent perfection, announcing and receiving the free grace of Christ offered in his sacrifice on our behalf, and accepting his commission to go and make disciples of all peoples.

Invocation and Adoration: The beginning of every service of Christian worship should not only involve a welcome for those gathered but also demonstrate hospitality for the presence of God in their midst.

Confession and Assurance: When we have confessed our sins, we are eager to hear God's word of pardon and assurance of his grace. Only the word of Christ's forgiveness can empower us to worship with and minister to one another in that space.

Word and Table: Having seen God for who he truly is, recognizing ourselves as having fallen short of his glory but having received afresh his word of pardon, we are ready to receive the nourishment of his Word and Table anew.

Affirmation of Faith: Once we have received the nourishment of God's Word and his Table, we respond by affirming our faith afresh

---

[40] Paul Basden, "'Something Old, Something New': Worship Styles for Baptists in the Nineties," in Furr and Freeman, *Ties That Bind*, 188, reflects on the lineage of stylistic trends in Baptist worship and concludes: "More than anything else, the purpose of worship determines the style of worship. Once a congregation decides its reason for gathering together on the Lord's Day, the style of worship will follow."

through corporate declaration of our doctrinal essentials (best articulated by the historic and ecumenical creeds) and corporate prayer for the needs of our community and our world.

Commission and Blessing: Lastly, we are sent as Christ's ambassadors back into the world. Instead of placing the burden to recall the fullness of the story on the sermon alone, we can seek to believe this story in its fullness throughout the service of worship itself.

Whole-Gospel Response

We need to go deeper on one embedded aspect of the gospel structure above. No doubt, many Baptists fear that a departure from a revivalistic structure for worship would mean a loss of gospel centrality in their gatherings. That would be a tragic loss indeed. To prevent such a loss, I would encourage Baptists to prioritize a weekly practice of the Lord's Table. If done well and supported by careful biblical and theological teaching, a weekly observance of the Lord's Table could create an opportunity for everyone to respond to the proclamation of the good news every week. In many instances of Baptist worship, only those willing to dedicate or rededicate their lives to Christ are called to respond fully to the preached Word. This represents a grave and worrying missed opportunity.

Every believer needs to be exhorted and encouraged to trust the gospel afresh *and to be given* the opportunity for an embodied response in worship.[41] The best of the Baptist tradition upholds this simple and essential conviction for true worship. Christ has imparted two ordinances for his body to practice in its times together. We would love to have cause to practice believer's baptism in every gathering of worship, so why do

---

[41] James K. A. Smith, foreword to Benson, *Liturgy as a Way*, 9–10, reflects perceptively: "Over the past couple of centuries, the church's worship—perhaps especially in Protestant evangelicalism—unwittingly mimicked the rationalism (and dualism) of modernity. . . . The metaphysics of modernity flattens the world, reducing human persons to information processors. And if we buy into this, we will 'worship' accordingly. The didactic will trump the affective; the intellect will crowd out the imagination; the body will be present as only a vehicle to get the mind in the pew. Welcome to the cathedral of Descartes."

we forsake practicing the other ordinance via such infrequent participation? The time has come to recover this biblical practice and restore it to the life of Baptist worship. At this point, it seems farfetched to suppose a regular practice of the Lord's Table would be in imitation of Catholic practice. Instead, we are missing out on the very evangelistic witness of the Table, for our regular practice of the Supper proclaims Christ's death and resurrection until he comes again (1 Cor 11:26). Of course, keen pastoral wisdom must be exercised in administration of the Table. Seekers should not be allowed to participate in the Table until they have trusted Christ for salvation and been baptized. But going forward with those receiving the bread and the cup might give seekers opportunity to receive prayer and counsel and then to trust Christ. We should not neglect or be embarrassed at this biblical practice, but instead trust that the Lord will use it more fully in our lives and the lives of those visiting our gatherings.

Whole-Gospel Hope

The Baptist movement has been marked by an abiding anticipation of Christ's return. We see this most readily in the origins of Baptist witness and Baptists' willingness to suffer persecution and marginalization for the sake of their convictions. In addition, the great missionary zeal that marks Baptist life evinces an awareness of living in the last days and the responsibility to pursue God's harvest in the time we have here. While these and other aspects of Baptist life indicate an eschatological focus, we could do more to see this abiding hope held up and promoted in our times of worship. We must embody more fully the prophetic witness of holy Scripture concerning the nature of our Christian hope. Namely, we must seek to give a balanced perspective on the reasons for this hope, for we look forward to Christ's return not only in anticipation of being fully with him but also to find relief and deliverance from the evils of this present age.

Today, it seems many Baptists are more at home in the world than were our historical forebears or are our brothers and sisters in the persecuted church. We would do well to embrace more forms of solidarity with the persecuted, the forgotten, and the oppressed in Christ's global church. Such efforts would necessarily involve forms of lament in our worship. We must acknowledge the powers and principalities of evil alongside the call to confess our individual sins (Eph 6:12). We need a thick language of description in our worship that gives a more comprehensive account of how broken the world actually is. When we are able to lament deeply, we open up new avenues to hope in Christ more fully. We will not celebrate our blessed hope with all the vigor and joy it invites without doing the hard work of facing and confronting the very real evils that plague our world today.

For such an outward-facing church movement, we spend far too little of our time together in prayer for the world, our country, or our neighborhoods. In this country, we are blessed to behold the amazing witness of the African American church tradition and its flourishing amid great suffering and injustice. We think of the amazing gospel songs and spirituals the African American church has given the world, and we must at the same time acknowledge that the beautiful hope embodied in these songs was birthed in a centuries-long, institutionalized, and economically incentivized evil. Out of the genocide, oppression, and exploitation of this community has come one of the most vibrant and life-giving expressions of Christianity in recent history. We do well to remember its sacrifice and learn from its indelible witness. To incorporate its earnest anticipation of Christ's reign and the deliverance of his saints would go a long way toward renewing Baptist worship today. Our worship needs to include dedicated times of lament and confession for systemic injustices in the world around us. Such an acknowledgment would then subtly frame the kingdom focus of our worship and help to maintain our priority for a heavenly citizenship above any citizenship of this world. Our songs and prayers would then cease to sound sentimental and trite but instead would demonstrate the biblical groaning so characteristic of the saints' song in the book of Revelation (chap. 5).

Conclusion

The simplicity and spontaneity of Baptist worship has often felt so fresh and freeing that we have been tempted to think of it as self-originating and wholly independent. Of course, it is not. Baptist worship issues from specific places and times. More than that, it has been animated, guided, and interrogated along the way by God's Word. We also find over and over that we are not the first to pursue such renewal—there is a great cloud of witnesses that has gone before us. We would do well to mend these connections today, for the sake not only of honoring Christ and his church but also of guarding our hearts in faithful worship and protecting our witness. Many streams of the Christian tradition hold up the historical maxim "*lex oriandi; lex credendi*," which translates loosely as "the rule of prayer determines the rule of faith." In other words, how we pray (and worship) affects and guides what we actually hold dear and depend on in our faith. Baptists need to acknowledge this reality.

Admittedly, the social, political, and cultural conditions surrounding Baptist churches today do not parallel closely those of the early church nor those immediately following the Reformation, but this is an encouraging sign that the movement is still advancing. In light of how far our missionary endeavors have taken us, we must develop a greater repository of faithful liturgical roots for our worship today. Such a cloud of witnesses should include a variety of brothers and sisters from past generations, different contexts, and distinct expressions. The Christian tradition will not choke out the rooted convictions of Baptist distinctives but rather will enrich the ground in which our simplicity and spontaneity might flourish anew.

8

Baptists, Baptism, and the Christian Tradition

MATTHEW Y. EMERSON

Oklahoma Baptist University

Introduction

Is it even possible to talk about "Baptist catholicity" or Baptists in relation to the Christian tradition when it comes to the theology and practice of baptism? Many, Baptists and non-Baptists alike, would answer
this question in the negative. From the perspective of many Baptists,
credobaptism[1] is the most important piece of evidence when arguing
that tradition is not in any sense authoritative. From the standpoint of
paedobaptists,[2] on the other hand, credobaptism is clear evidence that
Baptists and other baptistic traditions have erroneously followed their
own idiosyncratic interpretive maneuvers instead of understanding
Scripture in light of the rule of faith and the weight of tradition.

In contrast to both of these negative replies, this chapter seeks to
answer the opening question in the affirmative. Rather than seeing the
theology and practice of credobaptism as a departure from tradition, this

---

[1] The term *credobaptism* refers to the belief that baptism is reserved for
confessing believers and therefore not applicable to infants or very young children.

[2] The term *paedobaptism* refers to the belief that the children of confessing
Christian parents should be baptized, either in infancy or when the parents convert
to Christianity.

chapter will argue that credobaptism was seen by early Baptists as—and that it remains—a *recognition* and *restoration* of the most biblically faithful aspects of previous theologies of baptism. Credobaptism also represents a *reformation* of theologies and practices of baptism that preceded the early Baptists. While this argument could be made from a variety of perspectives—biblical, theological, or historical—due to the nature of this volume we will focus our attention on the historical perspective.

Our main goal is to demonstrate that early Baptists, and by extension their theological heirs, viewed credobaptism as reforming the Christian tradition of baptism, not as an outright rejection of that tradition. We will do so by examining the confessional statements of various early Baptists, noting the primary means by which they connected their theology and practice of baptism to the Christian tradition, and also their primary points of departure from it. We limit our inquiry to confessional statements: first, because of limited space; and second, because they indicate a kind of baseline consensus among different individual Baptists. We will argue that the early Baptists viewed credobaptism in continuity with the Christian tradition with respect to its covenantal symbolism, its signification of union with Christ and membership in his church, and its necessity for participation in the Lord's Supper. Early Baptists viewed credobaptism as reforming the Christian tradition with respect to the proper subjects and the mode of baptism.

Baptist Recognition of the Great Tradition on Baptism

Early Baptists did not see themselves as radically departing from the Christian tradition as a whole or the tradition on baptism in particular. Rather, in each of these cases they saw themselves like the rest of the Reformers and Reformational movements saw themselves—retaining what was biblical, rejecting what was not, and reforming doctrine and practice that had biblical warrant but had developed unbiblical aspects. While the magisterial Reformers focused on soteriology and, to an extent, ecclesiology, the so-called radical Reformers, including English

Baptists and biblical Anabaptists on the continent,[3] felt that Calvin, Luther, Zwingli, and their heirs had not sufficiently reformed regarding ecclesiology, especially in three primary areas: baptism, polity, and the relationship between church and state. These are intertwined, as they are concerned at the individual, local, and state levels with what is variously called personal responsibility before God or freedom of conscience.[4]

These two phrases indicate two sides of the same coin, namely, that the individual, and by extension the local church comprising believing individuals, is personally responsible before God for his thoughts and actions and thus should not be coerced by others in his beliefs or religious practices. On an individual level, this means the decision to repent of one's sins and trust in the saving work of Christ for deliverance is the responsibility of the individual and the individual alone. Because that act of repentance and faith is the means by which one enters into the new covenant, and because baptism is the sign of the new covenant, only those who make conscious professions of faith should be baptized. Ecclesiological corollaries to this foundational commitment relate to local church governance and religious liberty, but our focus will remain

---

[3] I refer specifically here to "biblical Anabaptists" rather than to "radical Reformers" as a whole in order to (1) acknowledge the variety within the radical Reformation and(2) distinguish biblical Anabaptists, including the Swiss Brethren and German Anabaptists such as Balthasar Hubmaier, from some of the more charismatic and radical Anabaptists such as Thomas Müntzer. The latter and his ilk were as much concerned with political revolution as they were with biblical reformation, while the former had more modest aims with respect to continuing the Reformation in the area of ecclesiology. Additionally, the so-called *Schwarmerei* were rooted in the experientialist movements of the late Middle Ages, while the biblical Anabaptists were more akin to the magisterial Reformers in their respect for Scripture's ultimate authority and the importance of the Christian tradition.

[4] This conviction has taken on a variety of manifestations in Baptist life, including shifts in both terminology and meaning. I use the more generic phrases "personal responsibility before God" and "freedom of conscience" to avoid identifying the core affirmation of this teaching with any of its particular manifestations throughout Baptist history, including "soul freedom," "soul liberty," or the like.

on the individual level and the sign of entrance into God's new covenant, baptism.

A survey of early Baptist confessions[5] will demonstrate a fundamental commitment both to (1) recovering and reforming baptismal theology and practice in a way that reflects biblical teaching and (2) retaining continuity with the Christian tradition on baptism where it exists. Before we turn to the various early Baptists and baptistic traditions, we need briefly to explore the theology and practice of baptism prior to their reform of it.

A Brief History of Baptism[6]

Baptism has been important to Christian doctrine and piety since the apostles. The New Testament provides a number of avenues for understanding baptism, from the historical realities of John the Baptist and Jesus in the Gospels and the earliest church in Acts to the theology and practice of baptism outlined in the Epistles and Revelation. The earliest church viewed baptism as integral to the Christian life, as evidenced in part by the instructions of the *Didache*: baptism is required for participation in the Lord's Supper (*Did.* 9.5), and the person being baptized is to fast and be tested (presumably in a manner anticipating the later use of written creeds) beforehand (*Did.* 7).

According to Gregg Allison, early Christians viewed baptism as serving "six purposes: the forgiveness of sins; deliverance from death;

---

[5] In addition to my own survey of early Baptist confessions, I rely on the work of Fowler, *More Than a Symbol*; and Riker, *Catholic Reformed Theologian*. While Fowler notes many of the historical sources included here, the argument of his book differs from the argument of this chapter, in that Fowler seeks to recover something he calls "baptismal sacramentalism," whereas I aim to demonstrate the continuity of credobaptism with the rest of the Christian tradition. In other words, our goals are different. I also find Fowler's definition of "baptismal sacramentalism" to be too close to baptismal regeneration. Riker's chapter on Keach's view of baptism will be used in my section on Keach. My argument could be considered a summary of Riker's in service of the larger argument of this chapter.

[6] For a comprehensive study of baptism in the early church see Everett Ferguson, *Baptism in the Early Church: History, Theology, and Liturgy in the First Five Centuries* (Grand Rapids: Eerdmans, 2009).

regeneration, or the new birth; the gift of the Holy Spirit; the renunciation of Satan; and identification with Jesus Christ."[7] Each of these was
understood to have biblical support. In Acts the "forgiveness of sins"
and the gift of the Holy Spirit are both closely associated, narratively
speaking, with faith and baptism;[8] deliverance from death finds a conceptual parallel with baptism in Rom 6:1–4; regeneration and baptism
are linked in Titus 3:5, and possibly John 3:5; and union with Christ
(and thus implicitly renunciation of Satan) is associated with baptism
in Rom 6:1–4.[9] Additionally—and in part because the early church
increasingly came to believe baptism was required for salvation and
effected *saving* grace in the person baptized—a number of adjustments
to the practice of baptism occurred. These included consecrating the
water, anointing the person being baptized with oil, laying hands on
the person being baptized, and requiring *catechesis* (up to two years) of
the person before baptism.[10]

Many aspects of the baptismal theology and practice noted above
seem to *imply* the person being baptized is an adult. Forgiveness of sins
is closely associated with conscious faith in the New Testament (e.g.,
Romans 10); renunciation of Satan by the person being baptized would
imply the ability of the individual to renounce; and *catechesis* implies the
person being baptized is able to recite and, at least rudimentarily, understand the catechism. In the early church, however, infant baptism quickly
became the norm. Origen (third cent.) cites the aforementioned necessity of baptism for salvation as a reason to baptize infants as quickly as

---

[7] Gregg R. Allison, *Sojourners and Strangers: The Doctrine of the Church*,
Foundations of Evangelical Theology (Wheaton, IL: Crossway, 2012), 325. Allison
cites Tertullian, *Against Marcion* 1.28, for the first four purposes. In support of the
latter two, he cites Tetullian, *The Shows*, and Basil the Great, *On the Spirit* 15.35, in
Gregg R. Allison, *Historical Theology* (Grand Rapids: Zondervan, 2011), 614–15.

[8] See Robert Stein, "Baptism in Luke-Acts," in Thomas R. Schreiner and
Shawn D. Wright, eds., *Believer's Baptism: Sign and Seal of the New Covenant in
Christ*, NAC Studies in Bible & Theology (Nashville: B&H Academic, 2006),
35–66, esp. 47–56.

[9] Allison discusses the link between Titus 3:5; John 3:5, and regeneration in
Sojourners and Strangers, 325.

[10] Allison, 326.

possible;[11] Cyprian (third cent.) says likewise,[12] as does Augustine (fifth cent.).[13] The oft-mentioned dissent of Tertullian to paedobaptism (*On Baptism* 18) is evidence that at least some Christians were already practicing paedobaptism by the end of the second century.[14] Tertullian's dissent comes on the grounds that children should be able to assent to the faith and consciously acknowledge and repent of their sins before being baptized.[15] Despite Tertullian's objections, it is clear the theology and practice of baptism turned to paedobaptism and to sacerdotalism[16] regarding its effects and necessity by the fifth century at the very latest.[17]

The Reformers firmly rejected the soteriological aspect of the late patristic and medieval theology of baptism. The Reformation thus affected baptismal views primarily with respect to the doctrine of salvation. Instead

---

[11] Allison, 327–28, citing Origen, *Homilies on the Gospel of Luke*, 14:5.

[12] Allison, 328, citing Cyprian, *Letters*, 58.2; 58.5.

[13] Allison, 328–29, citing Augustine, *On Marriage and Concupiscence*, 2.51, and *On Original Sin*, 21.

[14] Allison points out that there may be an even earlier reference to paedobaptism in Irenaeus, *Against Heresies* 2.22.4, where he references infants' being "born again of God." Allison, *Sojourners and Strangers*, 327n32, notes, though, that this is ambiguous.

[15] On Tertullian's view of baptism, see the discussion in Ferguson, *Baptism in the Early Church*, 336–50. Tertullian's reluctance to baptize infants is born out of a strong tie between the practice and repentance and faith, as well as Tertullian's insistence that Christian preaching brings about conversion and thus the necessity for baptism. Regarding the latter, infants cannot understand or be catechized, and so they should not be baptized. There is also in Tertullian a fear of postbaptismal sin that influences his thought.

[16] By this term I am referencing the belief that the sacrament's efficacy is related to its proper administration by a priest. This does not mean that those who affirm this view believe the sacrament's efficacy is dependent on the merits of the priest; rather, it functions *ex opere operato*, or regardless of whether the priest is morally upright. Still, baptism's effect is dependent in a sacerdotal view on the right administration of the sacrament, which includes the proclamation of the Word in conjunction with it *and* its performance by an ordained priest. To put it slightly differently, the priest serves a mediatorial role between the grace of God and its effect on the persons receiving the sacrament.

[17] On baptism in the early church, especially with respect to the shift from adult baptism to infant baptism, see Steven A. McKinion, "Baptism in the Patristic Writings," in Schreiner and Wright, *Believer's Baptism*, 163–88.

of seeing infant baptism as the necessary removal of original sin through the administration of the sacrament by a priest, the Reformers insisted on justification by faith alone. Baptism was still the external sign of covenant inclusion, but faith alone (as opposed to faith in conjunction with works, i.e., the seven sacraments of the Roman Catholic Church) was the operating mechanism of justification, the "inner reality."

The so-called radical Reformers[18] and early English Baptists agreed with this soteriological Reformation, and with the magisterial Reformers' ecclesiological reforms at least with respect to their rejection of the papacy and the elevation of tradition as a parallel authority with Scripture. But it was precisely in regard to this latter issue, the sufficiency of Scripture and its authority over tradition, that the radical Reformers and early English Baptists felt the magisterial Reformers had not gone far enough in their reformation project. Ecclesiologically, the theology and practice of baptism, church polity, and the relationship between church and state still needed reformation. Luther, Zwingli, and Calvin all give biblical grounds for retaining infant baptism.[19] Zwingli additionally mentions that rejecting infant baptism would (further?) divide the church.[20] Perhaps also the political climate of the late sixteenth and seventeenth centuries, in which Roman Catholic and Protestant governments were at war with each other, contributed to a premature ecclesiological halt in the Reformation

---

[18] Anecdotally, it appears many non-Baptists are under-informed about Baptist origins. Often the term "radical Reformers" is used without further distinction between the so-called biblical Anabaptists, spiritualist Anabaptists, and rationalist Anabaptists. Both modern Anabaptists and other baptistic denominations that claim Anabaptists as their forebearers do so almost exclusively in relation to biblical Anabaptists. As is often the case in polemical theology, though—and again, I am speaking anecdotally—the spiritualist Anabaptists, who were often much more radical in their politics and theology, are used as foils to paedobaptist and/or non-free-church positions. To state the point succinctly, Thomas Müntzer should not be taken as the radical Reformer exemplar; Balthasar Hubmaier and the Swiss Brethren (George Blaurock, Felix Manz, and Conrad Grebel, disciples of Huldrych Zwingli) would be more appropriate exemplars.

[19] On Luther, see Allison, *Sojourners and Strangers*, 330. On Zwingli, see Allison, 330–32. On Calvin, see Allison, 334–35.

[20] Allison, 331.

project. Whatever the reason, the Reformers did not reform baptism beyond rejecting its soteriological efficacy. The radical Reformers and early English Baptists saw a need for further reform. It is to them we now turn. Here our goal is primarily to demonstrate these groups' explicit desire for catholicity regarding baptism, rather than providing a description of their theology/ies of baptism.

Biblical Anabaptists

We take as our focal point in examining Anabaptists the confessions of one type of Anabaptist, the so-called biblical Anabaptists.[21] Melchior Hoffman and other spiritual Anabaptists, who tended to eschew authority and rely on ecstatic experiences, are often regarded today as exemplary of Anabaptism. But there is a fairly clear divide between biblical and spiritual Anabaptists, and it is the biblical variety we will discuss. There are at least two reasons for narrowing our focus to this specific group. First, and most importantly, the first group of General Baptists, led by Thomas Helwys, was in contact with biblical Anabaptists in Holland. John Smyth had originally brought the group to the Netherlands but then encountered and eventually attempted to join the Waterlander Mennonites. This led to another group in the church departing from Smyth and his remaining followers and returning to England under the leadership of Helwys as Baptists.

The Waterlanders wrote their own confessions, one in 1577 and a second version in 1580 or 1581. The impetus for writing lay in some

---

[21] Some Baptist historians would argue Anabaptists should not be considered in an essay of this nature, where our question is whether *Baptist* theologies of baptism are catholic. I include them here for two reasons. First, the question is with respect to credobaptism per se, not just about institutionally Baptist theologies of baptism. In that respect, we must consider Anabaptist theologies of baptism because they are the earliest known instances of credobaptism since the patristic era. Second, with respect to mode, even though Anabaptists used affusion rather than immersion, and some Baptists would therefore conclude that their method was still not baptism per se, the question of catholicity is primarily with respect to the nature of and qualifications for the person baptized.

developments in Menno Simons's thought. Simons, credited with organizing and leading north German Anabaptists after Melchior Hoffman's
disciples failed in their Anabaptist rebellion at Münster, became increasingly rigid in his understanding of church discipline and Hoffmanite in
his Christology.[22] At the same time, Faustus Socinus led a group of Polish
Mennonites to reject classic Christology and classic Trinitarianism. The
group of Mennonites that Simons had previously led to the Netherlands
fractured into four groups based on their response to these developments.
The Waterlanders rejected Hoffmanite Christology and the rigid discipline (i.e., immediate excommunication for egregious sins) of Simons
and wrote their confession of faith to make their positions clear on these
issues and to demonstrate the continuity of their thought with other
Protestants. Significantly, John Smyth asked for the 1580 confession to
be employed "to test the agreement of the English and the Mennonites."[23]
The Waterlander Confession was instrumental in John Smyth's thought.
While Smyth was not a Baptist for very long (if at all in the strict sense),
his life and thought stand at the fountainhead of early English Baptists,
even if sometimes in an antagonistic manner.

Another reason we should examine the biblical Anabaptists in particular is because of the thirty thousand Dutch exiles who had entered
England by 1562. According to Leonard and Lumpkin, "It is . . . certain
that Mennonites thronged to England as a refuge, and that they quietly
carried on their religious life for a time in the new land." But, as they
continue, "evidence is lacking that that they made many direct disciples
in England."[24] In other words, while we cannot say with certainty that
all of the Dutch refugees were biblical Anabaptists, or even Anabaptists,
nor can we prove any direct link between the Mennonite refugees and the
early English Baptists, we *can* say the rise of free church and credobaptist

---

[22] Hoffman supposedly taught that Christ appeared only in celestial flesh, not
in human flesh, thus reviving in some sense the Docetist heresy. See Lumpkin,
Baptist Confessions of Faith, 2nd rev. ed., 42.

[23] Lumpkin, 45.

[24] Lumpkin, 75.

positions happened fairly soon after the immigration of the Mennonite refugees to England.

Correlation does not equal causation, but we can at least note the proximity of Dutch migration to the rise of Baptist thought in England. For instance, as Leonard and Lumpkin note, Robert Browne's "pioneer experiment in congregationalism in 1580" happened in Norfolk County, a county recently overrun by Dutch artisans. And, after Browne's experiment failed, he fled to Holland. While his group disintegrated and he eventually conformed to the Church of England, another Separatist congregation formed in London by 1587 or 1588. This congregation elected Francis Johnson as pastor in 1592, but Johnson was arrested and most of the congregation fled to Amsterdam. (The reader should by now have noticed the continued back and forth between England and Holland and, perhaps, between English Separatists and Waterlander Mennonites.) There they elected Henry Ainsworth as pastor in 1595, and in 1596 they wrote A True Confession. This confession was subsequently used by the seven Particular Baptist Churches in London as a template for the First London Baptist Confession of Faith in 1644.

While this chain from Dutch Mennonites in Norfolk County to the First London Baptist Confession of Faith is much more tendentious than the explicit link between the Waterlander Confession and John Smyth's congregation in Holland, there is at least enough evidence to suggest the early English Baptists arose in a context where they would have been aware of biblical Anabaptist views.[25] Again, this is not to suggest direct influence of biblical Anabaptists on early English Baptists. That assumption is heavily contested in the scholarship on Baptist origins,[26] and we do not wish to assert it here. Our only aim is to say that, if we are to

---

[25] For this account see Lumpkin, 75–77.

[26] For discussion of Baptist origins, and particularly the relationship between Anabaptist thought and early English Baptist thought, see, for instance, Bebbington, *Baptists through the Centuries*, 25–41; Chute, Finn, and Haykin, *Baptist Story*, 11–20; Garrett, *Baptist Theology*, 8–16; and Roger G. Torbet, *A History of the Baptists*, 3rd ed. (Valley Forge, PA: Judson, 1963), 22–29. I tend to agree with Bebbington that "while there may be some verbal connection, there is no sign of any more substantial bond between the Anabaptists and the Particular Baptists.

examine a particular group of Anabaptists in relation to early English Baptist thought, it should be the biblical Anabaptists as exemplified by the Waterlander Mennonites.

We will consider here four Anabaptist confessions: the Schleitheim Confession (1527), Ridemann's *Rechenschaft* (1540), the Waterlander Confession (1580), and the Dordrecht Confession (1632). We have already given our rationale for considering the Waterlander Confession (WC) above. The Schleitheim Confession (SC) is the oldest known consensus Anabaptist document, while Ridemann's *Rechenschaft* (RR) and the Dordrecht Confession (DC) are generally acknowledged as significant, respectively, in early Anabaptist life (particularly in the Hutterite community) and in the modern American Mennonite movements.

Schleitheim states the following regarding baptism:

> First. Observe concerning baptism: Baptism shall be given to all those who have learned repentance and amendment of life, and who believe truly that their sins are taken away by Christ, and to all those who walk in the resurrection of Jesus Christ, and wish to buried with Him in death, so that they may be resurrected with him, and to all those who with this significance request it [baptism] of us and demand it for themselves. This excludes all infant baptism, the highest and chief abomination of the pope. In this you have the foundation and testimony of the apostles. Matthew 28, Mark 16, Acts 2, 8,16,19. This we wish to hold simply, yet firmly and with assurance.

We should also note the explicit mention of baptism as a prerequisite for being placed under the ban (SC 2) and for taking the Lord's Supper (SC 3). Additionally, SC articles 3 and 4 both reference renunciation of and separation from Satan, a common feature in Christian confessions and baptismal practices since the early church. Finally, SC exhibits a number of commonalities with other prior Christian confessions and Reformation documents, including the polemical statements about

---

There is greater scope for positing a link between the Anabaptists and the General Baptists" (31).

the pope, employed widely and liberally in most Reformation contexts (above, introduction, and SC 4); recourse to classical Christian doctrines such as divine immutability (SC 7); and reference to interpretive conclusions that reflect precritical hermeneutical methods (SC 6.3).

Rechenschaft is significant because it is one of the earliest Anabaptist documents to give a full, if attenuated, account of Anabaptist faith and practice. The earlier SC, as well as Hübmaier's Eighteen Dissertations (1524) and the Hutterite Discipline of the Church (1527), are mostly concerned with practical matters, even with respect to baptism, rather than with both doctrine and practice. *Rechenschaft* is comparatively significant in this regard. The confession begins by citing the Apostles' Creed (RR I.1), an important indication that the author saw himself and his Hutterite Anabaptist brethren in continuity with and dependent upon the Christian tradition, at least in terms of what we might call "primary doctrines." Regarding baptism (RR I.11), Ridemann states, "Baptism means the entrance into the covenant of grace of God and the incorporation into the Church of Christ. The 'right and necessary sequence is preaching, faith, rebirth, and baptism. Children cannot be baptized in the right way because they are not reborn through preaching, faith, and the Spirit.'"[27] Note the emphasis on covenant inclusion, ecclesial and Christological union, rebirth, and the work of the Spirit.

Waterlander, as Leonard and Lumpkin put it, is a "fairly elaborate and complete work."[28] It is thus one of the earliest Anabaptist confessions in the truest sense of the word; that is, it elaborates significantly on each doctrinal point and cites Scripture to support each of its stated beliefs. Waterlander begins with what can only be called a restatement, even a quotation, of the Christian tradition's consensus regarding theology proper and the doctrine of the Trinity, including references to the classic "incommunicable attributes" (e.g., eternity, omnipotence, immortality) in article I, to traditional Trinitarian distinctions with respect to the divine personal names in article II, and to the eternal relations of origin as the only biblically and dogmatically sufficient means of distinguishing

---

[27] As quoted in Lumpkin, *Baptist Confessions of Faith*, 2nd rev. ed., 41.
[28] Lumpkin, 45.

between the persons in article III.[29] Relatedly, article VIII relies on traditional language to describe the incarnation,[30] language reminiscent of Chalcedon (451) and the so-called *extra calvinisticum*.[31] Also exhibiting this kind of implicit catholicity are article XV on Christ's descent and resurrection and the use of the term "sacraments" to refer to baptism and the Lord's Supper (articles XXV, XXX–XXXIV). With respect to the latter, WC uses the traditional couplet of "external and visible actions" to signify the "internal and spiritual action [of] God" (article XXX).

Regarding baptism, WC XXXI addresses practice, particularly baptizing in the triune name and disallowing infant baptism. Article XXXII addresses "What Baptism Signifies Internally" and reads as follows:

> The whole action of external, visible baptism places before our eyes, testifies and signifies that Jesus Christ baptizes internally (Matt 3:11; John 1:33) a laver of regeneration (Eph 5:26; Titus 3:5) and renewing of the Holy Spirit, the penitent and believing man: washing away, through the virtue and merits of his poured out blood, all the spots and sins of the soul (1 John 1:7) and through the virtue and operation of the Holy Spirit, which is a true, heavenly (Isa 44:3; Ezek 36:27; Joel 2:28; John 7:38), spiritual and living water [washing away] the internal wickedness of the soul (1 Cor 6:11; Titus 3:5–7) and renders it heavenly (Phil 3:20), spiritual (Rom 8:9) and living (Eph 2:4, 5) in true righteousness and goodness. Moreover baptism directs us to Christ and his holy office by which in glory he performs that which he places before our eyes, and testifies concerning its consummation

---

[29] Lumpkin, 46–47.

[30] Lumpkin, 48.

[31] This term refers to the position that the incarnate Son remains omniscient, omnipresent, and omnipotent according to his divine nature while also becoming finite, locatable, and limited according to his human nature. Given that Calvin was writing around the same time, it is difficult to ascribe dependence in one direction or another here. In any case, the *extra calvinisticum* may more accurately be called the *extra patristicum* given the concept's ubiquity in the early church's Christological formulations. On this issue see Myk Habets, "Putting the 'Extra' Back into Calvinism," *SJT* 62, no. 4 (2009): 441–56.

in the hearts of believers and admonishes us that we should not cleave to external things, but by holy prayers ascend into heaven and ask from Christ the good indicated through it [baptism] (John 7:31): a good which the Lord Jesus graciously concedes and increases in the hearts of those who by true faith become partakers of the sacraments.

This article closely connects the external sign with the internal reality (both in its wording and in its repeated use of the term "sacraments"), and the realities signified by baptism are reminiscent of the six purposes for baptism in the early church as articulated by Allison. Like SC 3, WC XXXIII restricts participation in the Lord's Supper to those who have been baptized.

Similar signs of catholicity, both generally and with respect to baptism, are evident in DC. This "most influential of all Mennonite confessions"[32] draws on classic Christian language and scriptural citation for the doctrines of God and Christology (arts. I and IV), quotes the second article of the Apostles' Creed almost verbatim in describing the work of Christ (art. IV), uses the term "sacrament" (art. X), restricts the Lord's Supper to those who have been baptized (art. X),[33] and evidences continuity with the traditional "six purposes of baptism" in art. VIII.

Early English Baptists[34]

We are on much firmer footing when deciding which groups of early English Baptists to consider, since there are only two main streams: General and Particular. We will consider both of these groups below. First we will consider representative personal and corporate confessions

---

[32] Lumpkin, *Baptist Confessions of Faith*, 2nd rev. ed., 61.

[33] Article X restricts participation of the Lord's Supper to "the believer," but this is in all likelihood synonymous with "those who have been baptized," given the context and the reliance on previous Anabaptist documents.

[34] On baptism among seventeenth-century Baptists, including in creedal and confessional statements as well as in the thought of individual writers, see Fowler, *More Than a Symbol*, 10–32.

of General and Particular Baptists. Then we will consider the writings of Benjamin Keach. Although this is an exception to the confessional focus of the chapter, we include Keach because he was instrumental in the Particular Baptist movement in England and also influenced the wording of one of the most important early American Baptist confessions, the Philadelphia Confession of Faith (1742).

General Baptist Confessions

The first General Baptist confession comes from the group, led by Thomas Helwys, that broke from John Smyth's party in Holland.[35] While we could consider both Smyth's personal confession and his group's corporate confession, because of the ambiguity regarding their status as Baptists and because of the confessions' similarity to WC, we will begin with Helwys and his group. "A Declaration of Faith of English People Remaining at Amsterdam in Holland" was published in 1611 by Helwys on behalf of his group. The document is fairly brief, although that appears to have been common before the mid-1600s. The opening sections on theology proper and the Trinity are especially short, perhaps because the author assumed commonality with other Christian groups in that regard. More expansive articles appear related to Christology and ecclesiology. Regarding the former, the group may have sought to distinguish itself clearly from the Hoffmanite Christology prevalent in some Anabaptist movements and perhaps adopted by Smyth, while the latter section explains characteristic Baptist emphases such as congregational polity, believer's baptism, and participation in government. The main sign of catholicity, apart from the classic Christology evinced in article 8, is that the meanings of baptism and the Lord's Supper both are explained using classic "outward sign of invisible realities" language. Baptism in particular is "the outward manifestacion off dieing vnto sinn, and walkeing in newness off life" (art. 14).

---

[35] For an overview of English General Baptists, see Garrett, *Baptist Theology*, 23–50.

General Baptist churches in the Midlands formed the first General Baptist association in the mid-seventeenth century. At their meeting in 1651 they adopted The Faith and Practice of Thirty Congregations, apparently to combat opposition they were experiencing (from whom, it is not clear). Although there are seventy-five articles and a postscript, most of the articles are only one or two sentences long. In its brevity and its content, then, it has much in common with Helwys's A Declaration of Faith (1611). Interestingly, Faith and Practice is relatively unique among early Baptist confessions in that it hardly touches on the meaning of the ordinances (arts. 47–53) but instead focuses almost entirely on their proper recipients and modes. There is thus not much to say regarding catholicity and baptism with respect to this particular confession, other than that article 51 states, like the rest of the Christian tradition, that baptism signifies entrance into the visible church.

General Baptists in London, in view of the inroads of the Quaker movement, wrote their own confession in 1654, The True Gospel-Faith Declared According to the Scriptures. Significantly, "It is the first Baptist Confession to prescribe the laying on of hands for all baptized believers."[36] This practice provides a connection to early Christian practices related to baptism, which as we noted above included laying on hands by at least the fourth century. Additionally, article XII explicitly connects reception of the Spirit to the nexus of the "prayer of faith," baptism, and laying on hands.

The two best known General Baptist confessions from the seventeenth century are The Standard Confession (1660) and The Orthodox Creed (1678). The first, revised in 1663 and again by Thomas Grantham in 1678, exhibits the same kinds of statements about baptism as those found in The True-Gospel Faith, although in a more expansive manner. Once again we find a nexus of the "prayer of faith," baptism, laying on hands, and reception of the Spirit (art. XII). This confession also expressly commands baptism in the triune name (art. XI) and, like other confessions, ties baptism to a life of repentance and renunciation of fleshly desires and actions.

---

[36] Lumpkin, *Baptist Confessions of Faith*, 2nd rev. ed., 175.

Another General Baptist confession, the Orthodox Creed, was published in 1678 in response both to Matthew Caffyn's Hoffmanite Christology and increasingly Socinian views on the Trinity and to the publication of new confessions by the Particular Baptists. Written by Thomas Monck, the confession is more expansive than previous General Baptist confessions because of its explicitly antiheretical purpose. In other words, while earlier General Baptist confessions could be relatively brief in their articulations of the doctrines of God and Christ because of assumed common agreement, the Orthodox Creed by necessity is much longer. Articles I–VII cover theology proper, the Trinity, and Christology, and each article evidences classical Christian theism, classical Trinitarianism, and classical Christology. Classical concepts and grammar found in these sections include simplicity, "pure act," eternal relations of origin, reduplication, *communicatio idiomatum*, and Chalcedonian Christological formulations. The Orthodox Creed is also unique in its explicit affirmation and inclusion of the three ecumenical creeds (art. XXXVIII), although as previously noted other Baptist confessions drew on the language of the ecumenical creeds and councils in their doctrinal statements.[37]

The Orthodox Creed first addresses baptism with an article on it and the Lord's Supper as "sacraments" (art. XXVII). The initiatory ordinance is then described as a "sign of our entrance into the covenant of grace, and ingrafting into Christ, and into the body of Christ, which is his church; and of remission of sin in the blood of Christ, and of our fellowship with Christ, in his death and resurrection, and of our living, or rising, to newness of life" (art. XXVIII). This again accords with the six purposes of baptism in the early church delineated by Allison. Article XXVIII also commands baptism in the triune name, and its condemnation of infant baptism is repeatedly tied explicitly to Rome. Additionally, article XXXII once again ties together baptism, the prayer of faith, laying on of hands, and reception of the Spirit.

---

[37] For a discussion of what he describes as "vestiges" of patristic thought in early Baptist confessions, see Harmon, *Towards Baptist Catholicity*, 72–81.

Particular Baptist Confessions

While the Particular Baptist movement did not rise to public recognition until the 1630s,[38] and the first known Particular Baptist confession was not written until 1644, it is important to consider a confessional predecessor, written by Separatists with free church and baptistic convictions in 1596: A True Confession. This confession was written by the previously mentioned group of Separatist exiles in Holland and was used as a template by London Particular Baptists when they drafted the First London Baptist Confession of Faith (1644). A True Confession, like many of the others already mentioned, relies on classical theology proper, Trinitarianism, and Christology (arts. 2 and 9) and uses the term "sacraments" and the "external sign of an internal reality" formula to refer to baptism and the Lord's Supper (arts. 34–35). The description of the Lord's Supper prohibits participation of those who have not been baptized (art. 35).

The First London Baptist Confession of Faith (1644) evidences many of the same features as A True Confession. Classical definitions of theology proper (art. I), Trinitarianism (art. II), and Christology (art. IX) are used. The Calvinistic tendency of most Separatists is also on display, as in A True Confession. Additionally, First London's conclusion includes a strong statement on catholicity, noting the writers' epistemic humility and their desire to be united with all true Christians despite disagreements on baptism.[39] Unlike its predecessor, though, First London does not use the term "sacraments." Instead it repeatedly uses the term "ordinance"[40] to refer to baptism and the Lord's Supper. But in describing these two ordinances, First London uses the common language and concepts employed in other Baptist confessions and indeed in other Reformation documents. When speaking about baptism, article XL says that

---

[38] For an overview of English Particular Baptists, see Garrett, *Baptist Theology*, 51–108.

[39] See Lumpkin, *Baptist Confessions of Faith*, 2nd rev. ed., 136–37.

[40] The term "ordinance" is used in many of the other confessions discussed here, but usually in conjunction with "sacrament" and not in isolation.

it being a signe, must answer the thing signified, which are these: first, the washing the whole soule in the bloud of Christ. Secondly, that interest the Saints have in the death, burial, and resurrection; thirdly, together with a confirmation of our faith, that as certainly as the body is buried under water, and riseth againe, so certainly shall the bodies of the Saints be raised by the power of Christ, in the day of the resurrection, to reigne with Christ.[41]

This again accords with the six purposes for baptism in the early church noted by Allison.

Finally, Particular Baptists adopted a revision of the London Confession of Faith in 1689, commonly known as the Second London Confession of Faith (2LCF). This was due to a variety of factors, including the recently passed Edict of Toleration, but also because copies of the first iteration of the LCF were scant.[42] While the authors relied on what they could out of First London, they also appear to depend on the Savoy Confession and the Westminster Confession of Faith (WCF).[43] Second London, like its predecessor, contains an explicit call for catholicity, this time in the preface rather than the conclusion.[44] It again models this through, for instance, reliance on classical definitions of theology proper and Trinitarianism in chapter II and of Christology in VIII.2. In the latter case, it even quotes the Chalcedonian Definition (via quotation of WCF VIII.2). The Second London Confession also uses "reduplication" language in VIII.7.

---

[41] Lumpkin, *Baptist Confessions of Faith*, 2nd rev. ed., 155.

[42] Lumpkin, 217. On the relation of Particular Baptists to other Separatist and Reformed movements, as particularly evidenced in the writings of Hanserd Knollys, see Dennis Bustin, "Hanserd Knollys and the Formation of Particular Baptist Identity in Seventeenth-Century London," in Ian M. Randall, Toivo Pilli, and Anthony R. Cross, eds., *Baptist Identities: International Studies from the Seventeenth to the Twentieth Centuries*, Studies in Baptist History and Thought 19 (Milton Keyes, UK: Paternoster, 2006), 8–10.

[43] Lumpkin, B*aptist Confessions of Faith*, 2nd rev. ed., 218.

[44] Lumpkin, 226–27.

Chapters XXVIII, XXIX, and XXX deal with baptism and the Lord's Supper. Here again we see preference for "ordinance" rather than "sacrament" (art. XXIX), although there is a sacramental meaning attached to both.[45] The Second London Confession identifies baptism as a "sign of his [the believer's] fellowship with him [Christ], in his death, and resurrection; of his being engrafted into him; of remission of sins; and of his giving up unto God through Jesus Christ, to live and walk in newness of life" (art. XXIX.1).[46] This same article also prescribes baptizing in the triune name (XXIX.3). Somewhat uniquely, though, 2LCF does not limit partaking in the Lord's Supper to those who have been baptized as believers by immersion.[47]

One final aspect of early Particular Baptist life that must be mentioned is the theology of Benjamin Keach, a seventeenth-century Baptist theologian instrumental in authoring 2LCF and its subsequent revisions. We include him here because of his influence on 2LCF and also because his catechism and his tract about baptism, *The Glory and Ornament of a True Gospel Church*—attached to 2LCF in its later distribution—were instrumental in early Baptist life in both England and America.[48] D. B. Riker has demonstrated Keach's catholic and ecumenical spirit and his status as a theologian of Reformed thought of the Baptist variety in *A Catholic Reformed Theologian: Federalism and Baptism in the Thought of Benjamin Keach, 1640–1704*. While the entire argument is important,

---

[45] See art. XXX.7, which states that those who take the Lord's Supper take outwardly the bread and wine but also "inwardly by faith, really and do indeed, yet not carnally, and corporally, but spiritually receive, and feed upon Christ crucified, & all the benefits of his death; the Body and Blood of *Christ*, being then not corporally, or carnally, but spiritually present to the faith of Believers, in that Ordinance, as the elements themselves are to their outward senses." In Lumpkin, 294.

[46] Lumpkin, 291.

[47] Lumpkin, 218. On the seventeenth-century Particular Baptists and the relationship of baptism to the Lord's Supper in their thought see Peter Naylor, *Calvinism, Communion, and the Baptists: A Study of English Calvinistic Baptists from the Late 1600s to the Early 1800s*, Studies in Baptist History and Thought 7 (Milton Keyes, UK: Paternoster, 2003), 94–106.

[48] Lumpkin, *Baptist Confessions of Faith*, 2nd rev. ed., 221.

Riker in turn demonstrates Keach's broad catholicity with the Christian tradition[49] and with Reformed thought in particular.[50] Riker's evidence for this catholic spirit includes direct statements from Keach about his desire for catholicity, Keach's use of previous confessions and creeds, and his affirmation of Reformed thought, particularly in relation to covenantal and federal theology.

This puts Keach's credobaptism in an ecumenical and Reformational light. As Riker puts it, though Keach disagreed with "Orthodoxy" (i.e., including the broad acceptance of paedobaptism) about baptism, "he sees himself not as departing from [Orthodoxy], but rather as a theologian carrying on the work of the Reformation. He believes that the Reformers dealt with the more fundamental issues, but left undone subsidiary points, which the Baptists are handling."[51] Or, to put it slightly differently, Keach "only departed from the earlier established Reformed Orthodox thought where necessary to continue the work of the Reformation."[52] But when Keach deemed departure necessary, as with respect to baptism, he still evinced catholicity.

Among the evidences that Keach's view of baptism is catholic while also intending to reform, we note similarities to the previously examined confessions. For instance, Keach is willing to call baptism a "sacrament,"[53] one that signifies entry into Christ's visible church and therefore also serves as a prerequisite to the Lord's Supper.[54] On both of these points Keach cites various early Christian theologians, such as Cyprian, and more recent Reformed interlocutors such as Ursinus. He also maintains that baptism, in Riker's summation, is a rite "instituted in order to be a visible sign of an invisible grace already effected in the life of the believer, i.e., it is a sign that new life was given."[55] We thus see broad continuity with

---

[49] Riker, *Catholic Reformed Theologian*, 9–62.
[50] Riker, 63–110.
[51] Riker, 7–8.
[52] Riker, 127.
[53] Riker, 123–24.
[54] Riker, 125–26.
[55] Riker, 129. Riker subsequently cites Keach's own quotation of The Anglican Catechism on this definition.

respect to baptism's sacramental (but not sacerdotal) quality. Regarding the purposes of baptism, Keach again demonstrates catholicity with both the Christian tradition broadly construed and Reformed orthodoxy. Riker summarizes Keach's understanding of baptism's meaning: a visible sign of an invisible grace, a sign of union with Christ, a token of the "washing of our sins in the blood of Christ,"[56] a proclamation of faith in Christ's resurrection, an outward sign of a cleansed conscience, and the means by which persons enter into Christ's visible church.[57]

This survey of early Baptist baptismal theology leads us to agree with Stanley Fowler's assessment that

> early Baptist authors consistently argued against any kind of sacramentalism which posits an automatic bestowal of grace through baptism, but they did not deny that baptism has an instrumental function in the application of redemption. . . .
>
> Some early Baptists spoke more strongly than others, but there was among them a recurring affirmation that the reception of the benefits of Christ is in some way mediated through baptism. Their theology of baptism may not have been absolutely uniform, but they consistently asserted that God, by his Spirit, bestows spiritual benefit through baptism. Christian baptism was for them a human response to the gospel, but this human act of obedience did not exhaust the content of the event.[58]

Signs of Credobaptist Catholicity in Early Anabaptist and Baptist Thought

Given this summary of early Anabaptist and Baptist thought, there are at least four ways in which their credobaptism evidenced, not successionism and (naïve) biblicism but rather, a reformational catholicity. First, they shared with the Reformers (and indeed many of them

---

[56] Riker, 129, quoting Keach, *Gold Refin'd*, 81.
[57] Riker, *Catholic Reformed Theologian*, 129.
[58] Fowler, *More Than a Symbol*, 31–32.

thought of themselves as Reformers)[59] a commitment to rejecting all Roman Catholic notions of justification and their ecclesiological corollaries. This meant reforming the understanding and practice of both sacraments for all Reformed groups—including credobaptists. Second, early Anabaptists and early Baptists bear resemblance to one another in using the term "sacrament" and its standard definition to refer to baptism. While English Baptist confessions in the latter half of the seventeenth century, with the exception of The Orthodox Creed, ceased to use the term and used only "ordinance," they continued to refer to baptism using definitions ("visible sign of an invisible grace") and to articulate the purposes of baptism in ways that remained consonant with the term "sacrament." Given that many early biblical Anabaptists and most early English Baptists also explicitly articulated broad catholicity related to classical Christian doctrines (e.g. the Trinity, theology proper, Christology) and through reference to the three ecumenical creeds and the first four ecumenical councils, it should be taken as a catholic move for them to also use broadly catholic language when describing the meaning and purpose of baptism—even while attempting to reform its practice.

A third evidence of catholicity is the repeated notion that baptism is prerequisite for participation in the Lord's Supper.[60] Indeed, this may

---

[59] E.g., Keach, *Gold Refin'd*, 155, as quoted in Riker, *Catholic Reformed Theologian*, 127.

[60] So Anthony Clarke: "In the early days of Baptist congregations the accepted understanding was that the Lord's supper was open only to those who had been baptized as believers." Clarke, "A Feast for All? Reflecting on Open Communion for the Contemporary Church," in Anthony R. Cross and Philip E. Thompson, eds., *Baptist Sacramentalism 2*, Studies in Baptist History and Thought 25 (Milton Keynes, UK: Paternoster, 2008), 92. He lists Benjamin Cox as an example but then goes on to note there is no such "explicit connection between baptism and communion" (Clarke, 93) in the Second London Confession. Here we should also mention that this "close communion" position was not held universally by seventeenth-century Baptists, John Bunyan being one notable proponent of both open membership and open communion. See his *Difference in Judgement about Water Baptism Being no Bar to Communion* (1673). Clarke, 92n2. On the debates between Bunyan and other Particular Baptists, especially William Kiffin (or, Kiffen), about communion, see Naylor, *Calvinism, Communion, and the Baptists*, 101–3. This is again why we have used confessional statements to explore this

be *the* catholic principle regarding baptism, as it can be traced all the way back to one of the earliest postapostolic documents, the *Didache* (9.5). Relatedly, early Anabaptists and Baptists also retained or recovered many elements of the historic practice, including baptism in the triune name and, in later General Baptist practice, laying on hands. Finally, these confessions have demonstrated that their authors desired to express continuity with the Christian tradition regarding the purposes of baptism. The gift of the Holy Spirit, the remission of sins, the washing of sins in the blood of Christ, union with Christ, union with one another, and entry into the visible church are mentioned in many of the confessions surveyed.

This casts new light on the relationship of some early Anabaptists and many early English Baptists to the Christian tradition. Rather than radically rejecting the Christian tradition in relation to baptism, these radical Reformers desired to recover what had been lost, retain what was biblical, and reform what was not. We would go so far as to say, for the early Baptists, baptism had the same meaning as it did for all orthodox Christians throughout the early and medieval periods and into the Reformation period. It just needed reformation with respect to the subjects and the mode of baptism. Or, to say it differently, early Baptists retained the orthodox Christian view of the *theology* of baptism while insisting on reforming its *practice*.

---

issue rather than individual writers, as it is the former that give us some idea of the consensus.

9

Baptists, the Lord's Supper, and the Christian Tradition

MICHAEL A. G. HAYKIN
The Southern Baptist Theological Seminary

Ernest A. Payne, the doyen of English Baptist historical studies for much of the twentieth century, maintained that from the beginning of Baptist testimony in the seventeenth century there has never been unanimity with respect to the nature of the Lord's Supper and that no one perspective can justly claim to have been the dominant tradition.[1] If Payne's statement has in view the entire history of Baptist witness, in all of its breadth and depth, it may be regarded as roughly accurate. However, as soon as specific periods and eras are examined, the evidence demands that this statement be seriously qualified.[2]

The late Michael J. Walker has shown, for instance, that when it comes to nineteenth-century English Baptist history, "Zwinglianism emerges as the chief contender for a blanket description of Baptist attitudes to the

---

[1] E. A. Payne, *The Fellowship of Believers: Baptist Thought and Practice Yesterday and Today*, 2nd ed. (London: Carey Kingsgate, 1952), 61.

[2] Some of the material in this chapter has already appeared in Michael A. G. Haykin, *One Heart and One Soul: John Sutcliff of Olney, His Friends and His Times* (Darlington, UK: Evangelical Press, 1994), 294–300. For permission to use this material in this format I am grateful to Evangelical Press.

Lord's Supper."[3] The Swiss Reformer Huldrych Zwingli (1484–1531) regarded the bread and the wine as mainly signs of what God has accomplished through the death of Christ, and the Supper therefore as chiefly a memorial. In discussions of Zwingli's perspective on the Lord's Supper, some twentieth-century authors have maintained that Zwingli was not really a Zwinglian; that is, he saw more in the Lord's Supper than simply a memorial.[4] Be this as it may, a tradition did take its start from those aspects of his thought that stressed primarily the memorial nature of the Lord's Supper, and this tradition dominated Baptist thinking in the nineteenth century.

In the previous two centuries, however, quite a different view prevailed, namely, that associated with John Calvin (1509–1564).[5] In Calvin's perspective on the nature of the Lord's Supper, the bread and wine are signs and guarantees of a present reality. To the one who eats the bread and drinks the wine with faith, there is conveyed what they symbolize—Christ. The channel, as it were, through which Christ is conveyed to the believer is none other than the Holy Spirit. The Spirit acts as a kind of link or bridge between believers and the ascended Christ. Christ is received by believers in the Supper "not because Christ inheres the elements, but because the Holy Spirit binds believers" to him. But without faith, only the bare elements are received.[6]

---

[3] Michael J. Walker, *Baptists at the Table: The Theology of the Lord's Supper amongst English Baptists in the Nineteenth Century* (Didcot, UK: Baptist Historical Society, 1992), 3.

[4] See Derek R. Moore-Crispin, "'The Real Absence': Ulrich Zwingli's View of the Lord's Supper," in Philip H. Eveson et al., *Union and Communion, 1529–1979* (London: Westminster Conference, 1979), 22–34.

[5] Cf. William Henry Brackney, *The Baptists* (New York: Greenwood, 1988), 62–63.

[6] Victor A. Shepherd, *The Nature and Function of Faith in the Theology of John Calvin* (Macon, GA: Mercer University Press, 1983), 220. Other helpful studies on Calvin's theology of the Lord's Supper include B. A. Gerrish, "The Lord's Supper in the Reformed Confessions," *Theology Today* 13 (1966–1967): 224–43; John D. Nicholls, "'Union with Christ': John Calvin on the Lord's Supper" in Eveson et al., *Union and Communion*, 35–54; Hughes Oliphant Old, "Biblical Wisdom Theology and Calvin's Understanding of the Lord's Supper," *Calvin Studies* 6

"This Soul-Reviving Cordial":[7]
Some Seventeenth-Century Perspectives

Among the key texts that must be examined for an accurate understanding of seventeenth-century Calvinistic Baptist doctrine in general is the Second London Confession of Faith. Well described as the "most influential and important of all Baptist Confessions,"[8] this statement of faith was first issued in 1677 and later reissued by the Calvinistic Baptist denomination in 1689 as a declaration of its doctrinal position. Incorporating large portions of the Presbyterian Westminster Confession of Faith (1646) and the Congregationalist Savoy Declaration (1658), the Second London Confession was clearly drawn up in such a way as to indicate extensive areas of doctrinal agreement between the Calvinistic Baptists and these other Calvinistic bodies. Chapter 30 in the confession, which deals with the Lord's Supper, is an especially good example of the way in which the Calvinistic Baptists sought to demonstrate their fundamental solidarity with other communities in the Reformed tradition.

Following the Westminster Confession and the Savoy Declaration, the Baptist Confession denounces as unbiblical the Roman church's doctrine of the mass, its practice of private masses, its refusal to allow any but a priest to partake of the cup, and its dogma of transubstantiation.[9] After noting such errors regarding the Lord's Table, the confession then inculcates a right understanding of this ordinance: "Worthy receivers, outwardly partaking of the visible Elements in this Ordinance, do then also inwardly by faith, really and indeed, yet not carnally, and corporally, but spiritually receive, and feed upon Christ crucified & all the benefits of his death: the Body and Blood of *Christ*, being then not corporally, or

---

(1992): 111–36; B. A. Gerrish, *Grace and Gratitude: The Eucharistic Theology of John Calvin* (Minneapolis: Fortress, 1993).

[7] The quote is from Benjamin Keach, *Tropologia: A Key to Open Scripture Metaphors* (London: William Otridge, 1778), 621. For a recent edition of this work see Benjamin Keach, *Preaching from the Types and Metaphors of the Bible* (Grand Rapids: Kregel, 1972).

[8] W. J. McGlothlin, *Baptist Confessions of Faith* (Philadelphia: American Baptist Publication Society, 1911), 219.

[9] Second London Confession 30.2–6 (McGlothlin, *Baptist Confessions*, 270–72).

carnally, but spiritually present to the faith of Believers, in that Ordinance, as the Elements themselves are to their outward senses."[10]

Close comparison of this statement with the parallel statements in the Westminster Confession and the Savoy Declaration reveals two main areas of difference. The two earlier confessions use the term "sacrament" to describe the Lord's Supper, whereas in the Second London Confession this is altered to "ordinance."[11] Neither term is actually used in the New Testament, but the term "ordinance" appears to have been adopted to stress the divine institution of the Lord's Supper.[12]

The second change is an omission. This omission is best seen by displaying the relevant passages side by side in the following table, with the omitted words in italics.

Westminster Confession/Savoy Declaration*	Second London Confession[†]
The body and blood of Christ being then not corporally or carnally, *in, with, or under the bread and wine; yet, as really,* but spiritually present to the faith of believers in that ordinance, as the elements themselves are to their outward senses.	The Body and Blood of Christ being then not corporally or carnally, but spiritually present to the faith of Believers in that Ordinance, as the Elements themselves are to their outward senses.

* Westminster Confession of Faith 29.7 in *The Confession of Faith of the Assembly of Divines at Westminster*, ed. S. W. Carruthers (Glasgow, UK: Free Presbyterian Publications, 1978), 22–23; Savoy Declaration 30.7 in *The Savoy Declaration of Faith and Order 1658* (London: Evangelical Press, 1971), 41. There is one slight difference between the Westminster Confession and the Savoy Declaration. Where the former reads "in, with, or under the bread *and* wine," the latter has "in, with, or under the bread *or* wine" (italics added).

[†] Second London Confession 30.7, in McGlothin, *Baptist Confessions*, 272.

---

[10] Second London Confession 30.7 (McGlothlin, *Baptist Confessions*, 272).

[11] It should be noted that both the Westminster Confession and the Savoy Declaration do use the term "ordinance" in later paragraphs to describe the Lord's Supper.

[12] W. Morgan Patterson, "The Lord's Supper in Baptist History," *Review & Expositor* 66, no. 1 (Winter 1969): 26. Cf. Erroll Hulse's discussion of these two terms in "The Implications of Baptism," in Baruch Maoz et al., *Local Church Practice* (Haywards Heath, UK: Carey, 1978), 46–47.

The phrase omitted in the Second London Confession was intended to reject the Lutheran explanation of how Christ is present in the Lord's Supper.[13] In the view of Martin Luther (1483–1546), Christ's body and blood are present "in, with, and under" the bread and the wine. Contrary to the Roman dogma of transubstantiation, the bread remains bread; yet, in some way, it also actually contains Christ's body after the prayer of consecration. Likewise the wine contains his blood after this prayer, though it remains wine. Why the Second London Confession omits this phrase is not at all clear. Possibly it was thought that Luther's view was not entertained by any in the Calvinistic Baptist community during the seventeenth century and thus was omitted so as to avoid encumbering the confession with needless statements.

The differences between the three confessions, however, are minimal compared to what the confessions have in common. All three affirm that as believers partake of the bread and the wine, Christ is "spiritually present" to them and nourishing them. In other words, all three documents essentially maintain the perspective of John Calvin.[14] Moreover, similar remarks can be found in the writings of those who approved this confession in 1689.

Hercules Collins (d. 1702), pastor of Wapping Baptist Church, London, could state in his Orthodox Catechism (1680), a Baptist version of the Heidelberg Catechism, that in the Lord's Supper we are made "verily Partakers of his Body and Blood through the working of the Holy Ghost."[15] From Collins's perspective, although Christ's body is in heaven,

---

[13] For the broader Puritan rejection of Luther's position, see John F. H. New, *Anglican and Puritan: The Basis of Their Opposition, 1558–1640* (Stanford, CA: Stanford University Press, 1964), 60.

[14] Those who drafted these confessions would have understood the phrase "spiritually present" to mean "present by means of the Holy Spirit." See E. Brooks Holifield, *The Covenant Sealed: The Development of Puritan Sacramental Theology in Old and New England, 1570–1720* (New Haven, CT: Yale University Press, 1974), 131–32. For some remarks on the biblical basis of this perspective as it is found in the Second London Confession, see David S. Dockery, "The Lord's Supper in the New Testament and in Baptist Worship," *Search* 19, no. 1 (Fall 1988): 44–45.

[15] Cited in E. P. Winter, "Calvinist and Zwinglian Views of the Lord's Supper among the Baptists of the Seventeenth Century," *The Baptist Quarterly* 15, no. 7

we can have communion with the risen Christ in the Supper through the Spirit. Another who approved the confession was William Kiffin (also spelled Kiffen) (1616–1701), pastor of Devonshire Square Baptist Church, London, from the 1640s until his death, who held "a unique place of honour and influence" among the early English Calvinistic Baptists.[16] Like Collins, Kiffin could also assert that "the [Lord's] Supper is a Spiritual participation of the Body and Blood of Christ by Faith."[17] Along the same lines, Benjamin Keach (1640–1704), the leading apologist for Calvinistic Baptist views in the final decade of the seventeenth century, could state that in the Lord's Supper "there is a mystical Conveyance or Communication of all Christ's blessed Merits to our souls through Faith."[18]

The first paragraph of chapter 30 of the Second London Confession also has a detailed discussion of the importance of the Lord's Supper for the Christian life. There it is stated that the "Supper of the Lord Jesus, was instituted by him, the same night wherein he was betrayed, to be observed in his Churches unto the end of the world, for the perpetual remembrance, and shewing forth the sacrifice in his death, confirmation

---

(1953–1954): 327. On Collins and his ministry, see Ernest F. Kevan, *London's Oldest Baptist Church, Wapping 1633–Walthamstow 1933* (London: Kingsgate, 1933), 38–50, 64–68; Michael Haykin, "A Cloud of Witnesses: The Life and Ministry of Hercules Collins (d.1702)," *Evangelical Times* 35, no. 2 (February 2001): 21; Weaver, *Orthodox, Puritan, Baptist.*

[16] Barrie R. White, "William Kiffin—Baptist Pioneer and Citizen of London," *Baptist History and Heritage* 2, no. 2 (July 1967): 91. For Kiffen see the series of volumes by Larry J. Kreitzer, *William Kiffen and His World*, 6 vols. (Oxford, UK: Regent's Park College, 2010–2017).

[17] William Kiffin, *A Sober Discourse of Right to Church-Communion* (repr., Paris, AR: Baptist Standard Bearer, n.d., ca. 2006; originally pub. London: George Larkin, 1681), 35.

[18] Keach, *Tropologia*, 623. For Keach's importance as a Baptist apologist see Murdina D. MacDonald, "London Calvinistic Baptists 1689–1727: Tensions within a Dissenting Community under Toleration" (DPhil thesis, Regent's Park College, University of Oxford, 1982), 77. The major source of information about Keach comes from his son-in-law, the early Baptist historian Thomas Crosby; see his *The History of the English Baptists* (London, 1740), IV.268–314. For a more recent account of Keach's life, see especially Austin Walker, *The Excellent Benjamin Keach*, 2nd rev. ed. (Kitchener, ON: Joshua Press, 2015).

of the faith of believers in all the benefits thereof, their spiritual nourish-ment, and growth in him, their further ingagement in, and to, all duties which they owe unto him; and to be a bond and pledge of their commu-nion with him, and with each other."[19]

In this enumeration of reasons for the Lord's Table, the Second London Confession follows closely both the Westminster Confession and the Savoy Declaration. Christ instituted the Lord's Supper for five reasons, according to this paragraph. The Supper serves as a vivid reminder of and witness to the sacrificial death of Christ. Then, par-ticipation in the Lord's Supper enables believers to grasp more firmly all that Christ has done for them through his death on the cross. In this way the Lord's Supper is a means of spiritual nourishment and growth. Fourth, the Lord's Supper serves as a time when believers can recommit themselves to Christ. Finally, the Lord's Supper affirms the indissoluble union that exists between Christ and believers and also between indi-vidual believers.

One cannot come away from reading these paragraphs on the Lord's Supper without the conviction that those who issued this confession were deeply conscious of the vital importance of the Lord's Supper for the Christian life. It should also be noted that, in this hearty apprecia-tion of the Lord's Supper, these early Calvinistic Baptists stood squarely in the mainstream of Puritan thought. The Puritans generally regarded the Supper as a vehicle the Spirit employed as an efficacious means of grace for the believer, and thus they opposed the Zwinglian perspec-tive on the Lord's Supper.[20] For the Puritans and for the seventeenth-century Calvinistic Baptists, the Lord's Supper was indeed, in the words of Benjamin Keach, a "Soul-reviving Cordial."[21]

---

[19] McGlothlin, *Baptist Confessions*, 270.

[20] For the Puritan view of the Lord's Table, see Geoffrey F. Nuttall, *The Holy Spirit in Puritan Faith and Experience*, 2nd ed. (Oxford, UK: Basil Blackwell, 1947), 90–101; New, *Anglican and Puritan*, 59–76; Holifield, *Covenant Sealed*, 109–38; Hywel W. Roberts, "'The Cup of Blessing': Puritan and Separatist Sacramental Discourses," in Eveson et al., *Union and Communion*, 55–71.

[21] Keach, *Tropologia*, 621.

"His Soul-Refreshing Presence":[22]
Eighteenth-Century Baptist Eucharistic Thought

A random sampling of eighteenth-century Calvinistic Baptist reflections on the Lord's Supper reveals strong evidence that the perspective on the nature of the Lord's Supper we have already noted in the seventeenth century continued to prevail for much of the following century. Consider, for instance, the views of William Mitchel (1662–1705). Between 1688 and 1705, Mitchel evangelized many of the towns and villages throughout east Lancashire and the West Riding of Yorkshire with unremitting ardor from his base at Bacup, in the Rossendale Valley. In so doing he laid the foundations for a significant number of future Baptist churches. After his death his coworker and cousin, David Crosley (1669–1744), published Mitchel's *Jachin & Boaz* (1707), in which the latter set forth a summary of his doctrinal convictions.[23] Strongly Calvinistic, the treatise exercised considerable influence over the life and thinking of early Lancashire and Yorkshire Baptist congregations.

In the section of *Jachin & Boaz* dealing with the Lord's Table, Mitchel declares that in the Lord's Supper Christ's "Death and Blood

---

[22] The quote is from Anne Dutton, *Thoughts on the Lord's Supper, Relating to the Nature, Subjects, and Right Partaking of this Solemn Ordinance* (London, 1748), 33. For a good overview of the high regard in which the Lord's Supper was viewed by late seventeenth- and early eighteenth-century Dissenters see Margaret Spufford, "The importance of the Lord's Supper to Dissenters," in Margaret Spufford, ed., *The World of Rural Dissenters, 1520–1725* (Cambridge: Cambridge University Press, 1995), 86–102. See also Karen Smith, "The Covenant Life of Some Eighteenth-Century Calvinistic Baptists in Hampshire and Wiltshire," in William H. Brackney and Paul S. Fiddes, with John H. Y. Briggs, eds., *Pilgrim Pathways: Essays in Baptist History in Honour of B. R. White* (Macon, Georgia: Mercer University Press, 1999), 178–82.

[23] For further details about Mitchel, see W. E. Blomfield, "Yorkshire Baptist Churches in the 17th and 18th Centuries," in *The Baptists of Yorkshire*, 2nd ed. (Bradford/London; Wm. Byles & Sons/London: Kingsgate Press, 1912), 73–88; Ian Sellers, ed., *Our Heritage: The Baptists of Yorkshire, Lancashire and Cheshire* (Leeds, UK: Yorkshire Baptist Association/Lancashire and Cheshire Baptist Association, 1987), 10–11; B. A. Ramsbottom, *The Puritan Samson: The Life of David Crosley, 1669–1744* (Harpenden, UK: Gospel Standard Trust, 1991).

is shewed forth; and the worthy receivers are, not after a corporal and carnal manner, but by the Spirit and Faith, made Partakers of his Body and Blood, with all his Benefits, to their spiritual Nourishment and Growth in Grace."[24] Mitchel goes on to repudiate explicitly the Roman Catholic doctrine of the mass and to aver, in the exact words of the Second London Confession, that the Supper is "only a Memorial of that one Offering up of himself, by himself, upon the Cross, once for all."[25] Mitchel is thus quite happy to speak of the celebration of the Lord's Supper in memorialist terms, but his earlier statement shows that he is unwilling to regard it solely as an act of remembrance. Following Calvin and his Baptist forebears, he asserts that the Lord's Supper is definitely a means of spiritual nourishment and that at the Table believers, by the Spirit, do meet with Christ.

Another Calvinistic perspective on the Supper is found in *Thoughts on the Lord's Supper, Relating to the Nature, Subjects, and Right Partaking of This Solemn Ordinance* (1748), by Anne Dutton (1692–1765). A prolific author, Dutton corresponded with many of the leading evangelical figures of the eighteenth century—Philip Doddridge (1702–1751), Howel Harris (1714–1773), George Whitefield (1714–1770), and John Wesley (1703–1791)—encouraging them, giving them advice, and sometimes chiding them. On one occasion Whitefield confessed that "her conversation is as weighty as her letters." And Harris once wrote to her that he was convinced "our Lord has entrusted you with a Talent of writing for him."[26]

---

[24] W. E. Blomfield, "William Mitchill's 'Jachin & Boaz'—1707," *Transactions of the Baptist Historical Society* 3 (1912–1913): 161. This language is taken directly from the Westminster Shorter Catechism, question 96.

[25] Blomfield. For a brief discussion of Mitchel's views see Winter, "Calvinist and Zwinglian Views," 327.

[26] Cited in Stephen J. Stein, "A Note on Anne Dutton, Eighteenth-Century Evangelical," *Church History* 44, no. 4 (December 1975): 488–89. See also Michael D. Sciretti Jr., "'Feed My Lambs': The Spiritual Direction Ministry of Calvinistic British Baptist Anne Dutton During the Early Years of the Evangelical Revival" (PhD thesis, Baylor University, 2009). Most of Dutton's works have survived in only a few copies. Thankfully many of her works are currently available in a series of volumes compiled by JoAnn Ford Watson, *Selected Spiritual Writings of Anne*

Dutton devotes the first section of her sixty-page treatise on the Lord's Supper to outlining its nature. In this section Dutton argues that the Supper is, among other things, a "communication." "As our Lord is spiritually present in his own ordinance," she writes, "so he therein and thereby doth actually communicate, or give himself, his body broken, and his blood shed, with all the benefits of his death, to the worthy receivers."[27] Here Dutton affirms that Christ is indeed present at the celebration of his Supper and makes it a means of grace for those who partake of it with faith. As she later states in this treatise, in the Lord's Supper "the King is pleas'd to sit with us, at his Table."[28] In fact, so highly does she prize this means of grace that she can state, with what other Calvinistic Baptists of her era might describe as some exaggeration, that the celebration of the Lord's Supper "admits" believers "into the nearest Approach to his glorious Self, that we can make in an Ordinance-Way on the Earth, on this Side the Presence of his Glory in Heaven."[29]

The diary of Isaac Staveley, a young clerk and a member of Eagle Street Baptist Church, London, during the latter years of the pastorate of Andrew Gifford (1700–1784), provides a third witness to this perspective on the nature of the Lord's Supper. Written daily from February 24 to September 22, 1771, the diary opens a window upon "the interests, way of life, thoughts and activities which we may suppose to have applied to a considerable number of Baptists during the later part of the 18th century."[30] The center of Staveley's life was the Baptist fellowship to which he belonged, and his chief delight the sermons of Gifford and visiting ministers, of which he wrote extensive summaries in his diary. Participation in the Lord's Supper was also an important event for Staveley. After the evening sermon on March 3, for instance, the young clerk recorded that he and his fellow Baptists "came around the table of

---

Dutton: Eighteenth-Century, British-Baptist, Woman Theologian, 7 vols. (Macon, GA: Mercer University Press, 2003–2015).

    [27] Dutton, *Thoughts on the Lord's Supper*, 3–4.
    [28] Dutton, 21.
    [29] Dutton, 25.
    [30] L. G. Champion, "Baptist Church Life in London, 1771," *Baptist Quarterly* 18, no. 7 (1960): 300.

our dear dying Lord to feast on the sacrifice of his offered body, show his death afresh, to claim and recognise our interest therein, to feast on the sacrifice of his offered body as happy members of the same family of faith and love."[31]

Staveley was probably not aware of the fact that the phrase "to feast on the sacrifice of his offered body," which he uses twice in this short extract, had its roots in the soil of Calvin's theology of the Lord's Supper. In his magnum opus, *The Institutes of the Christian Religion*, the Genevan Reformer had written that the Lord's Supper confirms "for us the fact that the Lord's body was once for all so sacrificed for us that we may now feed upon it, and by feeding feel in ourselves the working of that unique sacrifice."[32] Such language, from both Staveley and Calvin, is foreign to a mindset that regards the Lord's Table as merely a memorial.

"His Flesh is Meat Indeed": The Witness of Baptist Hymnody

Eighteenth-century Baptist hymnology is also a good guide to Calvinistic Baptist eucharistic piety. Some of the richest texts that display this piety can be found in *Hymns in Commemoration of the Sufferings of Our Blessed Saviour Jesus Christ, Compos'd for the Celebration of His Holy Supper*, by Joseph Stennett I (1663–1713), pastor of a Calvinistic Seventh-Day Baptist Church that met in Pinners' Hall, London.[33] Stennett described

---

[31] Champion, 301–2.

[32] John Calvin, *Institutes of the Christian Religion*, vol. 2, trans. Ford Lewis Battles, ed. John T. McNeill, bk. 4, chap. 17.1 (Philadelphia: Westminster, 1960), 1361. I am indebted for this reference to Walker, *Baptists at the Table*, 9.

[33] On Stennett, see especially "Some Account of the Life of the Reverend and Learned Mr. Joseph Stennett," in *The Works of the Late Reverend and Learned Mr. Joseph Stennett*, vol. 1 (London, 1732), 3–36; R. L. Greaves, "Stennett, Joseph (1663–1713)," in R. L. Greaves and Robert Zaller, eds., *Biographical Dictionary of British Radicals in the Seventeenth Century*, vol. 3 (Brighton, UK: Harvester, 1984), 205–6; Bryan W. Ball, *The Seventh-Day Men: Sabbatarians and Sabbatarianism in England and Wales, 1600–1800* (Oxford, UK: Clarendon, 1994), 120–25; B. A. Ramsbottom, "The Stennetts," in *British Particular Baptists, 1638–1910*, vol. 1 (Springfield, MO: Particular Baptist Press, 1998), 136–138; Allen Harrington and

the church's celebration at the Table as a "perpetual memorial" of Christ's death, a death to be commemorated.[34] And the bread and wine he called "proper Symbols" and "Figures."[35] Yet Stennett could also say of these symbols:

> Thy Flesh is Meat indeed,
> Thy Blood the richest wine;
> How blest are they who often feed
> On this Repast of thine![36]

And he can urge his fellow believers:

> Sing *Hallelujah* to our King,
> Who nobly entertains
> His Friends with Bread of Life, and Wine
> That flow'd from all his Veins.
> His Body pierc'd with numerous Wounds,
> Did as a Victim bleed;
> That we might drink his sacred Blood,
> And on his Flesh might feed.[37]

Stennett does make it clear that the feeding involved at the Table is one of faith,[38] but this is realistic language utterly foreign to the later Zwinglian perspective.

Martha Stennett Harrington, "The Stennetts of England," accessed August 11, 2018, https://www.blue-hare.com/stennett/tpgindex.html.

[34] Joseph Stennett I, *Hymns In Commemoration Of the Sufferings Of Our Blessed Saviour Jesus Christ, Compos'd For the Celebration of his Holy Supper* (London: N. Cliff and D. Jackson, 1713), iii, 4.

[35] Stennett, 29, 20.

[36] Stennett, 35.

[37] Stennett, 23.

[38] Thus, in one of his hymns he can state (*Hymns*, 19):
    "Here may our Faith still on Thee feed
    The only Food Divine;
    To Faith thy Flesh is Meat indeed,
    Thy Blood the Noblest Wine."

Two hymns of Benjamin Beddome (1717–1795), pastor of the Baptist cause in Bourton-on-the-Water, Gloucestershire, for more than fifty years, can also be cited as evidence for what is clearly the most prevalent belief about the nature of the Lord's Supper among eighteenth-century Baptists. Beddome was a prolific hymn writer, and many of his hymns were still in use at the beginning of the twentieth century.[39] Although Beddome wrote only a few hymns that dealt specifically with the subject of the Lord's Supper, they are fairly explicit as to his view of its nature. In one he prays:

Oh for a glimmering sight
Of my expiring Lord!
Sure pledge of what yon worlds of light
Will to the saints afford. . . . .

May I behold him in the wine,
And see him in the bread.[40]

In another the invitation is given:

Come then, my soul, partake,
The banquet is divine:
His body is the choicest food,
His blood the richest wine.

---

[39] On Beddome and his ministry see Thomas Brooks, *Pictures of the Past: The History of the Baptist Church, Bourton-on-the-Water* (London: Judd & Glass, 1861), 21–66; William Boswell Lowther, "Benjamin Beddome," *The Dictionary of National Biography*, 1885–1886 ed., vol. 2 (repr. London: Oxford University Press, 1963–1964), 97–98; W. R. Stevenson and John Julian, "Beddome, Benjamin" in John Julian, ed., *A Dictionary of Hymnology* (London: John Murray, 1908), 121–24; Michael A. G. Haykin, "Benjamin Beddome (1717–1795)," in Michael A. G. Haykin, ed., *British Particular Baptists*, vol. 1 I167–82. One recent hymnal contains five of his hymns—see *Grace Hymns* (London: Grace Publications Trust, 1975), nos. 288, 351, 470, 496, 514.

[40] Benjamin Beddome, *Hymns Adapted to Public Worship, or Family Devotion* (London, 1818), no. 672.

Ye hungry starving poor,
Join in the sweet repast;
View Jesus in these symbols given,
And his salvation taste.[41]

Beddome did not hold to a Roman Catholic or Lutheran view of the "real presence." The bread and the wine, he asserted, are "symbols." Nevertheless, he did expect the Lord's Supper to be a place where the "sweet repast" of salvation is savored and Christ himself seen. The "realism" of the language in the first of these two stanzas especially bespeaks the conviction that Christ is present at the ordinance.

This Calvinistic view of the Table is still evident in hymns composed at the very close of the eighteenth century. Thomas Steevens (1745–1802), pastor of Colchester Baptist Church and early supporter of the Baptist Missionary Society, is said to have penned two thousand or so hymns.[42] Only a few of his hymns appear to have been published, but among them is this one, a eucharistic hymn that ends on a fabulous Trinitarian note of praise:

The sacred emblems shew
The bleeding Lamb of God;
The bread presents his flesh to view,
The wine his precious blood.

His flesh is meat indeed!
I eat, and find I live;
My soul, with such provision blest,
Can feed, and grow, and thrive.

And O! this gen'rous cup,
How it revives my heart!

---

[41] Beddome, no. 669.

[42] For his life and ministry see the anonymous "Memoir of the Rev. Thomas Steevens," *The Baptist Magazine* 9 (1817): 81–88; and Henry Spyvee, *Colchester Baptist Church—The First 300 Years, 1689–1989* (Colchester, UK: Colchester Baptist Church, 1989), 31–39.

I sit, and sip with holy joy,
And griefs and fears depart.

Spirit Divine! To thee
I owe eternal praise;
The eyes by which I see the whole,
Were given by thy grace.

Yes, and the Father's love
Demands a tribute here;
'Twas he who gave his Son to die,
To bring the rebel near.

To the mysterious Three,
The Co-Eternal One,
Sitting around the Saviour's board,
Be equal honours done.[43]

The first three stanzas of this hymn ponder the meaning of the Table. Like the other eighteenth-century hymn writers we have considered, Steevens is clear that the bread and wine are "sacred emblems."[44] But the realistic language denominates the Table as much more than a memorial. In a line clearly dependent upon Stennett, Steevens asserts, "His flesh is meat indeed!" The Lord's Supper is thus a place of spiritual life and nurture (stanza 2) and of renewal that provides victory over "griefs and fears" (stanza 3). Stanzas 4 and 5 reflect Steevens's realization that the cross involves the entire Trinity: consider, obviously, "the bleeding Lamb of God" (stanza 1), but also the "Spirit Divine" who enables blind eyes to see the meaning of Jesus' death and the loving Father who sent his Son to

---

[43] James Upton, *A Collection of Hymns*, 2nd ed (London, 1815), no. 333. This hymn is to be sung to the tune Aylesbury. For access to this rare hymnal I am grateful to Chris Fenner, Music & Media Archivist, The Southern Baptist Theological Seminary, Louisville, Kentucky, and Kathryn Sullivan of the Bowld Music Library, Southwestern Baptist Theological Seminary, Fort Worth, Texas.

[44] Either Steevens or James Upton, editor of the hymnal, titled this hymn "Looking through the Signs at the Lord's Table."

die for rebel sinners. Hence, as the final stanza declares, equal praise is to be given to "the mysterious Three/the Co-Eternal One."

A "Memorial of the Absent Savior": The Emergence of a Zwinglian Template[45]

The view that the Lord's Supper is primarily or merely a memorial began to become widespread in Calvinistic Baptist circles only during the last quarter of the eighteenth century. Abraham Booth (1734–1806), the influential London Baptist leader, stated in 1778 that the Lord's Supper was designed to be a "memorial of God's love to us and of Immanuel's death for us."[46] Twenty years later, the Yorkshire Baptist leader John Fawcett (1740–1817) declared in the minor spiritual classic *Christ Precious to Those That Believe* (1799) that the

> Lord's Table . . . is wisely and graciously designed to revive in our minds the remembrance of him who gave his life a ransom for our souls. This institution is happily contrived to represent, in a lively and striking manner, the love, the sufferings, and the death of our blessed Redeemer, together with the benefits which we derive from them. When we unite in this solemnity, all the springs of pious affection should be let loose, while we contemplate the dying agonies of the Prince of Peace. We should feel the sweet meltings of godly sorrow, and the warmest exertions of gratitude, love and joy.[47]

A most striking acceptance of the Zwinglian perspective on the Lord's Supper is found in a text written by John Sutcliff (1752–1814), pastor of the Baptist church in Olney, Buckinghamshire, close friend of William Carey (1761–1834), and one of the founders of the Baptist Missionary

---

[45] John Sutcliff, *On Obedience to Positive Institutions* (Circular Letter of the Northamptonshire Association, 1808), 6.

[46] Cited in Payne, *Fellowship of Believers*, 65.

[47] John Fawcett, *Christ Precious to Those that Believe*, 4th ed. (repr. Minneapolis: Klock & Klock, 1979), 230–31.

Society. Sutcliff also played a central part in bringing revival to the Calvinistic Baptists, far too many of whose churches were largely stagnant and somewhat moribund in the second half of the eighteenth century.[48] Titled *The Ordinance of the Lord's Supper Considered* and written in 1803 as a circular letter for the Baptist churches of the Northamptonshire Association, this text abounds in memorialist language—the Calvinist tradition hardly makes a showing. Sutcliff took for his guiding verse throughout this letter the statement of Christ in Luke 22:19: "Do this in remembrance of me." Seen through the lens of this text, the Lord's Supper is a "standing memorial of Christ. When you see the table spread and are about to partake of the bread and wine, think you hear Christ saying, 'Remember me.' Remember who he is. . . . Again: Remember what he has done. . . . Once more: Remember where he is, and what he is doing."[49]

The fact that Christ instructed us to remember him, Sutcliff continued, clearly "implies his absence." Moreover, if a friend who is going away leaves us with a small present prior to his departure and asks us to "keep it as a memorial of his friendship," then, even if the present has "little intrinsic worth, we set a high value on it, for his sake." Gazing upon this present aids in the "recollection of our absent friend." So it is with the ordinance of the Lord's Supper: it is designed "to draw our attention to, and assist our meditations upon an unseen Jesus."[50]

This emphasis upon Christ's absence, and thus upon the Supper as a place primarily for mediation and remembrance, dominates Sutcliff's thinking about the Lord's Table. In a catechism he wrote and first published in 1783, the Lord's Supper is said to be a "solemn eating of bread, and drinking of wine, in commemoration of the death of Christ."[51] And

---

[48] For a study of Sutcliff's life and ministry see Haykin, *One Heart and One Soul.*

[49] John Sutcliff, *The Ordinance of the Lord's Supper Considered. The Circular Letter of the Northamptonshire Association* (Dunstable, UK: J. W. Morris, 1803), 2, 3.

[50] Sutcliff, 3–4.

[51] John Sutcliff, *The First Principles of the Oracles of God, Represented in a Plain and Familiar Catechism for the Use of Children*, rev. Joseph Belcher (Whitchurch, UK: R. B. Jones, 1820), 14.

in a later circular letter of 1808, *On Obedience to Positive Institutions*, Sutcliff unequivocally states that baptism and the Lord's Supper are "memorials of the absent Saviour." In baptism "we behold Jesus dying for our offences, and rising again for our justification," and in the Supper "we see his body broken, and his blood shed for the remission of sins."[52]

Toward the end of *The Ordinance of the Lord's Supper*, Sutcliff also emphasizes that remembrance of what Christ has done for the believer should lead him or her to a renewed commitment to the Savior:

> To him who gave his life a ransom, it becomes you to devote your lives. Bought with a price, remember you are not your own. Resolve therefore in the strength of divine grace, to glorify God in your body and in your spirit, which are God's. Each time you approach this sacred ordinance consecrate yourselves anew to the service, honour and glory of the blessed Jesus.[53]

The Lord's Table is thus a place of reconsecration.

Finally, Sutcliff stresses that participation in the Supper is a matter of obedience to the command of Christ; it is an open avowal of one's "subjection to him as a Sovereign." As such he warns his readers: "Never treat the positive institutions of the Redeemer as matters of indifferency."[54] But, as Michael Walker has cogently shown with respect to the memorialist position in the later decades of the nineteenth century, such a position was generally accompanied by some degree of ambivalence with regard to the importance of the Table for the believer's Christian experience.[55] Thus, although Sutcliff sought to guard against indifference about the Supper, his perspective on the nature of the Table would in time help to foster such an attitude.

For only two brief moments does an inkling of the Calvinistic perspective on the Supper shine through in this strongly memorialist interpretation of the Table. Near the beginning of the tract it is stated that

---

[52] Sutcliff, *Obedience to Positive Institutions*, 6.
[53] Sutcliff, *Ordinance of the Lord's Supper*, 7.
[54] Sutcliff, 9.
[55] Walker, *Baptists at the Table*.

Christ "still often visits in a spiritual manner his saints in attending divine ordinances."[56] This statement reveals an awareness that the Supper is more than simply a memorial, but it remains undeveloped. Then, in a section of the tract dealing with those who, for no apparent reason, occasionally absent themselves from the celebration of the Supper, Sutcliff asks a pointed question: "Is not this the way to grieve the holy Spirit by which 'you are sealed unto the day of redemption'? That Spirit whose delight it is on one hand, to glorify Jesus; and on the other, to see him glorified by you."[57]

It may be the case that here Sutcliff simply has in view the fact that failure to be present at the Table constitutes an act of disobedience, and it is for this reason alone that the Spirit is grieved. On the other hand, does this question betray a belief that the Supper is a means by which the Spirit provides God's people with spiritual nourishment? An earlier statement of Sutcliff's, in a sermon titled "Jealousy for the Lord of Hosts Illustrated" (1791), does seem to indicate that Sutcliff had not totally ruled out as inadmissible a Calvinistic view of the Lord's Supper. Speaking of the Spirit as the "grand promise of the New Testament," he affirms that his "influences are the soul, the great animating soul of all religion. These withheld, divine ordinances are empty cisterns and spiritual graces are withering flowers."[58] Without the Spirit the ordinances of baptism and the Lord's Supper are devoid of any spiritual value for those who receive them. With him present, though, they become vehicles of blessing. Apart from these spare hints of the richer, Calvinistic view of the Lord's Table, however, Sutcliff's tract on the Supper marks a definite setting aside of this view in favor of the leaner memorialist perspective. And it presaged what would come to be the majority view among British Baptists in the nineteenth century.[59]

---

[56] Sutcliff, *Ordinance of the Lord's Supper*, 2.

[57] Sutcliff, 6; see also Sutcliff, *Obedience to Positive Institutions*, 8–9.

[58] John Sutcliff, "Jealousy for the Lord of Hosts Illustrated" (London: W. Button, 1791), 12.

[59] It is noteworthy that the two earliest articles on the Lord's Supper in the denominational paper of the Calvinistic Baptists, the *Baptist Magazine*, which began in 1809, are from a fully memorialist point of view. See T. W., "On the

Explaining the Shift to Memorialism

Michael Walker has argued that nineteenth-century British Baptists became enamored of the memorialist position from the 1830s onward in reaction to a revival of English Roman Catholicism and the emergence of Tractarianism in the Church of England, a movement open to Roman Catholic theology and piety.[60] When Sutcliff wrote his letter on the Lord's Table, however, neither of these events was even on the horizon. Why then did he embrace the memorialist position? Ernest Payne has suggested that eighteenth-century rationalism, with its "suspicion of the mysterious and inexplicable," may have been a major factor in the advance of memorialist views among Calvinistic Baptists.[61] It is indeed fascinating to observe that Joseph Priestly (1733–1804), one of the leading opponents of the mystery of the Trinity in this era, can speak of the Lord's Supper in terms identical to those of Sutcliff. The Supper, he maintained, was instituted by Christ "in commemoration of his death." It is intended to serve as a "memorial" of Christ's death and a means whereby Christians make a public declaration of their allegiance.[62]

Shaping Sutcliff's view of the Supper, however, was a major shift in British Baptist ecclesiology underway during the final decades of the eighteenth century.[63] This shift involved nothing less than the transformation of the Calvinistic Baptist denomination in the British Isles from

---

Lord's Supper," *Baptist Magazine* 2 (1810): 504–6; T[homas] G[riffin], "On the Lord's Supper," *Baptist Magazine* 3 (1811): 361–68.

[60] Walker, *Baptists at the Table*, 84–120.

[61] Payne, *Fellowship of Believers*, 64–65. For a similar argument see also Susan J. White, "Christian Worship since the Reformation," in Paul F. Bradshaw and Lawrence A. Hoffman, eds., *The Making of Jewish and Christian Worship* (Notre Dame, IN: University of Notre Dame Press, 1991), 194–95.

[62] Joseph Priestley, *Institutes of Natural and Revealed Religion (1772–1774)*, in *The Theological and Miscellaneous Works of Joseph Priestley*, vol. 2, ed. J. T. Rutt (New York: Klaus Reprint, 1972), 336–37.

[63] On this shift, see Michael A. G. Haykin, "The Baptist Identity: A View from the Eighteenth Century," *The Evangelical Quarterly* 67, no. 2 (1995): 137–52. The material in this paragraph and the next one is taken from this article. For permission to use this material, I am grateful to the late editor of this journal, I. Howard Marshall.

an inward-looking, insular body concerned primarily with the preservation of its ecclesial experience and heritage into a body of churches that was outward-looking, with hands outstretched to evangelical believers in other denominations and vitally concerned about the advance of Christ's kingdom throughout the earth.

Earlier Calvinistic Baptist authors such as Benjamin Keach had sought to orient their ecclesiology by means of those marks traditionally identified by sixteenth- and seventeenth-century Reformed theology as vital for a genuine church of Christ. From the vantage point of this theological tradition, a true church can be said to exist where God's Word is faithfully preached, the sacraments of baptism and the Lord's Supper are administered, and biblical discipline is exercised. Thus Keach, in the earliest Calvinistic Baptist book devoted primarily to issues of ecclesial polity, *The Glory of a True Church and its Discipline Display'd* (1697), maintained that a church of Christ is composed of "Converted Persons," is a community where the "Word of God and Sacraments are duly administered, according to Christ's Institution," and has "regular and orderly Discipline."[64]

While Sutcliff did not disagree with this way of reflecting on the identity of the church, it was the proclamation of the Word of God— evangelistic preaching in particular—that permeated his conception of the church's nature. It was such preaching of the Word that enabled the kingdom of God to move forward and occupy the realms of darkness and convert them into strongholds of light. This perspective is clearly seen in the reasons Sutcliff delineates for the existence of local churches. In an 1802 address by Sutcliff at the ordination of Thomas Morgan (1776–1857) to the pastoral oversight of Cannon Street Baptist Church, Birmingham, he specifically mentioned three reasons: "the honor of Christ, the advancement of his cause, and their [i.e., the church members'] own profit."[65] By

---

[64] Benjamin Keach, *The Glory of a True Church, And its Discipline Display'd* (London, 1697), iii, 6.

[65] John Sutcliff, "Introductory Discourse," in John Sutcliff, John Ryland, and Andrew Fuller, *The Difficulties of the Christian Ministry, and the Means of Surmounting Them; with the Obedience of Churches to Their Pastors Explained and Enforced* (Birmingham, UK: 1802), 3.

"the advancement of [Christ's] cause" Sutcliff has in mind uninhibited evangelism at home and abroad.

Again, in *Qualifications for Church Fellowship*, an 1800 circular letter Sutcliff drew up for the Northamptonshire Association, he maintained that local churches have been designed for two principal reasons: the upbuilding of believers and the "promotion of the cause of Christ at large."[66] A statement by one of Sutcliff's closest friends, Andrew Fuller (1754–1815), the leading Baptist theologian of that era, encapsulates well the Olney Baptist's thinking in this regard: "The *true* churches of Jesus Christ travail in birth for the salvation of men. They are the armies of the Lamb, the grand object of whose existence is to extend the Redeemer's kingdom."[67] Such an evangelistic force tended to downplay the importance of the Lord's Supper, an ordinance designed expressly for believers and, in the minds of increasing numbers of Baptists in the nineteenth century, an aspect of the Christian life that played little part in the evangelization of the lost. In the words of W. R. Ward, "To the devotees of the missionary Church, bent on the business of conversion, ordinances which did not convert (as by the end of the eighteenth century they mostly did not) were a matter of diminishing interest."[68] The memorialist view of the nature of the Lord's Supper was well suited to this growing ambivalence regarding its importance.

---

[66] John Sutcliff, *Qualifications for Church Fellowship* (Clipstone, UK: J. W. Morris, 1800), 3.

[67] Andrew Fuller, *The Promise of the Spirit, the Grand Encouragement in Promoting the Gospel* (Northamptonshire Baptist Association Circular Letter, 1810), in *The Complete Works of the Rev. Andrew Fuller*, vol. 3, ed. Andrew Gunton Fuller, rev. Joseph Belcher (1845 ed.; repr. Harrisonburg, VA: Sprinkle Publications, 1988), 359, italics added.

[68] W. R. Ward, "The Evangelical Revival in Eighteenth-Century Britain," in Sheridan Gilley and W. J. Sheils, eds., *A History of Religion in Britain, Practice and Belief from Pre-Roman Times to the Present* (Oxford, UK: Blackwell, 1994), 271. Nevertheless, it is fascinating to note that while this change in viewpoint about the nature of the Lord's Supper was taking place among the Calvinistic Baptists, many of their evangelical counterparts in the Church of England still held to a robust eucharistic spirituality. See Christopher J. Cocksworth, *Evangelical Eucharistic Thought in the Church of England* (Cambridge, UK: Cambridge University Press, 1993), 72–78.

Sutcliff had been privileged to play a central role in the transformation referenced above, in which the Calvinistic Baptists moved from being a largely static denomination preoccupied with the preservation of its ecclesial heritage to one passionately involved in the missionary advance of Christ's kingdom throughout the earth. It was a movement in which much was gained, but also something lost. For Sutcliff's own theology of the Lord's Supper was indeed a poor alternative to the rich perspective of his seventeenth- and eighteenth-century Baptist forebears, who had come to the Table believing that there Christ would meet them and give them something deeply satisfying and precious.

10

Baptists, Classic Spirituality, and the Christian Tradition

Dustin Bruce
Boyce College

Introduction

If theological retrieval may be described as retrieving classical theological resources for the sake of renewing the contemporary church's doctrine and practice, then engagement with the devotional classics may be described as mining the resources of the great tradition for the sake of renewing the spiritual lives of contemporary Christians. Just as a number of retrieval theologians have sought to "look back in order to move forward," recent years have witnessed a return to the classic devotional texts of the Christian faith in order to provide what is lacking in the modern church. In his 1978 *Celebration of Discipline*, largely credited with launching the spiritual formation movement among evangelicals, Richard Foster, a Quaker, remarked that a "lack of any real spiritual density led me, almost instinctively, to the Devotional Masters of the Christian faith."[1] While many evangelical Baptists would agree that Christians suffer from a "lack of spiritual density," most of us would not "instinctively" turn to the Christian spiritual classics as part of the solution. Perhaps we should.

---

[1] Richard J. Foster, *Celebration of Discipline: The Path to Spiritual Growth*, 3rd ed. (San Francisco: Harper Collins, 1998), xiii.

Wesleyan theologian Fred Sanders has suggested that evangelical Protestants take an "open but cautious" approach to the Christian spiritual classics.[2] This chapter will argue along similar lines, with particular application to evangelical Baptists. An "open but cautious" approach to engaging the spiritual classics recognizes the value inherent in what Philip Sheldrake has termed the "wisdom documents" of the tradition, while also recognizing that a Baptist's first commitment must always be to the authority of Scripture.[3] This approach should be marked by an openness to read widely across historical, doctrinal, and ecclesial lines in search of gospel truth wherever it may be found. However, a responsible approach must take into account that, while numerous writings outside the Baptist tradition may be read with great spiritual profit, other writings may be deemed "spiritual classics" but prove pointless at best and harmful at worse. In order to facilitate an "open but cautious" approach to engaging spiritual classics outside the Baptist tradition, the rule of faith will be appropriated as a guide.

Defining the Christian Spiritual Classics

For most compilers of Christian spiritual classics, the "Christian" label is primarily determined based on the author's self-identification with the Christian tradition. While self-identifying with Christianity is a start, it does not make the orthodoxy of a spiritual document a foregone conclusion. The problem with such a broad assumption can be seen in Richard Schmidt's *God Seekers: Twenty Centuries of Christian Spiritualities*. Schmidt writes, "By a Christian Spirituality, I mean any spirituality which sees God in Jesus Christ." He explains,

---

[2] Fred Sanders, "Reading Spiritual Classics as Evangelical Protestants," in Jamin Goggin and Kyle Strobel, eds., *Reading the Christian Spiritual Classics: A Guide for Evangelicals* (Downers Grove, IL: IVP Academic, 2013), 149, drawing his language from a popular evangelical approach to the charismatic gifts.

[3] Philip Sheldrake, *Spirituality and History: Questions of Interpretation and Method* (New York: Crossroad, 1991), 164.

> Just as there are various spiritualities among the religions of the world, so are there various spiritualities among Christians. Each spirituality has a different emphasis, asks different questions, and relates to God through Christ from a different angle. . . . It is not a matter of finding the true or right way to relate to God, but of finding the way that is most helpful to you at this time.[4]

While we can affirm legitimate variety within Christian spirivalty, such an uncritical affirmation of various spiritual traditions cannot be an option for evangelical Baptists. Relativism and a self-indulgent picking and choosing of spirituality fail to do justice to a commitment to the authority of Scripture. While the great majority of selections included by Schmidt are biblically faithful, his methodology for selection of Christian spiritualities allows him to include, for instance, Rosemarry Radford Reuther, a twentieth-century feminist theologian whose redefined concept of Jesus proves incompatible with evangelical doctrine.

Steve Porter offers a better definition of a Christian spiritual classic: a writing that (1) "is clearly attributable to a reborn follower of Jesus"; (2) "focuses on a biblical understanding of sanctification"; and (3) is attested by "a multitude of voices across Church history" for its "value for Christian living."[5] Porter's definition proves helpful, as long as his call for a "biblical understanding of sanctification" is not pressed to require too precise a theology of sanctification. Evangelical Baptists can disagree among themselves concerning what exactly constitutes such a "biblical understanding of sanctification." Requiring a very specific theology of sanctification would at the very least limit readers to devotional classics written since the Reformation. We want to affirm that Christians in another age and another place may have experienced God and been transformed by their experiences in true and helpful ways, despite their failure to express a developed doctrine of sanctification. In order to learn and grow from the cloud of witnesses represented by Christian spiritual

---

[4] Richard H. Schmidt, *God Seekers: Twenty Centuries of Christian Spiritualities* (Grand Rapids: Eerdmans, 2008), xvi.

[5] Stephen L. Porter, "Why Should We Read Spiritual Classics?" in Goggin and Strobel, eds., *Christian Spiritual Classics*, 16.

classics, we must limit the doctrinal requirement to essentials of the faith. And yet, we must take the apostle Peter's warning seriously when he alerts us "there will be false teachers among you, who will secretly bring in destructive heresies" (2 Pet 2:1 ESV). Furthermore, many devotional classics deal with aspects of theology other than sanctification, making a broader commitment to orthodoxy a more appropriate criterion. Borrowing from Porter and Sheldrake, we may define a Christian spiritual classic as a document written from an orthodox Christian perspective that has gained broad acclaim from across the Christian tradition as helpful for growing in wisdom and devotion to God.

The Spiritual Formation Movement, Spiritual Classics, and Baptists

The reading of devotional literature has a long history in the church.[6] When Augustine picked up Athanasius's *Life of Antony*, he encountered an example of someone who had given his all to follow Christ.[7] Martin Luther was heavily influenced by the German mystical tradition, reading the "pure and solid theology" of Johannes Tauler's sermons and editing an edition of the anonymous *German Theology*. Referencing that work, Luther claimed that "only the Bible and Augustine had taught him more about God, Christ, man, and all things."[8] John Wesley read Jeremy Taylor's *Rule and Exercise of Holy Living and Dying* and Thomas à Kempis's *Imitation of Christ* with great spiritual profit. Following the example of these and others, leaders within the spiritual formation movement have brought the spiritual classics to prominence within the past several decades. Baptists have maintained a marginal but steady presence

---

[6] James M. Houston, "A Guide to Devotional Reading," *Crux* 22, no. 3 (1986): 2–15.

[7] Athanasius, and Robert C. Gregg, *The Life of Antony and the Letter to Marcellinus*, Classics of Western Spirituality (New York: Paulist, 1980).

[8] Quoted in Stephen E. Ozment, *The Age of Reform (1250–1550): An Intellectual and Religious History of Late Medieval and Reformation Europe* (New Haven, CT: Yale University Press, 1980), 239.

within the movement, including within the lists of recommended devotional classics themselves.

When the spiritual formation movement went mainstream in 1978 with Foster's *Celebration of Discipline*, it was marked by a concern for the retrieval of classical devotional texts.[9] Foster and his colleagues possessed what John Webster has called an "attitude of mind" that searched the past for resources applicable to current challenges.[10] Commenting on the promise of the devotional classics for encouraging spiritual life, Foster claimed, "Somehow I sensed that these ancient writers lived and breathed the spiritual substance these new friends in our little fellowship were seeking so desperately."[11] Foster differentiated a "devotional" reading of ancient writers from an "academic" reading:

> To be sure, I had encountered many of these writers in academic settings. But that was a detached, cerebral kind of reading. Now I read with different eyes, for daily I was working with heartbreaking, soul-crushing, gut-wrenching human need. These "saints," as we sometimes call them, knew God in a way that I clearly did not. They experienced Jesus as the defining reality of their lives. They possessed a flaming vision of God that blinded them to all competing loyalties. They experienced life built on the Rock. . . .
>
> As I continued to soak in the stories of these men and women who were aflame with the fire of divine love, I began desiring this kind of life for myself. And desiring led to seeking and seeking led to finding. And what I found settled me, deepened me, thickened me.[12]

---

[9] Chris Armstrong, "The Rise, Frustration, and Revival of Evangelical Spiritual Ressourcement," *Journal of Spiritual Formation and Soul Care* 2, no. 1 (2009): 113, writes of the spiritual formation movement, "It started in the 1950s and 1960s. It 'broke out' in 1978 with the publication of Richard Foster's *Celebration of Discipline.*"

[10] John Webster, "Theologies of Retrieval," in *The Oxford Handbook of Systematic Theology*, ed. John Webster, Kathryn Tanner, and Iain Torrance (Oxford, UK: Oxford University Press, 2008), 591.

[11] Foster, *Celebration of Discipline*, xiii–xiv.

[12] Foster, xiv.

With the 1993 publication of *Devotional Classics*, Foster and James Bryan Smith introduced readers to excerpts from an array of classic spiritual writers from across the centuries.[13] While Foster and Smith's original anthology included five categories, Foster's 1998 work, *Streams of Living Water*, delineated six traditions that encompass "various dimensions of the spiritual life," including the contemplative tradition, the holiness tradition, the charismatic tradition, the social justice tradition, the evangelical tradition, and the incarnational tradition.[14] In their 2005 revised edition of *Devotional Classics*, Foster and Smith updated their work to include classic writings from each of these six streams.[15] Each stream includes devotional classics from across the centuries, beginning in the New Testament and extending to twentieth-century authors. Of fifty-two selected readings, two of their authors may be identified as Baptists: John Bunyan and Charles Spurgeon.

Recent years have witnessed publication of several editions and anthologies of classic spiritual writings aimed at making the Christian devotional tradition accessible to a new generation of readers. In 2011, Renovaré, the ministry begun by Foster, published *25 Books Every Christian Should Read: A Guide to the Essential Spiritual Classics*.[16] Of the twenty-five recommended books, only one, *The Pilgrim's Progress* by John Bunyan, comes from the Baptist tradition.

Before Foster and Smith released their suggested list of devotional classics, Peter Toon, an Anglican theologian, released his *Spiritual Companions: An Introduction to the Christian Classics* in 1990.[17] According to Toon, "There is a vast storehouse of heavenly and practical

---

[13] Richard J. Foster and James Bryan Smith, eds., *Devotional Classics: Selected Readings for Individuals and Groups* (San Francisco: Harper Collins, 1993).

[14] Richard J. Foster, *Streams of Living Water: Celebrating the Great Traditions of the Christian Faith* (San Francisco: HarperCollins, 1998), xvi.

[15] Richard J. Foster and James Bryan Smith, eds., *Devotional Classics: Selected Readings for Individuals and Groups*, rev. and exp. (San Francisco: HarperOne, 2005).

[16] Julia L. Roller, ed., *25 Books Every Christian Should Read: A Guide to the Essential Spiritual Classics* (New York: HarperOne, 2011).

[17] Peter Toon, *Spiritual Companions: An Introduction to the Christian Classics* (repr., Grand Rapids: Baker, 1992).

wisdom at our disposal in the spiritual classics, ready for us to digest and allow to mould us after the pattern of Jesus Christ."[18] In his work, Toon chooses what he regards as one hundred classics of spirituality drawn from the patristic period through 1939, from across the spectrum of Trinitarian Christianity. Of the one hundred selections, Toon includes three selections by two authors from the Baptist tradition—again, Bunyan and Spurgeon.[19]

Around the same time as Toon, Bruce Shelley, professor of church history at Denver Seminary, released *All the Saints Adore Thee: Insights from Christian Classics.*[20] Shelley cited a concern for "how miserably little today's candidates for ministry know about the saints" as his primary reason for compiling an anthology of fifty-two brief readings with historical introductions. Of Shelley's fifty-two selections, three are associated with the Baptist tradition: along with Bunyan and Spurgeon, he included Oswald Chambers (1874–1917).[21]

As the spiritual formation movement has expanded, interest in engaging the devotional classics has only grown. In 2013 Jamin Goggin and Kyle Strobel released a collection of essays titled *Reading the Spiritual Classics: A Guide for Evangelicals* in an effort to "create readers [of spiritual classics] who are able to read theologically, historically, practically, and spiritually for the glory of God."[22] Both Goggin and Strobel are associated with the Baptist tradition, with Goggin serving on staff at Saddleback Church, a Southern Baptist congregation, and Strobel serving on the preaching team at a church historically associated with Northern Baptists. However, the volume makes no denominational claims and

---

[18] Toon, 1.

[19] Toon (49–52, 159–60) recommends *Pilgrim's Progress* and *Grace Abounding to the Chief of Sinners* by Bunyan, and Spurgeon's *Autobiography.*

[20] Bruce L. Shelley, *All the Saints Adore Thee: Insights from the Christian Classics* (Grand Rapids: Baker, 1994).

[21] Chambers was the son of a Scotch Baptist pastor and converted under the ministry of Spurgeon. He also trained for the Baptist ministry at Dunoon College, entering in 1897. However, Chambers's ministry was mostly itinerant and parachurch-related, so his connections with the Baptist tradition are often overlooked. See Shelley, *All the Saints*, 237–38.

[22] Goggin and Strobel, eds., *Christian Spiritual Classics*, 12.

aims to serve the broadly evangelical community. Contributors hail from a variety of denominational backgrounds, including Baptist.

The Baptist Dallas Willard?

Perhaps the most prominent figure associated with both evangelical Baptists and the spiritual formation movement is Dallas Willard. In a recent biography of the late Willard, Gary Moon captures the tension that has sometimes existed between the devotional classics and traditional Baptist piety. Willard, who along with Foster has been associated with beginning the modern spiritual formation movement, was ordained a Southern Baptist minister in 1956 and pastored First Baptist Church of Thomasville, Missouri, from the fall of 1956 to February 1957.[23] As a college student at Tennessee Temple, Willard was given the book *Deeper Experiences of Famous Christians*, by James Gilchrist Lawson.[24] About this work Willard would later write, "It opened to me the inexhaustible riches of Christ and his people through the ages. This brought me, in turn, a world of profound Christian literature of much greater significance for the understanding and practice of life in Christ."[25] The book, Moon writes, exposed Willard to a "wide and not-very-Southern Baptist casting."[26]

---

[23] Gary W. Moon, *Becoming Dallas Willard: The Formation of a Philosopher, Teacher, and Christ Follower* (Downers Grove, IL: InterVarsity Press, 2018), 77. Willard would later say, "The fact that I teach in a university does not mean that I don't think of myself as a minister of the gospel. I'm there because of that." Dallas Willard, "The Great Invasion of the Kingdom of God: Blessedness [Fragment]," The Kingdom of God (Faith Evangelical Church, Chatsworth, CA, April 9, 1978), MP3, 10:00.

[24] James Gilchrist Lawson, *Deeper Experiences of Famous Christians* (Anderson, IN: Warner, 1911).

[25] Dallas Willard, "When God Moves In: My Experience with *Deeper Experiences of Famous Christians*," in *Indelible Ink: 22 Prominent Christian Leaders Discuss the Books That Shape Their Faith*, ed. Scott Larson (Colorado Springs, CO: Waterbrook, 2003), 50.

[26] Moon, *Becoming Dallas Willard*, 64.

Engagement with classic devotional authors would mark the remainder of Willard's life and ministry. Remarking on his "early days of ministry," Willard recalled, "I spent huge amounts of time absorbed in Scripture and in reading great spiritual writers." He continued, "I supposed in those days the two that meant the most to me were Thomas à Kempis and Charles Finney . . . I literally wore out their books. They were unreadable when I got done with them."[27] Foster remarked of Willard, "Over the years he had soaked himself in the devotional classics and was well acquainted with what I have come to call 'the great conversation about the growth of the soul' throughout the centuries. And he had thought more carefully than anyone I knew about the interfacing of this great tradition with our contemporary malaise."[28] While Willard's upbringing, ordination, and church ministry experience were in the Baptist tradition, his reputation as a theologian and author, to quote Moon, is "not-very-Southern Baptist." While he remained a committed evangelical, it appears that Willard's turn to the devotional classics occurred within a more broadly Christian context, and certainly not within an exclusively Baptist context.

John Bunyan as Baptist Devotional Author

When one thinks of devotional classics within the Baptist tradition, John Bunyan (1628–1688) and *The Pilgrim's Progress* come immediately to mind. *The Pilgrim's Progress* has been widely considered not only a devotional classic but a classic of literature as well. As demonstrated above, Bunyan's work appears in most collections of spiritual classics. According to W. R. Owens, "No other work in English, except the Bible, has been so widely read over such a long period."[29] Answering the question of

---

[27] Dallas Willard, "Finding Satisfaction in Christ," in *Preaching Today*, 2005, MP3, https://www.preachingtoday.com/skills/2009/february/findingsatisfactionin christ.html.

[28] Richard Foster, quoted in Moon, *Becoming Dallas Willard*, 169.

[29] W. R. Owens, introduction to John Bunyan, *The Pilgrim's Progress* (Oxford, UK: Oxford University Press, 2003), xiii.

"why Bunyan's work is essential," one author summarized, "*The Pilgrim's Progress* has been beloved for so many years because of the drama of its narrative, the truth and reliability of its doctrine, and its absolute reliance on Scripture."[30]

Bunyan first published his work in 1678, with a second part added in 1684. Since its publication, *The Pilgrim's Progress* has never gone out of print and has been translated into over two hundred languages. In his work, Bunyan gave the English language timeless phrases, such as "Vanity Fair," "the wilderness of this world," and "Slough of Despond." Furthermore, *The Pilgrim's Progress* proved influential in the British working-class movement and provided English soldiers in the First World War with a vocabulary to understand and express their situation.[31]

Bunyan not only wrote one of the most recognizable devotional classics but also was influenced by two devotional works considered classics in his own day. When he was married in the late 1640s, Bunyan's father-in-law gifted the young couple two well-known spiritual texts: Lewis Bayly's *The Practise of Pietie* and Arthur Dent's *The Plaine Mans Path-Way to Heaven*.[32] Bunyan read the works to great profit. Dent's work likely influenced Bunyan's technique of using dramatic dialogue to express concepts related to godliness.[33] Bayly's work introduced Bunyan to similar concepts, such as vices disguised as virtues.[34] As James Houston points out, while Bayly and Dent remain relatively unknown today, their influence remains "conspicuous and permanent" through Bunyan's work.[35] Bunyan, then, modeled for Baptists how to benefit from, and contribute to, the Christian devotional classics.

---

[30] "The Pilgrim's Progress," in Roller, *25 Books Every Christian Should Read*, 193.

[31] Owens, introduction to *Pilgrim's Progress*, xiii.

[32] Richard L. Greaves, "Bunyan, John (1628–1688)," in *ODNB*, acessed December 9, 2017, https://doi.org/10.1093/ref:odnb/3949.

[33] Christopher Hill, *A Tinker and a Poor Man: John Bunyan and His Church, 1628–1688* (New York: Knopf, 1989), 161.

[34] Hill, 164.

[35] Houston, "Guide to Devotional Reading," 4

Placing Christian Classics on the Baptist Bookshelf

In 1973 historian Richard Lovelace identified what he termed the "sanctification gap" among evangelical Christians. Lovelace claimed the evangelical church had "disconnected sanctification from conversion, and made it easy for men to enter the kingdom on the basis of simple faith and initial repentance. . . . However, they failed to reinsert sanctification in its proper place in the development of the Christian life, and left the engine with no power train at all."[36] Willard has echoed Lovelace's analysis using the language of discipleship. In *The Great Omission*, he writes, "For at least several decades the churches of the Western world have not made discipleship a condition of being a Christian. One is not required to be, or to intend to be, a disciple in order to become a Christian, and one may remain a Christian without any signs of progress toward or in discipleship."[37] While Lovelace and Willard were diagnosing a broader swath of Protestantism than that of evangelical Baptists, the assessment rings true for Baptists. Evangelical Baptists have experienced a sanctification gap, and the "spiritual resources of the past are a much-needed medicine."[38]

While Christians need spiritual encouragement from contemporaries who can sympathize with their contextualized weaknesses, their spiritual growth also benefits from hearing voices of spiritual encouragement who do not share the same modern or postmodern sensibilities. As L. P. Hartley observed in *The Go-Between*, "The past is a foreign country; they do things differently there."[39] Evangelical Baptists who see a need to "do things differently" can find great help from the foreign country of the past. As Gordon Smith has highlighted, "Twenty-first century Christians are . . . rediscovering some of the ancient practices of the church . . . that

---

[36] Lovelace, "The Sanctification Gap," *Theology Today* 29, no. 4 (1973): 363–69.

[37] Dallas Willard, *The Great Omission: Reclaiming Jesus's Essential Teachings on Discipleship* (San Francisco: HarperCollins, 2006), 4.

[38] Armstrong, "Evangelical Spiritual *Ressourcement*," 114.

[39] Leslie P. Hartley, *The Go-Between* (New York: New York Review of Books, 2002), 17.

may have been more typical of a Christian community that sought to live faithfully in a pagan environment."[40]

Some may question why the Bible is not the only "old" book evangelical Baptists need. Why is it so important for Christians to read those other old books written in a time and place so distant from our own? The words of C. S. Lewis, taken from his introduction to Athanasius's *On the Incarnation*, have proven somewhat of a classic answer: "Every age has its own outlook. It is specially good at seeing certain truths and specially liable to make certain mistakes. We all, therefore, need the books that will correct the characteristic mistakes of our own period. And that means the old books."[41] If this was true for a mid-twentieth-century Anglican, it must also be true for a twenty-first-century evangelical Baptist—and the need to apply Lewis's wisdom is perhaps more urgent for contemporary Baptists in light of their historical amnesia. As James Payton has quipped, "If evangelicalism were charged with being historically aware, there might not be enough evidence for a conviction."[42] While the Scripture is certainly the foundational element of evangelical spirituality, the "me and my Bible" reflex has proven ineffective in rooting evangelicalism doctrinally and spiritually. Eugene Peterson reflects on the foundational role of the classics, "Familiarity with the classics is essential to being able to carry on intelligent conversations with our sisters and brothers in Christ."[43] This "intelligent conversation" can be an important element in spiritual renewal.

Gerald Sittser presses Lewis's logic further into the realm of spirituality: "Every generation of believers faces the risk of becoming a prisoner to

---

[40] Gordon T. Smith, "Grace and Spiritual Disciplines," in Glen G. Scorgie, Simon Chan, Gordon T. Smith, and James D. Smith, eds., *Zondervan Dictionary of Christian Spirituality* (Grand Rapids: Zondervan, 2011), 226.

[41] C. S. Lewis, preface to Athanasius, *On the Incarnation*, Popular Patristics 3 (Crestwood, NY: St. Vladimir's Seminary Press, 1977), 4–5. Lewis argues that all contemporary writers share a similar outlook.

[42] James R. Payton Jr., "Reading Orthodox Spirituality," in Goggin and Strobel, eds., *Christian Spiritual Classics*, 139.

[43] Eugene H. Peterson, *Take and Read: Spiritual Reading—An Annotated List* (Grand Rapids: Eerdmans, 1996), 7.

its own myopic vision of the Christian faith, assuming that how it understands faith and practice is always the best."[44] While modern believers
and ancient Christian authors share "one Lord, one faith, one baptism"
(Eph 4:5), the Christian spiritual classics introduce readers to a way of
following Jesus located in a different context, with different resources,
challenges, and cultural climates. Porter, in what he refers to as the "pneumatological rationale" for reading the classics, argues, "Since the Spirit of
God uses various extrabiblical means to bring his presence and Word to
bear on human hearts, it is evident that one fitting mean would be the
writings of other Christ followers regarding a biblical understanding of
the way of holiness."[45] The classics raise different questions, even if drawing from the same scriptural source. As Sittser points out, "These believers can teach us truths about the Christian faith that we have not learned
yet or do not consider important. . . . History will show us that there is
more to the Christian faith than what we think and have experienced."[46]

The variety of Christian communities that have produced the
authors Christian spiritual classics is nothing short of stunning. Authors
have sought to delineate the classic writings in various ways in recent
years. Foster wrote of six "streams" of Christian spirituality drawn
together into a "mighty Mississippi of the Spirit."[47] Sittser finds eleven
different spiritual emphases within the history of the church.[48] Indeed,
Evan Howard has located at least fifteen different "schools of spirituality" within the Christian tradition.[49] While such diversity has benefits,
it also raises challenges.

---

[44] Gerald L. Sittser, *Water From a Deep Well: Christian Spirituality from Early
Martyrs to Modern Missionaries* (Downers Grove, IL: InterVarsity Press, 2007), 18.

[45] Porter, "Why Should We Read Spiritual Classics?" in Goggin and Strobel,
eds., *Christian Spiritual Classics*, 23.

[46] Sittser, *Water from a Deep Well*, 18.

[47] Foster, *Streams of Living Water*, xv. As previously stated, Foster identifies the
contemplative, holiness, charismatic, social justice, evangelical, and incarnational
traditions.

[48] Sittser, *Water From a Deep Well*, 18.

[49] Evan B. Howard, "The Schools of Spirituality," in Goggin and Strobel,
eds., *Christian Spiritual Classics*, 63, describes a "school of spirituality" as a "certain
approach to or community of faith which brings together features of spiritual life

Though several tributaries may flow into the spiritual Mississippi, to borrow Foster's analogy, not all streams are safe to drink. As Sittser states, "Not everything that has occurred in the history of the church has been true, right and good. Much said in the name of God has been errant; much done in the name of God has been abhorrent. *Strange* and *different* are not always the right words to use. Sometimes *misguided* and *destructive* are."[50] For those of us committed to the authority of Scripture, historical spiritual relativism is not an option.

Returning to Sanders's "open but cautious" approach, evangelical Baptists need an approach that allows us to judge a supposed work of the Spirit by the Scriptures.[51] As evangelicals, we desire to measure all things according to the Word of God. Unfortunately, that reflex, when applied to spiritual writings, may become nothing more than an unhelpful exercise in proof texting. Perhaps an approach that measures a work against the central message of the Scripture will prove a better option.[52]

The *Regula Fidei* and Christian Spiritual Classics

The rule of faith (Lat. *regula fidei*), found in the writings of the ante-Nicene fathers, refers to the "sum content of apostolic teaching" formulated for "public use in worship, in particular for use in baptism, and it outlines the authoritative articles of faith."[53] The rule, which was never recorded as a fixed creed, found clearest expression in the writings of Irenaeus and Tertullian. In his *Prescription against the Heretics*, Tertullian summarized the rule of faith as

---

into an organic whole and communicates them to a future generation of recognized followers."

[50] Sittser, *Water From a Deep Well*, 19–20.

[51] Sanders, "Reading Spiritual Classics," 149.

[52] Daniel H. Williams, *Retrieving the Tradition and Renewing Evangelicalism: A Primer for Suspicious Protestants* (Grand Rapids: Eerdmans, 1999), 23, describes the rule and the Scriptures as having a "symbiotic" relationship.

[53] Kathryn Greene-McCreight, "Rule of Faith," in *Dictionary for the Theological Interpretation*, 703.

that which prescribes the belief that there is only one God, and that He is none other than the Creator of the World, who produced all things out of nothing through his own Word . . . that this Word is called His Son, and, under the name of God was seen "in diverse manners" by the patriarchs, heard at all times in the prophets, at last brought down by the Spirit and Power of the Father into the Virgin Mary, was made flesh in her womb, and being born of her, went forth as Jesus Christ; thenceforth He preached the new law and the new promise of the kingdom of heaven, worked miracles; having been crucified, He rose again the third day; having ascended into the heavens, He sat at the right hand of the Father; sent instead of Himself the Power of the Holy Ghost to lead such as believe; will come with glory to take the saints to the enjoyment of everlasting life and of the heavenly promises, and to condemn the wicked to everlasting fire, after the resurrection of both these classes shall have happened, together with the restoration of the flesh. This rule, as it will be proved, was taught by Christ.[54]

The earliest Christians used the rule of faith as a hermeneutical key for the Christian Scriptures. The rule, borne out of the Scriptures, served the church by staking out boundaries for interpretation. J. Todd Billings describes the rule as a map marking the path that is Jesus Christ:

It is not a detailed map that knows all of the stops along the way. But this map is a sketch of our story, our journey: through it we know our path (Jesus Christ), our source of illumination and empowerment (the Holy Spirit), and have a foretaste of our final destination (a transforming vision of the triune God, which involves restoration of creation and communion with God). On this path we grow in the love of God and neighbor as we grow

---

[54] Tertullian, "Prescription against the Heretics," *ANF* 3.249.

into our identity in Christ, and we grow in the knowledge of and fellowship with God.[55]

While Billings's statement first and fundamentally applies to interpreting the Christian Scriptures, the application of the rule he describes has implications for reading the Christian spiritual classics as well.

Early Christians used the rule to guide their interpretation of Scripture, but the rule also expressed the church's identity. "Now the Christians trace their origin from the Lord Jesus Christ," Aristides (2nd. cent.) emphasized, leading into a presentation of the rule of faith addressed to the Roman emperor.[56] Use of the rule in baptism, Kevin Vanhoozer noted, illustrated its function as a means of identity formation: "The salient point . . . is that the baptismal candidate, in confessing the Rule, was thereby affirming the Christian theo-drama as the framework for understanding his or her new identity 'in Christ.'"[57] The rule served as a new frame of reference not just for Christian Scripture but for Christian experience as well.[58]

As accounts of Christian experience and, in some sense, interpretations of Scripture, the spiritual classics are governed by the rule of faith. As John O'Keefe and R. R. Reno have argued, "The rule of faith was a rule for life as well as a rule for reading scripture and teaching its meaning. It was a spiritual rule that guided the whole person toward fellowship with God."[59] The Christian spiritual classics are helpful because they offer accounts of just such fellowship. And the rule becomes helpful as it guides the interpretation of just such experience.

---

[55] J. Todd Billings, *The Word of God for the People of God: An Entryway to the Theological Interpretation of Scripture* (Grand Rapids: Eerdmans, 2010), 10.

[56] "Aristides: Basic Faith," in *Tradition, Scripture, and Interpretation: A Sourcebook for the Ancient Church*, ed. D. H. Williams (Grand Rapids: Eerdmans, 2006), 67.

[57] Vanhoozer, *Drama of Doctrine*, 204.

[58] Paul M. Blowers, "The Regula Fidei and the Narrative Character of Early Christian Faith," *Pro Ecclesia* 6, no. 2 (1997): 202.

[59] John J. O'Keefe and Russell R. Reno, *Sanctified Vision: An Introduction to Early Christian Interpretation of the Bible* (Baltimore: John Hopkins University Press, 2005), 128.

The rule of faith is certainly not the only doctrinal guide ever produced within the church, so what makes it suitable to the task? Why not the rulings of the creeds and councils of the early church? The rule of faith proves suitable for three reasons. First, the rule is ancient. Second, the rule is limited in scope to a "mere Christianity." Third, the rule possesses a narrative structure. For these reasons, which will we expound briefly, the rule of faith continues to serve as demarcation of distinctly Christian spiritual writings.

Ancient Pedigree

Any standard used to define Christian classics must have the capacity to operate within the full range of the Christian tradition. We have already established that a great benefit of reading the classics is the opportunity to engage a world outside of one's own time and place.

The rule of faith is old enough to encompass nearly everything written within the Christian tradition. It emerged in bits from the writings of the apostolic fathers as the first-century church responded to questions coming from both outside and within the church. By the late second century, the rule was used widely by the ante-Nicene fathers.[60] Most commonly associated with Irenaeus and Tertullian, the rule may also be found in the writings of Hippolytus, Clement of Alexandria, Origen, Novatian, and others.[61] According to Tertullian, the rule was passed down in the churches from the apostles themselves. It was only in the written defense of Christianity against heretics that it needed to be written down.

The most ancient Christian spiritual classics form some of the most precious and enriching accounts of spirituality the church possesses. Whatever standard one chooses must accommodate the writings of Ignatius of Antioch, the *Didache*, the *Epistle to Diognetus*, and the like. It may be safely presumed the rule of faith was in operation at the time

---

[60] Tomas Bokedal, "The Rule of Faith: Tracing Its Origins," *Journal of Theological Interpretation* 7, no. 2 (2013): 234.

[61] M. E. Osterhaven, "The Rule of Faith," in *Evangelical Dictionary of Theology*, ed. Walter A. Elwell (Grand Rapids: Baker Academic, 2001), 1043.

such material was written. Apart from the Scriptures themselves, there is no more ancient doctrinal basis for authenticating an expression of faith as Christian. Commenting on the ancient pedigree of the rule, D. H. Williams states, "Long before the apostles or ecumenical creeds, we find the regulating function of the Rule of Faith in the churches, expounding the cardinal points of theology which evangelical Christians still believe and confess to this day."[62]

"Mere" Christianity

Related to the necessity for a standard with an ancient pedigree, any basis of selection for inclusion within a truly Christian tradition must limit itself to what C. S. Lewis famously called "mere Christianity." For Lewis, the reading of only modern books proves not only unhelpful but dangerous. He elaborates, "A new book is still on its trial and the amateur is not in a position to judge it. It has to be tested against the great body of Christian thought down the ages, and all its hidden implications (often unsuspected by the author himself) have to be brought to light." According to Lewis, the mature reader should "have a standard of plain, central Christianity ('mere Christianity' as Baxter called it) which puts controversies of the moment in their proper perspective. Such a standard can be acquired only from old books."[63]

The rule of faith provides a helpful expression of what Lewis, echoing Baxter, refers to as mere Christianity. Everett Ferguson summarizes the rule as the "essential message . . . fixed by the gospel and the structure of Christian belief in one God, reception of salvation in Christ, and experience of the Holy Spirit."[64] The rule strongly affirms the Trinity, the Christocentric nature of salvation, the unity of the Old and New Testaments, and the biblical storyline of creation, fall, and redemption.

---

[62] Williams, *Retrieving the Tradition*, 87.

[63] Lewis, "Introduction," 4.

[64] Everett Ferguson, "The Rule of Faith," in *Encyclopedia of Early Christianity*, ed. Everett Ferguson, 2nd ed. (New York: Garland, 1997), 1003–4.

The rule does not attempt to answer every point of doctrine but does provide the context in which every point of doctrine may be understood. It sets forth the basics of what is and is not meaningfully Christian—and no more.

Narrative Structure

A notable feature of the rule of faith is its narrative structure: it has been described as a "basic 'take' on the subject matter and plot of the Christian story."[65] As opposed to a document like the Westminster Confession, the rule does not articulate doctrine point by point but affirms the overarching narrative of the Scripture and Christian experience. Paul Blowers, commenting on the narrative structure of the rule, states that it "served the primitive Christian hope of articulating and authenticating a world-encompassing story or metanarrative of creation, incarnation, redemption, and consummation."[66]

Christian spiritual classics tell the story of men and women throughout the centuries who have sought to live in the presence of God. Many, like Augustine's *Confessions* or Bunyan's *The Pilgrim's Progress*, are narratives of life with God, offered as helps for those whose narratives are still being written. Others, such as Thomas à Kempis's *Imitation of Christ* or Brother Lawrence's *Practice of the Presence of God*, introduce principles for life with God. Philip Sheldrake has commented that what makes classics endure is their ability to "effectively translate Christian ideas into life-style so that the connection between theory and practice is made explicit."[67] Spiritual classics function not merely to teach doctrine but to contribute to the story of one's life with God. The rule can serve as an effective tool for comparing the story line and plot of a potential classic devotional writing to that of Scripture.

---

[65] Greene-McCreight, "Rule of Faith," 703.

[66] Blowers, "The Regula Fidei and the Narrative Character of Early Christian Faith," 202.

[67] Sheldrake, *Spirituality and History*, 165.

Conclusion

As evangelical Baptists aim to close the sanctification gap, the spiritual classics of the church offer a compelling vision for life with God that we desperately need to see. As Bruce Demarest has exclaimed, "The wonderful fact is, *we are heirs of a two-thousand-year treasury of Christian devotional writings.*"[68] Engaging the writings of saints from across such a span can help loosen the bonds of the cultural captivity to which we all belong.[69] And yet, like any new experience in a foreign land, an "open but cautious" approach seems wisest. By appropriating the rule of faith, twenty-first-century Baptists may remain open to how the Spirit might use a devotional classic, while cautious against those writings that offer little to no spiritual profit. As Bunyan concluded his future classic, he wrote,

> What of my dross thou findest there, be bold
> To throw away, but yet preserve the Gold
> What if my Gold be wrapped up in Ore?
> None throws away the Apple for the Core.[70]

Baptists must avoid the temptation to throw away the gold within Christian devotional classics when they come across a little ore. *Tolle lege!*

---

[68] Bruce Demarest, *Satisfy Your Soul: Restoring the Heart of Christian Spirituality* (Colorado Springs, CO: NavPress, 1999), 257.

[69] Demarest, 258.

[70] Bunyan, *The Pilgrim's Progress*, 155.

11

Baptists, Denominational Structures, and the Christian Tradition

AMY CARTER WHITFIELD

Southeastern Baptist Theological Seminary

"Out of all the things that we shall study, I think tonight will be the most important."[1] With those words in 1974, W. A. Criswell introduced a Wednesday-evening teaching series at the First Baptist Church of Dallas, Texas, on ancient creeds and confessions of the faith. The series was titled "What We Believe: The Doctrines of the Church."

Criswell began the series with a two-part introduction, "Concerning Creeds and Confessions of Faith"[2] and "The Great Confessions of Christendom."[3] The first sermon provided two reasons creeds have been adopted throughout church history. First, creeds arise out of faith's desire for self-expression. He argued, "It is impossible for a man to accept the faith of Jesus Christ and not have on the inside of him a burning,

---

[1] W. A. Criswell, "Concerning Creeds and Confessions of Faith," (sermon, First Baptist Church, Dallas, TX, January 16, 1974), https://wacriswell.com /sermons/1974/concerning-creeds-and-confession-of-faith.

[2] Criswell.

[3] W. A. Criswell, "The Great Confessions of Christendom," (sermon, First Baptist Church, Dallas, TX, January 23, 1974), https://wacriswell.com/sermons /1974/the-great-confessions-of-christendom.

irrepressible desire to say something about it."[4] Second, appealing to Matt 10:32–33, Criswell asserted that creeds stem from the commandment to confess our faith publicly. Additionally, he offered five uses for confessions of faith: to help believers understand the Bible's teaching; to instruct children; to display the bond of union between churches; to distinguish the Christian faith from other religions; and to recognize heretical teaching clearly.

The second sermon covered the great confessions of Christendom at lightning speed. In one evening he presented an overview of the three "universally accepted" creeds (the Apostles', Nicene, and Athanasian Creeds), two Reformational confessions (the Augsburg Confession and the 1646 Westminster Confession), and seven Baptist Confessions of Faith (the Schleitheim, First London, Somerset, Second London, Philadelphia, and New Hampshire Confessions, and the Baptist Faith and Message). While many in the pews might have been familiar with some items on that list (at least the most recent Southern Baptist statement), Criswell spoke as if he were introducing them for the first time. The study, he said, was a new personal opportunity: "I have done all this . . . first for my own soul; this is the first time that I have ever studied such a thing as this."[5]

Criswell was a former two-time president of the Southern Baptist Convention and one of the most well-connected and highly respected preachers of his time. His church was one of the largest and most influential churches in the convention, and he had already served as pastor for three decades. Yet he seemed to indicate a relatively light engagement with the Christian tradition. Criswell was typical.

Baptists (particularly Southern Baptists) have held a loose association with the Christian tradition throughout much of their history, regularly and proactively choosing to maintain their distinctiveness. This disengagement from the broader Christian world—though there have been notable exceptions—often was attributable to a concern for maintaining Baptist doctrine. At times, Baptists also seemed driven by a general

---

[4] Criswell, "Concerning Creeds and Confessions."
[5] Criswell, "Great Confessions."

distaste for ecumenism. Positively, Southern Baptists' efforts to retain their distinctiveness appear to have been motivated by a desire to preserve their identity, build loyalty, and ensure growth. Yet their parochial preferences also inhibited their access to rich theological and devotional resources and unwittingly elevated Southern Baptist culture above the Christian tradition.

The preamble to the SBC Constitution states that its framers gathered in 1845 "for the purpose of carrying into effect the benevolent intention of our constituents by organizing a plan for eliciting, combining, and directing the energies of the denomination for the propagation of the gospel."[6] The plan called for focusing the energies of the denomination to spread the gospel. This plan developed not via the creation of an entirely new organization, but rather out of separation from an existing one. Northern Baptists with a controlling interest in the Triennial Convention had refused to allow slaveholders to serve as missionaries, and Baptists in the South believed that action "unwarranted by the Bible."[7] While their stated purpose did not mention slavery, the context of their founding implies the gospel they were zealous to spread would be accompanied by protection of Southern culture.[8] But while those gathering in Augusta, Georgia, were doing so from a posture of dissent, they believed they were continuing a rich Baptist heritage while those who sought to exclude them were breaking away.

In their 1845 address to the new convention, William Bullein Johnson, Thomas Curtis, Richard Fuller, and C. D. Mallary declared: "We have constructed for our basis no new creed; acting in this matter upon a Baptist aversion for all creeds but the Bible."[9] An early test to this principle came when The Southern Baptist Theological Seminary developed its Abstract of Principles in 1857, the first formal statement of

---

[6] "Constitution," Southern Baptist Convention, http://www.sbc.net/aboutus /legal/constitution.asp.

[7] Robert G. Gardner, *A Decade of Debate and Division: Georgia Baptists and the Formation of the Southern Baptist Convention* (Macon, GA: Mercer University Press, 1995), 34.

[8] Bill J. Leonard, *Baptist Ways: A History* (Valley Forge, PA: Judson, 2003), 189.

[9] 1845 SBC Annual, 14, 19.

faith within this particular cooperative body. Influenced by earlier Baptist confessions and appealing to Scripture, it was developed not to be used *by* the church but rather *for* it. It presented theological boundaries for faculty and established churches' confidence that their ministers would be trained under the guidance of Scripture. This statement was more for accountability to churches than corporate expression.

As they grew larger in number, Southern Baptists staked their claim geographically. While they traced their history to earlier Baptists, their camaraderie and expression carried a distinctly regional expression. They continued interaction with their Baptist brethren to the North, particularly at an intellectual level. In that context the broader landscape was open to considering the Baptist connection with the Christian tradition, but Southern Baptists were not the ones driving the conversation.

For example, at the 1885 Fourth Baptist Congress,[10] in New York, Edward Braislin of Newton Centre, Massachusetts, presented a paper on "Liturgy in Baptist Churches." He argued formal liturgical practices had waned in the face of the "advancing spirit of religious liberty." With freedom to worship, how to do so became an open question. He acknowledged Baptist churches were liturgical but that "it ought in all fairness to be said that Baptist liturgy [was] of a very inferior kind, in fact almost no liturgy at all." The question at hand was whether Baptist churches should join in a greater tradition rather than pursue their own liturgical expression. In his argument,

> The stately and beautiful symbols of Christian worship as of Christian dogma, which are the products of the Christian Ages, are not the property of any one church or denomination, but belong to all whom reverence prompts to worship God. Because

---

[10] The Baptist Congress was a think tank of Baptist intellectuals that met from 1882 to 1912. It offered a forum for academic engagement among Baptists, crossing regional denominational lines. With participants ranging from Walter Rauschenbusch and William Whitsitt to J. B. Gambrell and E. Y. Mullins, the congress allowed issues to be fleshed out through discussion and debate. Records of the proceedings are held at the Southern Baptist Historical Library and Archives in Nashville, Tennessee. See the Baptist Congress Proceedings Collection, AR 40.

I find the Apostles' Creed, and the Prayer of Chrysostom in the Episcopal "Book of Common Prayer," it does not follow that my use of them inclines me toward the Episcopal Church, or toward its aged mother, the Church of Rome. Chrysostom was of an older age than either, and the Apostles' Creed is older than Chrysostom. The Lord's Prayer, the Psalms and the Prophets are also in the Book of Common Prayer; shall I for that reason hesitate to use them? There are some products of the human soul to which no man or class can claim exclusive right. Among these are the sacred Scriptures, the sacred hymns, the sacred prayers of the people of God. The fruit of sanctified thought belongs to the church universal. No man's previous use of them, no man's abuse of them shall lessen their value to me.[11]

Responses were largely supportive, but only from others in the North. The Rev. R. S. MacArthur of New York said, tongue in cheek, "The question before us is not, shall we have a liturgy in Baptist churches, but shall we have a good liturgy?"[12] The use of liturgy, he said, was an issue of worship. Thomas Armitage defended the importance of freedom in worship but saw it as cutting both ways: Liturgy should not become so ritualistic that the absence of any particular element would hinder anyone's worship. But it also should not become stubbornly resistant to the introduction of new worship forms.

That this was being addressed in an academic setting rather than as a normal part of the ecclesial experience may suggest that churches were not practicing such principles far and wide. But even at this high level, it appears to have been considered primarily by those in the North. Churches in the South were largely absent from discussion of the broader Christian

---

[11] "Baptist Congress 1885," Baptist Congress Proceedings Collection, AR 40, Box 1, Folder 1.1: 72, Southern Baptist Historical Library and Archives, Nashville, TN.

[12] *Proceedings of the Fourth Baptist Congress, Held in the City of New-York, Nov. 1885* (New York: Century), 73. Located in Baptist Congress Proceedings Collection, Southern Baptist Historical Library and Archives, Nashville, Tennessee. Accessed October 4, 2018.

tradition, as they were having a different discussion. As Southern Baptist churches entered the twentieth century, growth and expansion became a greater focus than connecting with a broader tradition.

While the SBC was built on a foundation of cooperation within itself, connections outside the family did not extend naturally or easily. The boundaries were identified as doctrinal, but cultural identity was emphasized too as a way to increase in size and hold a monopoly on the region. The desire to protect the ethos of the "Southern Baptist way" developed into a desire to expand it. As Bill Leonard states, "The denomination of the defeated, itself born of schism and racism, had become God's 'last' and 'only hope' for evangelizing the world."[13] This movement borne of dissent turned its eye toward growing in strength. A way to accomplish this was cultural consistency, protecting a way of life and giving people a predictable religious experience they could replicate. The Southern Baptist movement would not distinguish itself and protect a culture, however, if it identified with the rest of the world. It had a greater chance to thrive if it developed a culture of its own and if that tradition could take precedence over others.

During the twentieth century, the churches of the Southern Baptist Convention may have diverged on doctrinal lines at times, but outwardly they offered a generic similarity in experience. When someone visited a Southern Baptist church, she knew where she was. The hymns were recognizable, the lingo was similar, and the Sunday School curriculum was the same as the Southern Baptist church across town. Even if the churches were not all exactly alike, they felt familiar because they had a common culture—"a bit of Dixie in every SBC congregation," as Stanley Grenz put it.[14] For a non-hierarchical convention that worked from the bottom up, that was quite a feat. The convention machine grew in size and power. The culture and tradition spread as tens of thousands of church

---

[13] Bill J. Leonard, *God's Last & Only Hope: The Fragmentation of the Southern Baptist Convention* (Grand Rapids: Eerdmans, 1990), 13.

[14] Stanley J. Grenz, "Theology and Piety among Baptists and Evangelicals," in *Southern Baptists and American Evangelicals*, ed. David S. Dockery (Nashville: B&H, 1993), 161.

front doors opened to a similar scene. A development like this does not happen by accident—it begins with a singular purpose and narrow scope. Southern Baptists did not simply eschew the broader Christian tradition; they replaced it with a tradition and liturgy of their own.

The Southern Baptist Convention of the 1910s wrestled with a growing world and a changing context, wondering how they should relate to those from other religious backgrounds. While Southern Baptists recognized their existence within a larger Christian tradition, they instinctively preferred to chart an independent course. This did not mean outright rejection of engagement with others, nor recognition of common bonds. But they did not see connection beyond their own boundaries or emphasis of a larger Christian family as the best way to advance their cause.

In 1910 the Episcopal Church proposed a World Conference, ultimately inviting more than a hundred denominations to participate.[15] Southern Baptists considered this invitation for six years as they pursued their own growth strategies, and their deliberations demonstrated how they viewed their role within a larger landscape. A special committee, which eventually became a standing committee, reported their ongoing interactions with the organizers of the movement and their developing thoughts about the endeavor. They avoided declining the invitation outright but never showed genuine interest in it.

Simultaneously, the convention was beginning to take cues from political and economic progressivism as a way for institutional growth in a grassroots system. The pursuit of denominational efficiency opened the door for convention leaders to move toward a more unified methodology. Efforts were made to streamline processes and develop a common experience for people in the pews at all Southern Baptist churches. Efficiency may have been the primary goal, but building a culture came with it. Annual reports of the Home Mission Board and Sunday School Board from that era evidence an ambition going beyond simple gospel

---

[15] "Historical Note," Guide to the World Conference on Faith and Order Collection, 1913–1927, University of Chicago Library, accessed November 20, 2018, https://www.lib.uchicago.edu/e/scrc/findingaids/view.php?eadid=ICU.SPCL.WRLDCONFTHORD.

expression to include the language of cultural expression. Geographic realities in the United States, combined with comity agreements with Northern Baptists, limited their territory. In other words, for the Home Mission Board, "home" meant the South. That was their mission field. They wanted to win as many people as possible from the region, and in a way that was culturally compatible with it. The historic traditions of Christendom may have not been disagreeable, but at times they were not compatible missiologically with the American South. Emphasis of a broader tradition might result in dilution of the host culture.

Initial reaction in 1912 to connecting with the greater Christian landscape demonstrated an open but cautious approach. Southern Baptists were happy to interact with other groups and thankful for "increasing spiritual unity among all the true followers of our Lord." They wanted to promote any union among Christians but went on to state, "We feel it only frank and just to say that many of the tenets which are regarded as divisive between ourselves and our brethren of other communions are and ever must be cherished and defended by us as the clear teachings of God's Word, and on these matters we can never evade or compromise."[16]

That same year, concern arose about interdenominational literature having too much influence among the churches. The Convention Lesson Committee desired to move away from any collaborative work with other traditions in the realm of Sunday School instruction. They believed they would do better developing their own teachers than allowing interdenominational training: "We must discover for ourselves the best way to serve the Convention and to protect and advance our special interests in the field."[17]

The Home Mission Board's report went deeper into the motivation for narrower denominational efforts. It is understandable that an organization focused on reaching local individuals would have parochial tendencies. But their language shows the extent of their views: "In a day when there is much confusion, the Home Mission Board seeks through its missionaries, its literature, and through every influence that it

---

[16] 1912 SBC Annual, 14.
[17] 1912 SBC Annual, 18.

commands, to conserve that loyalty to our denominational body that we believe is for the honor of God and the strengthening of our people to contribute great things for the preservation of American institutions, for the purifying of society and the salvation of the world."[18] Insular thinking was taking root, and the lines between denominational and regional loyalty were starting to blur. Rather than connecting with influence from the outside, the board wanted to develop itself as the influencer.

Additionally, the increase in European immigration to the United States affected Southern Baptists' view of engagement with the rest of the world. As strangers came to the region, a broader cultural concern about the spread of Catholicism became a narrow concern for Southern Baptists, particularly with respect to home missions. The HMB recognized that its mission was affected by a growing immigrant population and that it had a role in reaching the world from the home front. However, against the backdrop of a fear of socialism, Southern Baptists seemed pulled between advancement and protection. Those on the board knew they had something to offer immigrants from other nations, but they also wanted to fight off new philosophies taking root in their homeland. Their language suggested simultaneous desires to evangelize and fight off outsiders:

> We should adopt an adequate evangelism for the foreigners who come, but it is absolutely essential that we shall maintain in the South a dominance of evangelical faith that shall bless the nation and the world. While we send the gospel to other nations and gird ourselves to evangelize those who have come to us, we should pray God to give us the wisdom to protect our American civilization from a flood of Catholic aliens greater than we can assimilate and transform into a power for a Christian world conquest.[19]

In 1913 the SBC continued to consider the World Conference on Faith and Order but focused primarily on arousing deeper interest in

---

[18] 1912 SBC Annual, 259.
[19] 1912 SBC Annual, 281.

staking denominational ground. Sunday School was the front line for connecting with grassroots Southern Baptists, and the Committee on Sunday School Lessons made the case for moving away from outside literature. They argued all denominations should educate their people, and they addressed the SBC specifically: "This is a need common today in all denominations. It seems to us peculiarly needed among our own people, because we stand almost alone in our witness for certain great doctrines."[20]

The Home Mission Board also portrayed Baptists as having a special role in protecting Southern culture by leavening it with the gospel. Baptists, the board stated, must "hold their prestige and influence in quickening and lifting up our Southern civilization" by withstanding "unscriptural liberalism."[21] The message was that if one was loyal to the South, one should be loyal to the SBC, because it was through the SBC that the South would be preserved and protected via doctrinal purity.

In pursuing this mission, the board communicated that it could not support outside sources as the primary resource for missions education. While it allowed for supplementary study, it advocated a main missions curriculum that was specifically Southern Baptist. It is understandable that a body would want to communicate its values and methodology clearly, but the board had already demonstrated particular concern with potential waning allegiance among young Southern Baptists the previous year. "An examination of many of these undenominational books shows that a number of them not only minimize denominational loyalty, which is to be expected in such books, but that they frequently contain positive preachments that seem definitely intended to break down the spirit of loyalty to one's own denominational group."[22]

In the deliberations of 1914 and 1915 we find the clearest picture of where the convention stood on relating to Christianity at large. Consideration of the World Conference on Faith and Order coincided with a plan for developing uniform Sunday School lessons and the launch of a strategy for denominational efficiency. These three issues

---

[20] 1913 SBC Annual, 54.
[21] 1913 SBC Annual, 284.
[22] 1912 SBC Annual, 304.

were handled by separate committees but with overlapping members as well as similar goals and descriptive language.

It was the express view of convention leadership, backed by a majority vote, that the best use of Southern Baptist resources and energies was to focus on building a streamlined Southern Baptist system with identifiable and distinctive characteristics. There was openness to connecting with others in a spirit of warmth and encouragement but not to expending efforts or capital to join a movement or achieve a goal together. Doctrinal boundaries were always mentioned as a major reason, but not far behind was a sense that identity might be lost if one stepped into a religious melting pot.

A major development in 1914 was the report of a special Committee on Efficiency. The SBC's processes had outgrown the simplicity of the convention as originally conceived, and the move toward efficiency in Western government and industry seeped into ministry and mission as well. As H. Leon McBeth put it, "Consolidation was in the air in the early twentieth century, and Baptists breathed that air."[23]

The Committee on Efficiency dealt with structural questions and inner workings but also addressed the tension between Christian union and denominational efficiency. It understood that the call to be united with the greater Christian tradition came from a motive of peace and brotherhood and of connection with the past. The committee even rejoiced in unity as a goal and called for finding common ground while being clear about doctrinal differences, believing Baptists could not pursue Christian union by compromise.

The commitment to theological truth and doctrinal purity is impossible to ignore. Setting boundaries was not a passive effort. The committee drew lines, with a plan for how the denomination would work inside those parameters. More than simply telling churches not to cross a line, the committee sought to align values for the purpose of advancement. They encouraged seven principles: (1) loyalty to Christ; (2) complete autonomy "unembarrassed by entangling alliances with other

---

[23] McBeth, *Baptist Heritage*, 612.

bodies holding to different standards of doctrine and different views of church life and church order"; (3) singular focus on multiplying entities in pursuit of denominational control; (4) total alignment of all efforts and programs, "avoiding the weakness of vagueness and the diffusion of denominational strength into channels leading away from the churches"; (5) renewed emphasis on education and training about the work of the denomination; (6) calling all to greater commitment and giving to "enlarged plans for progress"; and (7) a goal of peace within the denominational boundaries. They stated, "Your Commission is persuaded that in this way the Baptists of the South can best conserve their strength and utilize it for the extension of the Kingdom in the establishment of the truth in every part of the earth."[24]

While leaders acknowledged the good that can come from outside relationships, the focus on building structures for efficiency and posterity won out in the end. Leaders seemed to view themselves as initiators of a coming movement more than as participants in a centuries-old one. The Home Mission Board asserted in its report, "Our day of destiny has come. The land is ours, if we will but task it. The future greatness and glory of the South is largely in the hands of Southern Baptists and what we do in a decade will decide largely what we shall be for a century. Our supreme task is the enlistment of our forces and resources for this worthy undertaking."[25]

While this statement was not specifically about the incorporation of great Christian traditions, it gives insight into the goals of the denominational leadership. The leaders' belief that the Southern Baptist Convention was uniquely equipped and particularly called to carry the truth of the gospel from their region to the ends of the earth, through their own cultural expression, led them to pursue expansion from within rather than connection with something bigger than themselves. While theological boundaries had straightforward appeal, the pull toward a streamlined structure and deeper loyalty were additional reasons to spend energy on themselves rather than connecting with others.

---

[24] 1914 SBC Annual, 77–78.
[25] 1914 SBC Annual, 331.

The 1915 Commission on the World Conference on Faith and Order, chaired by E. C. Dargan, reported no realistic expectation of a set date for joining efforts but proposed a standing committee for potential future engagement. The hand of the SBC was still cautious and barely open. In the same convention, the Commission on Denominational Efficiency (also chaired by Dargan) evinced the convention's stronger desires:

> With all of our schools active centers of denominational life and unity, with our denominational press enkindled by missionary and educational zeal, with Sunday schools and Young People's Societies, true to the churches and their divine mission, with a new high note for progress sounded out from every pulpit, with the spirit of a sound mind pervading all our intra-denominational discussions, we may joyfully hope for such progress as has never been witnessed in the history of Baptists anywhere since the first centuries. Your Commission joyfully believes that there are no practical difficulties in the way of the broadest and most generous cooperation in an effort to enlist the multitudes for service in the holy war to which we are peculiarly called in these times. The Baptists of the South are homogeneous. We hold the same standards of faith in all matters of religion. The millions of Southern Baptists, including our colored brethren, with one mighty voice, that might wake the sleeping nations, can repeat in unison, "One Lord, one faith, one baptism." There is nothing in the way of unparalleled advance over the entire field of our activities.[26]

Southern Baptists wanted more efficient and focused denominational machinery. While this certainly involved the advancement of mission, it also recognized that a larger and more effective body could protect the culture.

For example, the Baptist Sunday School Board continued to address the issue of denominationally produced lessons. According to Tennessee

---

[26] 1915 SBC Annual, 24–25.

Baptists' *Baptist and Reflector* news journal, "In recommending the organization of the 'Convention plan classes,' the report . . . declared that Baptist Sunday School classes should have as their aim only the teaching of God's word and the making of Baptists out of their members."[27] The report sounded an alarm: "Our Baptist people must ever remember that when Sunday school methods and teaching fail to make Baptists out of our people or in any respect emasculate or compromise Baptist truth or polity, right then they must lop off the methods and trim down the lesson matter without respect to anybody or any relations on the face of the earth."[28]

The board concluded its report by noting its exclusive use of Baptist authors in teacher training materials: "We uphold the wisdom of any Baptist policy that has as its distinct aim the giving to the world more Baptists and better Baptists by every possible opportunity that offers itself to our churches, and we submit our report with the assertion that no agency of this Convention is charged with greater Baptist responsibility than our great Sunday School Board which more largely than any other single factor must shape the Baptist thinking and the Baptist ideals of the common masses of our people."[29] For Southern Baptists, receiving from the traditions of the Christian world was not a priority; instead the priority was to develop from within and give the world what Baptists believed to be something better. Their sense of superiority was apparent when the Home Mission Board declared that they had outpaced all other denominations in evangelistic campaigns in cities "not only in enshrining Christianity in many hearts but in enshrining Christianity as interpreted by Baptist teaching and methods."[30]

Baptists do not exist in a vacuum. Guided by Scriptural belief and freed by the principle of autonomy, they have always been able to decide

---

[27] Fleetwood Ball, "Southern Baptist Convention: 'Heavenly Houston Entertains Baptist Body,'" *Baptist and Reflector*, May 20, 1915, final edition, accessed November 24, 2018, http://media2.sbhla.org.s3.amazonaws.com/tbarchive/1915/TB_1915_05_20.pdf.

[28] 1915 SBC Annual, 55.

[29] 1915 SBC Annual, 56.

[30] 1915 SBC Annual, 300.

how far they will go in linking hands with others, whether reaching across denominations or back in time. Each decision for relationship carries its own context. In a convention coming of age, with a growing mechanism and an ambition to win the South, the limits stopped at the front door. It cannot be denied that doctrinal standards were a priority. But neither can it be said they were the lone priority. The mission at home would be delivered through a culture, and that would happen only if the culture was preserved and distinctive.

In the decades to follow, the SBC increased the scope and size of its Executive Committee, consolidated fundraising efforts into one stream-lined mechanism (the Cooperative Program), and adopted the first Baptist Faith and Message. This opened the door for accepting practices that were shadows of those found in the Christian church at large, but with their own Southern Baptist flavor.

For example, in March 1927 the Promotion Committee of the Cooperative Program sponsored Church Covenant Month. They encour-aged churches to publish their covenants in church bulletins and read them aloud publicly with appropriate emphasis, "that in every way pos-sible the pastors and churches make loving, sympathetic and persistent effort to [impress] upon all our people the fundamental Christian virtues and obligations contained in the Covenant."[31] They distributed cove-nants through Baptist bookstores, using one that had accompanied the New Hampshire Confession of Faith. The goal was not to connect to a greater tradition but rather to buttress a new one. They saw the use of church covenants as a way to accomplish their goal of promoting and increasing loyalty to the newly developed Cooperative Program. They declared, "If we can restore the Church Covenant to its rightful place in the thinking and motives of our people we shall realize great spiritual growth and shall have little lack of the funds necessary to carry forward

---

[31] Walter M. Gilmore, "March, Church Covenant Month," in *Biblical Recorder*, February 2, 1927, 5. Accessed through Special Collections and Archives at the Z. Smith Reynolds Library, Wake Forest University, http://digital.olivesoftware.com /Olive/APA/Wakeforest/default.aspx#panel=home.

all of our interests."[32] Church covenants were not necessarily a connection with a great tradition but rather a way to draw Southern Baptist churches to denominational unity.

Over time, Southern Baptists came to defend the use of creeds or confessions, not necessarily for participating in broader traditions but rather as a way to defend the development of their own. They referenced such things rarely as expressions of worship but rather as clear definitions of boundaries. As the *Baptist and Reflector* wrote in 1928, "Arguments have been broadcast from within and without Baptist ranks berating the Convention for adopting a creed. It is a creed when it is used by the Convention for the control of its own agents, for determining its own membership and for guidance in framing and carrying out its own policies. And the Convention has an absolute, inherent, scriptural right so to use it as a creed."[33]

In the 1930s the observance of a church calendar took shape, but it was again distinctly Southern Baptist. Rather than connecting with others as part of a common worship experience, the calendar was designed to highlight denominational efforts and promote ministry efforts and missions causes. The goal was to bring unity within the boundaries, with little apparent interest in connection outside. The efforts were successful, as the calendar gave yet another opportunity for cultural uniformity. But the calendar was unique to the convention and was developed for pragmatic reasons instead of spiritual ones. Baptists were not connecting to a greater movement but rather connecting with each other as they became their own greater movement.

By the mid-twentieth century, Baptist newspapers in their editorial pages hosted discussions on the use of creeds, with a clear pattern. The Apostles' Creed might be respected as a litmus test for doctrinal orthodoxy, but the use of any liturgical practices in worship was suspect as a hindrance to the free expression of one's faith. Confessions or covenants might be employed, but they were distinctly Baptist and utilized

---

[32] Gilmore.

[33] "Creeds or Confessions, Which?" *Baptist and Reflector*, April 26, 1928, http://media2.sbhla.org.s3.amazonaws.com/tbarchive/1928/TB_1928_04_26.pdf.

to establish loyalty and clarity more than contemplation or reflection. Ultimately, as concern developed over theological liberalism, it appeared that culture was keeping the denomination together while the foundation of doctrine was struggling to hold.

Glenn Hinson observed in 1986 that while Baptists developed confessions of faith, and perhaps even modeled structures after creeds and confessions before them, they gave their own flavor to them. Rather than being spiritual declarations for the purpose of joining a cloud of witnesses, confessions were established pragmatically. As the denomination grew, a marker of identification was needed—and not identification with others but rather a distinctive identification of their own. Confessions were about putting a flag in the ground to stake a claim, not to join hands with others. Hinson encouraged his Southern Baptist brethren to consider reconnecting with traditions of old rather than confining themselves to typical interdenominational pushes. Historic ecumenical creeds such as the Nicene or Athanasian Creed, he said, could offer a place of connection. He even appealed to evangelism, stating, "The farther Southern Baptists reach out toward the world, the deeper they must sink their roots into the mainstream of Christian history. Otherwise they will find themselves withering."[34]

However, his argument did not get very far, and timing may have been the reason. The Southern Baptist Convention was embroiled in controversy in the mid-1980s, and there were other issues to be concerned with. There was not necessarily disagreement with the substance of ancient creeds, but neither were Southern Baptists considering fresh engagement with them. Their goal was a refreshing of their own statement of faith, a pinnacle of the movement that would come in 2000. But even then, it was presented as a boundary marker for doctrinal beliefs more than an expression of worship.

The World Conference on Faith and Order did eventually take place, but Southern Baptists did not attend. Cultural preservation of the early twentieth century gave way to cultural exportation a few decades later.

---

[34] Glenn Hinson, "Creeds and Christian Unity," *Journal of Ecumenical Studies* 23, no. 1 (Winter 1986): 36.

The progressive organizational growth strategy paid off, as the Southern Baptist Convention became the largest Protestant denomination in North America. And in 1974, midway through his ministry, W. A. Criswell taught the members of the First Baptist Church of Dallas about traditions they did not know. He challenged them, "You say, 'We don't have a creed.' That is funny. It is ridiculous! It is inane! 'Credo,' I believe."[35]

In 2003, O. S. Hawkins's convention sermon at the SBC Annual Meeting in Phoenix, Arizona, hinted at a potential dawning of willingness among Southern Baptists to consider the broader Christian tradition. He began with a reference to our spiritual forefathers' wrestling with the question of who God is and how answers came through the apostles, the Nicene Creed, and Athanasius.[36] This was the first time in SBC history that the ancient creeds were mentioned from the stage in a convention sermon. In the years since, churches have begun to incorporate those creeds into corporate worship, with Southern Baptists reciting them together and acknowledging their place in the Christian tradition. At the same time, the uniformity of a distinctly Southern Baptist culture has given way to a diversity of environments and experiences.

Desiring rootedness in the Christian tradition does not require trading in denominational identity. Southern Baptists are defined not by regional or sociological culture but by their foundational beliefs and unique system of cooperation. We can choose to connect with one another because we believe we can do more together than we can do apart, and we can choose to connect with the great cloud of witnesses before us because we learn from the larger body of Christ.

Criswell exhorted his congregation as they began their study, "If you'll stay with this and bring your mind and your heart, you're going to be blessed."[37] SBC churches can connect to traditions of the past and the union of the present, and receive the same blessing.

---

[35] Criswell, "Concerning Creeds and Confessions."

[36] O. S. Hawkins, "The Question for Our Time: Who Do You Say That I Am?" (sermon, 2003 Southern Baptist Convention, Phoenix, AZ, June 18, 2003), http://media2.sbhla.org.s3.amazonaws.com/annuals/SBC_Annual_2003.pdf.

[37] Criswell, "Concerning Creeds and Confessions."

12

Southern Baptists, Evangelicalism, and the Christian Tradition

DAVID S. DOCKERY

Southwestern Baptist Theological Seminary

The Southern Baptist Convention is the largest Baptist denomination in the United States and the world, comprising 15 million members and nearly 50,000 congregations in all fifty states. The Southern Baptist Convention maintains a visible presence among large segments of the South and in other regions of the United States. But Southern Baptists did not begin this way.

Baptist Beginnings

Baptists originated in England during the early seventeenth century.[1] One of the earliest groups of Baptists was led by John Smyth and Thomas Helwys, who sought asylum in the Netherlands. Both General and Particular Baptists emphasized religious freedom. Both were confessional, with Particular Baptists pointing to the London Confessions, while the 1678 Orthodox Creed served as the confessional framework for General Baptists.[2] The Orthodox Creed focused on how much Baptists

---

[1] See Chute, Finn, and Haykin, *Baptist Story*, 11–38.
[2] McBeth, *Baptist Heritage*, 66–69.

were like other Christians, affirming their agreement with the Apostles', Athanasian, and Nicene Creeds.[3]

Each group manifested strengths and weaknesses. The errant thinking among General Baptists tended more toward Socinianism and Arianism. The Particular Baptists veered off track by moving toward an anti-missionary mindset. Dan Taylor rescued the gospel for General Baptists; Andrew Fuller did the same for the Particulars. Both groups came together around the missionary movement led by William Carey. Together they rallied to support the development of the Foreign Missionary Society.[4]

Baptists first emerged in America in Rhode Island in the 1630s. By 1730–1740 there were eight congregations and about four hundred Baptists in America. In 1707 the first Baptist association was established in this country, in Philadelphia. Associations developed in the South shortly thereafter, beginning in Charleston, South Carolina, in 1751, followed by the Sandy Creek Association in North Carolina in 1755.[5]

In 1812 Adoniram Judson and Luther Rice began the missionary movement among Baptists in America, and the Triennial Convention was launched in 1814, with Richard Furman, well-known pastor of the First Baptist Church of Charleston, serving as the first president. These Baptists adopted the New Hampshire Confession in 1833. Differences developed regarding what it meant to be Baptist, as well as regarding the societal model of doing missions,[6] regarding where money should be invested to start new churches, and regarding whether church members who happened to be slave owners could be appointed as domestic or foreign missionaries. In 1844 these differences became obvious to all. Baptists in the South wanted a convention model in terms of organizational structure, wanted money to go to the South for the funding of new

---

[3] McBeth.

[4] David S. Dockery, *Southern Baptist Consensus and Renewal* (Nashville: B&H, 2009), 38–39; George, *Faithful Witness*.

[5] See Bill J. Leonard, *Baptists in America* (New York: Columbia University Press, 2005), 83–87.

[6] William R. Estep, *Whole Gospel for the Whole World* (Nashville: B&H, 1994), 49–76.

church starts, and wanted to be able to appoint slaveholders as missionaries. Across the Triennial Convention, these ideas were rejected by those outside the South.

Southern Baptist Beginnings

In 1845 the Southern Baptist Convention began when messengers gathered in Augusta, Georgia, and approved application for a charter from the State of Georgia, a charter approved officially in Richmond, Virginia, the next year. W. B. Johnson was elected as the first president. The Foreign Mission Board was established in Richmond while a Home Mission Board began in Marion, Alabama. This new Baptist group committed itself to one overarching purpose: "one sacred effort for the propagation of the gospel."[7] A convention model was adopted, something quite important and distinctive from Northern Baptists, with boards elected to oversee the different entities that would come into place. Nine state conventions had been formed prior to the formation of the new convention in the South.

The state conventions dominated Baptist life throughout the nineteenth century, largely because of the distance, travel, and communication required to conduct business within the new South-wide convention. In 1870, following the Civil War, some urged the Northern and Southern Baptists to come back together, but to no avail. While the slavery issue was no longer a matter of dispute, funding issues and the convention model of governance remained areas of tension and disagreement. Those in the South said to their brothers and sisters in the North that it was best if they, like Paul and Barnabas, went their separate ways, with the North adopting a societal model in contrast to the convention model.[8]

---

[7] The preamble of the original constitution of the SBC described its purpose as "eliciting, combining, and directing the energies of the whole denomination in one sacred effort, for the propagation of the gospel." The words remain an important part of the heritage of the SBC and powerful for contemporary Baptists. See Jesse C. Fletcher, *The Southern Baptist Convention: A Sesquicentennial History* (Nashville: B&H, 1994), 46–52; also McBeth, *Baptist Heritage*, 381–91.

[8] Chute, Finn, and Haykin, *Baptist Story*, 163–84.

The Southern Baptists developed and moved toward stability from 1845 until the beginning of the twentieth century. A commitment to cooperation and more efficient operations characterized the first half of the twentieth century. Southern Baptists rapidly expanded throughout the middle of the twentieth century, surpassing the Methodists as the largest Protestant denomination in the country. Theological disputes and controversy have characterized the convention from the 1960s to the present period. While some unnecessary fragmentation took place during this time, the majority of Southern Baptists affirmed efforts to recover biblical authority as a foundational commitment of the convention. Important steps to address an issue that had haunted Southern Baptists since 1845 took place during the final decade of the twentieth century as initiatives toward racial reconciliation occurred.[9]

The twenty-first century has seen ongoing attempts to wrestle with what it means to be Baptist, how to respond to change, how to deal with controversy, and how to relate to the broader evangelical community. It is to this final question that we now turn our attention.

Southern Baptists and Evangelicals

In 1983 James Leo Garrett Jr., E. Glenn Hinson, and James Tull put together a most important volume, published by Mercer University Press: *Are Southern Baptists "Evangelicals"?*[10] Though both Garrett and Hinson qualified their answers to this question, Hinson basically answered no while Garrett responded in a positive manner. The conversation focused on the uneasy relationship between Southern Baptists and American evangelicals. In 1993 a multiauthor volume extended the discussion from various perspectives, with contributions from Southern Baptist

---

[9] See the discussion in David S. Dockery, "Who Are Southern Baptists? Toward an Intergenerational Identity," *The SBC and the 21st Century: Reflection, Renewal, & Recommitment*, ed. Jason K. Allen (Nashville: B&H, 2016), 79–93. Portions of this chapter's summary of Baptist history are drawn from that work.

[10] See James Leo Garrett Jr., E. Glenn Hinson, and James E. Tull, *Are Southern Baptists "Evangelicals"?* (Macon, GA: Mercer University Press, 1982).

moderates and conservatives as well as representatives from across the broader evangelical community.[11] The book was titled *Southern Baptists & American Evangelicals: The Conversation Continues*. Much of this conversation involved an attempt to understand the evangelical community, who they are, and what they believe. In the next section of this chapter we will attempt to extend the 1983 and 1993 conversations in light of our context in the second decade of the twenty-first century.

Understanding Evangelicalism

Evangelicalism is a story of complexities. Who are these evangelicals? What do they believe? What does evangelicalism have to do with politics? How should evangelicalism be understood in light of denominational distinctives? What is the state of evangelicalism, and what are its future prospects? How do Baptists relate to this broader evangelical community?[12]

Evangelicals are men and women who love Jesus Christ, the Bible, and the gospel message. They are gospel people. Evangelicalism is a cross-denominational movement that emphasizes classical Protestant theology, which is best understood as a culturally engaged, historically shaped response to mainline liberalism on the one hand, and to reactionary fundamentalism on the other.[13]

Evangelicals are heirs of the Reformation of the sixteenth century; of Puritanism and Pietism of the seventeenth century; of the eighteenth- and nineteenth-century revivalists and awakening movements; and particularly of the post-fundamentalists coming out of the twentieth century's modernist/fundamentalist controversies.[14]

---

[11] David S. Dockery, ed., *Southern Baptists & American Evangelicals: The Conversation Continues* (Nashville: Broadman, 1993).

[12] See Dockery, *Southern Baptist Identity*; also Dockery, "Evangelicalism: Past, Present, and Future," *Trinity Journal* 36 NS (2015): 3–21.

[13] See Mark A. Noll, *American Evangelical Christianity: An Introduction* (Oxford, UK: Blackwell, 2001).

[14] Michael A. G. Haykin and Kenneth J. Stewart, eds., *The Advent of Evangelicalism: Exploring Historical Continuities* (Nashville: B&H, 2008).

Various efforts have been made to define what it means to be an evangelical.[15] In the simplest terms, as several others have somewhat facetiously noted, an evangelical is someone who identified with or liked Billy Graham; a liberal is someone who thought Billy Graham was a fundamentalist; and a fundamentalist is someone who believed Billy Graham to be apostate. Some have said we know evangelicals by the hymns they sing. Others have suggested that we know evangelicals by a particular kind of piety or experience—that is, we know them by their heart; we know them when we are with them. Some have described true evangelicals as "card-carrying" evangelicals.[16] Still others say we know evangelicals by these things but that one must also include their doctrine—we know evangelicals by what they believe.[17] I propose that there is some truth in all of these observations, agreeing with the latter group that doctrinal matters cannot be ignored.

While we connect the evangelical movement with the teaching of the apostles, the early church consensus as it developed through the great church councils, and the Reformation of the sixteenth century, evangelicalism is perhaps best traced to the revivals of the eighteenth century.[18] Though much has been made of the involvement of many evangelicals in the political arena, including the extremely insightful work by Kenneth Collins, *Power, Politics, and the Fragmentation of Evangelicalism,* evangelicalism is best understood, contrary to media reports, not as a political identity but as a confessional identity focused on (1) the gospel; (2) personal conversion or the response to the gospel; (3) the Bible as the source of that gospel message; and (4) service or activism, the living out of that

---

[15] Donald W. Dayton and Robert K. Johnston, eds., *The Variety of American Evangelicalism* (Downers Grove, IL: InterVarsity Press, 1991).

[16] George M. Marsden, "Contemporary American Evangelicalism," in *Southern Baptists and American Evangelicals,* 27–39.

[17] See David F. Wells and John D. Woodbridge, eds., *The Evangelicals: What They Believe Who They Are, Where They Are Changing* (Nashville: Abingdon, 1975), 9–19; also Kenneth S. Kantzer and Carl F. H. Henry, *Evangelical Affirmations* (Grand Rapids: Zondervan, 1990).

[18] See David W. Bebbington, *Evangelicalism in Modern Britain* (London: Unwin Hyman, 1989); Douglas A. Sweeney, *The American Evangelical Story: A History of the Movement* (Grand Rapids: Baker, 2005).

message (adapted from David Bebbington's evangelical quadrilateral).[19] Alister McGrath, in his fine book *Evangelicalism and the Future of Christianity*, suggests six core beliefs of evangelicalism:

1. Supreme authority of Scripture.
2. Majesty and lordship of Jesus Christ as the only Savior for sinful humanity.
3. The Trinitarian God—including the important work of the Holy Spirit.
4. Need for personal conversion.
5. Priority of evangelism and missions.
6. Importance of Christian community.[20]

The two Reformation doctrines of *sola Scriptura* (the Bible is the church's ultimate authority) and *sola fide* (salvation is by faith alone) still inform and shape twenty-first-century evangelicalism. These two defining emphases are often called the "material principle" (the gospel) and the "formal principle" (the Scriptures).[21] The seventeenth century added to these doctrinal essentials the need for personal, heartfelt, life-transforming, experiential faith. The movement known as Puritanism, similar to Pietism, stressed conversion and grace and downplayed liturgy and sacraments, maintaining that a conversion to faith in Jesus Christ impacts all of life.[22]

Both the Puritan and the Pietist movements were used of God to awaken a cold orthodoxy and revive scholastic Protestantism. While seeking to address spiritual decline in the Lutheran, Reformed, and Anglican churches, these movements stressed experiential faith, emphasizing prayer, warmhearted fellowship, and evangelistic zeal. The Pietists

---

[19] Bebbington.

[20] Alister McGrath, *Evangelicalism and the Future of Christianity* (Downers Grove, IL: InterVarsity Press, 1995).

[21] Bernard L. Ramm, *The Evangelical Heritage* (Waco, TX: Word, 1973), 23–40.

[22] See Bruce Shelley, *Evangelicalism in America* (Grand Rapids: Eerdmans, 1967); Edwin S. Gaustad, *The Great Awakening in New England* (New York: Harper and Row, 1957).

influenced the Moravians as well as the eighteenth-century revivals, including the conversion of John Wesley.[23] By the end of the eighteenth century, the most evangelistic of the churches in both North America and Great Britain were the Baptists and Methodists, clearly the fastest growing groups, even impacting the slave communities, in which, as Joel Carpenter has noted, Jesus was found to be a "rock in a weary land."[24] During this time (1792), William Carey set out for India, launching a worldwide missions movement that would shape what would become a global evangelical movement by the twenty-first century.[25]

The evangelical movements at the beginning of the nineteenth century looked somewhat different from the Reformation and post-Reformation movements two hundred years earlier. While the Reformed theology emphasis at Princeton, led by Charles and A. A. Hodge, along with B. B. Warfield, shaped the thought leaders of the day, evangelicalism as a whole placed greater emphasis on personal, warmhearted, experiential faith, as well as cooperation across denominational lines, aggressive evangelistic efforts, conversionist views of salvation, pious living, and revivalistic expectations. D. L. Moody became the most influential figure in this regard on both sides of the Atlantic in the nineteenth century, for not only his evangelistic preaching but also his social efforts, urban renewal, and transdenominational emphasis.[26]

Thus, by the time of the Civil War, Protestantism in both the North and the South could be equated with evangelicalism and evangelicalism could be equated with Protestantism. Indeed, historian William G. McLaughlin has dared to say that the story of American evangelicalism

---

[23] John R. Weinlick, "Moravianism in the American Colonies," in *Continental Pietism*, ed. F. Ernest Stoefler (Grand Rapids: Eerdmans, 1976), 123–63.

[24] Joel A. Carpenter, "The Fellowship of Kindred Minds: Evangelical Identity and the Quest for Christian Unity," in *Pilgrims on the Sawdust Trail*, ed. Timothy George (Grand Rapids: Baker, 2004).

[25] George, *Faithful Witness*.

[26] Michael S. Hamilton, "The Interdenominational Evangelicalism of D. L. Moody and the Problem of Fundamentalism," in *American Evangelicalism*, ed. Darren Dochuk, Thomas S. Kidd, and Kurt W. Peterson (Notre Dame, IN: University of Notre Dame Press, 2014).

during the nineteenth century is the story of America itself, with emphasis on rugged individualism, laissez-faire economic theory, the Protestant ethic regarding both work and morality, and millenarian hope in Manifest Destiny.[27] By the end of the nineteenth century, however, that was all changing.

As the twentieth century began, new movements were launched to revive, renew, correct, and sometimes even separate from the established Protestant denominations—which evangelicals viewed as growing more liberal and worldly. After the Civil War, evangelicals wrestled with the changes taking place all around them, including Darwinism, naturalism, biblical criticism, post-slavery society, pragmatism, and expanding urbanization and industrialization.

As the twentieth century began, the modernist/fundamentalist controversy moved publicly into full force. In 1910 the "five fundamentals" were clarified by northern Presbyterians, reflecting on earlier versions spelled out by the Niagara Prophecy Conference. These doctrinal tenets, which focused on the full and complete inspiration and authority of Scripture, the virgin birth of Jesus Christ, the deity of Christ, the atoning death and resurrection of Christ, and the historical reality of biblical miracles, were aimed at the primary challenges of liberalism. A series of 90 articles titled *The Fundamentals* (1910–1915), edited by R. A. Torrey and funded by Lyman and Milton Stewart, was well reasoned, serious, calm, thoughtful, not shrill, and generally quite persuasive.[28] More than thirty of these articles dealt with the nature of Scripture. Authors included what some considered to be more moderate voices, such as the Southern Baptist leader E. Y. Mullins and the British theologian James Orr.

In 1919, however, fundamentalist Baptist leader W. B. Riley said the five fundamentals were not enough. He also wanted to stress separatism, dispensationalism, and lifestyle taboos, which continue to be distinguishing marks for many segments of the fundamentalist movement nearly

---

[27] William G. McLoughlin, "Introductions," in *The American Evangelicals, 1800–1900*, ed. William G. McLoughlin (Gloucester, MA: Peter Smith, 1976).

[28] See R. A. Torrey, ed., *The Fundamentals*, 12 vols. (Los Angeles: Bible Institute of Los Angeles, 1917).

a century later.[29] In 1922 Harry Emerson Fosdick preached his famous sermon at the First Presbyterian Church of New York City, "Shall the Fundamentalists win? No!"[30] In 1923, representing the more conservative perspective, Princeton scholar J. Gresham Machen published *Christianity and Liberalism*, with the word *and* being key in the title, as Machen treated the subjects as two different religions.[31] In 1925 in Dayton, Tennessee, the Scopes trial gained the attention of the nation. The fundamentalists won the battle but seemingly lost the war.[32] Before the fundamentalist/modernist controversy, denominational distinctives were much more clearly recognized and understood:

- Lutherans: Word and faith
- Reformed and Presbyterian: sovereignty of God
- Anglicanism: prayer book and worship
- Baptists: Scripture, conversion, and baptism
- Quakers: inner light
- Methodists: heartfelt religion
- Holiness: piety and separatism
- Restorationists: New Testament church
- Pentecostals: though just beginning in the early twentieth century, emphasis on the power of the Spirit.[33]

Such clarity began to dissipate with the rapid fragmentation that followed the modernist/fundamentalist controversies and with the rise of a new generation of evangelical leaders who became more visibly identified following the Second World War.

---

[29] Timothy P. Weber, "William Bell Riley," in *Baptist Theologians*, ed. Timothy George and David S. Dockery (Nashville: Broadman & Holman, 1990), 351–65.

[30] Gary Dorrien, *The Making of American Liberal Theology: Idealism, Realism, and Modernity, 1900–1950* (Louisville, KY: Westminster John Knox, 2003), 203–8.

[31] J. Gresham Machen, *Christianity and Liberalism* (1923; reprint, Grand Rapids: Eerdmans, 1987).

[32] Edward J. Larson, *Summer for the Gods: The Scopes Trial and America's Continuing Debate over Science and Religion* (New York: Basic, 1997).

[33] David S. Dockery, "Denominationalism: Historical Developments, Contemporary Challenges, and Global Opportunities," in *Why We Belong*, 209–31.

In 1942 new winds began to blow with the formation of the National Association of Evangelicals, which created a type of evangelical ecumenism in which commonalities were seen to be more important than denominational distinctives. In 1947 a new theological seminary was founded by evangelist Charles Fuller, designed to create a new a scholarly evangelicalism. Fuller Seminary's young faculty included E. J. Carnell, Carl F. H. Henry, Wilbur Smith, and Harold Lindsell. The Evangelical Theological Society, with a shared commitment to biblical inerrancy, was birthed in 1949.[34] That same year, Billy Graham's evangelistic crusade in Los Angeles put Graham on the map, thanks to the unbelievable attention provided by the Los Angeles media. Now Graham had become the movement's spokesman, Henry the movement's theologian, and Harold Ockenga the movement's organizer. Others, such as Kenneth Kantzer, Ted Engstrom, and Bernard Ramm, to name a few, also carved out significant roles.

A 1957 New York crusade was pivotal for defining the non-separatist approach of Graham and the new evangelicals.[35] Fundamentalist leaders labeled Graham an apostate because he violated the separatist tendencies of the fundamentalist movement when he invited Roman Catholic and mainline Protestant leaders to sit on the platform at his New York crusade. This story is told with great insight by historian Grant Wacker in his work on Graham, *America's Pastor*.[36]

In 1959 Carnell, a brilliant theologian at Fuller Seminary, authored *The Case for Christianity* (which really should have had the inverted title of Machen's 1923 work, namely, "Christianity and Fundamentalism"). Carnell declared that fundamentalism was suspicious, separatistic, and divisive—pointing out it failed to agree on core beliefs, and thus declaring that fundamentalism was "orthodoxy gone cultic."[37]

---

[34] Millard J. Erickson, *The New Evangelical Theology* (Westwood, NJ: Revell, 1968), 13–45.

[35] See Matthew J. Hall and Owen Strachan, eds., *Essential Evangelicalism* (Wheaton, IL: Crossway, 2015).

[36] Grant Wacker, *America's Pastor: Billy Graham and the Shaping of a Nation* (Cambridge, MA: Belknap/Harvard, 2014), 12–15.

[37] E. J. Carnell, *The Case of Orthodoxy* (Philadelphia: Westminster, 1959).

By contrast, the new leaders of the evangelical movement, Billy Graham, Harold Ockenga, and Carl Henry (who wrote *The Uneasy Conscience of Modern Fundamentalism*), focused on core beliefs, stressing the importance of cooperation, scholarship, and cultural engagement. In the 1960s the mainline denominations had seemingly lost their way. Living amid the sexual revolution in a time of racial unrest, protests, rock and roll celebrations, love-ins, and sit-ins, the mainline denominations shifted their focus away from the gospel to social issues such as the Vietnam War, civil rights, and gender and sexuality.[38] The emphasis on issues other than the gospel, in the words of former *Los Angeles Times* writer Russell Chandler, moved the "mainline" to the "sideline" in the twenty-first century.[39]

Evangelical leaders in the middle of the twentieth century rejected fundamentalism while holding on to the fundamentals represented in the best of the Christian tradition that runs through the Reformation, Puritanism, Pietism, and the Great Awakenings.[40] Twentieth-century evangelicals could be characterized as historically orthodox, gospel-centered, culturally engaged, and transdenominational. Graham, Henry, and others stressed the importance of biblical inerrancy but viewed it as a matter primarily of evangelical consistency rather than of evangelical identity.[41]

It has been said that the evangelical movement is a protest against a Christianity that is "not Christian enough." The Puritans said this about the Church of England, claiming it was only halfway reformed. The revivalists maintained that the churches were full of unconverted

---

[38] See Helen Lee Turner, "Fundamentalism in the Southern Baptist Convention: The Crystalization of a Millennialist Vision" (PhD diss., University of Virginia, 1990).

[39] Russell Chandler, *Racing Toward 2001: The Forces Shaping America's Religious Future* (San Francisco: HarperCollins, 1992).

[40] Joel Carpenter, *Revive Us Again: The Reawakening of American Fundamentalism* (New York: Oxford, 1997).

[41] See Carl F. H. Henry, ed., *Revelation and the Bible* (Grand Rapids: Baker, 1958). Contributors included G. C. Berkower, F. F. Bruce, and Paul K. Jewett, among others.

people. Critiques of the traditional church and a call for renewal have been central features of evangelical-type movements for almost five hundred years.[42]

By the middle of the twentieth century, fundamentalism had grown hardline, harsh, and isolationist; the evangelical movement attempted to stress Christian unity instead, seeking to distinguish primary matters from secondary and tertiary ones. It is best to understand evangelicalism as a large umbrella group that includes many sub-movements and thousands of parachurch organizations. Princeton sociologist Robert Wuthnow brilliantly argued that a major restructuring of American religion had taken place by the end of the twentieth century.[43]

For evangelicals, as with historic orthodoxy throughout the centuries, the church's basic beliefs are centered and grounded in Jesus Christ. Evangelicalism can be understood in light of its historical meaning and ministry connectedness, but it also includes a truth claim, a theologically and historically shaped meaning. We cannot and must not miss the fact that evangelicals have focused on the authoritative Scripture and the gospel, understood in the person and work of Jesus Christ. Evangelicals believe that salvation is by God's grace alone through faith in Jesus Christ. By grace believers are saved, kept, and empowered for a life of service. Evangelicalism is more than an intellectual assent to creedal formulas, as important as that is. It is more than a reaction to error and certainly more than a call to return to the past. It is the affirmation of and genuine commitment to the central beliefs of orthodox Christianity, as these beliefs have been carefully and clearly articulated. These are the core strengths of the evangelical movement.[44] While there are other strengths, there are challenges and weaknesses as well that ought to be noted.

---

[42] Donald G. Bloesch, *The Evangelical Renaissance* (Grand Rapids: Eerdmans, 1973), 13–29, 101–58.

[43] See Robert Wuthnow, *The Restructuring of American Religion* (Princeton, NJ: Princeton University Press, 1988).

[44] John Stott, *Evangelical Truth* (Downers Grove, IL: InterVarsity Press, 1999), 13–34; McGrath, *Evangelicalism and the Future of Christianity*, 53–62.

Transdenominational and Entrepreneurial Evangelicals

Most denominations have been divided over whether evangelicalism as a movement has been a help or a hindrance to them. Forty years ago, Foy Valentine, then-leader of the Southern Baptist Christian Life Commission (forerunner to the Ethics and Religious Liberty Commission), claimed, "Southern Baptists are not evangelicals; that is a Yankee word."[45] Part of that claim had to do with the left-of-center leanings of most Southern Baptist leaders at the time, and part of it was a failure to understand the differences between evangelicals and fundamentalism. But the confusion seen in Valentine's response represents the confusion present among a variety of leaders across all denominational lines. During the time of the Great Awakenings and revivals in the eighteenth century with George Whitefield, the nineteenth century with D. L. Moody, and the twentieth century with Billy Graham, evangelicalism mostly functioned without a developed ecclesiology or a cooperative or shared funding approach, which created networks that worked through parachurch groups and around denominational structures.[46] The result has often been much duplication of effort, creating funding challenges, mixed loyalties, and numerous inefficiencies. Evangelicalism's transdenominational and entrepreneurial spirit has been viewed with confusion—then and now.

So-called card-carrying evangelicals are best understood as people committed not only to essential orthodox Christian beliefs but to transdenominational movements, special-purpose groups, and networks. These interlocking networks, more so than denominations, form the center of evangelicalism. D. L. Moody popularized these special-purpose-group movements. Billy Graham blessed and grew these organizations, which

---

[45] Quoted in Kenneth L. Woodward et al., "The Evangelicals," *Newsweek*, October 1976, 76.

[46] Kenneth J. Collins, *The Evangelical Movement: The Promise of an American Religion* (Grand Rapids: Baker, 2005), 34–40; also W. K. Wilmer et al., *The Prospering Parachurch* (San Francisco: Josey-Bass 1998).

emphasized lay leadership and entrepreneurial expansion.[47] Evangelicals rarely started new denominations but poured their energy into an untold number of organizations, many of which were started or enabled by the Graham Association.[48]

Evangelicalism in the twenty-first century, however, is anything but a unified, flourishing movement in North America. In fact, with the 2018 death of Billy Graham, the movement's unity seems to be in serious jeopardy.[49] While some aspects of evangelicalism are thriving, others are embattled. Some have lost their theological compass, having become untethered from both Scripture and tradition, resulting in a post-evangelical drift.[50] In addition, the media has compounded the confusion by continuing to use the term *evangelical* to describe political identities rather than theological or spiritual commitments.[51] Growth in evangelicalism is taking place primarily in minority and intercultural contexts.[52] Most primarily white congregations are in decline. Evangelicals must take heart and recognize the rapidly changing demographic patterns in this country, coupled with Christianity's expanding global context.

Changes in our context can be seen in technology, the economy, globalization, government, the social realm, population patterns, and elsewhere. Evangelicalism is not exempt from the impact of these changes. Important for missional and ministry collaboration is awareness that the movement's unity, or perceived unity, is threatened by politics, key

---

[47] Richard Mouw, *The Smell of Sawdust: What Evangelicals Can Learn from their Fundamentalist Heritage* (Grand Rapids: Zondervan, 2000).

[48] See David Aikman, *Billy Graham: His Life and Influence* (Nashville: Thomas Nelson, 2007).

[49] See Lon Allison, *Billy Graham: An Ordinary Man and His Extraordinary God* (Brewster, MA: Paraclete, 2018).

[50] See Kenneth J. Stewart, *In Search of Ancient Roots: The Christian Past and the Evangelical Identity Crisis* (Downers Grove, IL: InterVarsity Press, 2017).

[51] See Mark Laberton, ed., *Still Evangelical? Insiders Reconsider Political, Social, and Theological Meaning* (Downers Grove, IL: InterVarsity Press, 2018).

[52] See Soong-Chan Rah, *The Next Evangelicalism* (Downers Grove, IL: InterVarsity Press, 2009).

doctrinal differences, a variety of approaches to church and worship, methods of ministry, and diverse opinions on ethical and social issues.[53]

Because of this rapid cultural change, alternative trajectories are being offered to the church that in some ways are not unlike those offered in the initial decades of the twentieth century. Evangelicals will need to explore how they can ensure faithfulness to Scripture and the best of the Christian tradition while looking for ways to help apply these truths among the growing global church. It is a time to celebrate what God is doing cross-culturally, interculturally, and globally.[54]

A century ago, liberalism began to flourish by adapting the Christian faith to the changing culture, even identifying with it. Shaped by the influence of Friedrich Schleiermacher and Horace Bushnell, as well as their popularizers such as Harry Emerson Fosdick, Henry Ward Beecher, and Philips Brooks, liberalism and its wide-ranging influence seemingly had great momentum. By the time of World War I, half of all denominational leaders in America were self-identified liberals, as well as about one-third of all pastors and more than half of all publishing house leaders and college/seminary faculty. During this time the unique historic and orthodox claims of the Christian faith were rejected or redefined.[55]

In our world today, we see the rise of secularization, growing interest in a vast and amorphous spirituality, a new atheism, and the rise of the "nones" (those with no religious affiliation), all shaped by and within a postmodern culture.[56] While there are things for us to learn from the trends of the early twentieth century and from our own time period, before we rush toward the trending post-evangelical trajectories of our day it would be good to be reminded of the overall assessment of the progressive movement from H. Richard Niebuhr, one of the twentieth

---

[53] See Luder G. Whitlock, *Divided We Fall: Overcoming a History of Christian Disunity* (Philipsburg, NJ: P&R, 2017); John Dickerson, *The Great Evangelical Recession* (Grand Rapids: Baker, 2013), 11–122.

[54] Lamin Sanneh and Joel Carpenter, eds., *The Changing Face of Christianity* (New York: Oxford, 2005).

[55] Luigi Giussani, *American Protestant Theology* (Montreal: McGill-Queen's University Press, 2013), 53–99.

[56] James Emery White, *The Rise of the Nones* (Grand Rapids: Baker, 2014).

century's most profound thinkers: "Liberalism has created a God without wrath who brought men without sin into a kingdom without judgment through the ministry of Christ without an atoning cross."[57]

Yet, just as we need not fall into the waiting arms of a revisionist progressivism, so we would be equally wise to avoid a reductionistic fundamentalism.[58] Neither a new form of liberalism nor a reactionary fundamentalism is a wise option at this time. A big-tent vision needs wisdom to avoid moving unintentionally in the direction of an unhealthy inclusivism or heterodox universalism.

While recognizing how different the current context is from that of the mid-twentieth century, evangelicals need courage to affirm first-order essentials informed by the Christian tradition that have been believed and confessed throughout church history.[59]

Southern Baptists, Denominational Evangelicals, and Questions about the Future

The evangelical movement is understood largely as a grassroots kind of ecumenism that holds people together because of like beliefs and structures.[60] While evangelical theologians have done a magnificent job focusing on the truthfulness of Scripture, hermeneutics, the doctrine of revelation, and the importance of the gospel, for the most part evangelicals have not done a very good job articulating a theology of the church, especially of denominations. That weakness has led to an ambiguous understanding of how churches relate to one another and to structures within and outside of denominations, creating an uneasy marriage between the church, denominational organizations, and other institutions. Now we

---

[57] H. Richard Niebuhr, *The Kingdom of God in America* (New York: Harper, 1959), 193; also Sydney E. Ahlstrom, *Theology in America* (Indianapolis: Bobbs-Merrill, 1967), 587–618.

[58] Stott, *Evangelical Truth*, 13–34.

[59] Thomas Oden, *Rebirth of Orthodoxy: Signs of Life in Christianity* (San Francisco: Harper San Francisco, 2003).

[60] Mark A. Noll, *The Rise of Evangelicalism* (reprint; Downers Grove, IL: InterVarsity Press, 2018).

find ourselves in the second decade of the twenty-first century, with major changes in the way people think about denominations and denominationalism. This has also become the case among Southern Baptists.[61]

So, what does this say about the future of evangelicalism and the future of the SBC?[62] While denominationalism is in decline, denominations still matter; certainly some sense of structure matters. Former Yale historian Jaroslav Pelikan, in his important book *Spirit versus Structure*, maintains that Christianity needs structure in order to carry forward the Christian message.[63] Yet, if we focus too much on structure, we wind up in one ditch, leaning toward bureaucracy. If we focus too much on the other side, with too much emphasis on the Spirit, we move toward an amorphous kind of Christianity. So there must remain some place for denominational evangelicals like Southern Baptists who continue to emphasize denominational structures, even as we recognize the importance of variety in our ever-changing context.

Learning from One Another

Let us attempt to move the conversation in a more focused way to Southern Baptists and their relationship to the evangelical community. Southern Baptists are indeed evangelicals, but a distinctive kind of evangelicals. Southern Baptists are denominational evangelicals, the position maintained by James Leo Garrett in 1983 and by myself and others in 1993.[64] In contrast, many Baptist evangelicals such as Billy Graham and Carl Henry have been evangelicals first and Baptists second. Some evangelicals in this category, such as E. J. Carnell, former president of Fuller Seminary, made caustic statements about the cultic nature of Baptist life.[65] Henry and Graham probably spoke more frequently in churches outside the Baptist world than

---

[61] Dockery, *Southern Baptist Consensus and Renewal.*

[62] Dockery, *Southern Baptist Identity.*

[63] Jaroslav Pelikan, *Spirit versus Structure* (New York: Harper and Row, 1969).

[64] See David S. Dockery and James Emery White, introduction to *Southern Baptists and American Evangelicals*, 1–26.

[65] See E. J. Carnell, *The Case for Orthodox Theology* (Philadelphia: Westminster, 1959).

within. Southern Baptists as a whole, however, tend to be Baptists first and evangelicals second, which is what creates the questions and tensions for both "card-carrying, transdenominational evangelicals" as well as loyal Southern Baptists. I have somewhere read that Southern Baptists have this to say for themselves: their theologians still think their work should influence the church, and the church still cares what its theologians say. This is the reason for the title of the book put together by a dozen of Southern Baptists' finest thinkers, *A Theology for the Church*.[66]

So, what do these denominational evangelicals with a focus on Baptist churches have to say to evangelicals? To answer the question, I would like to turn back the clock to 1925, a setback year for evangelicals and fundamentalists with the public relations nightmare that followed the Scopes trial in Dayton, Tennessee. On the other end of the state, in Memphis, Southern Baptists at their annual convention adopted not only a new funding strategy known as the Cooperative Program but also their first denomination-wide confession of faith, the Baptist Faith and Message. While cooperation and doctrinal commonality both had been in place since the SBC's founding eight decades earlier in 1845, the convention now in a formal way declared that both conviction and cooperation mattered. The confessional statement, a process led by Southern Seminary president E. Y. Mullins, was needed to address mounting concerns about evolution and to clarify Southern Baptist doctrinal commitments in the midst of the modernist/fundamentalist controversy raging across the country.

The 1925 Baptist Faith and Message was largely a restatement of the 1833 New Hampshire Confession, with minor revisions. The Southern Baptist Convention in 1925, however, chose to move beyond the realm of classic doctrinal essentials, addressing not only the evolution question but also the importance of stewardship, cooperation, education, evangelism, missions, and social ministries.[67]

---

[66] See Daniel L. Akin, ed., *A Theology of the Church*, rev. ed. (Nashville: B&H, 2014).

[67] See the discussion in David S. Dockery, "Convictional Yet Cooperative: The Making of a Great Commission People," in *The Great Commission Resurgence: Fulfilling God's Mandate in Our Time*, ed. Adam W. Greenway and Chuck Lawless (Nashville: B&H Academic, 2010), 387–400.

In 2000, topics related to life, sexuality, and racial reconciliation were also included in the Baptist Faith and Message.[68] Might it be helpful for evangelicals, who have focused almost entirely on doctrinal essentials, to address the loss of a theological and ethical compass in some sectors of the evangelical world by rethinking the importance of some of these ministry and ethical issues for inclusion in doctrinal statements? Perhaps there are better ways to address some of these matters than those adopted by Southern Baptists, but it may also be that Southern Baptists and evangelicals have something to learn from each other at this point.

Evangelicals have clearly and helpfully addressed key issues of revelation, Scripture, the Trinity, and the gospel,[69] all of which were invaluable resources for Southern Baptists during the final three decades of the twentieth century, when Southern Baptists needed a theological renewal and realignment. Along with these foundational strengths, evangelicals have also demonstrated a weakness in the area of ecclesiology. Perhaps because of issues surrounding Landmarkism, both James P. Boyce and E. Y. Mullins wrote major volumes on systematic theology without sections on ecclesiology.[70] Still, in *Axioms of Religion* and *Baptist Beliefs*, Mullins addressed the topic of the church.[71] J. L. Dagg, W. T. Conner, Dale Moody, Duke McCall, John Newport, and James Leo Garrett, among others, have contributed constructive proposals to the doctrine of ecclesiology.[72] While transdenominational evangelicals including Methodists, Anglicans, Lutherans, Nazarenes, Presbyterians, and others have found shortcomings in Baptist polity and ecclesiology, evangelicals can strengthen their approach to ecclesiology by adopting Southern Baptists as dialogue partners in these areas. Indeed, many of the chapters in this volume create the opportunity for first steps in these directions.

---

[68] The Baptist Faith and Message had undergone one earlier revision in 1963 as well.

[69] Millard J. Erickson, *Christian Theology*, rev. ed. (Grand Rapids: Baker, 1989).

[70] Mullins, *Axioms of Religion*.

[71] E. Y. Mullins, *Baptist Beliefs* (Valley Forge, PA; Judson, 1925).

[72] For example, see James Leo Garrett Jr., *Systematic Theology: Biblical Historical, and Evangelical*, vol. 2 (Grand Rapids: Eerdmans, 1995).

One of evangelicals' biggest weaknesses grows out of the entrepreneurial and transdenominational mindset so ubiquitous in evangelical circles. While strengths in this approach have led to strong ministries among hundreds of parachurch organizations, none more so than the Billy Graham Evangelistic Association, it has also resulted in much competition, duplication, and inefficiency of operation. It has also created structures needing accountability. Moreover, it has tended to discourage the strengths, guidance, and direction that come from a common shared heritage. It is here that Southern Baptists in 1925 began positive steps of which evangelicals might take note. Reports in state Baptist papers at the time reveal that the adoption of the Baptist Faith and Message was seen as the major story coming out of the 1925 meeting. Though the convention also approved a twelve-page report from the Committee on Future Programs, chaired by M. E. Dodd, to develop a general outline of plans for the funding of denominational ministries, it was only barely noticed because of the attention given to the new statement of faith.

The Cooperative Program is a cooperative and collaborative partnership whereby churches across the Southern Baptist Convention combine financial gifts given to and through state conventions, which are then passed on to support missionaries, equip pastors and church leaders, enable educational institutions, and address benevolent, social, ethical, and moral concerns. The Cooperative Program for the past ninety years has been the denominational glue that pulls together nearly fifty thousand Southern Baptist congregations for the purpose of advancing the gospel around the world.[73]

Baptist churches may choose to form associations or conventions. Southern Baptist churches have organized local associations, state conventions, and a national convention. These churches actually do not join associations or conventions so much as choose voluntarily to cooperate through these entities. One cannot understand who Southern Baptists are apart from the distinctive idea of voluntary cooperation and participation in the Cooperative Program.

---

[73] Dockery, "Convictional Yet Cooperative."

The world in which we live has changed much since 1925. One thing that remains constant is the commitment to the Great Commission shared by Southern Baptists and evangelicals. The call for cooperative collaboration in the twenty-first century must be heard differently at this time in light of now-evident differences from the cultural homogeneity characterizing the early twentieth century. Once again, transdenominational evangelicals and the denominational evangelicals of the SBC have much to learn from one another in terms of doctrine and practice, worship and ministry, conviction and cooperation.

Southern Baptists and evangelicals in the twenty-first century represent various ethnic backgrounds, are young and old, come from small and large churches, and worship in rural communities and in sprawling metropolitan areas. Both groups include the highly educated as well as the undereducated, those who are well known and anonymous, both rich and poor, social-media magnets and Luddites, and theologians and practitioners. While Southern Baptists are primarily from the South and card-carrying evangelicals are primarily from areas outside the South, both groups can be found in the North, South, East, and West. Others will take note, however, if we love one another, celebrate our variety, and serve together in harmony, faithfulness, and heartfelt cooperation.[74]

Southern Baptists and evangelicals are both facing challenging times—extremely so in some sectors of each movement. Both are asking hard questions related to the present and the future. Together we must pray for wisdom as answers to these questions are pursued. A spirit of convictional cooperation and cooperative conviction will be needed by all. Our commitment to a convictional cooperation and a spirit of cooperative conviction might bring together the two different groups, perhaps through new and developing networks that can strengthen and augment established entities and structures in an auxiliary way.

Evangelicals and Southern Baptists can move forward in a hopeful manner if both remain convictionally connected to the full and complete authority of Scripture, the gospel, and the best of the Christian tradition

---

[74] Dockery, *Southern Baptist Consensus and Renewal*, 16–57.

articulated so clearly in this volume.[75] Southern Baptists will need to risk moving out of their insularity while strengthening their capacity for kingdom diversity. Evangelicals will need to strengthen their ecclesiology and reduce duplication and competition while developing a new spirit for, and structure to enable, more enhanced cooperation and collaboration. Both groups will need to move beyond competition and duplications for the good of the gospel, doing so in ways that will help us better understand and more effectively minister in and to the changing global context around us.

Learning more about one another, eliminating stereotypes and misunderstandings, strengthening trust, and learning to work afresh in cooperative ways will be essential. We must see one another as colaborers in the gospel. We must look for commonalities rather than rivalries. Both groups need fresh eyes, a cooperative spirit, and genuine convictional grounding. We will need conviction and cooperation, boundaries and bridges, denominational structures and networks that will be open to the fresh winds of God's Spirit. With his help, we must work through existing tensions, doing so in balanced, constructive, and hopeful ways.[76]

Evangelicals need to recognize that the Southern Baptist Convention, with its vast resources, has significant opportunity to lead the way in reaching the world for Christ. In addition, evangelicals must recognize that Southern Baptist academic institutions, particularly the convention's seminaries, exist primarily to serve Baptist churches. Evangelicals can learn much from Southern Baptists at this point, better connecting theology, church, missions, and ministry.

For the majority of Southern Baptists looking toward the evangelical world and also for evangelicals seeking to understand Southern Baptists, the two worlds may be just too different. Perhaps evangelicals are so

---

[75] See David S. Dockery, *Christian Scripture: An Evangelical Perspective on Inspiration, Authority, and Interpretation* (Nashville: B&H, 1995); Dockery, ed., *Southern Baptists, Evangelicals, and the Future of Denominationalism* (Nashville: B&H, 2011); Dockery and George, *Great Tradition of Christian Thinking*.

[76] David S. Dockery and Timothy George, *Building Bridges: Perspectives on Baptist Unity* (Nashville: Convention Press, 2007).

overly concerned with epistemology, revelation, and other theological matters in general that they will be less than appreciated by Southern Baptists. I live in both worlds and at times am prone to think that way. Perhaps the SBC is often overly concerned with piety, programs, evangelism, ministry, and missions. Some evangelicals may unfortunately be experiencing theological drift, and some in the SBC may at times appear too narrow in both their thinking and their relationships. If so, we must go our separate ways. I, for one, trust that will not be the case.

Toward Renewal in Our Thinking: The Place of Tradition

But please hear this word: we must realize that our struggles are not against fellow Christ-followers but rather against demons, secularism, and unbelief. What is at stake if we do not take our eyes off the intramural squabbles that seem to characterize most denominations and which have certainly characterized Southern Baptists for the past fifty years is a loss not only of unity within the Christian movement but also of the Christian movement's mission focus in the West. We need a fresh commitment to biblical orthodoxy; a historic, apostolic, and catholic Christianity; and a faithful transgenerational, transcontinental, and multiethnic movement that stands or falls on first-order issues.[77]

Without forsaking our denominational distinctives, we are called to a commitment to gospel commonalities that are more important than and precede those distinctives: a commitment to the divine nature and authority of God's written Word, the deity and humanity of Jesus Christ, a heartfelt confession of the Holy Trinity, the uniqueness of the gospel message, the enabling work of God's Spirit, salvation by grace through faith alone, the importance of the church and the people of God who are both gathered and scattered, the hope of Christ's return, and the sacredness of life and family. In this twenty-first-century context, it is essential that we learn to disagree graciously over our differences. We will likely

---

[77] Dockery, *Southern Baptist Consensus and Renewal*, 168–220.

not find ways to agree on a wide variety of secondary and tertiary issues. We must find ways to connect and re-create contexts of belonging for the multiple generations and various ethnic groups within the body of Christ.

Also needed for our day is the reclamation of a model of dynamic orthodoxy. The orthodox tradition must be recovered, one that is in conversation with the great history of the church, the great tradition that traces its way from Nicaea to Chalcedon, from Augustine to Bernard, to Luther and Calvin, to Wesley, the Pietists, and the revivals, resulting in what J. I. Packer and Thomas Oden have called the "one faith" that has been believed by all God's people in all places at all times.[78]

A recommitment to such a confessional integrity will help us recover a call to the unity of the Christian faith in accord with the Nicene affirmation that the church is one, holy, catholic, and apostolic. All of us in this changing twenty-first century world must recommit ourselves afresh to the oneness and universality of the church. This recommitment must be supported by the right sort of virtues: a oneness that calls for humility, gentleness, patience, and forbearance with one another, a love and diligence to preserve the unity of the Spirit in the bond of peace. We trust that God will help us to do so. Along with these virtues will come a global perspective that includes a renewed dedication to racial reconciliation in our country, looking forward to a day in which the great multitude from every nation, all tribes and all people groups and tongues, shall stand before the Lamb as proclaimed and promised in Rev 7:9.

Let us trust God to bring a fresh wind of his Spirit; to bring renewal to our theological convictions and to our shared work; to revive our ministry and service so that we can relate to one another in love and humility and thereby inspire true fellowship and community; and yes, to bring new life to Christians, churches, and denominational entities as well.

Let us join together in asking God to grant us a renewed commitment to the gospel, to the church, and to the best of the Christian tradition, bringing about a renewed spirit of cooperation for the good of God's people around the globe. Let us work together to advance the gospel and

---

[78] J. I. Packer and Thomas C. Oden, *One Faith: The Evangelical Consensus* (Downers Grove, IL: InterVarsity Press, 2004).

trust God to bring forth fruit from our labors, resulting in renewal among both Baptist and evangelical congregations and entities. Let us pray that these efforts will bear fruit for God's kingdom as we work together to advance the gospel and the work of the global Christian movement in the twenty-first century.

13

Baptists, Global Christianity, and the Christian Tradition

Soojin Chung

California Baptist University

Introduction

The year 2018 marked the first time Africa boasted the most Christians of any continent. Compared to 1910, when only 18 percent of Christians lived in the global South, by 2018 66 percent of Christians lived in the global South.[1] A new center of gravity lies in Africa, Latin America, and Asia, with the largest Christian communities now residing in the global South. The term "South" here denotes geographic location less than it does degree of access to wealth and resources.[2] Economically, these southern churches are poorer than their western counterparts. Theologically, they are more conservative and prone to supernatural orientation than western churches. Understanding global Christianity—in which Baptists long have been key participants—is important as we navigate questions about Baptists and catholicity because (1) Christianity's center of gravity has conspicuously shifted to nonwestern countries, reminding us that

---

[1] Todd M. Johnson and Gina A. Zurlo, eds., *World Christian Database* (Leiden/Boston: Brill, accessed March 2019).

[2] Philip Jenkins, *The Next Christendom: The Coming of Global Christianity* (Oxford, UK: Oxford University Press, 2011), 4.

293

catholicity must be understood not merely historically but also globally, and (2) global Christianity helps us see the massive challenges to maintaining unity amid wide-ranging cultural and theological differences. Approaches to Baptist catholicity that fail to consider global Christianity cannot sustain the church's mission of taking the whole gospel to the whole world.

This study of global Christianity not only examines the manifestations of Christianity worldwide but also assesses their implications for our current world. Rapid globalization, rising immigration, and a shifting paradigm of Christianity have all created new, exciting windows to the future, as well as new challenges.

Global Christianity and Women

One of the most significant themes in global Christianity is the central role of women. In 1999 Dana Robert argued that the "typical late twentieth-century Christian was no longer a European man, but a Latin American or African woman."[3] Historically, women were among the earliest converts to Christianity in the global South. Of Central American Pentecostal converts in the late twentieth century, more than 66 percent were women. The typical American congregation is 61 percent female and 39 percent male. According to Pew Research, women in the late twentieth century were more religious than men on all measures, including weekly church attendance, daily prayer, and belief in heaven.[4] While men assumed the formal, ordained religious leadership positions, women constituted the majority of active participants.

Historically, women have been important leaders in evangelistic and educational mission work. In Asia, interlocking social networks and gender

---

[3] Dana L. Robert, "Shifting Southward: Global Christianity Since 1945," *International Bulletin of Missionary Research* 24, no. 2 (2000): 50–58, http://www.internationalbulletin.org/issues/2000-02/2000-02-050-robert.pdf.

[4] "The Gender Gap in Religion Around the World," Pew Research Center, March 22, 2016, https://www.pewforum.org/2016/03/22/the-gender-gap-in-religion-around-the-world.

roles required missionaries to depend on local female leaders, since male foreigners were not allowed to contact upper-class women. In the 1870s, missionaries depended heavily on these women, who were local female evangelists and active agents in the development of Asian Protestantism rather than passive objects of proselytization.[5] Although there were limitations on women's leadership due to theological convictions and factors related to indigenous religious practice, women played a pivotal role as social and religious leaders despite their poor social status. Many were lower-class and/or widows, but they overcame social prejudice and gender discrimination through their spiritual power and authority. Sadie Kim of Korea, for example, was a prominent leader who organized women's church groups and taught Sunday school at Namsanhyun Church. She was also a social activist, organizing a Widows' Relief Association.

Female leaders from various backgrounds enjoyed close partnerships with foreign missionaries. Kollumba Kang Wansuk, a Christian activist and martyr in Korea, developed a unique spiritual authority despite being a woman from a traditional Confucian background. She worked closely with Father Jacob Zhou Wenmo and was treated with the highest regard and trust, a status few others enjoyed.[6] As a leader in her church, she taught theology and acted as a mediator. She was responsible for all matters regarding women in the church. She was also a model of chastity, an important element of Christian piety for Korean women at that time.[7] She was martyred due to her faith and, up until her death, zealously led both men and women into the church.

Candida Xu is one of the few seventeenth-century Chinese women whose public records are available to us, due to her royal lineage. Xu,

---

[5] Christine Sungjin Chang, "Hidden but Real: The Vital Contribution of Biblewomen to the Rapid Growth of Korean Protestantism, 1892–1945," *Women's History Review* 17.4 (2008): 575.

[6] Robert E. Buswell Jr. and Timothy S. Lee, eds., *Christianity in Korea* (Honolulu: University of Hawaii Press, 2007), 47. Father Zhou (1752–1801) was the first Chinese missionary priest sent to Korea. He changed his name to Father Ju to assimilate to the Korean context. He was killed in the Saenamteo area for his faith in 1801.

[7] Buswell and Lee, 53.

from a third-generation Chinese Christian family, was a granddaughter of Xu Guangqi (a Chinese scholar and bureaucrat, ca. 1600) and a friend of Matteo Ricci (a founder of Jesuit mission efforts in China). She was able to share the gospel with her husband, who became a Christian only two years before his death. Xu successfully combined Confucian and Christian social ideals by remaining a faithful widow to her deceased husband. This chastity was considered a virtue in both Confucianism and Christianity at the time. Xu became a model Christian as well as a model Chinese woman, showing filial piety and commitment to moral values.

While at times traditional Asian cultural norms and Christian values conflicted, the two value systems shared many similarities. Christian continuity with traditional Asian values allowed women to juggle their religious and their domestic lives. Christianity brought religious and cultural transformation to women in Asia and gave them a new sense of domestic and public identity.

Female missionaries from across various American denominations advocated holistic mission and spearheaded combined medical, educational, and evangelistic missions. While these female missionaries supported traditional evangelistic missions in the nineteenth century, they departed from the practice of an earlier period by advocating the social uplift of women as well. They systemized a missiology of education in order to encourage a holistic mission model. The optimism found in this unique missiology can be traced back to the post-Civil War social atmosphere. Empowered by a new social ambience and driven by their firm belief in a holistic mission, the faithful women involved in this movement sent educated female missionaries to many parts of Asia. The concept of "women's work for women" was based on the belief that education was crucial for the liberation of women around the world. Using education, these missionaries sought to elevate women's social status.[8] It was in this spirit that the Women's Foreign Missionary Society sent the first female physicians to Korea and founded in Seoul the world's largest

---

[8] Dana L. Robert, *American Women in Mission: The Modern Mission Era, 1792–1992* (Macon, GA: Mercer University Press, 1997), 132, 160.

women's university, now known as Ewha Women's University. While male missionaries like Henry Appenzeller engaged in educational ministry as well, female missionaries were the leading force in spreading global Christianity among women.

In many African countries, indigenization of Christianity was carried out primarily by female Christians. Dorothy Hodgson, in her *The Church of Women: Gendered Encounters between Maasai and Missionaries*, offers a compelling argument that the introduction of Christianity in Tanzania was not a gender-neutral encounter. Rather than being relegated to an inferior position, women gained power and authority by joining a spiritual community. For women, new leadership opportunities and a newfound identity in Christ both became major impetuses for conversion. Due to the mass conversion of females in Tanzania, Maasai tribal Christianity rapidly spread and lead to a heavily indigenized Christianity.

In summary, indigenous female leaders and female missionaries promoted a holistic mission theology, one that played a crucial role in spreading global Christianity and raising the social status of women. Despite numerous obstacles, women converted to Christianity due to both social and religious reasons and in turn played an instrumental role in the spread of global Christianity.

Global Christianity and Contextualization

Another prominent theme in the rise of global Christianity is the tension between contextualization and syncretism. On one level, global Christianity assumes inclusivity in that it acknowledges diverse forms of Christianity—it celebrates both locality and universality. At the same time, the authentication of diverse local expressions has been challenging at times. Exactly what degree of local expression can be allowed? Who makes the judgment call? Who has the authority to set church structures and guidelines for worship styles?

Missionaries and missiologists have been asking these questions for centuries. Christianity's introduction to Korea, for instance, generated an inevitable clash between two disparate worldviews. Because missionaries forbade ancestor veneration, locals viewed Christianity as a foreign intrusion threatening a Confucianist social order and a shamanistic religious system. In return, the missionaries' attitude toward traditional Korean religions was initially extremely negative. Appenzeller devalued traditional religions, insisting that Buddhism was derelict, Confucianism only divisive, and shamanism merely superstitious and lowly.[9] However, when the search for an indigenous name for God arose in Korea, most missionaries advocated for the method of assimilation and contextualization, which adopted one of the traditional names for the divine in Korea. Missionary John Ross advocated for this practice because he believed using a vernacular Korean word with which people were familiar would assist in the acceptance of monotheistic practice. Since Koreans already held the notion that *hananim* was the supreme God among countless gods and spirits, Ross saw an opportunity for critical contextualization. On the other hand, in the opinion of Horace Underwood, precisely because Koreans were familiar with the term it was prudent to avoid it altogether and create a new word for God. Nevertheless, natives began to use *hananim* in this way, and many missionaries sought to provide a compelling theological ground for the term. After testing several different names for the Christian God, Underwood finally accepted the term *hananim* in 1905.

One contemporary example that shows the challenging nature of inclusive/exclusive missionary practices occurred in 2010, during the Third Lausanne Congress on World Evangelization in Cape Town, South Africa. During the opening and closing events of the Congress, performers presented worship arts in indigenous worship style. They appeared in traditional African clothes with aboriginal dancers, with loud horns and drums resounding in the background. Although the event met with great enthusiasm by most delegates, there were lively discussions on the fine line between contextualization and syncretism.

---

[9] Sung-Deuk Oak, *The Making of Korean Christianity: Protestant Encounters with Korean Religions, 1876–1915* (Waco: Baylor University Press, 2013), 16.

Religious pluralism is not a new phenomenon in many parts of Asia and Africa. Christians in the global South have been struggling to address the complex issues of religious pluralism, religious persecution, and religious wars for centuries. However, the rise of global Christianity has presented new challenges to Christians worldwide, faced with the reality of religious pluralism in a world connected by increasing immigration and globalization. Christianity has become a world religion alongside other faiths such as Judaism, Islam, Hinduism, and Buddhism.[10] It is important to maintain both the locality and the universality of global Christianity without compromising the essential tenets of the Christian faith. If one form of locality, or one form of culture, dominates Christianity, it is no longer a mosaic but becomes a monopoly. Since its inception, Christianity has been a global movement that spread in its early days throughout Asia, Africa, and Europe. It was never confined to one region or language. This fluidity, or "translatability," is part of the very nature of Christianity. It is one of Christianity's strengths, as the faith is able to shape and to be shaped by various cultures.[11] Christianity always moves outward and is never stagnant.

Baptists and Global Christianity

What is the role of Baptists in the global spread of Christianity? In 2018 there were approximately 2.5 billion Christians around the world, comprising a third of the global population. The largest Protestant groups were Pentecostal/charismatic (13.5 percent of the total world population), followed by Anglican (3.8 percent), nondenominational (3.5 percent), and Baptist (3.4 percent) groups. Considering that many Baptists living in the global South identify themselves as both Baptist and charismatic, and considering that many nondenominational groups are Baptistic in

---

[10] Dana L. Robert, *Christian Mission: How Christianity Became a World Religion* (Chichester, UK/Malden, MA: Wiley-Blackwell, 2009).

[11] Lamin Sanneh, *Translating the Message: The Missionary Impact on Culture*, rev. ed. (Maryknoll, NY: Orbis, 2009).

their theology, the number of Baptists worldwide is well over 3.4 percent of the world's population.

The 1792 founding of the Baptist Missionary Society (BMS) was a groundbreaking achievement for Baptists. BMS sent notable missionaries around the world, and many aspects of the global spread of Baptists can be attributed to organized mission endeavors. Literature was another effective means to spreading Baptist witness around the world. The British and Foreign Bible Society (BFBS), founded in London in 1806, distributed Bibles around the world in vernacular languages.

The growth of Baptists in the global South was not only the consequence of systematic missionary efforts but was also due to various other factors including migration, the development of an efficient printing press, and new means of transportation. Railroads, steamships, and later automobiles and airplanes increased population mobility, allowing mass migration. Many Baptists residing in the global North moved to different countries for new opportunities, and the European and American diaspora was one of the most significant reasons for the growth of Baptists around the world. Many freed slaves, for example, migrated to Liberia, a haven for the victims of slavery and a safe place to practice the Christian faith. Lott Carey, a black Baptist pastor, was one of them. He migrated from Richmond, Virginia, and in 1822 established a Baptist church in Monrovia, Liberia's capital. Similarly, many black Baptists migrated from Halifax, Nova Scotia, to western Africa in 1792. David George, a former slave, had planted a church in Nova Scotia, a British colony. Then George led a group of Baptists and migrated to Sierra Leone, planting a church in the capital, Freetown. In general, this mass migration was driven not only by religious conviction but also by an urge to forge a better life.[12]

The following section will highlight Baptist activities in Asia, Latin America, and Africa. Although these three regions do not encompass the entire global South, an overview of activities there will demonstrate the diversity found in global Christianity.

---

[12] Bebbington, *Baptists through the Centuries*, 233–40.

Baptist Growth in Asia

In 1910 approximately 2.4 percent of the population in Asia was Christian. By 2010 that number had increased to 8.5 percent. Christianity in Asia is marked by varied historical development, intense religious persecution, and regional diversity due to political, socioeconomic, and cultural factors.[13] Asia was one of the earliest Baptist mission fields, and by 1904 Baptists in Asia and Oceania numbered around 160,000. By 2004 that number had increased to 5.3 million, seven times higher than the number of Baptists in Europe, the birthplace of Baptists.[14]

One of the world's major Baptist centers is in South Asia, particularly the hill country of northeast India. In the late nineteenth century, English and American Baptists evangelized the tribal people who had migrated there from China. Northeast India became one of the most successful mission fields worldwide for Baptists. Since the second decade of the twentieth century, a significant Baptist movement has been growing in the Indian states of Nagaland and Manipur. Today, Baptists are the largest Christian denomination in Nagaland, producing indigenous missionaries and utilizing a self-supporting, self-propagating, and self-governing model of cooperation. The broader Indian subcontinent has also been receptive to Christianity in general and Baptists specifically. Since the Indian subcontinent is religiously diverse, missionaries initially experienced difficulty evangelizing. With concerted efforts, however, Baptists have gained adherents from various faiths, including people from Hindu, Buddhist, Muslim, and animistic backgrounds.[15]

In Southeast Asia, where Theravada Buddhism dominates the peninsulas and archipelagoes, Christians are a small minority. With the closing of China after World War II, Baptists actively pursued their mission work in Thailand, Indonesia, Malaysia, Singapore, Vietnam, and Laos.[16] Most of the Christians in Southeast Asian countries are

---

[13] Todd Johnson and Kenneth Ross, eds., *Atlas of Global Christianity* (Edinburgh, UK: Edinburgh University Press, 2009).

[14] Chute, Finn, and Haykin, *Baptist Story*, 296.

[15] Wardin, *Baptists around the World*.

[16] Wardin, 149.

tribal people. In Thailand, for example, the majority of Christians are not of Thai descent but are tribal minorities. Almost half of all Baptists in Southeast Asia reside in Burma (known by its oppressive regime as Myanmar). Many of them are concentrated among three tribal groups in Burma: the Kayin (Karen), Chin, and Kachin. The ethnic Burmese are predominantly Buddhist, and tribal groups remain targets of religious persecution.

Baptists were the first Protestants to enter Burma, and the country was the first mission field for American Baptists. Adoniram and Ann Judson initiated this Baptist mission. Commissioned by the American Board of Commissioners for Foreign Missions in 1812, their subsequent conversion to Baptist views led them to resign from the board and join the American Baptists. In 1813 they settled in Rangoon, a major city of the Third Burmese Empire. Educational mission was one of the primary methods used by the Baptists. They established Rangoon Baptist College (1871), later renamed Judson Baptist College; Burman Theological Seminary (1836); Karen Theological Seminary (1845); and several Bible schools for various groups.[17] The literary mission was another successful venture. The Baptist Mission Press, established in 1816, published the Bible in five languages, books on church history, and catechisms. The Burma Baptist Missionary Convention, established in 1865, and the Karen Baptist Convention became the largest and most active bodies among the Baptists in Burma.

East Asia experienced significant Baptist growth despite the context of communist regimes and religious pluralism. In 1845 the Foreign Mission Board of the Southern Baptist Convention sent its first missionaries—S. C. Clopton and George Pearcy—to China. There the first wave of Baptist missionaries established the First Baptist Church of Canton. The mission flourished mostly among minority groups, particularly the Hakka people of the northern part of Guangxi province. One of the most notable Baptist missionaries to China was Lottie Moon, who settled in the port city of Dengzhou (now Penglai), in

---

[17] Wardin, 155.

Shandong. She advocated for contextualization and adopted a Chinese lifestyle, living among the locals in rural Chinese villages. The Woman's Missionary Union avidly supported her missionary efforts and collected Christmas offerings in order to send her assistance. Today the SBC's Lottie Moon Christmas Offering is the largest foreign mission offering of any denomination worldwide.

Baptists used education as one of their mission strategies in China. In 1906 the Foreign Mission Board of the Southern Baptist Convention and the American Baptist Foreign Mission Society established Shanghai Baptist College and Seminary (later renamed University of Shanghai). This university produced notable Chinese Christian leaders such as C. C. Chen and T. C. Wu, who returned to China after studying abroad. By 1927 there were more than one hundred Christian leaders serving in various capacities as pastors, missionaries, teachers, and doctors at Baptist institutions in China.[18] Although churches in China are divided between the Three-Self Church sanctioned by the government and the underground churches in private houses, Baptists remain active agents in both camps.

Baptist communities exist in some parts of western Asia, such as Israel, Lebanon, Syria, and Jordan, but in countries such as Iran, Iraq, and Afghanistan there is no official Baptist presence due to anti-western policies of Islamic regimes. Among these, Lebanon has the longest Baptist history, starting from 1895, when Said Jureidini established the first Baptist church in Beirut. Jureidini was a local photographer who became a Baptist while traveling to Chicago. He received financial help from the Baptist General Convention. Although growth was slow, the number of Lebanese Baptists steadily increased, and in 1955 the Lebanese Baptist Convention was born. Southern Baptists also established the MENA (Middle East/North Africa) Evangelism Ministry in Lebanon and founded an Arab Baptist Publication Center.

---

[18] Wardin, 96.

Baptist Growth in Latin America

Latin America's history of Christianity began with violence and forced evangelism. When conquistadors from Spain and Portugal subjugated the new continent in the first part of the sixteenth century, they viewed their work as a religious crusade and used force to Christianize the native people. Moreover, they enslaved the indigenous population and exploited them economically. Catholicism was introduced first, and it was not until the waning of Spanish power that Baptists from various countries gained influence in Latin America.

In the Caribbean, extensive mission activities unfolded among English-speaking blacks. In Jamaica particularly, indigenization was extremely successful, resulting in many self-supporting and self-governing local churches. In 1842 Jamaican Baptists established the Jamaican Baptist Missionary Society. Cuba also experienced a rapid growth of Baptists due to successful indigenization. Baptist churches in Cuba partnered with the Jamaica Baptist Missionary Society and later were supported by the Florida Baptist Convention and the SBC Home Mission Board. Today, Baptists and Pentecostals are the two largest Protestant denominations in Cuba.[19]

Baptists were among the first Protestant missionaries to enter Mexico. In 1864 James Hickey of the American Bible Society, Thomas Westrup, and two Mexican locals, Jose Maria Uranga and Arcadio Uranga, established the first Baptist church in Monterrey, also the first evangelical church in Mexico. Although Baptist work was abruptly halted during the revolution of 1910–1917, in the following years the mission was successful and became more localized. The National Convention of Mexico works among ten indigenous language groups and sends missionaries to various parts of Latin America to this day.

Central America was slower than Mexico to see Baptist growth. Many efforts faced fierce resistance from the government. In Guatemala, for example, many Baptist missionaries and individuals were deported for

---

[19] Wardin, 289.

their faith at the request of the Catholic clergy during the mid-1800s.[20] Before 1940 there was scarcely any Baptist mission activity among Spanish-speaking regions in El Salvador and Nicaragua.

Baptists played an important role in the rapid growth of evangelical faith in South America. In 1965 there were approximately 250,000 Baptists in South America; by 2007 that number had increased to 1.8 million. The most significant growth has occurred in Brazil, where Baptists number over 1.1 million, constituting more than 60 percent of Latin America's Baptists. In 1907 Brazilian Baptists organized the Brazilian Baptist Convention. This convention includes vibrant local leadership and a denominational structure similar to the SBC's. By the end of the twentieth century Brazilian Baptists had established more than forty educational institutions and sponsored schools throughout the country.[21]

Baptists in Latin America are experiencing new challenges as well as exciting windows of opportunity due to the renewalist movement, which emphasizes supernatural intervention of the Holy Spirit in daily life. At times Pentecostals and charismatics have infused Christianity with indigenous spiritism and Afro-Brazilian animism, often resulting in syncretism. A South American emphasis on spiritual gifts, miracles, and the prosperity gospel has affected Baptist practice. The renewalist movement fostered explosive growth of Protestantism, often resulting in vigorous mission efforts by the Catholic Church to reestablish its place in the religious marketplace. The fine line between contextualization and syncretism is a lived religious reality for Latin American Christians.

Baptist Growth in Africa

Christianity in Africa goes back to Pentecost, when Egyptians and Libyans were present to receive the Holy Spirit. Around AD 60, Christianity began to spread in North Africa, and around 400 the Ethiopian king

---

[20] Bebbington, *Baptists through the Centuries*, 241.
[21] Robert E. Johnson, *A Global Introduction to Baptist Churches* (Cambridge, UK: Cambridge University Press, 2010), 289–91.

Ezana made Christianity the kingdom's official religion.[22] Although the success of Christianity was short-lived due to Islamic expansion around 600, African Christianity is as old as European Christianity. Mission history in Africa is often intertwined with colonialism. The scramble for Africa, which occurred during the period of new imperialism from the late 1800s to the early 1900s, divided and conquered African territory and imposed European state religions. Mission churches should be distinguished from colonial churches, however, since the mission churches' goals were fundamentally religious, not political. Among mission churches, Baptists were pioneers.

Before World War I, the Baptist Missionary Society of Great Britain, the American Baptist Missionary Union, the Southern Baptist Foreign Mission Board, the Foreign Mission Board of the National Baptist Convention, and the Mission Society of German Baptists were active in parts of western and southern Africa. In western Africa, the majority of Baptists reside in Nigeria. Before World War I there was little Baptist missionary activity in western Africa except for that in Nigeria, Liberia, and Sierra Leone. Southern Baptists established their mission station in Nigeria in 1850, and, while growth was slow, by 1919 the Nigerian Baptist Convention was successfully born. Since the 1930s, Nigerian Baptists have grown exponentially, centered around Ogbomosho, home of the Nigerian Baptist Theological Seminary, Baptist Media Center, and various Baptist medical and educational institutions. The Women's Missionary Union, an auxiliary to the Nigerian Baptist Convention, has also played an indispensable role in the spread of Christianity.

Baptist missionaries were well received in equatorial Africa. They spearheaded missions in countries such as Cameroon and the Democratic Republic of the Congo. In addition to evangelism, educational and medical missions were established in the coastal areas and interior. Baptist presence in eastern and northern Africa, in comparison to other regions,

---

[22] Douglas Jacobsen, *Global Gospel: An Introduction to Christianity on Five Continents* (Grand Rapids: Baker Academic, 2015); Sebastian Kim and Kirsteen Kim, *Christianity as a World Religion: An Introduction*, 2nd ed. (New York: Bloomsbury Academic, 2016).

is weak. The biggest growth in East Africa has occurred among agriculturalists in Kenya, Tanzania, Uganda, Burundi, and Rwanda.[23] Due to government hostility in predominantly Muslim North Africa, Baptist presence there is meager. Southern African Baptists have experienced rapid growth in many areas, including South Africa, Malawi, Mozambique, and Zambia. Southern Africa continues to play an important role in supplying an indigenous missionary force to other African regions. Vernacularization of literature and the rise of charismatic movements have assisted the explosive growth of global Christianity in Africa.

Conclusion: Baptist Ecumenicity for Mission

In July 1974 more than 2,700 evangelical leaders gathered at the Palais de Beaulieu in Lausanne, Switzerland, to discuss the progress of world evangelization and to foster ecumenicity for world mission. The Lausanne Congress on World Evangelization was spearheaded by influential leaders such as Billy Graham and John Stott and brought together delegates from 150 nations. Subsequently, the Lausanne Covenant, a seminal missiological document to this day, was crafted by the drafting committee under Stott's leadership. The slogan of the Lausanne Congress was adapted from a phrase Stott used in the Lausanne Covenant: "Evangelization requires the whole church to take the whole gospel to the whole world."[24] The slogan was officially incorporated into the Manila Manifesto in 1989. The whole church includes the *global* Christian community, and mutual respect and partnership is essential to advancing the kingdom of God. A Baptist approach to catholicity informed by global Christianity underscores that we are a part of the *whole* church, the global church.

Baptists such as David Dockery and Timothy George have persistently emphasized the need to place Baptist identity in the *consensus fidei* of historic Christian orthodoxy, focusing more on the unity

---

[23] Wardin, *Baptists around the World*, 13.

[24] John Stott, *The Lausanne Covenant: Complete Text with Study Guide* (Peabody, MA: Hendrickson, 2012).

among evangelicals than on "denominational egocentricity." George has admonished that excessive denominational allegiance is "self-absorbing, self-justifying, and self-gratifying."[25] Continuity with the consensus of the early church and a historically informed faith based on the person and work of Jesus Christ must be kept as a priority.

The ultimate goal of Baptist ecumenicity is not unity per se but unitedly participating in the *missio dei*. The disunity of the church is lamentable not simply because disunity is deplorable but because it hinders the ultimate purpose of the church: participation in God's mission.[26] The global church exits in a post-Christendom context, which necessitates deep humility and vision for reconciliation. No one form of Christianity can claim preeminence—with Christianity moving away from privilege to diversity, the whole church must seek to attain unity for the sake of gospel advancement. The global church is essentially a mission, because we love and serve a missionary God whose love is always centrifugal.

---

[25] James A. Patterson, "Landmarkism's Sectarian Legacy: An Obstacle to Ecumenism in the Southern Baptist Convention," *Criswell Theological Review* 14, no. 2 (Spring 2017): 3–15.

[26] Joshua Searles, "Moving Towards an Ecumenism of Koinonia: A Critical Response to 'The Church: Towards a Common Vision' from a Baptistic Perspective," *Journal of European Baptist Studies* 15.2 (2015): 17–27.

14

Racial Tension, the Baptist Tradition, and Christian Unity

Walter R. Strickland II
Southeastern Baptist Theological Seminary

Introduction

Baptist catholicity situates Baptist identity within the broader Christian tradition. This chapter contributes to an abiding unity by exploring racial disharmony within the Southern Baptist Convention (SBC) and its connection to the development of the National Baptist Convention (NBC). This story conveys several dynamics that have reinforced racial division both within and between these ecclesiastical bodies. As a result, this account serves as an object lesson for understanding and pursuing unity while allowing for Christ-honoring diversity within Baptist life. Studying the relationship between Southern and National Baptists also will yield principles for forging a closer connection between Baptists and the diverse body of Christ at large.

The historical narrative is replete with successes and failures displaying the subtle power of habits subconsciously adopted from generation to generation. Daily patterns inherited from family and friends inform presuppositions that generate expectations for the status quo. This inheritance includes an array of ideas that must be scrutinized biblically in order to affirm the good and escape the undesirable patterns and biases of our forebears. This task is frightfully difficult because it is akin to describing the concept of wetness to a fish. As a result, escaping the state of racial disunity among Baptists, bequeathed through generations, will take intentional and sustained effort.

Countless well-intended Southern Baptists have begun the journey of reconciliation with deep conviction and enthusiasm but have encountered frustration due to the slow pace of change. Discouragement is inescapable when the complexity of racial tension is oversimplified and solutions prove unfruitful. The racial tension among Baptists will not diminish until a confluence of factors is considered as interconnected parts. At least three areas must be engaged in order to pursue unity today: (1) individual sentiment, (2) institutional involvement, and (3) theological tradition. The following essay illustrates how denominational (i.e., institutional) structures foster division as they reflect individual biases hardened by theological fortification. Despite these negative developments, this essay concludes with hopeful prescriptions for racial reconciliation.

Baptist Shift from Antislavery: Pre-1845

Before the SBC was established, Baptists drifted away from their largely antislavery First Great Awakening posture. This antislavery disposition was officially documented in 1785 when the Virginia General Committee, home to 20,000 of the nation's then-65,000 Baptists, affirmed that slavery was "contrary to the word of God."[1] Soon after, Baptists in the Carolinas and Georgia affirmed antislavery statements of their own and endorsed gradual emancipation.[2]

Among the South's Baptists, this antislavery posture began eroding in 1790 after a resolution on gradual emancipation was adopted by the Virginia General Association but failed to meet general approval of the

---

[1] Eva Sheppard Wolf, *Race and Liberty in the New Nation: Emancipation in Virginia from the Revolution to Nat Turner's Rebellion* (Baton Rouge: Louisiana State University Press, 2009), 97. While Virginia does not represent a consensus, it was a large, measurable cross-section of Baptists in the South.

[2] H. Shelton Smith, *In His Image, but . . . : Racism in Southern Religion, 1780–1910* (Durham, NC: Duke University Press, 1972), 47.

state's Baptist associations. This occasion marked the beginning of pro-slavery ripples throughout Baptist life.[3] From 1790 to 1831, local associations began splitting over the issue of slavery throughout the South. The tide changed on the matter in the aftermath of Denmark Vesey's failed revolt of 1822 and Nat Turner's murderous rebellion of 1831. This sea change demonstrates the power of the political climate in denominational discourse as non-Virginian Baptists stood with their brethren and began shifting their posture on slavery as if the Vesey and Turner incidents represented their own misfortune.

Northern and Southern Baptists reached a point of division after the American Baptist Home Mission Society (ABHMS) and later the Triennial Convention took a stand against slave ownership when Georgia Baptists nominated slave owner James Reeve to serve as a missionary. In the intense rhetoric of the American Baptist Anti-Slavery Convention, "Slaveholders stand under the 'contempt of mankind' and the 'displeasure of God.'"[4] The New York convention called upon Baptists in the South to "confess before heaven and earth the sinfulness of holding slaves; admit it to be not only a misfortune, but a crime."[5] Because of this evil, Northern Baptists could not "recognize [slaveholders] as consistent brethren in Christ."[6] Baptists in the South insisted that the ABHMS and their Northern brethren had violated their pact to remain neutral on slavery and as a response established their own denomination and mission boards.

Racial Tension within Southern Baptist Churches: 1845–1865

Inaugural SBC president William Bullein Johnson offered a public address to express the sentiment of the new convention, emphasizing three points: First, after articulating the painfulness of the division, Johnson insisted

---

[3] Smith, 48.
[4] McBeth, *Baptist Heritage*, 384.
[5] McBeth, 384–85.
[6] McBeth, 385.

upon the previously noted point that Northern Baptists had violated the constitutions of the mission societies by insisting on a specific position on slave ownership. Second, he claimed Southern Baptists were returning to the original Baptist missionary work. Third, because he was sensitive to the new body being dubbed the "slaveholding convention," Johnson claimed the purpose of the new convention was not for "upholding of any form of human policy" but for the "extension of Messiah's kingdom" (i.e., missions).[7] Despite Johnson's explanation, H. Leon McBeth, a sympathetic Southern Baptist historian, insists that "Slavery was the main issue. . . . [It] is a blunt historical fact."[8]

The SBC's development highlights the convergence of two genuine desires among Baptists in the South. On the one hand was a desire to take the gospel to those who had not heard it, while on the other hand was a desire to protect slavery as an institution. These sentiments, embodied by the majority of Southern Baptists, were institutionalized via the nearly immediate formation of mission boards and policies that allowed slave owners to be supported and commissioned to the field. In time, Southern Baptists' theological malformation, emboldened by slaveholding Christians, surfaced as Southern Baptists connected the value of humans to their social status and/or spiritual state, paradoxically deeming blacks worthy of both servitude and evangelization.

These irreconcilable theological presuppositions were evident in Southern Baptist churches, with belief in black inferiority reflected by worship practices, beginning with the seating arrangement. It was common for blacks to sit in the back of the church, often referred to as the "African corner" or "nigger pew." In larger churches blacks were forced to sit in the balcony, called "nigger heaven." Moreover, practice of the Lord's Supper confirmed a dysfunctional anthropology by racially segregating participants, thus signifying a supposed ontological gradation within God's people. Worshipers also routinely reconvened at the conclusion of morning services, and the authority of the pulpit was misappropriated to

---

[7] E. Franklin Frazier, *The Negro Church in America* (New York: Schocken, 1964), 25.

[8] McBeth, 382.

read slave codes, sets of rules for slaves based on the presupposition they were property rather than persons.

Black Christians responded to structural sin and theological dysfunction in the SBC with an institutional response of their own. In pursuit of dignity in corporate worship, blacks, primarily in the North but also somewhat in the South, established independent black churches and what became known as the "invisible institution," a series of secret all-black meetings.[9] Religious historian Leroy Fitts recognizes three types of public Baptist churches attended by blacks: (1) mixed churches, (2) predominantly black churches under white leadership, and (3) separate churches under black leadership. These three forms of "doing church" existed simultaneously, but the accelerating trend was to establish separate, all-black churches.[10]

---

[9] "Invisible institutions," also referred to as "hush harbors," were secret religious meetings held by enslaved Africans that were hidden from the oversight of their masters. The nomenclature signifies the secretive nature of this enterprise, as such gatherings were illegal and discouraged by masters fearful of revolt. In order to appease their masters, blacks continued attending the churches prescribed by their masters that promoted submission and docility but supplemented their worship experience with these secret meetings. It is important to note the development of this invisible structure in response to systemic ecclesiastical racism.

[10] Leroy Fitts, "The Exodus of Black Baptists," chap. 2 in *A History of Black Baptists* (Nashville: Broadman, 1985). This chapter focuses on Fitts's second category because its aim is to describe racial tension within the SBC that led to a new denominational structure, the NBC. All-black Baptist associations began to sprout in the 1830s on the heels of the Nat Turner rebellion. The estimated 150,000 black Baptists in 1850 began pouring into independent associations, especially after black and white relations became more tenuous when Baptists split in 1845 over the issue of slavery. The first black Baptist churches in the South predated the establishment of the SBC, which offered blacks a precedent after its founding. The first black Baptist congregation was established in 1758 on William Byrd's planation in Mecklenburg, Virginia, and the second, Silver Bluff Baptist Church, was founded by the famous George Liele in Silver Bluff, South Carolina. While the founding date of Silver Bluff Church is far from certain, it is commonly placed between 1773 and 1775, despite the church's cornerstone claiming 1750. In the West, the first black associations began to formalize later because racial tension was far less pronounced than in the South. See Anne H. Pinn and Anthony B. Pinn, *Fortress Introduction to Black Church History* (Minneapolis: Fortress, 2001), 68–69.

In this new ecclesiastical arrangement, African Americans could pray and sing together without fear of white congregants and at times be led by their "kinsmen in the flesh." Furthermore, the gospel of Jesus Christ was less likely to be used as a tool to manipulate slaves; rather, it was a message of hope—both in the present and for the future.

While the independent black church movement mitigated the sting of oppression to a degree, the racial dynamics were especially complex for black Baptist churches that remained in Southern associations. Retaining such churches in the SBC served as an ongoing means of controlling these newly established black congregations. Despite the long-held Baptist distinctive of local church autonomy, associational hierarchies regularly made decisions for black congregations, including appointing white ministers.[11] In rare cases, predominantly black churches were appointed a black minister, but those churches were also assigned white overseers to safeguard against feared revolt or insurrection.

Churches with black leadership were systemically excluded from cooperating within their associations because they were not allowed to send delegates to regular meetings. The exclusion of black leadership on every level of Southern Baptist life kept the SBC from considering the needs of black constituents and bred paternalism among white Southern Baptists. In essence, black Southern Baptist churches were anything but independent, and denominational structures were used as a means of upholding the status quo.

Among black Baptists, the off-putting activity of the SBC was not relegated to church polity or the nature of cooperation; it formalized into theological principles that serviced the twofold aim of pursuing "kingdom expansion" around the world and enslaving fellow men. In addition to theological features such as a revivalist approach to sin, conversion, and repentance, Southern Baptist theology upheld an anthropological dualism that simultaneously affirmed oppressive church practices yet allowed Southern Baptists to feel altruistic in their dealings with blacks.

---

[11] See McBeth, *The Baptist Heritage*, 390. For an extended explanation or find the proceedings of the First Triennial Meeting of the Southern Baptist Convention, 1846, 22.

Proslavery theology allowed for the abuse of blacks while promising them freedom in the life to come. In practice, this theological dichotomy determined that the slaves' bodies belonged to their earthly masters while their souls belonged to God.

The faith passed down from whites to blacks was carefully curated to convince black Christians of this dualism. To that end, Scripture passages highlighted for blacks mirrored the British Slave Bible. Such slave Bibles encouraged captives to remain docile by removing 90 percent of the Old Testament, including passages like those in Exodus that depicted God freeing his people from bondage. Moreover, 50 percent of the New Testament was eliminated, including verses such as Gal 3:28, which insists upon the unity and equality of those who are in Christ. Verses that remained highlighted servitude, including Eph 6:5, which commands, "Slaves, obey your human masters."

Beyond the selective texts included in slave Bibles and slavery-friendly catechisms (such as one known as Caper's Catechism), passages were commonly warped to appropriate the Christian faith for social ends. The curse of Ham (Gen 9:18–27) was used to claim that God, not man, had inaugurated the institution of human bondage. Moreover, it was argued, Noah's curse singled out blacks for perpetual service to whites. In Exodus, ongoing dependence of a slave to his master was illustrated via Israel's longing to return to servitude following its deliverance from Egypt.[12] Blacks were also taught that Jesus's silence on slavery despite its prevalence in his society was an affirmation of the practice. The apostle Paul's instruction to the saints to remain in the situation in which they found themselves when God called them (1 Cor 7:20) was misapplied to *slavery* despite Paul's clear reference to *marital* status. In addition, the book of Philemon was a common source for advocating what was referred to as the "Pauline mandate" for slavery. These teachings were intended to cultivate an eschatologically focused faith among

---

[12] Lester Scherer, *Slavery and the Churches in Early America: 1619–1819* (Grand Rapids: Eerdmans, 1975), 66. Some of the abuses were found in the pre–Civil War schoolhouse.

blacks and eliminate their desire for equitable social and ecclesiastical standing with whites.[13]

The Christian faith that blacks embraced was not dependent on the proslavery theology thrust upon them in Southern Baptist churches. While black Baptists clung to the fundamentals of sin, repentance, and sanctification, independent black churches, and especially the invisible institution, served as venues to forge a theological tradition that responded more appropriately to the condition and concerns of blacks.[14] The theological themes of the Second Great Awakening increasingly found a unique expression among African Americans. In particular, Christopher Evans cites a more egalitarian expression of brotherhood in the black Christian community.[15] Furthermore, African American theological formation aims to be holistic in scope and to contain no dichotomy between sacred and secular, as the resurrection of Christ profoundly transforms every facet of human existence.

Black Baptists also read Scripture with a participatory posture. In contrast to the bookish faith of many whites, who tended to read the text more analytically, blacks rehearsed biblical stories as if they themselves were God's people. For example:

> Slaves began identifying with the Hebrew people and declared themselves to be insiders in the scriptural drama. Their identification with the story established their identity within the people of God. In particular, the Exodus narrative holds a place of prominence among the Old Testament accounts because it demonstrates slavery to be against God's will and nature. As a result of God's unchanging character, the promise of deliverance was

---

[13] James H. Evans, *We Have Been Believers* (Minneapolis: Augsburg Fortress, 1992), 39.

[14] Pinn and Pinn, *Fortress Introduction*, 12.

[15] Christopher H. Evans, *Histories of American Christianity: An Introduction* (Waco, TX: Baylor University Press, 2013), 81.

certain, then and now, and this supposition blossomed within the African American Christian tradition.[16]

Thus proper application of the biblical story was to involve participation in the liberating work of God in blacks' own circumstances. This growing disassociation with white Christians set the stage for a large-scale migration following emancipation.

The Black Exodus from the Southern Baptist Convention: 1865–1895

The abuse black Southern Baptists endured resulted in their mass exodus from the SBC at the conclusion of the Civil War. Prior to ratification of the Thirteenth Amendment in 1865, black churches unaffiliated with white churches or associations were a rare occurrence, but at the conclusion of the war this became the norm, even in the South. As Albert Raboteau stated, "the "invisible institution" took on visible form." The networks of black congregations established to counteract the ecclesiastical abuse endured in white churches no longer had to be hidden.

The extent of the split between black and white Baptists in the South is illustrated by the demographic shift among South Carolina Baptists. In 1858 the Southern Baptist Conference of South Carolina counted 29,211 black church members; in 1874 there were 1,614.[17] While most blacks

---

[16] Walter R. Strickland II, "Methodological Development in African American Theology: The Influence of Past Historical Periods upon Contemporary Black and Womanist Thought," in *T&T Clark Handbook of African American Theology*, ed. Antonia Michelle Daymond, Frederick L. Ware, and Eric Lewis Williams (Edinburgh, UK: T&T Clark, 2019), 225.

[17] Albert J. Raboteau, *Canaan Land: A Religious History of African Americans*, Religion in American Life (Oxford, UK: Oxford University Press, 2001), 68. Parallel developments were occurring in Methodism. The AME church grew from a modest 20,000 members at the beginning of the Civil War to nearly 400,000 by 1884. See C. Eric Lincoln and Lawrence H. Mamiya, *The Black Church in the African American Experience* (Durham, NC: Duke University Press, 1990), 54. Another predominantly black Methodist denomination, the African Methodist

did not remain in white-led churches, some black churches stayed in their local Baptist associations in anticipation of a new dynamic in race relations after the Thirteenth Amendment was ratified. Unfortunately, hopes of a newfound equality were not actualized in the SBC. Paternalism was alive and well in Baptist life, driving blacks to establish a convention of their own.[18]

A National Convention for Black Baptists: 1895

Formation of the National Baptist Convention USA marked the formalization of a deepening cleavage between white and black Baptists that has yet to be overcome. Because supposed white superiority was inherent to the bylaws and sentiments held within the SBC, black Christians established a place to pray, sing, preach, and commune without the oppressive blanket of perceived inferiority. This constructive goal of establishing the NBC was clear in an address given by the convention's inaugural president, Elias Camp Morris, in 1899:

> I wish to repeat what I have said on several other occasions: that this Society [denomination] entertains no ill will toward any other Christian organization in the world. It seeks to be on friendly

---

Episcopal Zion Church, increased in membership from 20,000 to 200,000 from 1860 to 1870, the great bulk of its growth occurring in the South (Raboteau, *Canaan Land*, 68). Furthermore, a third major black Methodist denomination, the Christian Methodist Episcopal Church, claimed membership exceeding 103,000 by 1890 (Lincoln and Mamiya, *Black Church*, 63).

[18] One example of Southern Baptist paternalism was the 1894 Fortress Monroe Conference. This gathering of Northern and Southern Baptist delegates was to ease remaining tensions following the Civil War, as both sides had continually breached established geographical boundaries in their church planting and other mission efforts. Of the three accords from the conference, two involved ministry with black Baptists. Given that two-thirds of the conference agenda pertained to ministry with black Baptists, it is reasonable that delegates from black Baptist churches would have been invited to attend—but none had been. This "father knows best" mentality permeated the Southern Baptist disposition toward black Baptists. This egregious lack of representation was one of the primary motivating factors behind the formation of the National Baptist Convention in 1895.

terms with all, and the charge that this organization means to draw the color line, and thereby create prejudice in "Negro" Christians against "white" Christians, is without foundation.[19]

Between 1890 and 1906 church membership rose from 2.6 to 3.6 million among African Americans, who largely attended independent black churches that had no ties to white denominations. By 1906 the National Baptist Convention claimed more than two million congregants and represented more than 61 percent of all black churchgoers in America.[20] These statistics bear witness to the comprehensive nature of the split between white and black Baptists.

Fortifying the Divide

The overwhelming consequence of racialized denominationalism is that each convention has been conditioned to look after the interests of its dominant cultural group. These dynamics complicate racial reconciliation within both denominations and stifle rich catholicity. On the whole, the existence of two denominational structures creates difficulties for racial reconciliation because structures are not neutral—they influence the people who exist within them.

One challenge caused by racialized denominational structures is that beloved corporate worship traditions and operational procedures produce a stumbling block, as allegiance to the "way we have always done it" is seen as more valuable than forging a new way of mutuality between the established bodies. Segregated conventions left limited starting places from which to work toward racial unity because their structures had been forged in the midst of racial dissension. Among those invested in racial reconciliation, the status quo forces the paralyzing question, From which

---

[19] Elias Camp Morris, *Sermons, Addresses and Reminiscence,s and Important Correspondence, with a Picture Gallery of Eminent Ministers and Scholars* (Nashville: National Baptist Publishing Board, 1901), 93.

[20] Paul Harvey, *Through the Storm and Through the Night: A History of African American Christianity*, The African American Experience Series (Lanham, MD: Rowman & Littlefield, 2001), 72.

side do I begin working toward unity? This results in passionate individuals' losing their desire for unity as they work against an institutionalized culture.

The founding dispositions of each convention charted a course for dissonance between the two. At its inception, the SBC's framers believed they had the singular goal of "expanding the Messiah's kingdom" in mind. Their genuine hope was to expand God's kingdom by verbally proclaiming Jesus as Lord. In contrast, the founders of the NBC aimed to promote the spiritual health of blacks and also to develop skills and character traits among blacks in order to assert their full humanity in a nation marked by racial injustice.[21] While both conventions were convinced they were doing "Christian" work, accusations of truncating the gospel or needlessly conflating it with social concerns have continually complicated reconciliation.

A significant dynamic at play is the need for black Christians to "cast all their cares" upon the Lord and look to the resources of the faith to engage their problems. By contrast, white Christians could cast some of their cares, particularly social concerns, onto other institutions such as government, because it has consistently had their best interests in mind. So, white Christians sought to keep the gospel pure by looking to the faith to do what no other entity could do, namely, save souls. This divergence regarding the scope of the faith's work causes dissonance between the denominations, which ultimately causes disharmony.

Denominational entities also contribute to theological and methodological myopia, which perpetuates disunity. Both conventions maintain seminaries in which clergy can be successful at their educational pursuits without earnestly engaging brothers and sisters from other Baptist denominations. Furthermore, the theological insularity of seminaries is broadcast by denominational publishing houses that tend only to consider the needs of a racialized constituency. These institutional dynamics form a structural barrier to unity and have abiding contemporary consequences that are difficult to quantify. Conventions established to serve a

---

[21] Pinn and Pinn, *Fortress Introduction*, 77.

racialized segment of God's people provided a venue to coddle individual racial bias, promoted institutional insularity, and generated theological myopia in both contexts. The question arises, Where do we go from here?

Toward a Baptist Catholicity

The race problem in the twenty-first century is less about dismantling supposed white superiority and more about understanding the dynamics that have allowed the wounds of racism to fester for generations. While individual biases will always be a matter of contention, contemporary racial strife is often caused by those who unknowingly participate in racialized social structures and fail to oppose racist people. Denominational life is no different: large denominations such as the NBC and SBC operate with a sense of self-sufficiency, seldom looking outside themselves for resources. This leaves tension between the denominations unengaged, as structures isolate people and implicit racial biases are seldom challenged.

A confluence of racial biases that lead to feelings of superiority and structural independence breeds the false assumption that there is nothing to be gained from interacting with one another. The solution to racial tension in Baptist life, however, is not to destroy both denominations and create a new united structure. Rather, work must be done within the existing structures to position them to serve a broader constituency and eliminate strain between the conventions. This involves engaging individual biases, structural insularity, and theological myopia.

While the nuances of each denomination's work toward unity warrant their own extended exploration, the following steps toward catholicity are applicable to various Christian groups, with the NBC and SBC in the foreground. The following steps assume that the SBC of the twenty-first century does not share the sentiments of the denomination's founders regarding the right to slave ownership.[22] These steps also assume that the NBC harbors no willful abhorrence toward Southern Baptists, or whites in general. Rather, these steps assume the

---

[22] See the SBC's 1995 resolution on racial reconciliation.

denominational structures in place inhibit the relationships necessary to overcome individual and theological biases that emerge from isolation. These insights may be fruitful for fostering racial unity within each denomination but also aim toward a more robust catholicity between the NBC and the SBC.

Individual Bias

Racial tension commonly begins with individual bias. Racism and bias are distinct features in the racial landscape. Racism is overt and intentional, while bias is more easily overlooked because its proponents do not wish to promote racist sentiments. Despite people's intentions though, the consequences of both racism and bias are real. The damage of racial bias is often unacknowledged because it is falsely equated with willful racism, which most Christians desire to eliminate from their lives.

In 1 Corinthians 13 Paul makes a claim about believers that also applies to all of humanity when he says they "see in a mirror dimly" (13:12 ESV) and are "childish" (13:11 ESV) in their earthly existence. Human limitation emerges from our particularity as embodied beings. Each person comes from a particular geographic location, socioeconomic status, upbringing, time period, and racial background. Each of these characteristics "dims lenses" to some earthly realities while making people keenly aware of other circumstances. Our blind spots become biases and are accentuated if the possibility of having a blind spot is denied. These limitations are essential to what it means to be human.

Moreover, individual biases are amplified in community. The old adage is true: More is caught than taught. The more homogeneous a social group, the more likely it is their blind spots will overlap. A group of people who are uniformly blind is prone to deny anything said to exist in that area of blindness. Homogeneous environments exacerbate blind spots by buttressing casual assumptions and failing to situate them in an explicitly biblical framework. As a result, denying a personal blind spot is a denial of being human, so the question should not be, Do I have a bias? but rather, How am I biased?

Within each denomination, cultural and operational norms support the esteemed status quo. For example, within each convention dynamics exist in everything from preaching and worship styles to matters of polity controlling the distribution of funds to missionaries. Each denomination has grown accustomed to taking care of business in its own way. These dynamics foster a healthy denominational pride yet also can have negative consequences. Because conventions grow accustomed to "having always done it a certain way," an unspoken conclusion can develop that other denominational practices are inferior. This attitude is intensified by racial dynamics in America that systematically distance the races from one another. An air of superiority looms because there are few real relationships to overturn prejudgments. In essence, denominational lines minimize the possibility for racial reconciliation because of individual bias and its intensified nature in a homogeneous community.

Solutions to Individual Racism

Because all people "see in part," brothers and sisters who see God's Word and world from different perspectives need each other. Pride tempts each person to assume he or she sees objectively and that others see through a glass dimly. Unfortunately, the people of God rarely reap the benefits of mutual sharpening among brothers and sisters of diverse ethnicities. Segregated churches and denominations hold diverse (yet biblically allowable) positions on a range of subjects that breed awkward moments and unavoidable misunderstandings. Despite uncomfortable moments, the value of self-displacement must be understood as a necessary step toward overcoming blind spots and biases.

While nobody sees with pure objectivity, the people of God can continually identify the baggage humans are prone to add to the gospel; as a result of this work, the gospel of Jesus Christ is clarified. As Prov 27:17 states, "Iron sharpens iron, and one person sharpens another." It is evident that iron sharpens iron with great effectiveness across the lines of difference. The dynamic of mutual sharpening is best illustrated in the beauty of marriage. Two sinners come together and are refined and sanctified over time. Despite difficult moments, on the whole believers cherish the opportunity to be sanctified and uphold their marriage covenant before God. Unfortunately, many American Christians have bought into the norm of segregation in our country, and when conversation becomes uncomfortable across racial lines, Christians are prone to express their commitment to American segregated cultural norms rather than promoting the gospel of unity.

The church's inability to pursue racial reconciliation reveals a cavernous hole in our understanding of sanctification. In America, the struggle for racial reconciliation is a premier litmus test for spiritual maturity. A body of believers that worships across racial lines and expresses the "one anothers" of the New Testament paints a wonderful picture of the gospel's ability to overcome division. Moreover, a genuinely multicultural people has heeded the call of the apostle Paul in Phil 2:3–5: "Do nothing out of selfish ambition or conceit, but in humility consider others as more important than yourselves. Everyone should look out not only for his own interests, but also for the interests of others. Adopt the same attitude as that of Christ Jesus."

People in multiethnic spaces can put on Christ in a way that overcomes historical baggage, heals grudges, and forces believers to think on behalf of others. This requires the forgiveness and patience exemplified in Christ. Christians have a supernatural example in him of someone who resisted retaliation and absorbed the final blow of sinfulness in order to end the cycle of brokenness and hurt. Christlike selflessness is necessary to seek diverse brothers and sisters intentionally in order to expose biases and overcome racial tension for the advancement of God's kingdom.

Structural Insularity

Structures are not neutral; they exert a shaping force and help diagnose activity contrary to their stated goals. Like a cadence in the background, some adherents to a structure intentionally march in step. Others fall in line subconsciously, but it is important to note that structures resist change because people who uphold them have much invested in them.

In a real sense, structures indicate who can contentedly participate in a denomination in a long-term manner. Structures—comprising programming, curriculum, and ministries—are often constructed by those who have always been the system's beneficiaries. If decision makers share a nearly uniform set of concerns shaped by a similar experience, those who likewise share that experience will feel the most support from the structures in place.

If, for instance, the NBC and SBC became poised to serve a broader constituency, their structures would need to be reexamined, for as institutions refine goals, their practices, policies, and procedures must follow suit. Ensuring that systems support the full scope of a vision is imperative, because structures can myopically serve a single demographic with excellence without consideration of other groups. Moreover, structures are deceptive, as those who perpetuate structural myopia can do so unknowingly. It takes a representative of a vulnerable demographic to identify that group's vulnerability within an organization.

Solutions to Systemic Bias

Aligning institutional structures with an expanded vision that includes serving those beyond one's historic constituency takes effort. To ensure that new efforts are not mere passing fads, the relevance of new initiatives must be demonstrated in light of a denomination's established mission. Within Christian institutions, it is imperative that racial reconciliation be demonstrated as a biblically and theologically inspired goal, not one motivated by political or social pressure. The individuals who constitute the institution must be shown how this additional dimension fits into Scripture. If appropriate care is taken to execute this step, members of a denomination will grasp this essential biblical theme. As a result, application in personal and corporate efforts will naturally follow.

In complex organizations, it is important not to limit diversity efforts to a single person or office. While this is a more arduous path, decentralized efforts are far more effective than a centralized model that produces measurable results more quickly. While events and isolated efforts to support the new goal are important, the most enduring changes occur when each individual in every office is trained to execute his or her role in serving a broader demographic. A denomination-wide initiative reimagines what success looks like in the minutia of the entire organization and generates broad momentum for transforming systemic insularity.

By his grace, God has granted believers the resources to overcome limitations; in addition to Scripture and the Holy Spirit, he has given us one another. For this reason, when organizational structures and policies are created or examined, it is ideal to have participation from representatives of those groups the organization hopes to support. The cumulative scope of each individual's limited vision provides better odds that each demographic will be considered in decisions made. Organizations will be hard-pressed to create an environment in which various kinds of people can flourish if practices, policies, and procedures are not examined to ensure everyone benefits from the status quo, not only the majority.

Theological Bias

The effects of homogeneous communities extend into Scripture reading and theological formulation. Scripture readers often approach the task like any other, as self-interested people who privilege their findings over others'. As a result, reading the Bible and doing theology in a homogeneous group limits humanity's ability to understand all that God is doing in Scripture. The biblical text is far richer and more wonderfully complex than any individual or homogeneous group can discern. Yet, in denominationally affiliated seminaries, homogeneity of biblical interpreters is common.[23]

Contemporary Southern Baptists tend to downplay the role of context (denominational or otherwise) in Bible reading and theology because, historically, progressive Christians have inflated the place of context over Scripture itself. To avoid the same error, evangelicals may insist theology

---

[23] This observation is intended not to critique the existence of denominational seminaries but to acknowledge that they can easily become echo chambers that cease to equip students to serve the whole people of God.

and Bible study are noncultural realities. But contextual realities have always been at play, influencing Scripture reading and theology, as well as other Christian practices such as discipleship and education. Therefore, a particular context has become inherent to each denomination. The question becomes, what context is dominant? The most popular or influential culture in a denomination tends to become the baseline or measure from which all cultures are judged. As a result, that dominant culture is mistakenly considered culturally neutral.[24] In the quest to avoid cultural captivity in Scripture reading or theologizing, it may appear advantageous for each Christian to align himself with the dominant culture in his denomination—because that culture is assumed to be normal.

But being part of the "normal" culture can breed an inflated view of self that produces a subconscious (or at times conscious) form of cultural supremacy. The "normal" cultural perspective is then asserted in biblical, organizational, and cultural interpretation. A temptation for those who embody the "normal" culture is attempting to judge the validity of nondominant cultures. It is common for minority cultures to be accepted insofar as their biblical and theological contributions match the dominant culture. Denominationally, the effect is multifold. First, this phenomenon generates a theology that engages only the inquiries of a particular dominant cultural group while masquerading as a "universal" theology of all people. Second, because denominational theological formulation can become parochial, theology can become a means of justifying denominational activity rather than setting a biblical course of action.

Solutions to Theological Bias

Learning to cherish a tradition yet look beyond its theological biases is a necessary skill for the theologian who serves within a denominational context. Perhaps for the first time, the people of God can gain a fuller perspective of how God is working in his world when they see that the

---

[24] It is important to note that the dominant culture is not always the dominant culture in the United States as a whole but rather the dominant culture within the institution in question.

Christian worldview is sufficiently robust to engage all of life in every context—this is a theological endeavor.

People from different backgrounds raise unique questions and bring different experiences to the table. As diverse groups surround the Word of God—the source of truth—and submit to its claims on their lives, the Holy Spirit cultivates biblical wisdom in each individual to engage life's circumstances in light of the risen Lord. As burdens are borne across the lines of difference, new opportunities arise to theologize on behalf of others in ways that illuminate Scripture's implications for each participant's life.

Conclusion

History bears witness to the development of the NBC and the SBC. Although these parallel entities emerged from sinful circumstances, the hope of the gospel offers a way forward for these denominations—and others that have become insular. In the contemporary moment, both desire to counter America's legacy of racism by searching for biases on individual, structural, and theological levels. The interconnectedness of these dynamics requires leaders from both denominations not to settle for addressing one but to address them all. While the world's rationale for pursuing racial unity is accompanied with a guilt-laden punitive tone, believers are driven by Christ's prayer of catholicity that we might all be one (John 17:21).

15

Baptist Contributions to the Christian Tradition

Jason G. Duesing
Midwestern Baptist Theological Seminary

Introduction: The Thorough Reformers?

"Of all persecuted sects, the Baptists stand forth as most prominent, simply and only because they aim at a more complete and thorough reform than any others ever attempted."[1] John Q. Adams, pastor of Baptist churches in New Jersey and New York, offered this statement in a published series of lectures that reflected a widespread sentiment among Baptist churches in the latter part of the nineteenth century—namely, that Baptists were the most consistent Protestants and that all other corners of the Christian tradition should therefore conform to their views. The idea of Baptists as the "thorough Reformers" gained popularity during these days of ascendant Landmarkism but continued even after that successionist tradition faded from prominence—so much so that non-Landmarkers also used this idea of thoroughness as a defense of Baptist distinctives.

Yet, while at its root the idea of being "thorough Reformers" conveys fidelity first to the Bible over tradition, and has proved helpful

---

[1] John Quincy Adams, *Baptists: The Only Thorough Religious Reformers* (New York: Sheldon, 1876), 21.

over the last five hundred years in a number of areas, the idea has also proved unhelpful. Some of the "thorough Reformers" have been *too* thorough, communicating a tradition of exclusivity (in the negative sense of that term)—a kind of "truer Christian" mentality. In these expressions, Baptist contributions to the Christian tradition have led to more conflict than aid.

In this chapter I aim to review how Baptist contributions to the Christian tradition have been both helpful and unhelpful, with a view toward identifying how present and next-generation Baptists should make future contributions. To begin, I will present a brief survey reviewing the history of the relationship of Baptists to the Christian tradition.

It's Complicated: Baptists and the Christian Tradition

The history of the relationship of the Baptist tradition to the broader Christian tradition is complicated. In the nineteenth century, the most prominent evangelical voice in America was the president of Brown University, Francis Wayland (1796–1865). A Baptist who wrote on Baptist distinctives and furthered Baptist missions, Wayland was known for his reformation of Brown and his textbooks on ethics and political philosophy. In Wayland's day, Baptists in Rhode Island and throughout the nation were no longer seen as dissenters from the Christian tradition but instead were now in the main of evangelical life in America. Thus Wayland, in his *Notes on the Principles and Practices of Baptist Churches* (1857), could claim that "the theological tenets of the Baptists, both in England and America, may be briefly stated as follows: they are emphatically the doctrines of the Reformation, and they have been held with singular unanimity and constancy."[2]

The Landmarkers would go further in asserting Baptist exclusivity, as we will note, but other non-Landmarkers would as well. E. Y. Mullins

---

[2] Francis Wayland, *Notes on the Principles and Practices of Baptist Churches* (New York: Sheldon, Blakeman, 1857), 16.

(1860–1928), writing on "The Contribution of the Baptists to American Civilization," asserted, "Baptists have been the only adequate interpreters of the Reformation."[3] Even Charles Spurgeon (1834–1892), not known for a strident Baptist posture, would say, "We believe that the Baptists are the original Christians. We did not commence our existence at the Reformation, we were Reformers before Luther or Calvin were born; we never came from the Church of Rome, for we were never in it. We have an unbroken line up to the apostles themselves! We have always existed from the very days of Christ, and our principles, sometimes veiled and forgotten like a river which may travel underground for a little season, have always had honest and holy adherents."[4]

While variation did exist in the forcefulness of such claims, this pattern of Baptists' expressing their distinctives in the Christian tradition as the "thorough Reformers" marked a difference from the first Baptists. In seventeenth-century England, early Baptists crafted their first confessions of faith not to show how accurate and thorough they were but rather for the purposes of survival and validation, to show how much they had in common with other churches in the Christian tradition.[5] The Orthodox Creed (1679) of the General Baptists, while certainly putting forward Baptist convictions regarding the "ceremonies" and "government of the church," was written primarily to "unite, and confirm all true Protestants in the fundamental articles of the Christian religion, against the errors and heresies of the Church of Rome."[6] Likewise, the London

---

[3] E. Y. Mullins, *The Contribution of the Baptists to American Civilization* (Philadelphia: American Baptist Publication Society, 1907), 6 (also included as chap. 16 in Mullins, *Axioms of Religion*, 1908).

[4] Charles H. Spurgeon, "Public Meeting of our London Baptist Brethren," Sermon 376, Metropolitan Tabernacle Pulpit, April 2, 1861, *Spurgeon's Sermons*, vol. 7, comp. Classic Christian Library, 225.

[5] See G. Stephen Weaver, "Baptists as Thorough Reformers: The Reformation as Source of Seventeenth Century Baptists" (paper presented at the 69th Annual Meeting of the Evangelical Theological Society, November 17, 2017, Providence, Rhode Island).

[6] An Orthodox Creed: Or, A Protestant Confession of Faith (London, 1679), transcribed by Madison Grace, Center for Theological Research, Southwestern Baptist Theological Seminary (Fort Worth, TX, 2006).

Confession of the Particular Baptists (1644) sought first to defend beliefs as orthodox, showing common belief in Trinitarian Christianity, before ever getting to the unique Baptist practice of the church.[7]

The nineteenth century did produce some who expressed a more balanced understanding of the relationship of Baptists to the Christian tradition. In 1881 John A. Broadus (1827–1895) was invited to address the American Baptist Publication Society at its meeting in Indianapolis, Indiana. His sermon, "The Duty of Baptists to Teach their Distinctive Views," speaks of some "Baptist brethren" who, in their zeal for their denomination, were often "violent" and "bitter" in their defense of Baptist distinctives.[8]

In light of this complex history of how Baptists have understood their relationship to the Christian tradition, next I will review exactly what I have in mind when I refer to the Christian tradition, before looking specifically at how Baptists have made both helpful and unhelpful contributions.

Seated around the Fire: Building on a *Consensus Quinquesaecularis*

In the seventeenth century, Lutheran scholar Georg Calixtus advocated for the term *consensus quinquesaecularis* to describe the core doctrines held by Christians for the first five hundred years following the close of the New Testament, as represented by the historic creeds formulated during that time.[9] The idea of a *consensus quinquesaecularis* is a good starting place for defining the Christian tradition. In that vein, the Niceno-Constantinopolitan Creed (381) describes the church in four attributes:

---

[7] London Baptist Confession of Faith (1644).

[8] John A. Broadus, *The Duty of Baptists to Teach their Distinctive Views* (Philadelphia: American Baptist Publication Society, 1881). References in this paper to Broadus's sermon are adaptations and revisions from my introduction to *Upon This Rock*, ed. Jason G. Duesing, Thomas White, and Malcolm B. Yarnell III (Nashville: B&H Academic, 2010).

[9] Translated as "consensus of the first five centuries." See Timothy George, "Why I Am an Evangelical and a Baptist," in *Why We Belong*, 97.

one, holy, catholic, and apostolic. These traits are a helpful starting place for defining the basics of the church in the Christian tradition. In particular, the catholicity of the church is important, for "[universal] came to be used synonymously with 'orthodox'" as a descriptor of the church.[10]

Todd Billings, at the end of Scott Swain and Michael Allen's helpful *Reformed Catholicity*, provides an instructive picture of this sense of *catholic*. He writes:

> I sometimes describe this dynamic in terms of an underground water table: many American Christians today think that they do not have to occupy any particular tradition, but can pick and choose from many traditions—like digging a hole here and there looking for water. But when one learns to really inhabit a tradition with depth, one can hit the "catholic water table." At that point, Baptists, Pentecostals, Roman Catholics, Reformed, and Orthodox can all find areas of common ground, even amid real and significant ongoing differences.[11]

This idea of catholicity is helpful for thinking of the Christian tradition as a whole, and for thinking of its wholeness.

C. S. Lewis, in explaining his mere Christianity, conceived the traditions of Christianity to be

> like a hall out of which doors open into several rooms. If I can bring anyone into that hall I shall have done what I attempted. But it is in the rooms, not in the hall, that there are fires and chairs and meals. The hall is the place to wait in, a place from which to try the various doors, not a place to live in. For that purpose the worst of the rooms (whichever that may be) is, I think, preferable.[12]

---

[10] Mark Dever, *The Church: The Gospel Made Visible* (Nashville: B&H Academic, 2012), 18.

[11] J. Todd Billings, "Rediscovering the Catholic-Reformed Tradition for Today," afterword in Allen and Swain, *Reformed Catholicity*, 153.

[12] C. S. Lewis, preface to *Mere Christianity* (London: Macmillan, 1952), preface.

Timothy George provides a related metaphor that further complements the topic of this chapter. Commenting on a resilient Landmark tendency toward isolation among Baptists, he writes:

> There is a strand in Baptist life that celebrates fences while neglecting foundations. Now, I am all in favor of Baptist distinctives . . . but I would like to see a stronger emphasis on the basics—the Bible, the Trinity, salvation by grace. It is possible . . . to believe strongly in the separation of church and state while . . . putting a question mark around the bodily resurrection of Jesus. Fences have their place, but without a solid foundation the fences will not long endure.[13]

Therefore, in thinking about the Christian tradition, a Bible-prioritized confessional consensus serves as a foundation for the universal, orthodox, catholic church. From this foundation over the centuries have come many traditions—rooms off the great hall, fences built upon this foundation— that allow for vibrant fellowship while sharing the water table, or common ground, of the Christian tradition. With a greater understanding of these preliminary matters, we can now examine examples, both unhelpful and helpful, of how Baptists have contributed to this Christian tradition.

Resetting Landmarks:
Unhelpful Baptist Contributions

"Pendleton was the prophet, Graves the warrior, and Dayton the sword-bearer" in a movement of ecclesiological significance among Baptists in the nineteenth century called Landmarkism.[14] These three, driven by the admonition in Prov 22:28 to reset ancient doctrinal standards, formed the

---

[13] Timothy George, "Baptists and Ecumenism: An Interview," *Criswell Theological Review* 14, no. 2 (Spring 2017): 90, http://www.centerforbaptistrenewal .com/blog/2017/4/6/baptists-and-ecumenism-a-discussion-with-timothy-george.

[14] William W. Barnes, *The Southern Baptist Convention 1845–1953* (Nashville: Broadman, 1954), 103. Portions of this section have been adapted from my chapter in Jason K. Allen, ed., *The SBC in the 21st Century* (Nashville: B&H Academic, 2016).

great triumvirate that sought to establish local churches upon the original landmarks of a scriptural church—namely, Baptist distinctives.[15] In the late 1850s, Landmark views were spreading rapidly, with great influence throughout the southeastern United States, at the hand of J. R. Graves's popular periodical, *The Tennessee Baptist.* Many in the Southern Baptist Convention were concerned with the implications of the Landmark situation, but few Baptists responded, and prior to the Civil War a Landmark expression of Baptist identity pervaded the churches.[16]

Writing on Graves and his colleagues, James E. Tull observed that few "features of Landmark ecclesiology are more striking than its definition of the character of the church as . . . local only."[17] To be sure, the Landmarkers wrote extensively on the term *ecclēsia* and its use in the New Testament. J. R. Graves saw only "*one* possible literal meaning to the Greek—that of a *local* organization."[18] An important implication of Graves's understanding of the local church is that churches not organized according to his understanding of New Testament principles are not true churches.[19]

Graves did not hold to a doctrine of the universal or catholic church. He spoke of it, but only to assert his belief that such an entity cannot exist. References to Paul's persecution of the church, as in Gal 1:13, Graves believed, were an indication not of the universal church but of

---

[15] H. Leon McBeth, *A Sourcebook for Baptist Heritage* (Nashville: Broadman, 1990), 316–27.

[16] See Kenneth Vaughn Weatherford, "The Graves-Howell Controversy" (PhD diss., Baylor University, 1991).

[17] James E. Tull, *High Church Baptists in the South*, ed. Morris Ashcraft (Macon, GA: Mercer University Press, 2000), 14.

[18] J. R. Graves, *Old Landmarkism* (repr., Texarkana, TX: Bogard, 1880), 28, 32.

[19] At that time Graves was only asking if Baptists can "recognize those societies, not organized according to the pattern of the Jerusalem Church . . . as the Church of Christ." See J. R. Graves, "Mass Meeting at Cotton Grove June 24, 1851," *The Tennessee Baptist* 7, no. 45 (July 19, 1851). But only a few years later Graves stated that all paedobaptists and groups of unbaptized believers are not churches. See J. R. Graves. "Baptist Carolla," *The Tennessee Baptist*, ca.1851, cited in Fred W. Kendall, *A History of the Tennessee Baptist Convention* (Brentwood, TN: Tennessee Baptist Convention, 1974), 115–16.

the local church in Jerusalem.[20] When speaking about passages in the New Testament that refer to the body of Christ, such as 1 Cor 12:13–14, Graves refused to identify these as references to a universal church. In this case he employed his generic-use argument and stated that to "understand the 'body of Christ' here to refer to a local church . . . meets all the requirements of the passage . . . but to understand it of a Church Invisible, it meets none of the requirements of the passage."[21] After further explication of his view, Graves concluded there is no passage that affords ground for the idea of a universal church on earth.[22]

The denial of a church catholic is an unhelpful contribution to the Christian tradition, for at least two reasons. First, while not the primary emphasis in the New Testament, there is such a thing as the universal church. Regarding passages that refer to the body of Christ, for example, consider Graves's contemporary interlocutor and challenger, theologian J. L. Dagg. In his *Manual of Church Order*, a volume written in part to collide with the "rising power of Landmarkism,"[23] Dagg asserts that in Rom 12:4–5, the "body of Christ" to which Paul referred is not solely the local church at Rome but all individual Christians.[24] Dagg offers several reasons for why the argument that Paul was speaking only of the local Roman assembly is faulty. First, Paul himself was not a member of this church, yet he said in this passage, "We being many are one body in Christ."[25] Second, to understand the text in this way "converts the beautiful figure which the Holy Spirit employs to represent the union between Christ and his people, into a monster, having one head and many bodies."[26]

---

[20] J. R. Graves, *Intercommunion: Inconsistent, Unscriptural and Productive of Evil* (Memphis: Baptist Book House, 1881), 128–39.

[21] Graves, *John's Baptism: Was it from Moses or Christ? Jewish or Christian?* (Memphis: Baptist Book House, 1891), 78–83.

[22] Graves, *Old Landmarkism*, 32.

[23] Tom J. Nettles, "Preface to the New Edition of Manual of Theology," in J. L. Dagg, *Manual of Church Order* (repr., Harrisonburg, VA: Gano Books, 1990).

[24] Dagg, 110–11.

[25] Dagg, 111.

[26] Dagg, 111.

Instead, Dagg explains that Paul meant to describe the body of Christ as one body with many members. Dagg reaches his conclusions through a hermeneutic that seeks the simplest reading of any text.[27] Dagg concludes, therefore, that his understanding of the church as universal is found in the New Testament. The church universal includes all local churches—not in an organization but rather in individual members. However, all local churches do not constitute the entirety of the universal church, for this term refers to Christians in heaven and on earth as well as those who are not members of a local church.[28]

Second, the conclusions of Landmarkism regarding the local and universal church perpetuated a need for Baptist churches to identify their unique connection to the New Testament and the history of Christianity. That is, if only Baptist churches are true churches, then where does one find those churches in history? The result was successionist theories identifying any sect in history characterized by something like Baptist distinctives as a part of the unbroken "Trail of Blood."[29] W. Morgan Patterson, in his 1969 *Baptist Successionism: A Critical View*, explains:

> For Baptists, the nineteenth century was replete with disputes both with fellow Baptists and with non-Baptists. . . . In this forensic arena Baptists had to defend their doctrines, their prac- tices, and their history, as well as to refute the false charges made against them. . . . In the interdenominational strife Baptists lacked the weapons and advantages of culture, status, and a noble history with which to retaliate against their opponents. However, this deficiency could in large measure be overcome by an unbro- ken linkage of Baptists to the Christians of the first century.[30]

Such efforts constituted a significant portion of Baptist engagement with the Christian tradition in the nineteenth century—engagement that was,

---

[27] Dagg, 105, 108.

[28] Dagg, 121.

[29] J. M. Carroll, *The Trail of Blood* (Lexington, KY: 1931).

[30] W. Morgan Patterson, *Baptist Successionism: A Critical View* (Valley Forge, PA: Judson, 1969), 69–70.

in my estimation, largely unhelpful. This isolationism and elitism served only to perpetuate confusion about how a Baptist should understand the history of Christianity, the creeds and confessions of the early church, and brothers and sisters in non-Baptist gospel-preaching churches.

Further, these boasting "thorough Reformers" also diverted Baptist churches from the heretofore Baptist tradition of seeking consensus in core doctrines while at the same time engaging in further reform with regard to the doctrine of the church. One cannot reform the Christian tradition when claiming exclusive privilege to it. Herein lies the greatest irony of the Landmarkers: in seeking to move away from Roman Catholicism and its claims of an unbroken succession of tradition handed down through the papacy, Landmarkers prioritized their own successionist tradition over the very thing that made them Baptist in the first place, namely, elevation of the Bible over tradition.[31]

Church Health and Religious Liberty: Helpful Baptist Contributions

Although Baptists have made unhelpful contributions to the Christian tradition, with the Landmark movement being just one example, they have made helpful contributions as well. In contrast to the discord of the nineteenth century, Baptists have served other churches via a healthy articulation of the place of the local church in the lives of Christians, while at the same time seeking to defend the freedom of other churches and religions to disagree. These two contributions—a healthy ecclesiology and religious liberty—serve ends beyond showing how the Baptist tradition is more thorough in its Reformation efforts. In short, Baptists have contributed to the church catholic when they have sought to build local churches and defend the freedom of religion with the gospel and for the gospel.

In essence, I am summarizing what evangelical Baptists have discussed often in the late twentieth and early twenty-first centuries, namely,

---

[31] Patterson, 72–74.

Baptist distinctives and Baptist identity. Thus, I am aiming not to say anything new but rather to reassert and affirm the path whereby future Baptists can continue to make helpful contributions to the Christian tradition. Baptist historians and theologians regularly discuss what exactly constitutes a list of Baptist distinctives. In the seminary classes I teach, after weeks of building a case for the value of the Baptist tradition, despite its many flaws and errors in history, I conclude each term by summarizing what identifies the Baptist tradition:

> (1) A people of the Book who preach the gospel and have found it helpful to summarize what the Bible says about the Christian life in confessions of faith. (2) The practice of believer's baptism by immersion as the entrance to a (3) believer's church that is (4) free and separate from the state and thus advocates religious freedom for all in society while (5) seeking to share the gospel with all in society and to the ends of the earth in an intentional and organized Great Commission focus of evangelism and missions. All done through (6) biblical cooperation among churches.

These points are concomitant with other interpretations of unique Baptist contributions to the Christian tradition. As the Center for Baptist Renewal's manifesto of Evangelical Baptist Catholicity states,

> We affirm the distinctive contributions of the Baptist tradition as a renewal movement within the one, holy, catholic, and apostolic church. These distinctives include the necessity of personal conversion, a regenerate church, believers' baptism, congregational governance, and religious liberty.[32]

---

[32] Stamps and Emerson, "Evangelical Baptist Catholicity," art. 4. The Center for Baptist Renewal explains, "Other Baptist groups and theologians have utilized the notion of 'Baptist Catholicity' or 'Bapto-Catholicity' (see, for example, the manifesto for Re-Envisioning Baptist Identity [1997]), but we are seeking to stake a claim for a particularly *evangelical* expression of this impulse," http://www .centerforbaptistrenewal.com/baptist-catholicity-renewal.

For the purposes of this chapter, I condense all of these distinctives into the two categories of church health and religious liberty, both advocated by Baptists for and from the gospel.

Church Health

In some ways, the greatest contribution of Baptists to the church catholic is a call to focus on and live within the church local, in a way not in opposition to the church universal. Drawing on C. S. Lewis's model, Baptists have provided helpful contributions when they call others to join their rooms for fellowship and for talking about their walls, tables, and chairs. Advocacy for healthy enclaves is not an end unto itself but rather a call for welcoming outposts in which Christians may live, debate, love, and define. The Reformed evangelical theologian Richard Mouw sees this as especially important for contemporary evangelicalism. He writes that a "'thin' generic evangelicalism has to be strengthened by taking seriously the various 'thick' confessional streams that feed into the evangelical movements." [33] Mouw recognizes the concern of many evangelicals for the distractions that can come from an all-encompassing focus on detailed ecclesiology, but "there is plenty of evidence today that when we start with a theology that only features the shared evangelical convictions, we are left with a movement that can easily be blown about by every wind of doctrine." [34]

Another evangelical theologian, Carl F. H. Henry, also saw the value of ecclesiology for evangelicals, particularly Baptist ecclesiology. He said,

> To "become" a Baptist is more exciting than to become a Roman Catholic, or even a Protestant of traditions into which one is "born." . . . Reliance upon Scripture to reveal the saviourhood and lordship of Jesus Christ, and his plan and purpose for mankind, is more than the first tenet of authentic Baptist belief; it is

---

[33] Richard J. Mouw, *Adventures in Evangelical Civility* (Grand Rapids: Brazos, 2016), 146–47.

[34] Mouw, 147.

the foundation stone for the other principles which, if unsettled, jeopardize the total Baptist spiritual structure.[35]

If there is therefore a need and even a welcomed opportunity (from other evangelicals at least), how are Baptists to cultivate their ecclesiology in ways that contribute to the Christian tradition? The nineteenth-century Baptist theologians J. L. Dagg and John Broadus again help us.[36]

In his *Manual of Church Order*, Dagg wrote with regard to the relationship of ecclesiology to other doctrines:

> Church order and the ceremonials of religion, are less important than a new heart; and in the view of some, any laborious investigation of questions respecting them may appear to be needless and unprofitable. But we know, from the Holy Scriptures, that Christ gave commands on these subjects, and we cannot refuse to obey. Love prompts our obedience; and love prompts also the search which may be necessary to ascertain his will.[37]

As evangelical Protestants, we are rightly often first in line to affirm that the doctrine of the church is less important than a heart twice born. Our Reformation heritage hands us five *solas*, and to think of an additional *sola ecclesia* is contrary to the movement itself. As such, evangelicals are not as often quick to affirm that wrestling with and arriving at sure ecclesiological convictions, as Dagg suggests, is a worthwhile exercise. Why then should we study the doctrine of the church? To answer this, we must clarify ecclesiology's rightful place among, and functional posture toward, other doctrines.

As one reads and studies the Bible, a growing realization dawns that some doctrines are more significant than others—in terms not of truthfulness or ultimate value but of priority. In 2004 Albert Mohler provided a word of great clarity with his article "A Call for Theological Triage and Christian Maturity." Here he explains:

---

[35] Carl F. H. Henry, "Fifty Years a Baptist," in Russell D. Moore and Tom J. Nettles, eds., *Why I Am a Baptist* (Nashville: B&H, 2001), 209–11.

[36] The remainder of this section is an adaptation of my chapter in Allen, *SBC in the 21st Century.*

[37] Dagg, *Manual of Church Order*, 12.

Given the chaos of an Emergency Room reception area, someone must be armed with the medical expertise to make an immediate determination of medical priority. Which patients should
be rushed into surgery? Which patients can wait for a less urgent
examination? Medical personnel cannot flinch from asking these
questions, and from taking responsibility to give the patients with
the most critical needs top priority in terms of treatment. . . .

A discipline of theological triage would require Christians to
determine a scale of theological urgency that would correspond
to the medical world's framework for medical priority.[38]

Mohler then unveils a method for organizing doctrines in three levels:
first-order (fundamental truths of the Christian faith), second-order
(areas where believing Christians may disagree, but with division, e.g.,
ecclesiology), and third-order doctrines (areas where believing Christians
may disagree yet remain in fellowship, e.g., eschatology). This idea of
theological triage has proven helpful for navigating seasons of theological
foment and fellowship.

To examine this further as it relates to ecclesiology, consider John
Broadus's address on the duty of Baptists, in which he observes that
Christ's commands to the disciples consisted of what he termed both
"the internal and the external elements of Christian piety." The internal
elements, Broadus explains, are more crucial to the Christian faith as they
relate to individuals and their relationship to their Creator. However,
Broadus clarifies that any primacy given to the internal elements does not
mean the external elements have little value or lack importance. Broadus
reasons that if Christ and his apostles gave commands relating to external
elements such as the "constitution and government" of churches, then it
"cannot be healthy if they are disregarded."

Therefore, as one reads and studies the Bible, one has the growing
realization that the local church functions as a repository not only to

---

[38] R. Albert Mohler Jr., "A Call for Theological Triage and Christian Maturity,"
Albert Mohler (blog), May 20, 2004, https://albertmohler.com/2004/05/20/a-call
-for-theological-triage-and-christian-maturity-2.

receive and transmit the internal or first-order message of the gospel to the current generation but also to preserve that message for future generations. The external or second-order commands given to order and govern the church are essential for this task, even though they are not as important as the internal or first-order message.

When Paul wrote to Timothy to instruct him in "how one ought to behave in the household of God," Paul described the local church as the "pillar and buttress of the truth" (1 Tim 3:15 ESV). The idea of the local church functioning as a pillar (Gk. *stulos*) and buttress (Gk. *hedraiōma*) creates a picture of an intentionally designed (i.e., ordered) structure that, through its strength, has been prepared both to uphold (i.e., present or proclaim) an object as well as to protect (i.e., preserve) it. Jesus's promise in Matt 16:18 (ESV) that "the gates of hell shall not prevail against" the church reinforces the idea that the local church has been given as an indestructible fortress of strength, held together by Jesus Christ himself (Col 1:17).

As a result, Jesus and his apostles have given commands of an external or second-order nature that must be taught and implemented. But for what purpose? The object given to the local church to uphold and protect is the "truth." The truth is the message of eternal life—the substance of the internal or first-order commands of Christ (1 Tim 2:4; 2 Tim 2:25). The New Testament teaches that this truth was, and is, to be handed over or delivered from one generation to the next through the local church.

Luke spoke of this at the beginning of his Gospel, writing to assure Theophilus of the certainty of the things he had been taught. Luke stated that he had written an "orderly account" of the things that "those who from the beginning were eyewitnesses and ministers of the word" had "delivered" (Gk. *paredosan*) to Luke and others (Luke 1:1–4 ESV). Likewise, Paul instructed Timothy and the Ephesian church to "guard [Gk. *parathēkēn*] the good deposit," a reference to the entire message of the gospel he had taught and given to them. In a broad sense, the purpose of all of Paul's letters is to deliver the truth not only to his immediate recipients but also to all who would read his letters and implement their commands in local churches (Col 4:16). Jude reinforced the notion that the truth is the object the local church exists to proclaim and protect. In Jude 3 he explained that "the faith," or the gospel message of eternal life, had been delivered (Gk. *paradotheisē*) to the saints. That is to say, the internal or first-order command of salvation through Jesus Christ had been handed down to Christians who live out the Christian life in local churches. Jude stated that this delivering was done "once for all" (Gk. *hapax*), referencing the complete and final nature of the message rather than the idea that the message had no further need of transmission.

In sum, these New Testament commands that speak of the truth are primary or, in Mohler's triage analogy, first-order and essential. However, the external commands that speak clearly to the order, practice, and health of the local church, while secondary, should not be considered unessential. As Dagg said, they are "less important than a new heart," yet the local church has a duty to carry forth and teach disciples to observe these second-order commands in obedience to Matt 28:20, for, though second-order, they were nonetheless given by the Lord Jesus, and, as Dagg reminds, our love for Christ and for his disciples, present and future, prompts our joyful obedience.

How does ecclesiology relate to other doctrines? The answer is found in the heart and practice of the mission of the local church herself. In a sentence, the local church, the "pillar and buttress of truth," exists to "guard the good deposit" and "deliver" it to future generations. Understanding ecclesiology's rightful place among other doctrines and how the gospel-centered nature of the church positions that doctrine in service to the Great Commission is only the grand beginning of studying the doctrine of the church.

Religious Liberty[39]

When Thomas Jefferson replied in 1802 to a letter from the Danbury Baptist Association on the topic of freedom of religion, he likely did not realize the weight that his reply's best-known phrase would carry. He

---

[39] This section is an adaptation of my introduction in *First Freedom: The Beginning and End of Religious Liberty*, ed. Jason G. Duesing, Thomas White, and Malcolm B. Yarnell III (Nashville: B&H Academic, 2016).

referenced in his letter a "wall of separation between church and state," and subsequent generations have debated those words endlessly.[40]

Whether Jefferson foresaw the impact his words would have, he clearly meant to protect the free practice of religion and to counteract the continued establishment of state churches. In that sense, Jefferson's wall has served as a foundation of religious freedom in the United States.[41]

The building of Jefferson's "wall" has origins in the sixteenth-century Reformation and the expansion of that movement among English dissenting believers—some of whom traveled to the New World in the seventeenth century. The state church system extended to the colonies as well, and thus the building of the wall endured many stoppages. Indeed, after Roger Williams left the Baptist church in Providence, he continued to call for religious freedom in the colonies. As McGloughlin notes, "In the fight for separation of church and state in New England, the Baptists were only one of several battalions of dissenters. Ultimately, however, they proved to be the most consistent, the most numerous, and the most effective."[42] To wit, John Clarke and Obadiah Holmes of the Baptist church in Newport, Rhode Island, would even spend time in jail, and Holmes would endure a public beating in Boston for his beliefs.[43]

Writing in 1645 to the city of Providence, Williams used the metaphor of a ship at sea to describe how he thought one should understand the relationship of religion to the state:

---

[40] Thomas Jefferson, "To the Danbury Baptist Association," January 1, 1802, in *The Papers of Thomas Jefferson*, vol. 36 (Princeton, NJ: Princeton University Press, 2009), 258.

[41] For this brief overview I was helped immensely by Matthew L. Harris and Thomas S. Kidd, eds., *The Founding Fathers and the Debate over Religion in Revolutionary America* (Oxford, UK: Oxford University Press, 2012). See also Thomas S. Kidd, *God of Liberty: A Religious History of the American Revolution* (New York: Basic, 2010); William G. McLoughlin, *New England Dissent, 1630–1833: The Baptists and the Separation of Church and State*, 2 vols. (Cambridge, MA: Harvard University Press, 1971); and Philip Hamburger, *Separation of Church and State* (Cambridge, MA: Harvard University Press, 2002).

[42] McGloughlin, *New England Dissent*, 1:8.

[43] John Clarke, *Ill Newes from New England* (London, 1652), 51.

There goes many a ship to sea, with many hundred souls in one ship, whose weal and woe is common, and is a true picture of a commonwealth, or a human combination of society. It hath fallen out sometimes that both papists and protestants, Jews and Turks, may be embarked in one ship; upon which supposal I affirm, that all the liberty of conscience, that ever I pleaded for, turns upon these two hinges—that none of the papists, protestants, Jews, or Turks, be forced to come to the ship's prayers or worship . . . if they practice any. I further add, that I never denied, that notwithstanding this liberty, the commander of this ship ought to command the ship's course, yea, and also command that justice, peace and sobriety, be kept and practiced, both among the seamen and all the passengers.[44]

This advocacy and argument increased the popularity of separation between the state and church, making way for new ideas about religious liberty by the dawn of the eighteenth century and the First Great Awakening of the 1730s. The 1763 conclusion of the French and Indian War brought further economic and political tensions between the British motherland and the colonists, resulting in the Boston Tea Party and the forming of the First Continental Congress. The colonists declared and won their independence, and among many new ideas for this nation, the ground was cleared for the wall of separation to arise.

As Thomas Kidd and Matthew Harris note, "The two most celebrated confrontations over religious establishment and religious liberty took place in Massachusetts and Virginia."[45] Key building blocks in the formation of the wall of separation followed. In Massachusetts, Baptist pastor and mobilizer for disestablishment Isaac Backus wrote *An Appeal to the Public for Religious Liberty* in 1773. Following the war, in 1786 Thomas Jefferson brought his bill titled Act for Establishing Religious Freedom, which ended the state-established church in Virginia.

---

[44] Roger Williams, "Letter to the Town of Providence," January 1654–55, *Letters of Roger Williams* (Providence, RI: 1874), 278–79.

[45] Harris and Kidd, *Founding Fathers*, 12.

Once the U.S. Constitution was ratified, its first amendment, adopted in 1791, ensured the free exercise of religion on a national level. Still, states such as Connecticut and Massachusetts refused to adopt the disestablishment partition fully, though they did grant free exercise from this time. In that same year, Baptist pastor John Leland, a friend of Jefferson and James Madison, published his influential *The Rights of Conscience Inalienable*, explaining why he and the other Baptists were willing to risk their livelihood for religious liberty:

> First. Every man must give an account of himself to God, and therefore every man ought to be at liberty to serve God in that way that he can best reconcile it to his conscience. If government can answer for individuals at the day of judgment, let men be controlled by it in religious matters; otherwise, let men be free.

> Second. It would be sinful for a man to surrender that to man, which is to be kept sacred for God. . . .

> Third. But supposing it was right for a man to bind his own conscience, yet surely it is very iniquitous to bind the consciences of his children—to make fetters for them before they are born, is very cruel. . . .

> Fourth. Finally, religion is a matter between God and individuals: the religious opinions of men not being objects of civil government, nor any ways under its control.[46]

Upon Jefferson's 1800 election as president, the Baptists in Danbury, Connecticut, wrote him, sharing that "they hoped that Jefferson's victory might signal a rising tide of religious liberty that would ultimately transform the New England states into bastions of freedom."[47] In reply, Jefferson famously reflected that, with the approval of the First Amendment, the American people built a "wall of separation

---

[46] John Leland, *The Rights of Conscience Inalienable* (1791).
[47] "Introduction" in Harris and Kidd, *Founding Fathers*, 20.

between church and state."[48] By 1821 Connecticut disestablished the Congregational Church. Massachusetts was the last state to recognize the wall, doing so in 1833. Thus Baptists labored to ensure the freedom of religion in this country not only for their churches but also to ensure that those in the other churches of the Christian tradition, and even other religions, could freely consider the gospel.

Conclusion: The History of Future Baptist Contributions

In 1994 L. Russ Bush, then-academic dean of Southeastern Baptist Theological Seminary, served as president of the Evangelical Theological Society. His presidential address, "The History of the Future," offered a helpful reminder: "We are living and making the history of the future. What we teach and do today will be what future Christians consider to be their heritage."[49]

In this same sense, Baptists today are living and making the history of future Baptist contributions to the Christian tradition. They could proceed in the unhelpful direction of the Landmarkers, advocating an isolationist Bapto-centrism that triumphantly asserts themselves as the most "thorough reformers." If pursued, such steps would build strong the fences of Baptist distinctives. Yet they would obscure the core and common doctrines of the Christian tradition. In C. S. Lewis's hall of mere Christianity, such unhelpful contributions would remove future Baptists to an annex or even a separate building. Yes, such Baptists would have fireplaces and fellowship of sorts, but not around common doctrines rooted in a shared tradition. In short, their pursuit of isolated ecclesiology would be an end unto itself.

On the other hand, Baptists could follow the way of Dagg and Broadus. Understanding and advocating the doctrines Baptists share with other Christians, future Baptists can contribute to gospel advance

---

[48] Jefferson, " Danbury Baptist Association," 258.
[49] See L. Russ Bush, "The History of the Future or What Should We Do Now?," *Journal of the Evangelical Theological Society* 38, no. 1 (March 1995): 3.

through their advocacy of healthy ecclesiology and religious liberty. David Dockery and Timothy George have written that as Baptists are "anchored in their own heritage,"[50] they can help renew the Christian tradition from within.[51] Baptists serving this way will sound like Carl F. H. Henry, who believed

> Baptists are not so much interested in promoting the Baptist denomination as such in the world as in advancing the one church that Christ heads through the Baptist witness. But we should not feel that to realize this purpose requires surrender either of Baptist distinctives or denominational fervor.[52]

Yet this irenic approach should avoid the side effect of silencing Baptists in the advocacy of their convictions. Recall that in Broadus's day he noted how the Landmark excessiveness caused other Baptists to retreat, "scarcely ever making the slightest allusion to characteristic Baptist principles," being "afraid of appearing sensational in their own eyes, or in those of some fastidious leaders . . . shrink[ing] from saying the bold and striking things they might say, and ought to say."[53] While in this chapter I have been speaking as a Baptist concerning Baptist engagement with the Christian tradition, I think it appropriate also to say to other traditions, following Broadus's warning, not to forget or overlook the Baptist tradition in the pursuit of catholicity. To put it another way, while it is true, and the thrust of this presentation, that Baptists must engage with care and charity, it is also true that often other traditions neglect the value or potential contributions of the Baptist tradition. This is especially true when what the Baptist tradition may contribute, by way of a healthy ecclesiology, is a call to a lower church or even the breaking of long-held traditions.

---

[50] David S. Dockery and Timothy George, *Theologians of the Baptist Tradition* (Nashville: B&H Academic, 2001), xv.

[51] George, " Evangelical and a Baptist."

[52] Henry, "Fifty Years a Baptist," 211.

[53] Broadus, *Duty of Baptists.*

Given that 2017 marked the five hundredth anniversary of the Protestant Reformation, perhaps the best way to conclude thinking about the future of Baptist contributions to the Christian tradition is with a call to *semper reformanda secundum verbum dei* (Latin for "always reforming according to the Word of God").[54] In the centuries following the Reformation, various Protestant traditions built upon the Reformation by calling their churches to exist in such a state. All groups should always seek ongoing reformation, as thorough as the Scriptures direct, along the way seeking to contribute that which is helpful to brothers and sisters in other enclaves of the Christian tradition. We do so by drawing upon our common commitment to the Scripture and the shared Christian confessional tradition. To be sure, there will remain disagreement, and sometimes the contribution needed will be sharpening and corrective, but what should be prized is the fact that these are disagreements among a family of reformers in the Christian tradition. To share the Baptist vision of Timothy George:

> Yes, by all means, let us maintain, undergird, and strengthen our precious Baptist distinctives . . . but let us do this not so that people will say how great the Baptists are but rather what a great Savior the Baptists have, what a great God they serve.[55]

As we set forth to live and make the history of the future Christian tradition, may Baptists set out to become that kind of "thorough Reformer."

---

[54] See R. Scott Clark, "Always Abusing Semper Reformanda," *Tabletalk* (November 1, 2014); and Michael Horton, "Semper Reformanda," *Tabletalk* (October 1, 2009).

[55] George, " Evangelical and a Baptist," 109.

16

Conclusion: Toward an Evangelical Baptist Catholicity

Matthew Y. Emerson and R. Lucas Stamps

Retrieving the Past, Renewing the Present, and Readying for the Future

Retrieval for the sake of renewal is the watchword of this volume. When we speak of renewing Baptist life, we do not intend to communicate that the Baptist movement is dying and somehow in desperate need of our efforts to revive it. No, in many ways, the Baptist movement is as alive as ever, with many exciting stories to tell in terms of evangelistic fervor, missionary endeavors, cultural engagement, and theological education.[1]

But every movement this side of glory is always in need of greater renewal and a more thorough reformation. We believe one of the most fertile sources for this kind of renewal is the Christian tradition—not only in terms of our own rich Baptist heritage, but also in terms of the Reformation, medieval, and patristic traditions that lie behind it. As we retrieve the past, and harvest it for doctrinal and liturgical "best practices," as it were, then we will find new inspiration in our efforts to interpret and apply the Scriptures for our own day.

---

[1] Portions of this conclusion originally appeared on the website for the Center for Baptist Renewal, accessed June 9, 2019, http://www.centerforbaptistrenewal.com/baptist-catholicity-renewal.

To the degree the Baptist movement is experiencing decline or attrition, the essays in this volume do not constitute a comprehensive solution. But they may offer a partial remedy. The conviction beneath all these essays is that one path to renewal is found by revisiting first principles—those fundamental convictions and practices that Baptists share in common with all Christians, even as they are given particular shape by our own Baptist distinctives. As Morgan and Ferguson's essay demonstrated, the deepest and richest soil for renewal is to be found in holy Scripture and its teaching on the unity of the church: loved by the Father, bought by the Son, and indwelt by the Holy Spirit. The other essays in this volume have suggested Baptists also have much to receive—as well as much to give—in the great collection of traditions that constitute the one, holy, catholic, and apostolic church. The doctrinal, interpretive, liturgical, sacramental, and spiritual heritage of the centuries belongs as much to Baptists as to any other communion in the body of Christ. "For all things are yours, whether Paul or Apollos or Cephas or the world or life or death or the present or the future—all are yours, and you are Christ's, and Christ is God's" (1 Cor 3:21–23 ESV).

Challenges to the church's witness, unity, and catholicity remain, including interdenominational disagreements, a crisis of holiness, racial strife, and theological conflicts. But Christ himself promised to build his church and that the gates of hell would not prevail against it. Therefore, we have hope.

Evangelical Baptist Catholicity: A Proposal

To this end, we wish to offer a more positive statement about the prospects of Baptist catholicity[2] from a conservative evangelical perspective.

---

[2] Once again, we want to make clear that by "catholicity" we mean universality and wholeness. It is not a reference to the Roman Catholic Church. It is simply a reference to the whole body of Christ across space and time.

We offer the following eleven theses as a kind of program for an evangelical Baptist catholicity.[3]

1. We affirm the ontological priority of the triune God and the epistemological priority of his inspired, inerrant, and infallible Word. Christian faith begins, is carried forth, and ends in God—in his being and works—and is made known to us in Holy Scripture.

2. We affirm the centrality of the gospel—the good news of salvation through the incarnation, life, death, and resurrection of the Son of God—for Christian faith, life, and worship.

3. We affirm the fundamentals of reformational theology, especially as they are expressed in the great *solae* of the Reformation: fallen humanity can be saved by grace alone through faith alone in Christ alone on the basis of Scripture alone to the glory of God alone.

4. We affirm the distinctive contributions of the Baptist tradition as a renewal movement within the one, holy, catholic, and apostolic church. These contributions include emphasis on the necessity of personal conversion, a regenerate church, believers' baptism, congregational governance, and religious liberty.

5. We encourage a critical but charitable engagement with the whole church of the Lord Jesus Christ, both past and present. We believe Baptists have much to contribute as well as much to receive in the great collection of traditions that constitute the holy catholic church. We believe that we are "traditioned" creatures and that we should move beyond the false polarities of an individualistic modernity and a relativistic postmodernity.

6. We affirm that all people, including those of every race, ethnicity, and gender, are created in God's image and, if they have repented and believed in Christ, are brothers and sisters together in the one body of Jesus Christ through the Holy Spirit. Catholicity includes all believers around the whole globe throughout all history. It includes people of

---

[3] These theses function as a working document for the Center for Baptist Renewal. Their inclusion here should not be taken to mean that all the authors in this volume would endorse the statement. See Emerson and Stamps, "Evangelical Baptist Catholicity."

every culture and ethnicity, women and men, young and old, and those with disabilities. Everyone in Christ is included in the pursuit of unity in Christ's church. Because of this shared *imago dei* and because of Christ's saving work among all nations, peoples, and tongues, we believe that one major task of Baptist catholicity is to promote racial unity, especially within the body of Christ.

7. We encourage the ongoing affirmation, confession, and catechetical use of the three ecumenical creeds and the scriptural insights of the seven ecumenical councils. We believe these confessional documents express well what Thomas Oden called the "consensual tradition"—the deposit of faith taught in Holy Scripture and received by the church throughout space and time.

8. We believe Baptist worship should be anchored in Holy Scripture and informed by the liturgical practices of the historic church. We believe Christian worship should be Word-centered. In worship, we read, preach, sing, pray, and show forth (through the ordinances) the Word of God. We further believe Baptist worship could benefit from incorporating historic practices such as lectionary readings, observance of the liturgical calendar, corporate confession of sin, the assurance of pardon, the recitation of scriptural and historic prayers (especially the Lord's Prayer), and the corporate confession of the faith (expressed in the ecumenical creeds and other confessional documents).

9. We affirm the two ordinances or sacraments instituted by Christ,[4] baptism and the Lord's Supper, and believe that they function as signs and seals of God's grace, expressions of individual faith, and bonds of the church's covenantal unity in Christ. As such, these ordinances are not empty signs or mere symbols but tangibly demonstrate our union with

---

[4] The earliest Baptists, among both the General Baptists and the Particular Baptists, used the language of "sacrament" to reference baptism and the Lord's Supper. In doing so, they meant to communicate that these ordinances are means of grace utilized by the risen Christ to strengthen and confirm the faith of believers. They did *not* mean to convey that the sacraments are automatically effective, that baptism is regenerative, or that the elements of the Lord's Supper become the physical body and blood of Christ. See Matthew Emerson's and Michael Haykin's essays in this volume for more on Baptist approaches to the sacraments.

the risen Christ and with his body, the church. Other Christian practices, such as confession of sin, confirmation in the faith, the ordination of church officers, Christian marriage, and the prayerful anointing of the sick may also frame a life of Christian faithfulness, but should not be considered sacraments.

10. We affirm the continuity of God's works of creation and redemption. Therefore, we affirm the goodness of all honorable vocations, the importance of embodied habits and rituals, and the value of aesthetic beauty for Christian life and worship.

11. We believe all Christians should pray for and seek Christian unity across ecclesial and denominational lines and that Baptists should not reflexively reject principled, ecumenical dialogue with other Christian traditions.

As we retrieve the past, we seek to renew the present and to ready ourselves for the future, when all of God's people will at last be one even as our great triune God is one (John 17:11).

APPENDIX

Baptists, Bapto-Catholic Baptists, and the Christian Tradition

STEVEN R. HARMON

Gardner-Webb University

NOTE FROM THE EDITORS: This appendix is a response to the idea of an "evangelical Baptist catholicity" from Steve Harmon, author of Towards Baptist Catholicity *and one of the most prominent voices in the broader academic conversation about Baptist catholicity. While Harmon is not Southern Baptist and thus holds some theological views that do not coincide with those of the editors, of B&H Academic, or of the BF&M 2000, we desire to place our project in conversation with the wider work on Baptist catholicity in the academy. This appendix is an attempt to do so, and we are grateful to Dr. Harmon for responding and clarifying where he sees both common ground and difference between our project and his own, as well as others who are part of the Baptist catholicity conversation. For our understanding of that common ground and difference, see the introduction to this book.*

I first became aware of the interest of the editors of this book in seeking an "evangelical Baptist catholicity" by which their Southern Baptist communion might be renewed in May 2014. It was brought to my attention that Matthew Emerson had posted an appreciative and critical response to my 2006 book *Towards Baptist Catholicity: Essays on Tradition and the*

Baptist Vision[1] on his blog.[2] In a post on my own blog, I offered some initial responses to Emerson's questions and critiques.[3] That initial interchange, for which I remain grateful, provides an appropriate point of departure for writing about "Bapto-Catholic Baptists" and the continuation of this trajectory beyond *Towards Baptist Catholicity* and to a pan-Baptist engagement of the larger Christian tradition.

Towards Baptist Catholicity and "Evangelical Baptist Catholicity"

Emerson began his post with this:

> I recently read Steve Harmon's *Towards Baptist Catholicity: Essays on Tradition and the Baptist Vision*. I'm beginning some sustained work with my friend and colleague Luke Stamps on Baptist life and its relationship to the larger Christian tradition, and Harmon's collection of essays is one of the most prominent works on the subject. In this post I hope to affirm much in Harmon's book, but also offer some pointed questions and critiques from a different perspective (i.e., conservative Southern Baptist evangelical) than his own.

Emerson affirmed my perspectives on "the need to position Baptist life within the larger body of Christ . . . not only on a theological level . . . but on a liturgical level"; my critique of an uncritical embrace of certain

---

[1] Steven R. Harmon, *Towards Baptist Catholicity: Essays on Tradition and the Baptist Vision* (Studies in Baptist History and Thought, vol. 27; Milton Keynes, UK: Paternoster, 2006).

[2] Matthew Y. Emerson, "Steve Harmon and Baptist Catholicity," *Biblical Reasoning: Biblical and Systematic Theology According to the Scriptures* (blog), May 13, 2014, downloaded June 4, 2019, https://secundumscripturas.com/2014/05/13/steve-harmon-and-baptist-catholicity/.

[3] Steven R. Harmon, "Matthew Emerson on *Towards Baptist Catholicity*," *Ecclesial Theology* (blog), May 14, 2014, downloaded June 4, 2019, https://ecclesialtheology.blogspot.com/2014/05/matthew-emerson-on-towards-baptist.html.

aspects of modernity that had become intertwined with the Baptist tradition, especially in North America; and my commendation of the non-coercive liturgical (as well as catechetical) use of the ancient ecumenical creeds in the life of Baptist churches, along with other liturgical practices that form worshipers in Christian faith and faithfulness. He also raised a question about my rationale for commending particular liturgical practices and offered critiques regarding what Emerson termed matters of epistemology, but which related in particular to my characterization of the interrelationship of Scripture, revelation, tradition, authority, and community. In the remainder of this first section I draw from my initial blog response to Emerson's questions and critiques in order to clarify the relationship between what this book characterizes as "Evangelical Baptist catholicity" and my own work on Baptist catholicity.

The Role of Liturgical Practices

Emerson wrote, "I would have liked to see more engagement with Augustine's view of formation, where it is not only our cognitive faculties but also and sometimes primarily our repetitive bodily habits that transform us." I concur with Emerson—and Augustine and James K. A. Smith, whom he cites in this connection—on the role of embodied liturgical practices in the holistic Christian formation of persons.[4] There is a reductionistic cognitive emphasis in the Baptist appropriation of Zwingli on the anamnestic function of the Supper as a memorial meal, for example, that extends to other dimensions of worship. I am on board with efforts to resist such a reduction. I grant that there is something of a lingering cognitive emphasis in the chapter on worship in *Towards Baptist Catholicity*—for example, "As worshippers have the divine story imprinted upon their consciousness and find their place within this story week after week over a long period of time, they are formed in the faith and fitted for the practices that constitute the Christian life."[5] However,

---

[4] James K. A. Smith, *Imagining the Kingdom: How Worship Works*, Cultural Liturgies, vol. 2; (Grand Rapids: William B. Eerdmans, 2013).

[5] Harmon, *Towards Baptist Catholicity*, 157.

the overarching concern of that chapter was the retrieval in contemporary Baptist worship of the patristic coinherence of liturgy and theology as summarized in the formula *lex orandi, lex credendi* drawn from Prosper of Aquitaine. The theological formation of Christians through what happens in worship was a particular point of application. Thus, there is a focus on the cognitive in that chapter, but it is not intended to be exclusive of the other dimensions of formation through liturgical practices. A broader application is suggested by my descriptive and prescriptive definition of worship therein as "the participatory rehearsal of the story of the Triune God."[6] I tweaked that definition of worship slightly for a somewhat different application in a chapter on the function of Scripture in the life of the church in my more recent book *Baptist Identity and the Ecumenical Future*, where it is expressed as "the participatory rehearsal of the *biblical* story of the Triune God."[7] In employing this definition in my classroom teaching, I have modified it further: "the participatory *enactment* of the biblical story of the Triune God." The more broadly suggestive term in all three versions of the definition is "participation." The practices of worship are intended to draw us into ever-fuller participation in the life of the triune God, a participation that cannot be merely cognitive. When I first responded to Emerson's blog post, I was in the midst of preparing a response to Sarah Coakley's *God, Sexuality, and the Self: An Essay 'On the Trinity'*,[8] the first volume in her projected four-volume systematic theology *On Desiring God*, for a panel discussion of the book.[9] A significant contribution of Coakley's work is her recovery of a neglected dimension of the patristic concept of the Trinity, namely its pneumatic orientation in which the Spirit draws us ever more fully into participation in the life of the triune God through practices of prayer and asceticism.

---

[6] Harmon, 155.

[7] Harmon, *Baptist Identity*, 60–63, emphasis added.

[8] Sarah Coakley, *God, Sexuality, and the Self: An Essay "On the Trinity"* (Cambridge: Cambridge University Press, 2013).

[9] Published as Steven R. Harmon, "*Ressourcement Totale*: Sarah Coakley's Patristic Engagement in *God, Sexuality, and the Self*," *Perspectives in Religious Studies* 41, no. 4 (Winter 2014): 413–17.

I am on board with this too, and see it as connected with my proposals about the role of liturgical practices.

Scripture and Divine Revelation

Emerson noted what he regarded as "a problematic dichotomy between God's authority and the authority of Scripture." My intention in distinguishing between the ultimate authority of the triune God and the derivative authority of the Scriptures was not to dichotomize them, but rather to characterize properly the dynamic and integral relationship between them in an economy of revelation. He rightly pointed out that speech-act theory has a finely nuanced way of doing this, as seen not only in the work of Kevin Vanhoozer, which Emerson mentioned in this connection, but also Stanley Grenz among evangelical theologians. I do, however, think it important to qualify the relationship between revelation *qua* revelation and Scripture's participation in that revelation in a way that is not "direct," and that qualification is related to my response to Emerson's concerns about my treatment of the relationship of Scripture and tradition.

Scripture and Tradition

Revelation, in Christian understanding, is mediated. To be sure, revelation is first and foremost God speaking and acting, but this speaking and acting is received, remembered, and recorded by a community that mediates revelation by handing on—traditioning—what it has received, remembered, and recorded. My characterization of the coinherence of Scripture and tradition is not intended as an anthropocentric account of Scripture's participation in divine revelation, for the Spirit is at work among the people of God in their traditioning of revelation. Emerson was concerned that my perspective on the coinherence of Scripture and tradition in the formation of the New Testament canon "prioritizes tradition in the canonical process rather than the Spirit-led recognition of God's special revelation in the biblical books." I do not intend to suggest that the canon was merely decided by the tradition of the church in the fourth-century regional synods and episcopal communications that were affirmations of a long-developing consensus in the early church, with substantial second- and third-century attestation to the early formation of this consensus. Nor do I mean that these second- and third-century traditioning processes that forged this consensus were something other than the activity of the Spirit in the life of the church. The coinherence of Scripture and tradition belongs just as surely to the rubric of pneumatology as does biblical inspiration.

Authority and Community

Emerson wrote that I "seem to root the church's beliefs about the Trinity, Christology, and Scripture in a communitarian practice rather than in revelation." Here what I intend is not a contrast between the authority of the community and the authority of divinely given revelation, but rather one between the authority of the community and the authority of the individual. Furthermore, the community that functions in a pattern of authority is not community per se, but a community that is actively seeking to participate ever more fully in the reign of God by bringing its life together under the rule of Christ through the guidance of the Spirit. This vision of Christian community belongs, I think, to the essence of the Baptist vision and serves to correct a reductive individualism that became intertwined with the Baptist tradition in the wake of the Enlightenment, especially in its North American instantiation. Here it is also important to keep in mind that the concrete ecclesial community of reference from which I write is the Cooperative Baptist Fellowship, which has its origins in controversy within the Southern Baptist Convention in the 1970s through early 1990s. Emerson's concrete ecclesial community of reference is the continuation of one trajectory within that tradition; mine is one with a trajectory that once coexisted with it but has continued differently. That different trajectory has historic affinities with mainline Protestant liberalism, and I think the way forward for this trajectory is along the lines of postliberal theology—thus my invocations of George

Lindbeck that give Emerson pause. A postliberal/narrative influence on me who is somewhat close to home for Baptists is the late theologian James Wm. McClendon Jr., whose thought, along with moral philosopher Alasdair MacIntyre's work on the contested nature of a "living tradition," is significant for me. I agree that if Emerson's "conservative Southern Baptist evangelical" trajectory is to engage fruitfully the issues I treated in *Towards Baptist Catholicity*, it will have to be done in a different manner—not along the lines of McClendon but probably in a postconservative path as exemplified by Vanhoozer. But I think that when the two trajectories, postliberal and postconservative, take up the concerns that are important to both Emerson and me, they are angled toward many of the same ends. Thus, in this postliberal and postconservative common interest in catholicity is the potential for good developments in intra-Baptist relations as well as in Baptist interdenominational ecumenical relationships.

Church-Dividing Doctrinal Differences

Emerson was also concerned that I "slide over doctrinal differences with Roman Catholicism and Orthodoxy." I do not mean to suggest that there are no significant remaining church-dividing matters of doctrine, though I do think that the *Joint Declaration on the Doctrine of Justification* issued in 1999 by the Lutheran World Federation and the Catholic Church (subsequently joined by the World Methodist Council in 2006 and the World Communion of Reformed Churches and the Anglican Communion in 2017) has rendered soteriological objections moot.[10] While Mariological concerns do remain significant, the progress in mutual understanding of one another's perspectives on the role of Mary in the life of the church reflected in that section of the report from the 2006–2010 conversations between the Baptist World Alliance and the Catholic Church offers

---

[10] Lutheran World Federation and Roman Catholic Church, *Joint Declaration on the Doctrine of Justification* (Grand Rapids: William B. Eerdmans, 2000).

hope that this too is not insurmountable.[11] Rather, my intention with the final chapter of *Towards Baptist Catholicity* (titled "'What Keeps You from Becoming Catholic?' A Personal Epilogue") was to make clear my conviction that there are more significant reasons than doctrinal disagreement with Catholicism, Orthodoxy, or Anglicanism for remaining Baptist (or some other tradition) instead of following the yearning for a fuller qualitative catholicity to Rome, Constantinople, or Canterbury. In that chapter I suggested that seeking the visible unity of the church at present calls for fuller cultivation of this catholicity within our divided churches rather than moving to another church we might believe already possesses that catholicity to a greater degree than our own. That conviction I developed more fully in *Baptist Identity and the Ecumenical Future*. In relation to the theme of the present book, I would venture the suggestion that this conviction should apply not only to ecumenical work across denominational lines, but also to intradenominational Baptist divisions. The fact that some Southern Baptist theologians and some Baptist theologians no longer affiliated with the Southern Baptist Convention are seeking the fuller cultivation of catholicity within their respective Baptist communions holds promise for more visible forms of unity across this and other Baptist divides—as well as for the repair of unity between Baptists and other Christians who are heirs to the larger Christian tradition.

"Bapto-Catholic Baptists" and the Ongoing Trajectory of "Baptist Catholicity"

Towards Baptist Catholicity functioned as something of a travelogue of my own journey as a Baptist theologian toward a "catholic" Baptist identity. This was not a journey I could make alone; it called for traveling companions, and I began to discover that other Baptist theologians had been seeking such an identity. I interacted with their work in my writing of

---

[11] See, for example, Baptist World Alliance and Catholic Church, "The Word of God in the Life of the Church: A Report of International Conversations between the Catholic Church and the Baptist World Alliance 2006–2010," §§ 132–61, https://www.bwanet.org/images/pdf/baptist-catholic-dialogue.pdf.

Towards Baptist Catholicity, and in its first chapter I identified them and outlined our commonalities: (1) the recognition of tradition as a source of theological authority, (2) affirmation of the liturgical and catechetical use of the ancient ecumenical creeds as expressions of this tradition, (3) attention to liturgy as the context for formation by this tradition, (4) the location of tradition's authority in the life of ecclesial community, (5) advocacy of a sacramental theology, (6) retrieval of tradition as a resource for constructive theology, and (7) a commitment to a "thick" approach to ecumenical convergence, based not on lowest common denominator agreements between churches but rather on the effort to understand their genuine differences and to find in them the pathways to a shared Christian tradition.[12] I appropriated the label "catholic Baptists" for theologians whose work was characterized by those marks from a book chapter by Curtis Freeman, in which he wrote: "I suggest that Baptists may more easily explore the vast resources of Christian spirituality and that other Christians may more readily receive the unique contributions of Baptist spirituality if we attempt to think of ourselves (at least experimentally) as (little *c*) catholic (little *b*) baptists."[13] Others, including the editors of this volume, have employed the term "Bapto-Catholic" to describe not only such Baptist theologians but also Baptist church communities that have sought fuller catholicity in their worship, work, and witness.[14]

In the thirteen years since publication of *Towards Baptist Catholicity*, the number of Baptist theologians whose work intersects substantially with the features of "catholic baptist" or "Bapto-Catholic" theological identity has grown beyond the eight North American and five British Baptist theologians I named in the introductory chapter of that book as

---

[12] Harmon, *Towards Baptist Catholicity*, 6–17.

[13] Curtis W. Freeman, "A Confession for Catholic Baptists," in Furr and Freeman, *Ties That Bind*, 85.

[14] Cameron H. Jorgenson, "Bapto-Catholicism: Recovering Tradition and Reconsidering the Baptist Identity" (PhD diss., Baylor University, 2008); Nathan Nettleton, "Free-Church Bapto-Catholic," *Liturgy* 19, no. 4 (2004): 57–68 (Nettleton's article is about the South Yarra Community Baptist Church in Melbourne, Australia).

the fellow travelers I had discovered among my theological colleagues.[15] Several younger Baptist theologians have written doctoral dissertations, a number of them subsequently published, that identify with and/or develop many of these features of Baptist catholicity.[16] Meanwhile, some

---

[15] Harmon, *Towards Baptist Catholicity*, 17, where I named Curtis Freeman, Timothy George, Barry Harvey, Mark Medley, Elizabeth Newman, Philip Thompson, D. H. Williams, and Ralph Wood in the United States and John Colwell, Anthony Cross, Christopher Ellis, Paul Fiddes, and Stephen Holmes in the United Kingdom.

[16] Jorgenson's dissertation cited in a previous note (Jorgenson, "Bapto-Catholicism") has subsequently been joined by a noteworthy number of dissertations by Baptists and others in the free church tradition that address the intersection of ecclesiology and ecumenical theology in a "bapto-catholic" or "catholic baptist" fashion and/or engage Catholic theology constructively, in many cases influenced by James Wm. McClendon, Jr.'s construction of Baptist identity: Scott W. Bullard, "A Re-membering Sign: The Eucharist and Ecclesial Unity in Baptist Ecclesiologies" (PhD diss., Baylor University, 2009), published as *Re-membering the Body: The Lord's Supper and Ecclesial Unity in the Free Church Traditions*, Free Church, Catholic Tradition (Eugene, OR: Cascade Books. 2013); Jeffrey W. Cary, "Authority, Unity and Truthfulness: The Body of Christ in the Theologies of Robert Jenson and Rowan Williams with a View toward Implications for Free Church Ecclesiology" (PhD diss., Baylor University, 2010), published as *Free Churches and the Body of Christ: Authority, Unity, and Truthfulness*, Free Church, Catholic Tradition (Eugene, OR: Cascade Books, 2012); Aaron James, "Analogous Uses of Language, Eucharistic Identity, and the Baptist Vision" (PhD diss., University of Dayton, 2010), published as *Analogous Uses of Language, Eucharistic Identity, and the 'baptist' Vision*, Studies in Baptist History and Thought (Milton Keynes, UK: Paternoster, 2014); Derek C. Hatch, "E. Y. Mullins, George W. Truett, and a Baptist Theology of Nature and Grace" (PhD diss., University of Dayton, 2011), published as *Thinking with the Church: Toward a Renewal of Baptist Theology*, Free Church, Catholic Tradition (Eugene, OR: Cascade Books, 2017); Jonathan A. Malone, "Changed, Set Apart, and Equal: A Study of Ordination in the Baptist Context" (PhD diss., University of Dayton, 2011); Andrew Donald Black, "A 'Vast Practical Embarrassment': John W. Nevin, the Mercersburg Theology, and the Church Question" (PhD diss., University of Dayton, 2013); Amy L. Chilton, "Practiced Theological Diversity: Jon Sobrino and James Wm. McClendon Jr., on Theology as a Particular, Christological, Holistically Self-Involving Practice of the Church" (PhD diss., Fuller Theological Seminary, 2015); Spencer Miles Boersma, "The Baptist Vision: Narrative Theology and Baptist Identity in the Thought of James Wm. McClendon, Jr." (ThD diss., Wycliffe College, University of Toronto, 2017). For another perspective that draws on the Puritan/Reformed trajectory

of the theologians I mentioned in this connection in *Towards Baptist Catholicity* have extended this trajectory in fresh directions in their own work. Curtis Freeman has published a pair of books commending to Baptists a catholicity that is orthodox (but generously so, concerned more with the centrality of Christ than the peripheral boundaries between orthodoxy and alternatives), trinitarian, sacramental, and ecumenical[17] and exploring the gift of dissent that Baptists have offered to the world as a contribution to the flourishing of democracy.[18] Elizabeth Newman's recent books have given attention to the ecclesial practice of hospitality,[19] the retrieval of the Catholic Saint Teresa of Avila as a resource for engaging a broken church and world,[20] and the centrality of contemplation and worship to the mission of Christian higher education.[21] Barry Harvey set forth his own perspectives on what Baptist catholicity entails in a book titled *Can These Bones Live?: A Catholic Baptist Engagement with Ecclesiology, Hermeneutics, and Social Theory*[22] and has offered a retrieval of Dietrich Bonhoeffer as a resource for the church's life in the world that transcends the co-opting of Bonhoeffer's legacy by both the "right" and the "left" of American Christianity.[23] Paul Fiddes has contributed to a Baptist constructive theology of the

---

in the Baptist tradition to critique of some of these "bapto-catholic" or "catholic baptist" proposals, see Gordon Lansdowne Belyea, "Living Stones in a Spiritual House: The Priesthood of the Saint in the Baptist *Sanctorum Communio*" (ThD thesis, Wycliffe College/University of Toronto, 2012).

[17] Freeman, *Contesting Catholicity*.

[18] Curtis W. Freeman, *Undomesticated Dissent: Democracy and the Public Virtue of Religious Nonconformity* (Waco, TX: Baylor University Press, 2017).

[19] Elizabeth Newman, *Untamed Hospitality: Welcoming God and Other Strangers* (Grand Rapids: Brazos Press, 2007).

[20] Elizabeth Newman, *Attending the Wounds on Christ's Body: Teresa's Scriptural Vision* (Eugene, OR: Cascade Books, 2012).

[21] Elizabeth Newman, *Divine Abundance: Leisure, the Basis of Academic Culture* (Eugene, OR: Cascade Books, 2018).

[22] Barry Harvey, *Can These Bones Live?: A Catholic Baptist Engagement with Ecclesiology, Hermeneutics, and Social Theory* (Grand Rapids: Brazos Press, 2008).

[23] Barry Harvey, *Taking Hold of the Real: Dietrich Bonhoeffer and the Profound Worldliness of Christianity* (Eugene, OR: Cascade Books, 2016).

communion of saints[24] and played a key role in shaping the substantial and groundbreaking report from Phase II of the international ecumenical dialogue between the Baptist World Alliance and the Catholic Church, for which he served as editor.[25]

In my own work beyond *Towards Baptist Catholicity*, I have provided a general readership introduction to ecumenism and in my most recent book, *Baptist Identity and the Ecumenical Future*, offered a more explicitly ecumenical perspective on Baptist identity—not only in terms of what Baptists gain from the gifts of the whole church, but also in terms of what the whole church gains from the gifts stewarded by the Baptist tradition. One of the gifts I suggested that Baptists might receive from the larger Christian tradition is attention to the function of "magisterium"— an authoritative teaching office—in the church, which already functions in Baptist communities in a distinctively free church manner that is largely unrecognized and that can be more fully exercised. I argued that in addition to the Roman Catholic magisterium and its functional equivalents in Eastern Orthodoxy and Magisterial Protestantism, there is a free church practice of magisterium which localizes teaching authority in the gathered congregation. Such a free church magisterium gives attention to doctrine in the sense of McClendon's characterization of

---

[24] Paul S. Fiddes, Brian Haymes, and Richard Kidd, *Baptists and the Communion of Saints: A Theology of Covenanted Disciples* (Waco, TX: Baylor University Press, 2014).

[25] Baptist World Alliance and Catholic Church, "The Word of God in the Life of the Church: A Report of International Conversations between the Catholic Church and the Baptist World Alliance 2006–2010," *American Baptist Quarterly* 31, no. 1 (Spring 2012): 28–122. The report from the 2006–2010 conversations is also published in *Pontifical Council for Promoting Christian Unity Information Service* 142 (2013): 20–65; on the Vatican web site, downloaded May 28, 2019, http://www.vatican.va/roman_curia/pontifical_councils/chrstuni /Bapstist%20alliance/rc_pc_chrstuni_doc_20101213_report-2006-2010 _en.html; and on the Baptist World Alliance web site, downloaded May 28, 2019, https://www.bwanet.org/images/pdf/baptist-catholic-dialogue.pdf. On the influential role of Fiddes in shaping this and other reports from ecumenical dialogues with Baptist participation, see Steven R. Harmon, "Trinitarian *Koinonia* and Ecclesial *Oikoumenē*: Paul Fiddes as Ecumenical Theologian," *Perspectives in Religious Studies* 44, no. 1 (Spring 2017): 19–37.

doctrine as "a church teaching as she must teach if she is to be the church here and now."[26] I envisioned this free church magisterium as a minister-facilitated practice of theology by the members of local church communities seeking the guidance of the Spirit in their efforts to imagine what it will look like to follow Christ in their context. In facilitating this local practice of theology, pastors help the congregation to hear discerningly voices from elsewhere in the whole church that provide resources for bringing congregational life more fully under the rule of Christ. I identified those voices in terms of this nine-fold typology: (1) ancient creeds that stem from the early church's rule of faith; (2) historic Reformation confessions and catechisms, along with more recent confessional statements from various denominations; (3) confessions of the Baptist tradition; (4) Catholic magisterial teaching; (5) the liturgical texts of other traditions; (6) the reports and agreed statements of bilateral and multilateral ecumenical dialogues, at both the national and international levels; (7) contextual theologies that emerge from social locations other than the context of the local Baptist church engaged in this practice of theology; (8) ecclesial resolutions on ethical issues adopted by diverse church bodies; and (9) the lived Christian lives of the saints.[27] Regarding the role of socially-located contextual theologies, I wrote:

> It is especially important that these theologies be heard and not silenced, for they are a necessary check on the blind spots that may come from the social location of our own community when it is not intentionally interdependent with the global church. For Baptist communities in North America and Europe, this might mean deliberately seeking out and reading the theologies of liberation that emerge not only in Latin America but in many other contexts where oppression is a reality the practices of the church must address; black theology in its American and African developments; the various efforts by Asian theologians

---

[26] James Wm. McClendon, Jr., *Systematic Theology*, vol. 2, *Doctrine* (Waco, TX: Baylor University Press, 2012), 23–24.

[27] Harmon, *Baptist Identity*, 180–88.

to contextualize the faith in non-Western cultures; feminist, womanist, and *mujerista* theologies; and the growing body of theological literature by Christians whose sexual orientations likewise represent differing social locations within which they seek to bring their life under the lordship of Christ. Voices from other social locations must also be weighed, but unless a community hears them and refrains from silencing them, its capacity for weighing its own voices will be diminished.[28]

Catholicity, from the Greek *katholikē*, which means "according to the whole," has to do with the wholeness of the church. Unless the diachronic and synchronic completeness of the voices of the whole church are heard in the local church conversation about what it will mean to be the church of Jesus Christ here and now, the local church is not experiencing this dimension of catholicity—the wholeness of the church. I have recently finished coediting a book that collaboratively envisions what it might look like for local congregations to practice the "Free Church Magisterium" that I proposed in *Baptist Identity and the Ecumenical Future*. In this forthcoming book, titled *Sources of Light: Resources for Baptist Churches Practicing Theology*, a diverse group of twenty-three Baptist theologians (including some of the "catholic Baptist" theologians I identified in *Towards Baptist Catholicity*) contribute chapters that imagine how Baptist communities might draw on the resources of the whole church more intentionally in their congregational practice of theology.[29] These resources include theologies that attend to the social locations of followers of Jesus Christ. They also include the church's efforts to bring its life together under the rule of Christ in its practices of confessing and teaching the faith, navigating moral disagreement, identifying saintly examples for living the Christian life, ordering its life as a worshiping community, and seeking more visible forms of Christian unity across the divisions of the church. The ongoing trajectory of "Baptist catholicity" has for me

---

[28] Harmon, 186.

[29] Amy L. Chilton and Steven R. Harmon, eds., *Sources of Light: Resources for Baptist Churches Practicing Theology*, Perspectives on Baptist Identities, no. 3 (Macon, GA: Mercer University Press, forthcoming 2020).

come to mean this sort of inclusive catholic wholeness, as well as the things I emphasized in *Towards Baptist Catholicity*.

Catholicity as Pilgrimage for Bapto-Catholics, Evangelical Baptists, and the Whole Church

In *Baptist Identity and the Ecumenical Future*, I also gave attention to the gifts offered by the Baptist tradition to the whole church. Among the proposals I made in that book was this: that one of the distinctive ecclesial gifts that Baptists have to share with the rest of the church is the way they do theology as a relentlessly pilgrim community that resists all overly realized eschatologies of the church.[30] Our ecclesial ideal is a church fully under the rule of Christ, which we locate somewhere ahead of us rather than in any past or present instantiation of the church. Baptists are relentlessly dissatisfied with the present state of the church in our pilgrim journey toward the community that will be fully under the reign of Christ.

We may conceive of the catholicity of the church in terms of this pilgrim church vision. While "Bapto-Catholics"/"catholic Baptists" and advocates of "evangelical Baptist catholicity" may have significant disagreements, we are fellow pilgrims, seeking together the renewal of our Baptist churches and of the whole church through our quest for a fuller catholicity than can help us move closer to the church that is fully under the rule of Christ. May this book help its readers toward that end, through Jesus Christ our Lord.

---

[30] Harmon, *Baptist Identity*, 213–42.

NAME AND SUBJECT INDEX

EDITORS AND CONTRIBUTORS

Editors

Matthew Y. Emerson, Oklahoma Baptist University
Christopher W. Morgan, California Baptist University
R. Lucas Stamps, Anderson University

Contributors

Dustin Bruce, Boyce College
Soojin Chung, California Baptist University
David S. Dockery, Southwestern Baptist Theological Seminary
Jason G. Duesing, Midwestern Baptist Theological Seminary
Matthew Y. Emerson, Oklahoma Baptist University
Kristen A. Ferguson, Gateway Seminary of the Southern Baptist Convention
Timothy George, Beeson Divinity School
W. Madison Grace II, Southwestern Baptist Theological Seminary
Steven R. Harmon, Gardner-Webb University
Michael A. G. Haykin, The Southern Baptist Theological Seminary
Christopher W. Morgan, California Baptist University
Rhyne R. Putman, New Orleans Baptist Theological Seminary
Patrick Schreiner, Western Seminary
R. Lucas Stamps, Anderson University
Walter R. Strickland II, Southeastern Baptist Theological Seminary
Amy Carter Whitfield, Southeastern Baptist Theological Seminary
Taylor B. Worley, Trinity International University
Malcolm B. Yarnell III, Southwestern Baptist Theological Seminary